D0757949

INQUIRY INTO MEANING
An Investigation of Learning to Read

in memory of

Catherine Molony and Gil Klausner

INQUIRY INTO MEANING

An Investigation of Learning to Read

Anne M. Bussis
Edward A. Chittenden
Marianne Amarel
Edith Klausner

Educational Testing Service
Princeton, New Jersey

LEA LAWRENCE ERLBAUM ASSOCIATES, PUBLISHERS
1985 Hillsdale, New Jersey   London

Lawrence Erlbaum Associates, Inc., Publishers
365 Broadway
Hillsdale, New Jersey   07642

Library of Congress Cataloging in Publication Data
Main entry under title:

Inquiry into meaning.

 Reports the investigations and findings of the ETS
Collaborative Research Project on Reading.
  Bibliography: p.
  Includes index.
  1. Reading (Primary)—Research.   2. Reading (Primary)
—Case studies.   3. Children—Books and reading—Research.
I. Bussis, Anne M.
LB1525.I52   1985   372.4'1   84-25943
ISBN 0-89859-504-5

Printed in the United States of America

Contents

Preface

The ETS Collaborative Research Project on Reading was a 6-year investigation that brought researchers and educators together in classroom studies of young children learning to read. This book sets forth the rationale, methods, empirical findings, and theoretical outcomes of that collaborative venture.

The Research has several unusual features as compared with most studies of beginning reading, but all of these stem from the fact that the project focused on readers rather than on methods of reading instruction or on various subskills presumed necessary for reading. Our decision to focus on individual readers originated in the assumption that knowledge and skill can never flow directly from the teacher or curricular materials to the student, no matter how well designed the materials or how well planned the instruction. Ultimately, learning is a constructive act that depends on the learner's contribution of meaning. Educational research on reading has typically been concerned with questions other than the learner's contribution, or else it has tended to assume that the majority of learners construct similar meanings from objectively similar situations.

A research focus on readers carries several methodological consequences. It implies the need for evidence of a child's understandings and manner of functioning across the full range of classroom activities. It requires a study over time, in order that patterns may emerge from the documented evidence and the relationship of reading to the reader's broader purposes and meanings may be discerned. A focus on readers also calls for the in-depth study of relatively few learners rather than gathering more limited data on a great many children. It means, in effect, an approach using naturalistic methods and procedures that can be sustained over time. Naturalistic research encompassing almost 2 years of a child's classroom life is one of the unusual features of the ETS study.

The project also differs from most reading studies in its collaborative nature. Practitioners were centrally involved in all phases of the investigation, from planning and instrument development through data collection and analysis. Fortunately, collaborative methods are no longer rare in educational research, but collaboration as conceived here differs somewhat in both form and intent from most such endeavors. We undertook a collaborative venture not for the sake of teachers' professional development nor for the purpose of studying teachers and teaching, but in the interest of studying children's learning.

Research of this nature is optimally carried out in settings where children have an opportunity to express the meanings they bring to and take from instructional encounters, and where teachers give priority to observing children's expressions of meaning and learning. That teachers in the study were generally good observers of children is undeniable. Many considered professional development to be synonymous with improved observational capabilities and had sought to improve their own skills by participating in inservice programs that offer support and guidance for observation. Although the collaborating teachers in the study may be considered an unusual group in this respect, the children they observed were not unusual. Equally important, *what* the teachers observed was ordinary behavior that occurred during the normal course of classroom life.

In summary, every facet of the research (the focus on readers, the naturalistic methodology, the collaborative design, and the selection of teachers) was intended for the single purpose of gaining a better understanding of how children learn to read. Researchers and practitioners alike developed professional insights and broadened their perspectives as a result of the study, but the anticipation of this outcome is not what sustained the research. Few events in life present as complex or engrossing a challenge as trying to understand how learning occurs, and hindsight suggests no other purpose would have kept such an intense collaborative effort viable over such a long period of time.

Organization of the Book

The book is divided into three major sections, each of which stands as a relatively independent unit. PART I (Chapters 1–4) describes the theoretical rationale, design, and procedures of the study.

PART II presents a distillation of the research findings in the form of a theory about the nature of beginning reading and about the resources children bring to bear in learning how to read. The introduction to the theory (Chapter 5) opens with short summaries of the learning progress of two children and a brief overview of similarities and differences among children that were uncovered by the study. This evidence sets the stage for presenting a conception of reading within the broad context of skill learning in general. The theory is then elaborated under the following chapter headings: Knowledge Resources that Support the Skill of Reading (Chapter 6), The Orchestration of Knowledge in Reading (Chapter 7), and Stylistic Influences in Learning How to Read (Chapter 8).

PART III presents case studies of the learning patterns and progress of four children (Chapters 10–13). The introduction to the case studies (Chapter 9) provides sufficient background information about the research for readers to understand the nature and basis of each study. In highlighting characteristics particular to individual children, the four studies also illustrate the kind of detailed evidence that gave rise to the theory. Thus, PART III may be the most logical starting point for those who like to go from concrete instances to theoretical formulations rather than vice versa.

Acknowledgments

Where a personal pronoun seems called for in the text of this report, the pronoun "we" is used for good reason. The design, conduct, and outcomes of the reading study represent the combined thought and effort of many persons. First and foremost among them are colleagues who comprised the senior project staff at ETS—Edward Chittenden, Marianne Amarel, and Edith Klausner. Their respective authorship of individual studies is indicated in PART III, but it would be impossible to untangle each person's several contributions to PART II. Chittenden's and Klausner's construction of final coding schemes to analyze children's oral reading is an identifiable piece of work that clearly led to important insights. I am basically responsible for the analysis of style dimensions. Beyond that, however, the theoretical formulations in PART II reflect ideas that evolved in discussions over several months and years and are no longer traceable to a specific individual or point in time. My last responsibility in the study has been to give these ideas final formulation and to articulate them.

Rosalea Courtney and Gita Wilder are other ETS staff members who contributed much to the study. Courtney was an observer for both the pilot study (the first 3-year phase of work) and the operational study (the second 3-year phase), and she supported virtually every aspect of the work at ETS throughout the project's history. Wilder joined the project staff for the operational phase of the research, assuming responsibility as an interviewer, an observer, and a leader of one of the data integration teams.

The study's ability to stay alive and healthy for several years also owes much to the secretarial skills of Marilyn Brennan. There are probably few research projects that have had as many pieces of data come through the typewriter as has this particular project. Our thanks, too, to Betty Maest, who helped prepare the final manuscript for publication.

Colleagues outside of ETS also played an important role in supporting the research. Patricia Carini's central contributions to the study are discussed in Chapters 2 and 4. Courtney Cazden, Susan Florio, Patricia Minuchin, and Lee Shulman agreed to act in an advisory capacity when the data integration methods were being examined and adapted for use. Discussion with members of this advisory committee, both individually and as a group, helped ETS staff members to pinpoint and clarify many methodological issues. Vito Perrone provided a forum and atmosphere for presenting the ongoing work of the project at annual meetings of the North Dakota Study Group on Evaluation. And Lillian Weber's insights into children's learning served as a continuing stimulus to our own thinking.

In the long run, however, major credit for the project's existence belongs to collaborators in the field, though tracing specific contributions to specific individuals would be just as impossible for this group as it is for ETS staff. Suffice it to say that the fundamental task of observing was carried out primarily by those in the field and that they are mainly responsible for both the quality of data on individual children and for the integration of those data. The list below includes all non-ETS collaborators who participated in the research. The names of those who participated in the last 3 years of the research (the operational phase) are indicated with an asterisk.

New Rochelle and Hartsdale, New York

Robert Bisson	Hildie Popolla
Wilma Heckler	Penelope Wax
Sherrin Hersch	Lois Zabriskie
Celia Houghton	

New York City

*Beth Alberty	Ann Hazelwood	Esther Rosenfeld
Jacquelyn Ancess	Bette Korman	*Alice Seletsky
*Howard Budin	Bryna Linnet	*Susan Soler
*Geraldine Charney	Catherine Molony[1]	*Leslie Stein
Ann Cook	Lucy Mato	Michael Trazoff
*Virginia Cramer	Deborah Meier	Marsha Van Benschoten
*Virginia Crosswaithe	*Carole Mulligan	*Vivian Wallace
*Pamela Cushing	Norma Nurse	*Susan Weissman
Nancy Desplantes	*Theodora Polito	

[1]Deceased

North Bennington, Vermont

*Patricia Carini	Diana Natko
*Jessica Howard	Toby Wood

Paterson, New Jersey

*Mary Burks   Ora Pipkin
Linda Lewis   Irene Reynolds

Philadelphia

*Jessie Agre   *Rhoda Kanevsky   Ernestine Rouse
Dorothy Ballard   Bessie King   Ruth Rubenstein
Lillian Barbour   *Debra Klinman   Vivian Schatz
*Virginia Bommentre *Carol Leckey   *Lynne Strieb
Cynthia Boyce   *Peggy Perlmutter   Jean Uhling   .
*Gibson Henderson   Frances Raynak   *Edith Williams
Virginia Jamison   Ellen Reese

Research that involves many people and spans several years requires patience on the part of individuals in supporting institutions and agencies who are responsible for monitoring its progress. Such work is costly, and concrete results are long in materializing. Thus, we gratefully acknowledge not only the patience but the encouragement of Marjorie Martus, formerly with the Ford Foundation, of Joseph Dominic at the National Institute of Education, and of the administration of the Research Division and College Board Division at Educational Testing Service.

*Anne M. Bussis
(Project Director)
Princeton, New Jersey*

Permissions

The authors gratefully acknowledge the kindness of authors, illustrators, and publishers in giving permission to reproduce their materials in *Inquiry into Meaning: An Investigation of Learning to Read.* An unqualified acknowledgment indicates that nonexclusive world permission was granted.

BURKE PUBLISHING COMPANY LTD.: Text from *In the Village,* by Hilde Heyduck-Huth, published by Burke Publishing Company Ltd. ISBN-0-222-79966-8. Copyright © Burke Publishing Company Limited, 1969. Permission restricted to first printing and in English language only.

EDUCATORS PUBLISHING SERVICE, INC.: Text and artwork from *Ben Bug,* pp. 1–5, by Barbara W. Makar. Reprinted by permission of Educators Publishing Service, Inc. from *Ben Bug, A Primary Phonics Reader,* by Barbara W. Makar. Copyright © 1968 by Educators Publishing Service, Inc., Cambridge, Massachusetts 02238.

GRANADA PUBLISHING LIMITED: Approximately 100 words and 2 illustrations from *The Three Brothers,* pp. 4–7 (First Folk Tales 8) by Mollie Clark; for approximately 200 words and 2 illustrations from *The Lost Dog,* pp. 2–5, by Sheila McCullagh. Reprinted by permission of Granada Publishing Limited, 8 Grafton, London W1, England.

GROSSET & DUNLAP, INC.: Text from "Little Red Riding Hood," p. 58, in *The Grosset Treasury of Fairy Tales,* 1977. Reprinted by permission of Grosset & Dunlap, Inc. Copyright © 1982, by Grosset & Dunlap, Inc.; and text and artwork from *Mr. Pine's Mixed Up Signs,* p. 7, published by Scholastic Book Services Edition, 1972. Copyright © 1961 by Grosset and Dunlap, Inc.

INQUIRY INTO MEANING
An Investigation of Learning to Read

RATIONALE, DESIGN, AND PROCEDURES OF THE READING RESEARCH

1 A Research Focus On Meaning

Teaching begins with an understanding of learning, and teaching practice matures as experience broadens and deepens the practitioner's understanding. Though there is no substitute for the insight gained from experience, educational research has always sought to expand the body of practical knowledge with its own brand of insight. The goal is not just a potpourri of "findings" but the kind of theoretical insights to which every science aspires—in this case, a foundational theory of learning. Despite the roots of promising theory that exist in related disciplines, a coherent theory of learning which proves its mettle in the classroom has thus far eluded educational research.

Part of the theoretical failure stems from a historic reluctance of researchers to move out of the laboratory and into the classroom (Hawkins, 1966). Several investigators have called attention to this problem (e.g., Cazden, 1979; Simons, 1979; White, 1979), and many have taken corrective action. Other people attribute the failure in part to a pursuit of false goals, noting that educational researchers have often searched for the kinds of universal laws that characterize physical science, when there is little reason to believe that such universality characterizes the human condition at all (Mishler, 1979). Both problems are real and both are troublesome, but underlying these problems is a deeply ingrained perception of research that generates much of the trouble.[1] The perception is the legacy of Positivism and Behaviorism writ large across the annals of social science, and the legacy unfortunately receives continuing support from an attitude that penetrates almost every segment of society, including the realm of educational administrators and policymakers.

---

[1]See, especially, Chein, 1972, and Strike, 1974, for detailed analyses of this trouble source.

The attitude in question may be likened to a problem of double vision or double standards. On the one hand, we all tend to think of ourselves as rational, sensitive people, who act reasonably most of the time and try to make our lives as meaningful as possible. Nothing causes us to grumble more bitterly than to be treated like "robots" or "machines." On the other hand, we are captured by an image of technological progress that is embodied in electronic robots and machines. And caught by this image, we begin to speculate. "If only technological know-how could be brought to bear on stubborn educational problems, the problems might yield." "If only we could manage the classroom as efficiently as we manage computers, equity concerns might disappear." There is no doubt that modern technology can be used to creative ends in the classroom, but we fall into an easy trap when we begin to perceive children as the machines and teachers as the technicians. Where this perception prevails, we begin to treat students in ways we resent being treated and to undermine the talent that is teaching. The results are predictable: little enthusiasm or substantive learning on the part of students; and teachers who either become disillusioned and leave the profession, who become disheartened but struggle on, or who mindlessly begin to enact the technician's role.

The robot image of progress also perpetuates the myth that better technology leads inevitably to better theoretical understanding and insight. Einstein's theories exploded that view of scientific progress over 60 years ago, and few physical scientists have returned to it since.[2] Technology results *from* theory, not necessarily *in* theory; and to believe the reverse (that technical advance leads inexorably to theoretical advance) is to embrace a reductionist view of science that predates Einstein but lingers on in the field of education and in society at large. The appeal of this perspective to an analytic-minded society can perhaps best be summarized by two major tenets of the reductionist way of viewing things.

An original tenet: If it exists, it can be measured; and if we measure it, we will understand it better.

A more recent tenet: If it can be learned/taught, it can be analyzed into component parts; and if we break it up into component parts, it can be learned/taught more efficiently.

Virtually any product of complex learning can be reduced to component parts by logical analysis, for analytic logic is a powerful invention of the mind. But a fallacy occurs when the analysis is automatically assumed to be a blueprint of how the learning was achieved in the first place. This fallacy is often devastating for instruction, because it tends to confound information with knowledge, knowledge with skill, and exercises to promote information acquisition with the

---

[2]See Polanyi (1958, pp. 9–15) for a brief account of how Einstein's theory exploded the reductionist view of scientific progress. For a more detailed account that supports Polanyi's main thesis, see Pais' (1982) biography of Einstein.

exercise of judgment and the type of practice that underlies skilled achievements.[3]

Technology can of course be a stimulus to theory development, but only insofar as new techniques uncover relevant information and present it in usable forms. Since educational research lacks coherent theories of classroom learning, new techniques that enter the field primarily reflect greater sophistication in statistical theories and conceptions of measurement.[4] Potentially powerful as these techniques may be for some purposes, they usually entail the reduction of human behavior to test scores, rating scales, preconceived observation categories, or other representations that can be statistically manipulated. And this reduction usually leads researchers off the trail of learning theory, because it leaves them with little information that credibly reflects the meaning and intentionality of human learning. In effect, it leaves them with little subject matter to study.

Kaplan (1964) pointed to the trail of fruitful theory several years ago when he identified meaning as the distinctive subject matter of social science. The following discussion incorporates much of this basic argument.

PERSONAL MEANING IS THE SUBJECT MATTER OF EDUCATIONAL RESEARCH

Physical scientists encounter exceedingly complex phenomena, but not phenomena that mirror human thought processes. Neither atoms nor rocks nor stars construct symbolic representations of the universe and then act in accordance with the meanings they have constructed. Physical scientists simply do not deal with symbolic representations and meanings in the subject matter they study. They deal with physical events. Human acts, on the other hand, are only incidentally physical in nature, and it is only in rare circumstances that we ever attend to their actual physical properties. First and foremost, human acts are characterized by the meaning and intention of the persons who perform them. Sometimes we may interpret another person's meaning incorrectly, but it is nonetheless meaning to which we attend rather than the physical properties of movement or speech.[5] Whereas all forms of matter exhibit activity, human existence is distinguished by the fact that people intend and signify something by what they do.

---

[3]Distinctions between information, knowledge, and skill are discussed in Chapter 5.

[4]Various methods derived from anthropology that are currently being used in classroom research represent an exception to this general observation.

[5]The difference between speech and language exemplifies the distinction between physical reality and the reality of meaning. Speech sounds are physical events. Language is a symbolic event, a set of meaningful relationships we abstract from speech. If these relationships cannot be detected, as happens in listening to a foreign language being spoken, then we hear only incomprehensible sounds and not talk. Both speech and language are real, but they are real in different ways.

This distinctive quality of human life implies that personal meanings are the subject matter of educational research and the stuff from which fruitful theories must be spun. It's not that there are two different kinds of understanding at work in science, one appropriate to inanimate matter and the other to psychological events. By definition, all understanding is psychological in nature. A more apt depiction is that the social scientist has two different things to understand: what behaviors signify from the standpoint of the person(s) involved, and what those significations imply from the standpoint of a transcendent conceptual framework. The first task involves the clarification of personal meanings. The second task involves the formulation of comprehensive theory. No matter how elaborate our methodological and statistical designs may be in pursuing the second task, results will be disappointing unless the first task is attended with care. Even the most ambitious research program will miss the mark if it leaps over meaning and intention in a rush to formulate comprehensive theory.

To illustrate this twofold task more concretely, suppose researchers wished to determine early indications of spatial reasoning ability, and they set out to do so by studying young children's drawings. Important characteristics to note in this hypothetical situation are the following: (a) the goal involves the formulation of a higher-order conception that goes beyond children's drawings, but (b) drawings alone are assumed to be the critical subject matter to study and interpret. The investigators collect scores of drawings and proceed to classify them on the basis of such criteria as complexity of objects represented and various indices of spatial perspective. A significant number of drawings appear to be nothing but scribbles, however, and so a "scribble" category is added to the classification. Without belaboring details, let us say that the "scribble" category is eventually interpreted as indicating little evidence of spatial ability within the age range studied. The classification scheme may even be tried again on a larger number of children (with similar results) and subsequently used in a school system. Children who produce a certain percentage of scribble drawings are then given special assistance and instruction in spatial representation to help them overcome their apparent disability.

But let us look at a particular "scribbler" more closely. The child creates a recognizable picture of an airplane or car or truck and then hastily draws circular lines over the picture. With some probing, we discover that the scribbled swirls are intended to represent the movement of air around the vehicle. Further observation and questioning yield identical findings for a great many children. This closer look leads to an unhappy conclusion. Because personal meanings were not clarified, the conceptual scheme generated by research has wound up with an interpretive account of "scribbles" rather than of "vehicles in motion." Moreover, the drawing of vehicles-in-motion is now being remediated by special school instruction. For all we know, other categories in the conceptual scheme may represent equally plausible but erroneous accounts of drawing behavior that are being accommodated in schools by equally superfluous instruction.

The illustration above is greatly simplified, but it does not grossly distort, in principle, the sequence of events that occurs in many research projects. Other illustrations could point up other sequences that end in similar outcomes. Although "explanation" is the goal of any science, the verb *explain* has two distinct denotations: to clarify intention, and to give comprehensive interpretations. Educational research is obliged to engage in both tasks. When the behavior under investigation is sufficiently circumscribed, and when the problem and the age levels of interest suggest that persons will be reasonably aware of their intentions and able to articulate them, then questioning people may be a perfectly adequate way to clarify intention. If these conditions don't hold, then the clarification of meaning becomes a primary job of inference and theory construction in and of itself.

Theories of personal meaning (whether derived by questioning or inference) necessarily precede theories of a more comprehensive order in social science. The case for naturalistic methods of inquiry in research rests on the ability of such methods to capture and preserve clues to personal meaning. Without these clues, the central subject matter of educational research evaporates. We are left with little to contemplate, little to theorize about, little to "explain" in any sense of the word.

Because personal meaning is an ambiguous concept, obvious in some respects yet vague in others, it deserves closer scrutiny. The remainder of the chapter examines this concept, first circumscribing "meaning" from the perspective of contemporary theory in several social science disciplines, and then narrowing to consider "personal meaning" within the confines of personal construct theory.

THE CENTRALITY OF MEANING IN CONTEMPORARY THEORIES OF SOCIAL SCIENCE

In the late 1950s, three converging lines of research convincingly challenged the precepts of Behaviorism and propelled new theories to the foreground of scientific interest. Each of these lines of work emphasized the significance of meaning in slightly different ways, but collectively they mark the beginning of what is regarded here as the body of "contemporary theory" in social science.

One line of research can be traced to the publication of Chomsky's *Syntactic Structures* (1957), a theoretical work that stimulated new directions in the field of linguistics and the birth of a related discipline (psycholinguistics). Chomsky's theory posits that grammar is a set of rules for transforming the underlying meaning of thought into intelligible language forms. Used by a speaker, these rules generate intelligible utterances that reflect the speaker's meaning. Used by a listener, these same rules generate predictions about the speaker's utterances. Chomsky, of course, did not assume an extended knowledge of textbook grammar on the part of individuals; he was referring to tacit or implicit knowledge that people possess about the structuring of their native language. It is this understanding of structure, rather than knowledge of individual words, that holds the most essential clues to language meaning. A person may know many individual words in a foreign language, for example, but such knowledge is of little avail in conducting everyday conversation. To comprehend a language readily and to speak it fluently require a firm grasp of the grammatical rules that structure the language.

Chomsky's theory was put to the test almost immediately in careful studies of infants' language development.[6] Although the details of language behavior varied from child to child, psycholinguists were able to discern primitive rules that predicted the structure of each child's utterances. Moreover, commonalities among the grammars indicated a systematic progression in the structuring of the children's utterances. Further studies with older children revealed that the process of learning grammatical rules extends through the elementary school years, at least up to the age of 10. Since grammatical rules are not consciously formulated knowledge, and since young children's grammatical rules are not fully elaborated (they lead children to make errors no adult speaker would make), it seems clear that children do not learn the rules of their speech directly from adults. Rather, the implication is that children construct the rules that transform meaning into language for themselves, forming closer and closer approximations to the complex rules of an adult speaker.

Other psycholinguistic studies demonstrated that the comprehension of speech cannot be accounted for entirely by the sound waves emanating from a speaker but depends in large measure on the listener's active contribution of meaning. One of the most convincing demonstrations of this fact comes from one of the simplest experiments. Pollack and Pickett (1964) recorded ordinary conversations in an anechoic chamber to ensure the acoustic fidelity of the audio reproductions. The researchers then played excerpts from these recordings for listeners who knew nothing about the context of the original conversations. Though the physical stimuli were undistorted, and though listeners could hear the recordings as many times as they wished, the listeners were not very accurate in identifying the words spoken in the conversational excerpts. Lacking a context in which to place the sounds they heard, the listeners had difficulty anticipating language structures that might be uttered and thus experienced difficulty understanding what actually was uttered. Evidence from this study and other seminal investigations (e.g., Fodor & Bever, 1965; and Garrett, Bever, & Fodor, 1966) supports the notion that the ability to comprehend ongoing conversation presumes the ability to think along with the speaker and to predict the meanings that the speaker is likely to realize in language form.

---

[6]Representative studies include the work of Brown and Bellugi (1964), Chomsky (1970), Menyuk (1969), and Bloom (1970). See Cazden (1972) for a comprehensive presentation of this research and Bussis et al. (1981) for a briefer discussion; both writings are intended for educational audiences.

These developments in the field of language turned some widely accepted ideas upside down. They directly disputed the assumption that imitation and reinforcement are the primary mechanisms of language learning, and they brought didactic methods of language instruction into question. As conceived in contemporary theory, the initial achievement of learning language, as well as every subsequent act of speech and speech comprehension, depends on the individual's generation of meaning.

A second line of research that has shaped contemporary theory emphasizes the individual's active construction of knowledge and meaning equally as much as the work on language. This is the body of research stimulated by Piaget and his colleagues in Switzerland.[7,8] The word "meaning" rarely appears in Piaget's writing, but it seems fair to say that he construed meaning as synonymous with thought. And thought, according to the theory, is synonymous with personal action and with the mental structures children develop to represent both their action and the information gained through action. As modes of action and mental structures change with development, the nature of thought and meaning also changes. Each qualitative change constitutes a stage of development, and inherent to each stage are characteristic possibilities and constraints in the ways a child can understand and make sense of the world.

Piaget's theory thus implies not only that understanding and sense are constructed by the child but that they are relative to particular stages of development. And this idea, in turn, suggests educational implications. Some views of intelligence implicitly assume that intellectual growth amounts to a steady increase in the kind of logic that marks adult thinking. Piaget's theory of qualitative shifts in the child's understanding paints a very different picture of intellectual growth and (by implication) of the educator's role. A child's expression of "illogical" and "inaccurate" ideas may, in fact, signal meaningful comprehension with respect to the child's stage of development. More importantly, since the theory stresses action as the key to intellectual growth, a child's exercise of the reasoning powers characteristic of a given stage is considered crucial for advancement to the next stage. Thus, attempts to teach children ideas and answers that are logically correct by adult standards may be far from helpful. To the extent that children cannot assimilate and understand the ideas but only parrot them, such attempts may actually discourage the exercise of genuine rationality. And to the extent that the exercise of genuine (stage-appropriate) rationality is discouraged, children's intellectual development is impeded.

The third line of research forming contemporary theory is by far the most diverse with respect to both its origins and the directions it has taken. Initial

---

[7]Although Piaget's research spans six decades, he did not formulate his systematic theory until the early 1950s; and outside of a few scholarly circles, his theory remained relatively unknown in this country until Hunt introduced it to American audiences in *Intelligence and Experience* (1961).

[8]The educational literature contains several books and articles on Piaget's theory. See, for example, Athey and Rubadeau (1970), Furth and Wachs (1974), and Sigel (1969).

phases of this work are commonly identified as "cognitive psychology," a term that gained popularity during the sixties and that appropriately connotes a concern with many cognitive functions of the brain: memory, perception, decision making, information processing. The early group of cognitive psychologists[9] drew on a substantial body of theoretical research in perception, memory, and personality (the legacy of many of those who had resisted Behaviorism[10]) and consolidated this work with theories evolving from research on information processing (a new field of interest generated by the advancement of computer science). If one had to summarize the import of this first phase of cognitive psychology in two sentences, the message might read as follows. Nothing that is meaningful in the world "impresses" itself on the human brain. Rather, the brain "constructs" meaningful patterns from the information it receives; within certain physiological and developmental limits, it "decides" how best to organize meaning in memory; it "determines" what meanings to expect in the future on the basis of the meaning it has already constructed and stored; and it "intends" what to do next on the basis of its expectations and purposes.

No psychologist documented these theoretical conclusions more thoroughly or painstakingly than Neisser (1967), and no one saw the limitations of cognitive psychology at the time more clearly than he did. The two limitations he discerned, methodological and substantive, were intimately connected. The substantive problem was a failure to come to grips with the intentional aspect of human functioning. While intention was assumed, it was inadequately handled and not well understood. Neisser describes this limitation in the following way:

> If what the subject will remember depends in large part on what he is trying to accomplish, on his purposes, do not predictions become impossible and explanations ad hoc? If we give no further account of these purposes, how can we tell what he will think of next? (p. 304)

The crux of the problem, as Neisser saw it, could be traced to the classical procedures of experimental psychology and measurement. Participants in the usual learning experiment were assumed to have a single motive—to learn the experimental task they were supposed to solve, given the implied or stated alternatives that were set by the experimenter. Neisser notes that experimental situations are very different in this respect from ordinary situations of daily life. He continues:

---

[9]It would be unwieldy to identify all those who have made significant contributions to cognitive psychology, but important theoretical works during the first twenty years of the field include Bruner, Goodnow, and Austin (1956); Miller, Galanter, and Pribram (1960); Neisser (1967); and Weimer and Palermo (1974).

[10]Among those who developed integrative theories at odds with the mainstream of Behaviorism were Allport (1937); Kohler (1947); Lashley (1954); Murphy (1947); and Tolman (1948).

In itself, this is hardly a devastating criticism. Experiments need not imitate life. In fact, the art of experimentation is the creation of *new* situations, which catch the essence of some process without the circumstances that usually obscure it. The question in this case is whether the essence has truly been caught. The simplifications introduced by confining the subject to a single motive and a fixed set of alternative responses can be justified only if motivation and cognition are genuinely distinct. If—as I suppose—they are inseparable where remembering and thinking are concerned, the common experimental paradigms may pay too high a price for simplicity. (p. 305)

The publication of Neisser's work roughly marks the beginning of an ongoing trend in research that has moved along several different fronts while maintaining general theoretical compatibility. This trend built on cognitive theory forged in preceding decades, and (consciously or not) it took Neisser's challenge seriously, pioneering many new methods of study. In several instances, new methods have signaled the emergence of new or reconceptualized disciplines (e.g., sociolinguistics, ethnomethodology and the sociology of language, computational linguistics, artificial intelligence). Irrespective of methodological differences, investigators associated with this trend have started with the assumption that people generate meaning, and they have sought to examine specific ways in which meaning influences the everyday comprehension of objects and events, of written material, and of ordinary discourse.[11] The work thus far has had two main emphases. It has elaborated specific kinds of meaning (knowledge and assumptions) that people necessarily "fill-in" for themselves to make sense of objects, events, text, and discourse. And it has pointed to social and cultural influences that effect the nature of these "filled-in" meanings.

A confusing note in this ongoing work stems from the rather specialized vocabulary that has evolved within each methodological approach. Not only are methodological descriptions and theoretical conceptions couched in complex terminology, but different approaches use different terms to connote basically similar concepts. For example, the network of meanings that is assumed to direct thought and action has been variously referred to, among other things, as a "schema," "script," and "frame." Tannen (1979) traces the origins of some of these terms to specific approaches and investigators, but she then proceeds to summarize matters in the following way: "all of these complex terms and approaches amount to the simple concept . . . that, based on one's experience of the world in a given culture (or combination of cultures), one organizes knowledge about the world and uses this knowledge to predict interpretations and relationships regarding new information, events, and experiences" (pp. 138–139).

---

[11]See Bobrow and Collins (1975); Spiro, Bruce, and Brewer (1980); and Freedle (1979) for representative compendiums of this research and theory.

The overview presented in these few pages glosses over details of theories, and it ignores important differences between major theories, disciplines, and substrands within disciplines. The only intent of the summary is to highlight a message about the brain that has been conveyed by social science for over 25 years. Based on research in the areas of memory, perception, thought, language development, and language comprehension, this view of the human brain is so well documented that it is accepted as a ''given'' by most social scientists.

* The brain constructs perceptions and thought (as opposed to behaving like a sponge).
* The brain's central function is to create meaning.
* Meaning arises through the perception and interpretation of patterns, or relationships, in events.
* Anticipation and intention exert a directing influence on the brain's activity.

Although meaning is a relative matter that may shift character from one context or culture to another, from one developmental stage to another, and from one individual to another, there would appear to be nothing relative about its function in life. People in every culture and at every age strive to make their experience as meaningful as possible in whatever circumstance they find themselves. Such a message constitutes substantial reason for educators and educational researchers to be concerned with the meanings children construct in classroom environments.

Having said this, however, problems still remain. Every day, teachers encounter children in the same classroom, from the same cultural milieu, at the same developmental stage, and within the same general range of ability who nonetheless approach learning tasks and materials in very different ways. As argued previously, comprehensive explanations that account for these variations in learning necessarily depend on understanding variations at the level of individual meaning. But how is personal meaning to be regarded beyond the generalities stated above? And how does the teacher or researcher come to understand personal meaning? Such questions are directly addressed by Kelly's (1955) theory of personal constructs.

Although Kelly's ideas slightly predate contemporary theory (as defined here), they foreshadow it in almost every important respect. The reasons for reaching back to this particular theory are considerations of comprehensiveness and heuristic value. Kelly was a clinician, and his theory encompasses the general arena of living and learning that is the clinician's concern. Whereas specialized work in such areas as perception, memory, and language is essential to theoretical progress in understanding human functioning, specialization necessarily narrows one's way of talking about human functioning. And for those who seek to understand children's classroom learning, broader rather than narrower perspectives seem most helpful. Equally important, Kelly's theory contains valuable leads for designing studies of individual children in the classroom. The discussion that follows is thus an attempt to recast contemporary theory at a level of personal meaning and to suggest some practical guidelines for the study of individuals.

THE PSYCHOLOGY OF PERSONAL CONSTRUCTS[12]

Kelly's theory deals primarily with people's symbolic representations (or "personal constructs") of the world, but it originates in his broader view of reality. He was not a philosophical idealist who saw a shadowy world composed only of people's fleeting thoughts. The universe really exists in Kelly's theory, and he believed that humankind was gradually coming to understand it. But for Kelly, existence itself implied a further conviction that permeates his entire theory. To say that something exists is to say that it is dynamic, that it is continually going on and changing with respect to itself. In other words, it exists in time and can be measured along the dimensions of time. Because change through time is Kelly's very definition of existence, it means that his theory needs no special explanations of why people are motivated to act. Action and change are the qualities that define our existence in the first place.

If personal construct theory affirms the reality of the universe, it is even more emphatic about the reality of human conception. People's thoughts also "really exist," and they are the most distinctive characteristic of human life. As the theory makes clear, however, there is a continually changing correspondence between what people really think exists and what really does exist. The universe thus involves an interesting relationship wherein one part, the living person, is able to represent another part, the physical and social environment. Such a formulation emphasizes the creative capacity of living things to represent the environment rather than merely to respond to it. And it is with this assertion of creative capacity that the formal theory of personal constructs begins.

Anticipation and Construing

Kelly's fundamental postulate states that the ongoing activities of human life are psychologically channeled by the ways in which a person anticipates events. The cornerstone of his thinking thus prefigures contemporary theory, for it assumes that anticipation directs thought and action. Kelly's favorite metaphor for capturing this future-oriented aspect of human life is the "person-as-scientist." People in their everyday living engage in much the same activity as the scientist on the

---

[12]Discussion here covers only selected aspects of Kelly's theory.

job. They try to predict events in order to gain some measure of control over their destiny. Since life, for Kelly, makes sense only as it is seen in the perspective of time, it follows that anticipation should be the psychological heartbeat of human existence. For if persons are to make their way through the changing passage of time, they must be able to anticipate events. When they find themselves in a situation that makes little sense and that they cannot anticipate effectively, they become confused, sometimes anxious, often hesitant to act at all.

A person anticipates events by construing their replications. By "construing," Kelly means placing an interpretation on something; and by "replications," he implies that events repeat themselves. If people could detect no threads of continuity in the ongoing universe, then there would be no way to segment time, and life would be totally undifferentiated. But the universe does repeat itself. People do perceive recurrent themes in the flow of events, and they construct interpretations about those perceived themes. They mark them as meaningful in some way and thus phrase the experience of time.

For the newborn infant, the first construed themes or replications of events probably revolve around the biological rhythms of life. And in the dawn of history, people perhaps began to comprehend the universe by noting the recurrence of day and night, the cycle of the seasons, or (as Kelly speculates) the beating of their own pulse. Whatever such beginnings may be or may have been, the theoretical principle stands. When people construe repeated patterns in the ongoing flow of events, they construct an interpretation of those events, and these interpretations, in turn, become the means or ways of anticipating future events. The interpretive structure becomes an anticipatory construct.

Construct Systems

A construct system embraces the total network of a person's constructs, and it includes tacit as well as verbal constructs. Kelly reiterated this point throughout his writing, but it can hardly be overemphasized. Construing is not to be confounded with verbal formulation. Virtually all of the infant's experience and many realms of adult experience are represented in inarticulate form. We would be hard pressed, for example, to explain exactly how we propose to breathe, to digest our dinner, to dance a rhumba, or to play tennis. Such explanations are beyond our power to articulate well, because we cannot anticipate these matters within the same subsystem (of grammatical rules) that we use for communication. Yet all of these are individually structured processes, and what one anticipates has a great deal to do with the course they take.

Similarly, personal construct systems are characterized not only by knowledge (by *what* a person anticipates and understands), but also by stylistic features (by *how* one conducts commerce with the world). Some stylistic features are determined by the way the construct system is organized. Other style characteristics are undoubtedly determined more by biological make-up, coming close to what is implied by the old-fashioned word "temperament" (energy level and pace of action, for example). Whatever their origin, these stylistic features are often more salient to others than to the person involved. Unless a particular way of interacting with the world is foiled by external circumstances or specifically brought to an individual's attention, it often remains on the periphery of awareness. And some styles may be so deeply ingrained that they rarely if ever surface to conscious awareness. Although people are generally oblivious of how they go about things, the how is an integral aspect of personal meaning that pervades every realm of life and learning.

Learning

Kelly's theory deals with learning in the claim that a person's construct system varies as he or she successively construes the replications of events. Kelly thus asserts that construing is itself a process that occurs through time; and as it occurs, it creates changes in the individual's construct system. Combined with the theory's fundamental assumption that constructs determine behavior, this corollary means that learning necessarily takes place. As Kelly expresses it, "learning is not a special class of psychological processes; it is synonymous with any and all psychological processes."[13] Thus, the significant question to be asked is *what* a person has learned, not *if* a person has learned.

Kelly goes on to say that while learning and experience are synonymous, neither can be deduced from the parade of episodes that marches through a person's life. Experience is not constituted by ongoing events in and of themselves; it is constituted by a person's successive construing of events. If an individual fails to construe repeated themes in certain events that impinge on his or her life, then those events (no matter how compelling they may seem from someone else's perspective) will not enter the person's experience in any meaningful way. And two people exposed to the same physical events may construe them in very different ways. They may come away from the same situation with two quite disparate sets of learning and experience. Likewise, individuals may construe different happenings in much the same way and thereby share similar meanings and exhibit similar behaviors. It is similarity in the construing of events that provides the basis for similar perceptions and actions, and not similarity or sameness of the events themselves.

The Contextual Nature of Meaning

Since constructs are interpretations of relationships that exist in the ongoing events of the world, it follows that the elements of relationship are embedded in events of the world. In other words, meanings arise from contexts and are

---

[13]Kelly, op. cit., p. 75.

therefore contextually constrained. The idea of contextual relativity appears as a formal corollary in personal construct theory, though it certainly was not original with Kelly. The contextual nature of meaning has been a subject of speculation by psychologists since psychology began, and by philosophers for centuries prior to that. It is a major contention of contemporary theory and has stimulated a new surge of research interest and activity during recent years.

The fact that meanings arise from contextual relationships does not wed a person only to the literal and palpable events of life, however. The power of symbolic representation implies that individuals can transform contexts in imaginative ways and thereby create new meanings. If this were not so, people would never be able to generate and understand metaphoric meaning as easily as they do. At a more profound level, of course, people would never open up new realms of meaning in art nor pursue new worlds of understanding in science. A distinctive feature of human thought, as compared with the thought of animals, is its reflexive character, its ability to turn on itself as an event that can be construed. And in this reflexive capacity lies the imaginative potential to perceive new contexts of meaning. Kelly talks more of learning and experience than he does about meaning per se, but the burden of his entire theory speaks to both the tangible and intangible contexts of meaning that people conceive as reality. The human capacity to generate new contexts of meaning was expressed explicitly in contemporary theory by Neisser's formulation that the mechanisms of imagination are continuous with those of perception.

Choice, Change, and the Validity of Construct Systems

Personal construct theory views choice as an ongoing process in the evolution of construct systems. In any given situation, people choose for themselves that interpretation through which they anticipate the greater possibility for definition or extension of their system. Kelly's discussion of these terms clearly equates "definition" with the securing or consolidation (in extreme form, rigidifying) of previous interpretations, and "extension" with openness to new interpretations. Openness to new interpretations and new events involves the satisfying anticipation of having dared something, of extending one's capabilities, of fuller understanding, and so on. But it also involves the risk of abandoning familiar ground, and the anticipation of such risk is experienced as anxiety, however fleeting. To have a novel idea about familiar events or to learn something totally new therefore requires an outlook on the world that is tipped in the direction of affirming interest and attention.

People cannot, of course, seek the new at every turn. They need to consolidate their resources in familiar territory, or they would have no resources at all. This principle of consolidation and extension suggests that learning which evolves over any substantial period of time will be a process of growth and plateaus rather than one of uninterrupted progress. By logical extension, it implies that instructional provision for securing a child's established capabilities in an educational setting is equally as important as the provision for new engagements.

Although Kelly assumed that people learn by virtue of being alive, he did not go to the extreme of assuming that all learning is equally valid. Personal construct theory regards validity to be a function of structural properties of a construct system. Of the many structural characteristics Kelly discusses, permeability is the most important. A construct is permeable to the extent that it will admit new elements into the relational structure while remaining sufficiently defined to hold its practical value in anticipating events. To the extent that it admits new elements in this fashion, it is adaptable to new realms of life and to the changing face of familiar realms. Generally speaking, then, it is adaptability that provides the most reliable gauge of the growing validity of a person's constructs.

On the Understanding of Others

Kelly believed that the clues to personal meanings are found in a person's behavior. But he also believed it is necessary to look at behavior in certain ways in order to ascertain those clues. The part of his theory that deals with "how to look" contains the most explicit implications for research methodology.

Kelly's view on the matter of understanding others rests on a simple logical tautology. People come to understand one another in exactly the same way that they come to understand anything else—by construing patterns of relationship in the ongoing events of the world. The only difference in this particular case is that the ongoing events of interest happen to be the events of another person's behavior. A construct is someone's abstraction of reality that itself is real but not visible. Behavior, on the other hand, is clearly visible, and behavior is governed by constructs. Hunting for a person's abstractions of reality thus entails a search for patterns of similarity and contrast that keep being repeated in the things a person does and says.

The discernment of behavioral themes in this manner provides the only basis for what Kelly regards as genuine *interpersonal understanding*. By definition, such discernment requires a significant time period, because it is impossible to understand a person's characteristic anticipations of life after 5 minutes' or a day's acquaintance. Kelly also points out that interpersonal understanding implies only that one person is able to construe another person's outlook, not that one person necessarily shares another person's outlook. Quite often, the partners in a marriage, friendship, or working relationship have decidedly different ways of viewing the world, yet they come to understand and to anticipate each other's way of thinking about things. But interpersonal understanding can also be a relatively one-sided affair, and this situation often arises in relationships between an adult and a child. An observant teacher, for example, generally construes a child's thinking more effectively (at higher levels of abstraction) than a child construes the teacher's thinking.

As far as the conduct of research is concerned, Kelly's theory implies that systematic observation and documentation are the first steps toward understanding another person's thinking. We observe the events of an individual's behavior over some significant time period (whatever period seems called for by the problem under study) and try to record those events as faithfully as possible. The next step is one of inference. We abstract relationships from the documentary records that weave discrete and otherwise disjointed episodes into a coherent pattern. If the abstractions made on the basis of initial behavioral records fail to predict relationships in the later documentation, and episodes don't cohere over time, then it is necessary to reconsider the events. The main danger Kelly warns against in the process of making inferences and abstracting relationships is the tendency to make comparative interpretations.

Often, comparative interpretations come in the guise of statements about what a person *doesn't do,* as compared with what others do or what someone thinks should be done. Statements such as "doesn't pay attention" and "doesn't cooperate" are typical examples. Although the behaviors giving rise to this kind of interpretative statement may well recur in an individual's record, the interpretation itself yields little insight into what the person may have been attending to or trying to accomplish when he or she "wasn't attending" and "wasn't cooperating." Some comparative judgments are inevitable, especially in the realm of stylistic features of behavior (e.g., "speaks slowly"); but a preponderance of normative statements about the individual defeats the purpose of inquiry into personal meanings. As Kelly succinctly summarizes the aim of such inquiry:

> We cannot, of course, crawl into another person's skin and peer out at the world through his eyes. We can, however, start by making inferences based primarily upon what we see him doing, rather than upon what we have seen other people doing. (p. 42)

A practical issue for research on personal meanings is the definition of a behavioral event. At what level of detail is behavior to be described? The theory of personal constructs helps with this problem, for it states that constructs have a limited "range of convenience." That is, a particular construct is not useful for anticipating all aspects of the world, but applies only to some limited portion of the world and therefore governs only a limited portion of the person's behavior. The definition of a behavioral event thus hinges on the nature of the constructs under study. Constructs having an extended range of convenience require a broad overview of behavior, whereas constructs having a relatively narrow range of convenience require a more focused and detailed description of behavior.

The process of observing and recording raw data and then making inferences from the data is hardly an original idea. It is a model of research and theory construction that has characterized advance in every one of the physical sciences. But it is a model that has rarely been applied to individual behavior in educational research, primarily because educational research has tended to skip the step of clarifying personal meanings. One outstanding example of the model's application at the individual level occurred a few years after Kelly's writing, in the initial wave of psycholinguistic research. Investigators documented the speech behavior of a small number of individual children and then inferred from these raw data the grammatical rules that structured the utterances of each child. Eventually, this work led to the abstraction of higher-level theory concerning the general progression of language acquisition.

In principle, this model has also been put to use in several areas of contemporary research that trace their methodological orgins to anthropology. There is an important difference in the intent of much of this work, however. Although individuals have been studied, the major goal has been to clarify contextual influences that shape common understandings (those meanings shared by a group of people), rather than to clarify the personal meanings of individual group members. Kelly addressed this difference in drawing a distinction between interpersonal understanding and common understanding.

Common understanding implies that two people construe an event or series of events in basically the same way; they place a similar interpretation on it. Common understanding does not imply that one person understands the thinking of another. Kelly illustrates this difference with the example of driving. People anticipate the action of other drivers on the road with reasonable accuracy, yet they don't understand other drivers' thinking in an interpersonal way at all. What they do is understand the contexts of traffic in a manner that is roughly analogous to other drivers. Their respective interpretations of road situations are similar enough at least to allow for the coordinated movement of traffic most of the time. When an element of uncertainty enters the scene to jar someone's confidence in the interpretation of a particular traffic context, then the person becomes acutely aware that it is impossible to anticipate the understanding of other drivers, and he or she slows down. If people fail to register the elements that produce an uncertain context, and an accident ensues, they become painfully aware that strangers in cars have little basis for anticipating one another's thinking.

The limitations on common understanding—the fact that it takes us so far and no further—does not diminish its importance in life. The events of the world keep on happening, and people come to construe literally thousands of these events in similar ways. Without such common grounds of understanding, people would have no basis on which to communicate or to coordinate their actions with those around them. By itself, however, common understanding illuminates an individual's meanings only to the degree that it illuminates the collective meanings shared by the culture or social group of which the individual is a member. Used as a research tool for discerning personal meanings (for detecting themes in the recorded events of a person's behavior), common understanding provides a basis for making inferences about certain events. But it is a tool that requires judicious use. If research investigators simply take it for granted that other people construe situations in much the same way that they (the investigators) do, research results may reflect the compounding of one erroneous inference after another.

SUMMARY

This chapter has ranged across several fields (science, philosophy, social science) to underscore the reasons and theoretical wherewithal for focusing educational research on the meanings students derive from their instructional environments. The reasons for such a focus are many and varied, but the most fundamental reason is stated in the opening paragraph of the chapter—namely, the failure of research to forge a coherent theory of normal, everyday, classroom learning. The first section of the chapter attributes this failure in part to a national preoccupation with technological progress and the widely shared misconception that theoretical insight will follow on the heels of more sophisticated teaching techniques and testing methods. Although modern technology clearly has a place in the classroom, its usefulness for theoretical understanding hinges on the degree to which it provides information about the meaningful and intentional aspects of learning.

Building on the work of a philosopher of science (Abraham Kaplan), the chapter next argues that personal meaning is the essential subject matter of social science and that no theoretical progress is possible as long as research methods obscure rather than illuminate this subject matter. The power of naturalistic research methods stems from their potential to preserve clues to meaning and thus to shed light on what the social scientist must ultimately explain.

The remainder of the chapter expands on the concept of meaning. It does so first by tracing three diverse lines of research investigation that, together, pushed concepts of meaning to the foreground of theoretical attention. The three lines of investigation discussed are linguistic research, research stimulated by the work of Piaget and his colleagues, and the broad field of experimentation loosely associated under the banner of cognitive psychology. This section ends with four assumptions, currently espoused by most theorists, that highlight the centrality of meaning in human functioning.

Contemporary theories often emphasize a particular cognitive function (language, perception, memory) and/or are expressed in complex and abstract terminology. For this reason, the chapter turns to Kelly's Theory of Personal Constructs for a final exposition on the concept of meaning. Although Kelly's work predates contemporary theory, it prefigures almost every major contemporary assumption about the nature and significance of meaning. Moreover, Kelly's terminology and concepts tend to capture more of the whole individual and therefore seem more appropriate for those who strive to understand multiple facets of children's classroom behavior. And from a practical standpoint, Kelly's theory (particularly his ideas about interpersonal understanding and common understanding) suggests several implications for the conduct of classroom research. Specific ways in which these suggestions were implemented in the ETS Collaborative Research Project on Reading are described in the next three chapters.

REFERENCES

Allport, G. *Personality: A psychological interpretation.* New York: Holt, 1937.

Athey, I., & Rubadeau, D. *Educational implications of Piaget's theory.* Waltham, MA: Ginn-Blaisdell, 1970.

Bloom, L. *Language development: Form and function in emerging grammars.* Cambridge, MA: MIT Press, 1970.

Bobrow, D., & Collins, A. (Eds.). *Representation and understanding: Studies in cognitive science.* New York: Academic Press, 1975.

Brown, R., & Bellugi, U. Three processes in the child's acquisition of syntax. *Harvard Educational Review,* 1964, *34,* 133–151.

Bruner, J., Goodnow, J., & Austin, G. *A study of thinking.* New York: Wiley, 1956.

Bussis, A., Chittenden, E., Courtney, R., & Metz, K. *Let's look at children, II: A guide to theory and classroom observation.* Menlo Park, CA: Addison-Wesley, 1981.

Cazden, C. B. *Child language and education.* New York: Holt, Rinehart & Winston, 1972.

Cazden, C. B. Learning to read in classroom interaction. In L. B. Resnick & P. A. Weaver (Eds.), *Theory and practice of early reading* (Vol. 3). Hillsdale, NJ: Lawrence Erlbaum Associates, 1979.

Chein, I. *The science of behavior and the image of man.* New York: Basic Books, 1972.

Chomsky, C. Reading, writing, and phonology. *Harvard Educational Review,* 1970, *40,* 287–309.

Chomsky, N. *Syntactic structures.* The Hague: Mouton, 1957.

Fodor, J., & Bever, T. The psychological reality of linguistic segments. *Journal of Verbal Learning and Verbal Behavior,* 1965, *4,* 414–421.

Freedle, R. (Ed.). *New directions in discourse processing* (Vol. II). Norwood, NJ: Ablex, 1979.

Furth, H., & Wachs, H. *Thinking goes to school: Piaget's theory in practice.* New York: Oxford University Press, 1974.

Garrett, M., Bever, T., & Fodor, J. The active use of grammar in speech perception. *Perception and Psycholinguistics,* 1966, *1,* 30–32.

Hawkins, D. Learning the unteachable. In L. Shulman & E. Keislar (Eds.), *Learning by discovery: A critical appraisal.* Chicago: Rand McNally, 1966.

Hunt, J. McV. *Intelligence and experience.* New York: Ronald Press, 1961.

Kaplan, A. *The conduct of inquiry.* San Francisco: Chandler Publishing Company, 1964.

Kelly, G. A. *The psychology of personal constructs* (Vol. 1). New York: W. W. Norton, 1955.

Kohler, W. *Gestalt psychology.* New York: Liveright, 1947.

Lashley, K. S. Dynamic processes in perception. In E. D. Adrian, F. Bremer, & H. H. Jasper (Eds.), *Brain mechanisms and consciousness.* Springfield, IL: Charles C. Thomas, 1954.

Menyuk, P. *Sentences children use.* Cambridge, MA: MIT Press, 1969.

Miller, G. A., Galanter, E., & Pribram, K. H. *Plans and the structure of behavior.* New York: Holt, Rinehart & Winston, 1960.

Mishler, E. Meaning in context: Is there any other kind? *Harvard Educational Review,* 1979, *49,* 1–19.

Murphy, G. *Personality: A biosocial approach to origins and structure.* New York: Harper, 1947.

Neisser, U. *Cognitive psychology.* New York: Appleton-Century-Crofts, 1967.

Pais, A. *'Subtle is the Lord. . .' The science and the life of Albert Einstein.* New York: Oxford University Press, 1982.

Polanyi, M. *Personal knowledge: Towards a post-critical philosophy.* Chicago: University of Chicago Press, 1958.

Pollack, I., & Pickett, J. The intelligibility of excerpts from conversation. *Language and Speech,* 1964, *6,* 165–171.

Sigel, I. The Piagetian system and the world of education. In D. Elkind & J. Flavell (Eds.), *Studies in cognitive development.* New York: Oxford University Press, 1969.

Simons, H. D. Black dialect, reading interference, and classroom interaction. In L. B. Resnick & P. A. Weaver (Eds.), *Theory and practice of early reading* (Vol. 3). Hillsdale, NJ: Lawrence Erlbaum Associates, 1979.

Spiro, R., Bruce, B., & Brewer, W. (Eds.). *Theoretical issues in reading comprehension.* Hillsdale, NJ: Lawrence Erlbaum Associates, 1980.

Strike, K. E. On the expressive potential of behaviorist language. *American Educational Research Journal,* 1974, *11,* 103–120.

Tannen, D. What's in a frame? Surface evidence for underlying expectations. In R. Freedle (Ed.), *New directions in discourse processing* (Vol. II). Norwood, NJ: Ablex, 1979.

Tolman, E. C. Cognitive maps in rats and men. *Psychological Review,* 1948, *55,* 189–208.

Weimer, W. B., & Palermo, D. S. (Eds.). *Cognition and the symbolic processes.* Hillsdale, NJ: Lawrence Erlbaum Associates, 1974.

White, S. H. Old and new routes from theory to practice. In L. B. Resnick & P. A. Weaver (Eds.), *Theory and practice of early reading* (Vol. 2), Hillsdale, NJ: Lawrence Erlbaum Associates, 1979.

2
The Collaborative Design and Research Participants

When the ETS staff first decided to engage in classroom research on beginning reading, it was assumed that teachers would be essential to such an effort. The reasoning behind this assumption is discussed in Chapter 1 and may be summarized as follows. Research that focuses on individual children's learning is necessarily concerned with the meanings a child construes in the instructional environment of materials, activities, social relationships, and teaching episodes. The meanings construed in discrete instructional encounters interweave through time to form more general patterns of anticipation and interpretation. And these more general patterns, in turn, are revealed by the child's actions over time. As the person who is in contact with children regularly, over significant periods of time and in a variety of classroom and school contexts, the teacher clearly has the best single vantage point for discerning the meanings children bring to instructional events and the patterns that characterize their behavior.

Specifically, the teacher shares with children many meanings particular to certain contexts in the classroom and school. Because these meanings tend to enter the domain of common understanding rather quickly, and are rarely discussed after the first few weeks of school, they often remain obscured to an external observer. Moreover, the relationship that obtains between teacher and children in a classroom is of a special order, akin to a tacit social contract in which certain expectations and privileges are implicitly acknowledged by all parties (child, teacher, parents, school officials, and community at large). This special relationship allows the teacher to participate in children's learning and to glimpse their thinking in a manner barred to most other adults. Thus, teachers not only share important grounds of common understanding with children, they have unique opportunities to establish interpersonal understanding.

In principle, this assumption about the teacher's perspective holds across the board. In practice, however, teachers differ in the degree to which they act upon the unique opportunities afforded by their position. They may not act because they are discouraged, sometimes prevented, from doing so by other demands on their teaching time and attention. Or, they may not act because they consider it relatively unimportant to observe and try to make sense of children's behavior, or because their classrooms are structured in such a way that there is not much overt behavior to observe. Whatever the reason or reasons, a teacher's failure to observe the signs of children's meanings and thinking correspondingly diminishes the value of the teacher's perspective for understanding children's learning.

In practice, then, we sought collaboration with teachers who consider children's meanings instructionally relevant and who try to make those meanings accessible to observation. The condition of being accessible to observation is best fulfilled in settings that offer children explicit opportunities to make certain decisions about their work and to follow through on those decisions. Thus, teachers who collaborated in the ETS reading research provide for some degree of choice on a child's part, they value observation as a means of assessment, and they use information they observe about children's choices as one basis for their instructional decisions.

No matter how capable an observer a teacher may be, however, there is still only so much one person can observe about a given child in a situation that requires attention to 30 or more children. The very nature of the teacher's participatory relationship with children may also preclude a view of the learner from other informing vantage points. Strengths external to the teacher must therefore be capitalized on if research is to yield a balanced perspective. For example, the person who is knowledgeable about children's learning and experienced in classroom observation can provide invaluable accounts of a child's activities, just as the researcher who is knowledgeable about relevant theory can add another essential perspective. These considerations recommend a design of team collaboration in research on children's learning, and that is the general design we had in mind as we began to organize the study.

Practitioners who fit the qualities described above had participated in previous ETS research projects,[1] and we enlisted their participation and recruitment help in the reading study. These practitioners were associated with programs of inservice education that support observational capabilities and provide guidance in creating curricular opportunities for meaningful choice on the part of children. The constraint of geographic location (reasonable commuting distance from Princeton), and the fact that we wished to concentrate the study primarily in city schools, further determined the selection of collaborators. Given these determin-

---

[1]A description of one such project appears in Bussis, A., Chittenden, E., and Amarel, M. *Beyond surface curriculum: An interview study of teachers' understandings.* Boulder, CO: Westview Press, 1976.

ing factors, the group that initially joined ETS staff in the research consisted of teachers, advisors, and other supervisory personnel who were (or had been) affiliated with one of the following programs: the Teacher Center in Greenwich, Connecticut; Community Resources Institute in New York City; Creative Teaching Workshop in New York City; the Workshop Center for Open Education at City College in New York City; the Follow Through Program in Paterson, New Jersey; the District Six Advisory Center in Philadelphia; and the Prospect School and Center for Education and Research in North Bennington, Vermont. Inclusion of the Vermont group was an exception as far as geographic location is concerned, but it was crucial to the collaborative enterprise. Patricia Carini (Founder of the Prospect School and Director of the Center) not only made central contributions to the study's methodology, she and her staff offered seminars on the theory and practice of observation that provided another source of ongoing support for many collaborators.

COLLABORATION IN THE PILOT STUDY

The research was conducted in two distinct phases: a 3-year pilot phase, and a 3-year operational phase. The pilot study officially began in the summer of 1975, when collaborators met for a 2-week planning conference. One important outcome of the conference was a strategy for data collection organized around the concept of "team units" that could function in semi-autonomous fashion.

A team consisted of a classroom teacher, a field-based observer (usually an advisor associated with one of the inservice education programs), and a member of the ETS research staff. Each team was responsible for documenting the progress of one or two children in the teacher's classroom, according to guidelines constructed and/or reviewed by the entire collaborative group. This strategy proved to be efficient in the pilot study and was subsequently used throughout the rest of the research.

A second outcome of the conference was agreement on major forms of data collection and the drafting of preliminary guidelines. Primary attention was devoted to guidelines for a "Descriptive Interview," the study's principal means for obtaining the teachers' observations of the children in each classroom whose progress was being followed. Plans also called for the observer member of the teams to document each child's actions periodically. The teacher and ETS team members were also to obtain oral reading samples from each child at specified intervals throughout the year. A final form of data collected by the teacher was work produced by each child: samples of drawing, painting, writing, and three-dimensional constructions.

These data collection procedures were tried, revised, and refined as necessary for 18 months. Ways of transcribing the data and preparing them for data analysis were also worked out at the ETS office. At the end of this period, we were reasonably satisfied that the plan and procedures could operate smoothly and accomplish what they were intended to accomplish. The pilot study began with 37 teachers, 18 field-based observers, and 58 children. After trial-testing the interview and observation procedures with this large group for 6 months, we continued intensive data collection with a reduced number of collaborators and children for the next 12 months.

Collaborating teachers in the pilot study were from 12 schools in six localities. New York City and Philadelphia accounted for 8 schools, and the remaining sites were Bennington, Vermont; Hartsdale, New York; New Rochelle, New York; and Paterson, New Jersey. The student population was predominantly black in 7 schools, predominantly white in 2 schools, and racially balanced in 3 schools.

During the last 18 months of the pilot study, the staff turned full attention to methods of data analysis and integration, and Patricia Carini assumed a key role in the research at this time. The staff of the Prospect Center had been working with teachers on the development of several processes for describing and summarizing children's work and observations of their classroom activity. In the spring of 1977, Carini tailored these procedures for purposes of analyzing the cumulative interview, observation, and work sample data on individual children in the pilot study. She conducted the first collaborative sessions at which the procedures were tried, and she consulted on subsequent revisions of the procedures made by ETS staff. (See Chapter 4 for a detailed description of the data analysis and integration procedures used in the study.)

COLLABORATION IN THE OPERATIONAL PHASE OF RESEARCH

The research began a second 3-year cycle (the operational phase) in the fall of 1978. As the study moved into this phase, the scope of data collection was restricted to 26 children in 13 classrooms located in five schools (two schools in New York City, two in Philadelphia, and the Prospect School in North Bennington, Vt.). Because data collection for all children continued for more than 1 year, it was necessary to stipulate either that collaborating teachers taught combined grade levels (e.g., K–1, 1–2) and thus would retain the study children for 2 years, or that they taught adjacent grade levels within the same school, so that the study children would pass from one teacher to another. Two children were followed in every classroom, and the focus of work was limited mainly to children who were entering kindergarten or first grade.

Data collection procedures that had been field-tested and revised in the pilot study were used in the operational research. So, too, was the team strategy of data collection, with one modification. Whereas the Descriptive Interview with teachers had sometimes been conducted by the observer member of a team in the pilot study, the interviews were always conducted by the ETS member of each team in the operational phase of research. Data collection for most children spanned a period from September of one school year to February of the next school year. There were exceptions, however, and the design remained flexible enough to accommodate continued data collection for a full 2 years on a few children, mainly those who were in kindergarten when the operational study began. Table 2.1 shows the composition of teams, the school site, and the children's grade level during the first year of operational research.

The team arrangement facilitated the work in many ways. Among other things, it allowed for the decentralization of administrative responsibility involved in data collection. Specific dates and times for interviews and observations were scheduled by the team members involved rather than being channeled through some central person at ETS. Likewise, the interviewer member on each team assumed responsibility for such things as making sure teachers had needed

TABLE 2.1
Data Collection Teams in Year I (Operational Phase)

Interviewer	Observer	Teacher[a]	Child[b]	Site	Grade Level
Bussis	Alberty	(1)	Rita	NYC	1
			Tim		1
Chittenden	Alberty	(2)	Rob	NYC	1
			Jane		1
Amarel	Budin	(3)	Kate	NYC	1
			Peter		K
Chittenden	Wallace	(4)	Carrie	NYC	K
			Kris		1
Wilder	Budin	(5)	Sharon	NYC	1
			Tommy		1
Amarel	Wallace	(6)	Reggie	NYC	2
			Margo		2
Bussis	Courtney	(7)	Yvonne	NYC	3
			David		4
Klausner	Courtney	(8)	Susan	Phila	K
			John		K
Klausner	Courtney	(9)	Colin	Phila	1
			Crystal		1
Bussis	Courtney	(10)	Murray	Phila	1
			Toni		1
Amarel	Hendersen	(11)	Debbie	Phila	1
			Louis		1
Klausner	Klinman	(12)	Jack	Phila	1
			Tanya		1
Klausner	Leckey	(13)	Alex	Vt.	1
			Alma		1

[a]Names are omitted in order to ensure the children's anonymity. A fourteenth teacher joined the study in Year 2, as the teacher of Susan and John.

[b]Pseudonyms are used.

tapes and tape recorders to obtain oral reading samples from the children. Without such diffused administrative responsibility, it seems likely that the data collection effort would have bogged down before it ever got off the ground. Moreover, the team arrangement allowed for flexibility in certain substantive decisions. For example, the contexts of some observations by the external observer were designated in the guidelines as "optional," to be determined by the team members. And the selection of specific texts children read in several oral reading samples was left to the judgment of the teacher and interviewer. Such flexibility of design guaranteed that certain critical decisions could be made by those best informed about the children in question.

Although decentralization of this kind was essential, total group planning and consensus on the general guidelines for data collection were equally important. As already mentioned, the planning, tryout, and revision of procedures and procedural guidelines took place during the pilot study, with considerable input from all collaborators, and final decisions agreed to by the entire group. Because of the extensive nature of this preliminary work together, planning for the operational phase of research was primarily a matter of reviewing guidelines, making further specifications where needed, and deciding on a time schedule. With the exception of three teachers and one observer (who were generally familiar with the previous work), everyone in the operational study had also participated in the pilot study.

CHILDREN IN THE STUDY

The sample of children was restricted to native English speakers during both phases of the research, and it excluded those with severe emotional or intellectual handicaps as well as those who exhibited signs of being precocious readers. Teachers in the pilot study chose the children whose progress was followed by the teams. Generally speaking, the teachers selected children they thought would be "interesting" to follow, and their choices did indeed prove interesting— ranging from quiet children who often go unnoticed in a classroom, to children with clear preferences and capabilities, to children who exhibited motor coordination patterns (in drawing and writing) that are often associated with learning disabilities, to so-called "nonverbal" children who are also frequently identified as those who will have difficulty in learning to read. Although the teachers' selections were encompassing, they could not ensure the kind of ordinariness that random sampling is intended to guarantee. Thus, for the operational phase of research, each teacher selected one study child, and the other child was selected at random among eligible children of the opposite sex from the child chosen by the teacher.

Data were collected on 84 children throughout the project's 6-year history. Nineteen of these children were in the middle and upper elementary grades when

TABLE 2.2
Children's Grade Level at Time of Entry
into the Study

Grade Level	Pilot Phase	Operational Phase	Combined Phases	Subset of 40 Younger Children
Kgn	10	4	14	(8)
1st	20	18	38	(28)
2nd	11	2	13	(4)
3rd	8	1	9	
4th	4	1	5	
5th	5		5	
	58	26	84	(40)

their progress was documented, and their records do not figure in the theoretical formulations about beginning reading that are presented in Part II.[2] A few children moved away or were switched to different classrooms in the midst of documentation. And data collection for several children in the pilot study continued only long enough to accomplish a particular aim of that phase of the research. A subset of forty (40) thus constitutes the more fully documented group of younger children on which our theory of beginning reading is based. Twenty-three of these children were studies in the operation phase of the research, and 17 were studied in the pilot phase. The majority were studied during the period of their first- and second-grade years in school. Table 2.2 shows the grade-level distribution of children in the pilot and operational phases of research and in the subset of 40.

The subset of 40 younger children is divided evenly between boys and girls. Two of the children attended school in North Bennington, Vt., and the rest attended public schools either in New York City or Philadelphia. Approximately two-thirds (26) are black and one-third (13) white; one child is of Native American descent. They represent a range of low- to middle-income families, but most of the group clusters in the lower half of that range.

Although the children were within a normal range of intellectual and emotional functioning, this is not to imply that "normal" children lead wholly tranquil lives. Almost every child experienced emotional and/or physical stress at some point during the research. Such stress varied from relatively mild mishaps, anxieties, and frustrations common in childhood, to fears and pains associated with more serious traumas (a parent's death or illness, a family dwelling

---

[2]Some older children were very literate and proficient readers, and some were still struggling with the skill of reading. The documentation of these older children served to keep a spectrum of later reading accomplishments and problems in full view, as a backdrop for thinking about issues of beginning reading.

destroyed by fire, the deprivations and uncertainties that attend financial poverty). While the children were dealing with their share of life's problems, however, they also displayed their share of enthusiasm, curiosity, humor, stubbornness, interest, competitiveness, and kindness in classroom interactions and encounters. On the whole, we believe they represent a reasonably healthy, well-functioning, resilient group of children.

The Children's Reading Instruction

All of the children in the subset of 40 were in heterogeneously grouped classes, and some were in "mainstream" classes that included individuals with special problems. More importantly, the children's teachers were quite similar in five key aspects of their instructional practice in beginning reading.

1. They provided a range of reading material in the classroom and encouraged children to select from this range, either all of the time or during specified times each day. Typically, this range included alphabet and counting books, picture storybooks, information and reference books, classic children's literature, and a variety of easy-to-read trade books and beginning reading series.

2. They had a "free reading" period each day during which children were expected to be engaged with books on their own, either reading them or looking at pictures (for those who were not yet reading). Some teachers tended to emphasize the quiet nature of this time, and some permitted children to read aloud softly to each other if they wished. Many alternated between these two conditions over the course of the year.

3. They worked at least some of the time on an individual basis with children, hearing each child read and/or discussing what the child had read.

4. They read to the class each day and usually followed up with a brief group discussion of the book or story. Insofar as possible, they varied the selections between well-written literature and interesting information books.

5. They expected children to write, either every day or two or three times a week. Some teachers spent more time on writing than others, but all supported it to some extent, both as an expressive medium in its own right and as an approach to reading. Children usually would begin writing by dictating their sentence(s) or words to an adult (teacher or aide) and then copying what was written down for them.

In combination, these five practices mean that teachers in the study provided children with several perspectives on the written word. The practices also mean that the teachers encouraged children to exercise intelligence in choosing, deciphering, and making sense of books and writing.

Beyond the commonalities just described, the teachers' reading programs varied greatly. Fourteen teachers are represented by the group of 40 children.

Five of these teachers taught in schools that emphasized an analytic approach to reading and therefore required a structured program of phonic instruction. (Two of the five used the more indirect method of phonic instruction represented by the *SRA* reading program, and three used the direct method represented by the *Lippincott* program.) A sixth teacher used the *Bank Street* basal readers as core materials for her instructional work with reading groups. Another teacher built her program almost entirely around the *Breakthrough to Literacy* books and materials, which reflect a language experience approach. The other seven teachers relied on easy-to-read trade books and several beginning reading series as entry points for the children. Three of these seven teachers taught supplementary phonic lessons to subgroups of children on a systematic basis, usually concentrating this instruction more in the first half of the year. The remaining four generally provided phonic instruction to children on an individual basis, as needed. A more detailed account of the instructional practice of individual teachers appears in each of the child studies presented in Part III.

3 Data Collection Procedures

Chapters 1 and 2 assert that systematic observation and documentation of behavior constitute the first step toward understanding the meanings a child construes in his or her instructional environment. But exactly what does one observe, and how are these observations documented? How are the multiple documentations of observed behavior synthesized and interpreted? This chapter and the next address these fundamental questions.

A prior question in deciding what to observe is determining the boundaries of the observation and data collection effort. The continuities and contrasts children perceive between home, community, and school will clearly color their expectations and interpretations of classroom experience. On the other hand, a child's school experience has integrity in its own right, and it is the realm of a child's life that educators have the power to influence directly. From a theoretical standpoint, moreover, choice is an ongoing process in the development of construct systems, and change can occur anywhere throughout the system, producing bigger or smaller ripple effects depending on the particular constructs involved in change. The principles of ongoing choice and capacity for change underlie all educational endeavors, for without them education would obviously be a relatively trivial matter. These principles further suggest that setting boundaries on observation and data collection is more of a practical problem than a theoretical one. In the long run, such boundaries depend on the purposes of the research or educational endeavor, the resources available to conduct the endeavor, and various ethical issues involved in extending observations beyond the school to other realms of a child's life (even assuming parental permission). For purposes of the reading study, we set boundaries around behavioral information that is readily accessible to every teacher—i.e., the child's functioning within the classroom and (to a lesser extent) the school at large.

Within the boundaries of classroom/school behavior, the study sought to sample both broad and limited aspects of a child's functioning. The documentation on each child in the study thus consisted of four kinds of data: teacher interviews, observations made by the external observer, samples of work produced in the classroom, and tape-recorded samples of oral reading. Although guidelines for the Descriptive Interview with teachers were perfected within the first few months of the pilot study, other guidelines for data collection evolved over longer periods of time. Discussion here focuses on the final procedures that were used in the operational phase of the research.

THE DESCRIPTIVE INTERVIEW

At regular intervals throughout the period of data collection, the ETS member of each team unit interviewed the teacher about the two children in the study.[1] The procedure was somewhat similar to a debriefing process, with interview guidelines divided into three parts and several broad topics of discussion, as follows:

   I Salient Observations
  II General Behavior Topics
      A. Physical/Gestural Characteristics
      B. Affective Expression
      C. Peer/Adult Relationships
      D. Activities
      E. Methods of Working
      F. Progress in School Work (other than reading)
 III Language and Reading Topics
      A. Listening Patterns
      B. Language (Speaking)
      C. Language (Writing)
      D. General Reading Patterns
      E. Reading Competence, Strategies, Skills

Though the guidelines were structured in the sequence listed above, the interviews did not necessarily proceed in that order. Every interview began in Part I, as indicated, with a request for significant observations the teacher had made over the preceding weeks. The idea was to get immediately to those things the teacher considered most important to report about the child. Depending on the nature of those observations, the interviewer then turned to related topics within the guidelines, rather than proceeding down the list sequentially. For example, if the teacher began the interview with a description of some interesting work the

---

[1]See Chapter 2 for a description of the data collection "teams" and the method of selecting two children from each classroom for the study.

child had done, the interviewer might ask specific questions about the child's method of working (Part II, Topic E). After discussing other topics in Part II that seemed pertinent to the sense of the discussion, the interviewer would then move on to talk about some topics in Part III. Or, if the teacher's salient impressions were mainly concerned with reading, the interviewer moved directly to related topics in Part III and eventually worked backwards to Part II. The full guidelines, with leading questions and probes related to each discussion topic, are presented at the end of this chapter.

Since the guidelines were not used as a checklist, no single interview aspired to cover all topics. Some topics (e.g., physical characteristics) were usually discussed at the initial interview and only mentioned in passing thereafter. Other topics (e.g., reading strategies) did not enter the interviews until the child exhibited the relevant behaviors, but from then on would be updated at each interview. Although considerable information about every topic was obtained over the course of the first year of data collection, the study placed a premium on the teacher's and interviewer's judgment in deciding what was most important to discuss at any given interview. The interviews were tape-recorded and lasted approximately 60 minutes per child.

The design called for a minimum of seven interviews per child, five during the first year of data collection and two during the second year. Two additional interviews were conducted for those few children whose progress was documented for a full 2 years (mainly those who were in kindergarten when the operational study began). Interviews were spaced according to the following schedule:

Year 1	October	(middle to end of month)
	December	(first half of month)
	February	(first half of month)
	March/April	(late March or early April)
	May/June	(late May or early June)
Year 2	October	(middle to end of month)
	January	(middle to end of month)
	————end of data collection for most children————	
	March/April	(late March or early April)
	May/June	(late May or early June)

Preparation for the interviews on the teacher's part included reviewing the guidelines, organizing observational notes or other forms of records that had been made, and collecting work samples that were typical or especially revealing of the children. The interviewer was responsible for preparing a written report of each interview which then became part of the child's documentary record, along with whatever work samples the teacher submitted as documentation. In addition, the interviewer was responsible for writing a description of the teacher's schedule of instruction during a typical day, making an inventory of the books and other instructional materials available in the room, and drawing a floor plan to show the classroom arrangement. All of these documents (instructional schedule, inventory of instructional materials, and floor plan) were revised as needed during the period of data collection and maintained with the child's documentary record.

During the interview itself, the ETS interviewer's role was to keep the guidelines in focus and to elicit (when necessary) specific examples supportive of the teacher's statements. Although the teachers obviously made many kinds of statements during the course of an interview, it is possible to identify five general categories that were grounded in different kinds and amounts of supporting data. One type of statement dealt with simple historical facts—e.g., "has read three books since we last talked," or "has chosen to work with Lego lately." These statements were often spontaneously elaborated with appropriate detail; or, if not, prompted a request for further detail (what books were read, what kind of reading behaviors were exhibited, what did the child do with Lego, and so on). Other statements were more on the order of a summary or condensation of many behavioral incidents. Thus, if the teacher characterized a child's interactions as "being on the periphery of groups" or "being in the thick of things," such a statement would usually be tied to several discrete examples of a similar nature.

Still other statements dealt more with the child's apparent intentions, expectations, and interpretations of classroom life and learning. This type of statement might take many forms—e.g., "seems concerned about things being predictable and orderly"; "wants to understand how things fit together"; "has a strong sense of personal agenda." Whatever the exact form and content of these statements, they represented the teacher's interpretation of some pattern that had been perceived in the child's behavior. Questioning in these instances usually elicited diverse examples that covered a range of activities.

Occasionally, teachers would have a feeling or hunch about a child that was virtually impossible to document with concrete illustrations—e.g., "always seems willing to read, but I think something is bothersome about the situation." These hunches sometimes proved fleeting and remained unsubstantiated; but sometimes they turned out to be very astute intuitions that became concretely evident later on. Finally, some statements were almost the reverse of the hunch without solid evidence. These occurred in the reporting of a specific event that seemed out of character for the child or that otherwise puzzled the teacher. Like the hunches, such episodes sometimes proved isolated curiosities with little significance in the accumulated weight of the total record. Sometimes, however, they marked the beginning of an important transition in the child's school life.

Another function of the interviewer was to support the reporting of ordinary events. Almost every teacher began an interview at one time or another with the statement, "I don't have much to report this time." Since the teachers usually had a great deal to report, we finally understood this disclaimer to mean that nothing "exciting" or "extraordinary" had happened since the last interview. In an era when almost everything is claimed at the very least to be "sensational," it is easy to understand a teacher's occasional hesitancy to report rather humdrum events. Such support as was needed at those times, however, was usually needed only to encourage the *reporting* of ordinary events, not the observing of the ordinary.

The teachers were generally quite skilled in noticing the commonplace details of a child's behavior; and it is just this ordinary quality that strengthened the value of the teacher interview data. The excerpt below is illustrative.

> Kris's notebook is pretty sloppy, but I don't think he's a scattered child. He doesn't lose things . . . and he's neat about his clothes. Last week I happened to watch him take his sweater off. He placed it carefully on the table, folded it in thirds as you might do in a store, and then neatly placed it on his bin. . . He just seemed to assume that this is the way one takes a sweater off.

Folding a sweater and putting it away is certainly not a very exciting event, and it seems far removed from anything resembling reading behavior. But it is in noticing just such details and connecting them to other details (e.g., contrasts of neatness and sloppiness in other contexts) that larger and more significant patterns are often perceived.

Perhaps the most important quality that marked much of the interview data is one that could not be elicited by questioning or encouraged by support. This is the quality of being able to disentangle instructional intentions from children's actions, and it is well illustrated in the record of a first-grade child who was in the pilot study. During the initial interview, the teacher reported as follows:

> In class meetings, Dana is restless and talkative . . . but he likes rhyming and playing with words he hears. If I say "QUIET" at meeting, Dana will often say "smiet, wyet, piet" and so on. And the other day, when a child brought up the story of the boy who cried "Wolf" . . . Dana sat there and hooted "woooooolf" "woooolf" to himself. . . . So he hears beginning and ending sounds. For example, he knew *brother* started with "b," and he knew "p" and "t" were the beginning and ending of *paint*.

Although Dana talked when he was not supposed to at meetings, the teacher did not see him only through the template of classroom management rules. Rather than reporting that he was "inattentive," she noticed what he said. And in this instance, she linked what she observed to an ability that seems advantageous for learning how to read—the ability to identify sounds.

As it turned out, Dana foiled her initial instructional plans and predictions. Although he continued to play with words in what he construed as a playful context, he balked at sounding out words when reading aloud. As reported later in the year:

Dana can use a sounding out strategy in trying to identify words, but often he simply stops dead when he comes to a word he doesn't know, and you have to press him to sound it out. Sometimes I press him, but it usually goes nowhere and he'll just say, "I don't know." So usually I tell him right away, because I know it won't go anywhere. . . . I really think it's a practical thing with him. If he doesn't know, he *really doesn't know*—and I might as well tell him.

In this excerpt, Dana is not simply a child who fulfilled or disappointed the teacher's instructional expectations. Rather than seeing "stubbornness" in his actions, she observed a person with a preferred style of learning—a person who doesn't want to guess if he doesn't know.

We have tried to suggest something of the nature of the interview data, in addition to describing the interview procedure, because such data are not typical in research on children's learning. The other data collected in the reading study are of a more familiar variety or their nature is more self-evident.

NARRATIVE OBSERVATION ACCOUNTS

The observer member of each data collection team was a person experienced and skilled in classroom observation. Although most observers had also had training in the use of classroom observation instruments, the skill referred to here is that which results in a narrative account of the child's activities over a period of approximately 20 minutes. Such observations provide a "slice of life" view of the child that is similar in intent to the data provided by television. Both sources of observation (a person and a television camera) have distinct advantages and limitations in research, but the advantages of the person outweighed those of the camera for purposes of the collaborative study.

The observer recorded two periods or episodes of a child's activity during each of six classroom visits, yielding a total of 12 observations per child.[2] The observations were spaced at roughly the same intervals as the interview, and guidelines specified the general context in which a child was to be observed during each time period. As mentioned previously, however, the guidelines also provided leeway for decisions to be made by the data collection team. The schedule of observations and the specified contexts are shown below.

Yr. 1	*Observation A*	*Observation B*
October:	A free choice activity (e.g., sand, blocks, clay, painting, tinker toys, games)	A more constrained, "skill-type" activity such as writing, workbook exercises or math activities
Dec/Jan:	Formal reading instruction (small group or one-to-one interaction, as appropriate)	A group situation that involves discussion and listening

[2]Some observers made extra observations on the days they visited a classroom. Thus, 12 observations was a minimum per child.

March:	A "favorite" free choice activity	Quiet reading time
May:	Formal reading instruction or quiet reading time	Optional
Yr. 2		
October:	A free choice activity	Formal reading instruction or quiet reading time
January:	Formal reading instruction or quiet reading time	Optional

SAMPLES OF WORK

Evidence of children's understandings and meanings is also found in the work they produce in the classroom. Thus, samples or copies of work that was judged to be typical or particularly illustrative of the child's functioning were collected by teachers throughout the course of data collection. These were primarily examples of writing, drawing, painting, and worksheets, but also included photographs of three-dimensional constructions when these were a prominent part of the child's activity and interest. Teachers provided information about the context of the work, when and how it was undertaken, and the extent to which it was assigned or self-initiated. Although we sampled across all modes of work, a more extensive file was kept for any medium (e.g., writing, drawing) that was clearly preferred by the child.

ORAL READING SAMPLES

Tape-recorded samples of the child reading aloud were obtained by teachers on at least five occasions: three times during the first year of data collection and twice during the second year. The teachers chose some texts, and the child chose others. Although the guidelines specified five samples and a minimum of 2 selections per sample, most tapes contained more than 2 selections, and many teachers obtained more than five samples. The minimum oral reading data obtained by the teacher for each child was therefore five samples and 10 selections (2 per tape). In reality, however, the cumulated tapes for the majority of children contained about 15 selections, and some ranged as high as 25 selections.

The following definitions established guidelines about the nature of text material the children read.

Instructional Level: This selection is from reading material the teacher normally uses for instruction and for judging a child's progress. The difficulty should be such that the child can handle it but will probably make errors as well.

Preferred Material: This selection is typical of the material a child often selects on his or her own during free reading times. (The child may choose it if he/she wishes.)

Difficult/Interesting: The content of this selection is something the teacher judges will be of interest to the child, but the difficulty is fairly high in relation to the child's proficiency.

Most Difficult Material: This selection may be from any book, but it represents the hardest material the child can read with reasonable proficiency.

The suggested schedule for obtaining reading samples and the specified text materials for each sample were as follows:

	Selection A	*Selection B*
Oct/Nov	Instructional Level	Preferred Reading
Jan/Feb	Instructional Level	Preferred Reading
April/May	(ETS staff obtains oral reading on standard texts)	
June	Instructional Level	Diffic/Interesting
September	Instructional Level	Same "D/I" Selection as read in May/June
Dec/Jan	Most Difficult	Preferred Reading

The guidelines concerning text selections sometimes had to be stretched. For example, if a child typically spent free reading period perusing books with interesting pictures but very difficult text, the teacher usually chose what she thought would be appropriate for the "preferred reading" selections. A final set of guidelines had to do with the degree of assistance given a child. For most selections, the teacher gave only enough assistance to keep the reading going. In one selection designated as an "instructional level" text, however, the teacher offered the kind of clues, prompts, pointers, and assistance that was typical of her normal reading instruction.

The teacher also provided standard information about every selection the child read, as well as comments about anything unusual in the child's performance. The form used for this purpose is shown in Fig. 3.1.

Standard Oral Reading Selections

During April and May of the first year of data collection, the ETS interviewer member of each team obtained an oral reading sample on a standard set of selections. The texts represented different genres of children's books and were, in almost every case, unfamiliar to the study children. Three of the texts were within a difficulty range we judged would be accessible to "most school chil-

```
                                        ETS Collaborative Research Project on Reading


                          INFORMATION ABOUT ORAL READING SAMPLES
                     (This form should be completed for each selection the child reads)


                                                    Date: _____


         Teacher:_____        Child:_____
                                                      (pseudonym)

         Title of Book:_____


         Name of Series or Publisher:_____
                                        (E.g., SRA; Lippincott: Bowmar: Monster Series)


         Page numbers of passage read:_____


         Type of Selection:     _____    _____   _____
         (see guidelines)     Instructional Level   Preferred Rdg.  Difficult/Interesting


         Comments:  (Please comment on tape or in writing below)

            Who chose selection?

            Familiarity of selection to child?

            Remark on anything unusual in the child's performance or on relevant behavior
            not discernible from the tape alone (e.g., exclusive attention on the teacher
            rather than the text for clues; pointing to each individual word; covering up
            the text while pointing to words; child's attitude or reaction to the experience).
```

FIG. 3.1.   Oral Reading Information Form

dren'' at the end of first grade.[3] These three constituted the core selections given to every child. Depending on how the child performed, the interviewer either stopped after the core set or branched to more difficult books. One of the harder books featured nonsense poems, and the other two were storybooks. Since the interviewers had visited the classrooms on several previous occasions, there were few problems in establishing sufficient rapport so that the child could read comfortably.

The core set of standard selections included a conventional storybook (*Big Dog, Little Dog*); a book written with the kind of constrained spelling patterns

---

[3]Children who were in kindergarten were not given the standard oral reading selections until the end of the second year of data collection.

that characterize beginning texts in programs of linguistic and phonic instruction (*Ben Bug*); and a book in which the plot is conveyed partly by pictures and partly by text (*Blackboard Bear*). Only the beginning portions of the first two books were designated for the reading sample, though many children insisted on reading both books through to the end.

SUMMARY

The data collection plans may be summarized in terms of the primary responsibilities of the three members of the documentation team. The teacher was responsible for reviewing the interview guidelines, reviewing and organizing observational notes made for each child, and collecting work samples prior to each Descriptive Interview. Another major responsibility was obtaining the oral reading samples. Responsibility for focused observations and narrative accounts of the child's activity in various classroom settings was assigned to the observer member of the team. The ETS interviewer assumed general administrative responsibility for data collection and was specifically responsible for conducting and writing up the Descriptive Interviews, for gathering other kinds of descriptive information about the classroom (e.g., a general inventory of instructional materials), and for conducting the standard oral reading sessions.

GUIDELINES FOR THE DESCRIPTIVE INTERVIEW (PARTS II & III)

II GENERAL BEHAVIOR TOPICS

A. Physical/Gestural Characteristics
    —typical posture, bearing
    —pace of movement
    —forcefulness/impact of physical presence
    —gestural characteristics
    —eye contact
    —voice qualities (e.g., loud, soft, fluent, halting)
    —voice tone/inflection
B. Affective Expression
    —characteristic disposition and how expressed
    —how is anger expressed, controlled
    —how is affection expressed
    —general level of energy
C. Relationships
    —how does child relate to (fit in with) whole class
    —what social situations does child seek in work/play
    —do other children seek out child
    —relationship to adults
    —does approach/interaction vary in different settings? at different times?
D. Activities
    —what does child do in classroom when there is an opportunity to choose

---

(*continued*)

GUIDELINES FOR THE DESCRIPTIVE INTERVIEW (cont.)

  —breadth and depth of activities
  —what are unusual activities for the child to engage in
  —what are things child has never engaged/attempted in classroom
E. Method of Working
  —how does child organize self for work
  —how does child carry through on work
  —does child seek feedback about work? when? from whom?
  —does child ask for help with work? when? from whom?
  —does child use help that is offered? how?
  —evidence that child ''knows what he knows''—can gauge own capabilities
  —how does child demonstrate capabilities
F. Summary of Progress in School-Related Work (other than reading)
  —differential/even progress
  —unusual accomplishments, activities
  —unusual difficulties, blockings

III LANGUAGE AND READING TOPICS

A. Listening Patterns
  —when stories are read
  —when directions are given
  —during class discussions
  —in peer groups
  —in one-to-one interactions with adults
B. Language (Speaking)
  —does child speak a lot/little
  —does child talk more in some situations than in others
  —does child talk differently to adults than to peers
  —does child talk to self while working
  —does child engage in imaginary conversation with self/animals/objects
  —play with sounds/puns/jokes/riddles
  —extent of vocabulary and facility in speaking
  —does child tend to influence/sway other children or adults by the use of language (e.g.,
   by convincing argument, use of nuance or turning a phrase, name-calling, swearing)
  —any thematic topics of conversation
C. Language (Writing)
  —evidence of and interest in quasi-writing
  —does child like to dictate stories/captions/sentences
  —evidence from dictation that child understands how written language is separated into
   words? how words are grouped into sentences?
  —interest in representing letters/words on paper (e.g., on drawings)
  —hesitancy/firmness of writing—motor control
  —physical orientation of writing (e.g., backward, forward, up or down)
  —spacing within and between words
  —accuracy/nature of errors in child's spelling
   —evidence of invented spellings
   —spellings reflect pronunciation/dialect
   —spellings reflect overgeneralized rules (e.g., ''swimmed'')
   —evidence of attempt to combine known words into spelling of new words (e.g.,
    ''peapull'')

GUIDELINES FOR THE DESCRIPTIVE INTERVIEW (cont.)

—where does child go for help with spelling (dictionary, teacher, peers)
—does child write spontaneously or only when assigned
—any thematic topics in writing
—any recurrent forms/conventions in writing (e.g., once upon a time)

D. General Reading Patterns
    —evidence of quasi-reading
    —what books/other reading matter has child engaged
    —is reading material usually child's or teacher's selection
    —if child's selection, how does child go about choosing books
    —where does child obtain reading material (classroom, home, library)
    —does child like to read aloud? If so, to self or others?
    —social context of reading—alone or in group
    —does child want to share what he/she has read or heard read? How shares?
    —does child read spontaneously or only when assigned

E. Reading Competence, Strategies, Skills
    —significant features in reading (include recent accomplishments)
    —evidence of comprehension (overall meaning of text)
        —meaningful intonation in reading aloud
        —retells story
        —relates story to own experience
        —insightful comments/questions
    —strategies for monitoring/maintaining meaning
        —thumbs through book before reading
        —starts back at beginning of sentence or phrase if error occurs
        —scans backward/forward in text; scans pictures
        —guesses and plows ahead or slows down and stops in difficult text
    —word identification strategies
        —sounds out words
        —uses picture clues
        —substituted words are graphically similar to words in text
        —waits until someone supplies word
    —concentration and energy in reading
    —fluency and rhythm in oral reading
    —help sought by child outside of text and pictures—e.g., use of other children/adults/classroom resources
    —reactions to reading instruction

4 Data Analysis and Integration Procedures

The overall purpose of the study was to place learning how to read within the context of particular readers. This goal presumes the ability to illuminate the network of meanings (understanding, expectations, intentions, knowledge, styles, and interests) that a particular child brings to bear on learning in the classroom. The theoretical rationale of the research, as described in Chapter 1, assumes that a person's meanings are revealed in patterns of action over time. Thus, the aim of data integration was to identify major themes or patterns that cohered in the data for each child.

Many of the data analysis and integration procedures used in the study are based on methods originally developed by Patricia Carini for her own research on individual children (see Carini, 1975, 1979). Because Carini had also adapted the methods for use with teachers in programs of in-service professional development, we knew that the procedures were practicable and that they made sense to practitioners. During the last 18 months of the pilot study, we therefore turned full attention to examining the rationale of the procedures and adapting them specifically for purposes of the reading study. This effort involved ETS staff, Carini, subgroups of collaborators, and an advisory group of research colleagues outside ETS.[1]

The pilot phase of work culminated in a formal study of the data integration process, in which two groups of collaborators independently integrated data for the same two children.[2] ETS staff and collaborators met for 2 weeks, devoting a

---

[1]This external research group included Courtney Cazden, Susan Florio, Patricia Minuchin, and Lee Shulman.

[2]Both children had been followed for more than 1 year in the data collection phase of the pilot study.

full week to each child's record of documentation. The actual integration process was conducted 4 days during each week, and the groups came together on the fifth day to compare results. Composition of the groups was changed from one week to the next. Each of the four resulting integration groups was led by an ETS staff member, and another ETS researcher monitored the ongoing processes each week to check on the consistency of specific procedures. Consistency between the groups and comparability of the patterns identified for each child were satisfactory enough to warrant use of the procedures in the operational phase of research.

DESCRIPTIVE ANALYSES OF ORAL READING AND WORK SAMPLES

Data integration required some way of incorporating concrete samples of a child's work and oral reading into the documentary record of teacher interview data and narrative observational accounts. This task was accomplished by descriptive analyses.

A preliminary step to descriptive analysis was deciding which reading selections and work samples to analyze. The ETS interviewer prepared an inventory of the oral reading tapes for each child, listing every reading selection together with brief remarks about the reading. This inventory became part of the documentation and was used to select "key" readings for the child. Key readings included at least the core set of standard selections that had been obtained by the interviewer (*Big Dog, Little Dog; Ben Bug; Blackboard Bear*) and from 6–10 selections that had been obtained by the teacher. These latter selections spanned the period of data collection and were chosen on the basis of their informative value in revealing significant aspects of the child's reading. Usually, the most informative selections were texts which the child could handle reasonably well but which were challenging enough to prompt errors.

In choosing work samples, the child's investment in the work was a primary factor that entered the decision. The number of pieces selected for descriptive analysis as well as the medium selected (e.g., writing, drawing) depended on how much the child had produced and whether he or she clearly preferred a particular medium. (Work in preferred mediums was generally the most revealing.) The final selection of work samples was made either by the entire data collection team or by the teacher and the interviewer.

Descriptive Analysis of Oral Reading

Description of the oral reading selections followed guidelines formulated by ETS staff. The interviewer made a notational record of each key selection in preparation for the analysis. That is, the text of the selection was typed, and a record of the child's actual reading was then superimposed on the typed text by means of a notational system.[3] Collaborators had a copy of the notational record for reference as they listened to each selection, so that they did not have to concentrate on deciphering the child's words. Descriptive analysis was accomplished by small groups of collaborators (usually five or six), with guidelines directing attention to the following aspects of the child's performance.

1. Interactions with the adult (teacher or interviewer):
   —How does the child ask for and/or utilize help from the adult?
   —How does the child manage the adult generally? (e.g., responsiveness to adult comments, engaging the adult in conversation about the story or other matters).
2. Apparent interest and investment in the story or pictures as contrasted with investment in the task of reading per se (i.e., assuming the ''role'' of the reader).
3. Evidence of self-monitoring at the word level. For example:
   —Returning to read text previously omitted;
   —Spontaneous remarks about the text or own performance (e.g., ''This is hard!'' ''ain't that right?'').
4. Evidence of comprehension or monitoring of comprehension at the level of the overall story. For example:
   —Spontaneous comments on relation of the pictures to the story;
   —Comments connecting one part of the story to another;
   —Questions about concepts or pictures not understood.
5. What does the child do when he/she encounters difficulty? (e.g., slows down, engages adult in conversation, plows ahead, skips lines).
6. Comment on the child's language and enunciation, voice quality, expressiveness, flow of reading.

These guidelines were not intended to restrict the collaborators' comments, but only to ensure attention to certain facets of the reading not adequately handled by technical coding procedures. The descriptive analysis proceeded in rounds. Collaborators took notes as the tape selection was played through twice without interruption. Notes about the reading were then shared, discussed, and clarified as necessary. On the second round of note taking, the tape was stopped and portions replayed as many times as requested by participants. Observational notes were again discussed, and the chairperson of the group (usually an ETS staff member) was then responsible for organizing these notes into a written summary of the selection.

---

[3]Notational records were also used by ETS staff later on for purposes of technical coding and analysis.

Description of Work Samples

The same general procedure was used to analyze work samples, although guidelines did not direct attention to any predetermined aspects of the work. Rather, attention was often tuned for the analysis by a procedure Carini calls a "reflection conversation."[4] A reflective conversation literally centers on the personal reflections and associations of group members concerning a particular concept or topic. The topic chosen for reflection depended on the particular piece of work being analyzed. Sometimes, the topic coincided with the medium of the work sample itself (e.g., writing, drawing, painting) or with an idea suggested by the medium (e.g., authorship, line, color). other times, the topic was suggested by the particular subject matter of the work (e.g., ship, family, superhero). Whatever the topic, the point of such conversations was to enlarge each person's thinking about the nature of the work and the potential meanings it might hold.

The analysis of the work sample then proceeded on as descriptive a plane as possible, with collaborators in the group commenting on various features of the work. Although comments became more interpretative as the analysis progressed, each interpretative comment had to be grounded back to previous description or it was not allowed to enter the final record. The chairperson of the group was responsible for periodically summarizing the observations and for organizing them into a written description. Because the chairperson's job was especially demanding in these analyses, the chair rotated with each work sample.

If a child produced several similar pieces of work within a relatively brief period, the entire collection was often analyzed as a single unit. This adaptation of the procedure helped immeasurably in the group's ability to cover the work of prolific children. An example of the outcome of a descriptive analysis that considered a collection of work is shown in Table 4.1.

OVERVIEW OF THE DATA INTEGRATION PROCESS

Data integration for most children was also accomplished by small groups of collatorators. Each group included the three people who had been involved in data collection (teacher-observer-interviewer) and at least three other collaborators who were not acquainted with the child. The process was carried out either at extended meetings of 3–5 days (during vacation periods) or else during a series of weekend meetings. Meetings began in the spring of Year 2 (after data collection for most children was completed) and continued through the summer.

---

[4]See Carini (1979) for a description of the rationale and details of this procedure. Primarily because of time constraints, the procedure was not used as frequently in the reading study as Carini typically uses it.

TABLE 4.1
A Descriptive Analysis of Work Samples

Summary: Pencil Drawings

Integration Meetings: Day 2
Participants: Agre, Alberty, Bussis, Cramer, Stein, Weissman

This summary covers an array of 16 pencil drawings, most of them done in the month of May. We know from an interview that these were done by choice during intervals between assigned activities. Tim tended to finish his assigned work early and then would opt to draw during the remainder of the period. The sixteen drawings appear on ten sheets of drawing paper, sizes 9 × 12 and 12 × 18.

Except for one drawing that seems to be an underground scene and one that depicts little robot-like creatures at a lunch counter, the drawings are of figures and (some) objects suspended in space, with no background to fix their location. Most of the drawings on a given page contain more than one figure, although some figures are crossed out . . . as if Tim rejected these particular renditions. A few figures are colored in crayon.

    Themes: Superheroes (Batman, Spiderman, Thor); space figures/objects; and prehistoric-looking creatures that are either dragons or dinosaurs. In several of the pictures, two or more of these thematic elements appear together (e.g., spaceman and dragon). Some of the space figures have helmets and sword-like weapons that give them a medieval appearance.

    Detailed Description: See the description/impressions of one drawing contained in Pat Carini's report from our Fall meeting.

Tim does not have just one style of drawing, but uses lines in many way. There are curved and circular lines, lines flowing in opposition, angular and zigzag lines, stripes, and intersecting lines that form grids. Some lines are sketchy and tentative; others are sure and definite. Lines are used to show the motion of objects dropping down and of figures springing/flying up. Zigzags, grids, scallops, and webbed lines are used to depict detail. The lunchroom scene shows unusual perspective,* with the lunch counter curving around in diverging lines that clearly give the illusion of background depth.

The drawings show attention to detail, especially in facial features/expression and in dress/costume. Many erasures also testify to a concern for details.

Although figures are detailed, the drawings as a whole have an incomplete and unfinished look. Several factors combine to produce this unfinished impression—the fact that most of the drawings lack a background, that both sides of the drawing paper have been used in many instances, and (as noted previously) that there are crossed out figures and erasures. We know that the drawings were also stuffed haphazardly into his cubby. Overall, the group's impression was that Tim seemed to be drawing for himself, perhaps practicing certain aspects of his technique with figures.

TABLE 4.1 (*Continued*)

Because of the lack of background, many figures appear suspended in space. Motion lines indicate that other figures are either flying or (more typically) springing up into space. Despite this indication of springing or flying, however, there is a definite stiff and static quality to Tim's figures . . . as if they were posing in mid-air.

In many instances, the superheroes, space figures, and dragons are equipped with both weapons and protection (helmets and swords, fire-breathing capability, fierce teeth, spiny projections), suggesting the possibility of fierceness and impending combat. But, like his earlier superhero books, the possibility doesn't materialize in the drawings. There is no instance of physical contact between figures, and only one instance of contact at a distance (with Spiderman's web entangling a gorilla-like creature). Most figures face front, but even the profile views lack direct visual contact between protagonists. Moreover, the potential for power and fierceness of many figures is often balanced by some weakness or vulnerability—ineffectual appendages in the fire-breathing dragon, weapons missing the target, etc. The static quality of the figures and lack of background also serve to render the potentially harmful harmless and to mute the idea of battle.

The unfinished character of the drawings, the coupling of figures from different realms and ages (superheroes from comics, futuristic spacemen, prehistoric dragons), and the hint of combat that never materializes on paper—all of these factors suggest that the action of the story takes place in Tim's mind and that he uses the drawings to depict various characters in the drama for his own enjoyment. As seemed true of his early dictation books and the paintings, Tim's artistic skill is invested in rendering portraits. The details and context of the implied action remain publicly unstated.

The group also thought that there was a certain whimsical quality about the two drawings that contained a background—the underground scene, and (especially) the scene of the tiny robots at a lunch counter.

---

*Unusual perspective was also noted in an assigned book, *All About Me*—i.e., a picture of a TV sitting on a bureau, and a back view of a boy looking out of a window at rain outside.

Prior to the meeting for a given child, ETS staff sent each collaborator a complete chronological record of the interviews and narrative observations, together with xeroxed copies of selected work samples. Because the observations reported by the teacher and external observer constituted the record of broadest scope with respect to the time and settings it encompassed, the integration process began with a consideration of this record. (Typically, the record was between 70–90 single-spaced typewritten pages.) Collaborators read the observation record in advance of the meeting to identify patterns in the data. A pattern was defined as the recurrence of similar observations over time, across settings, or across data sources (teacher and observer). Especially prominent patterns often spanned all three criteria (time, settings, and data sources).

The integration meeting began with each member of the group listing the particular patterns he/she had identified and illustrating each one with examples from the documentation. The descriptive word or phrase used to label each pattern was called a "heading" (for reasons to be discussed below). When all the headings had been listed and clarified, it was a relatively easy task to discern areas of considerable overlap (where several headings in effect referred to the same data), as well as headings that were unique and those that seemed generally related but had different emphases or nuances. The group decided on mutually acceptable headings as descriptors for patterns that clearly overlapped most of the lists, and these headings were temporarily set aside along with headings unique to one or two lists. The chairperson then allowed a generous time period for discussion that focussed on the middle ground of agreement—those headings that had elements in common but differed in significant respects. At the end of the discussion, the group agreed on two or three patterns that captured important commonalities running through this middle ground of agreement.

The tool for achieving further clarification was a procedure called "charting." The group selected one of the headings that had been agreed upon and charted through the data with it. That is, each collaborator took a different section of the documentary record (10–20 pages) and underlined every datum that supported the heading. As each person, in turn, read the data he/she had underlined, these were listed with brief identifying phrases and page references on a large chart that everyone could see. By working through the entire record together in this manner, the group became more familiar with the data and could discuss any part of parts of the record that were unclear or that occasioned very different interpretations.

After charting through the data once as a whole group exercise, collaborators worked in pairs or individually to chart additional headings. Each subgroup also prepared a large chart that listed the supporting data for a particular heading, and the charts were used to report back to the full group. This first charting of headings thus resulted in a graphic and detailed presentation that permitted patterns to be examined, evaluated, and assessed in relation to headings that had not yet been charted.

For a change of pace and perspective, the group next turned attention to work samples. In comparison with observational data, which are statements about a child, work samples are relatively direct statements of meaning by a child. Two or three samples of work (either single pieces or collections of work) were analyzed by the procedures described previously. The resulting descriptions of work were then compared to the headings that had been charted. The purpose was to map aspects of the child's work to headings identified in the observational data, where there was an appropriate fit between the two, and to discern additional patterns suggested by the work descriptions.

The group then reconsidered the overall configuration of patterns. Headings were added, discarded, combined and redefined, or reconfirmed in light of the first charting results and the work sample analyses. New descriptive labels were designated as headings if necessary, and the new set of headings was charted through all the data (observations and work samples) a second time. The patterns defined by this second charting constituted the thematic description of the child's *total record.*

The next phase of the integration process was devoted exclusively to the documentation considered most relevant to beginning reading. The work began with descriptive analyses of key oral reading selections (as described previously). Descriptions of the child's oral reading were examined for patterns, and these patterns were given tentative heading designations. The group then delineated those portions of the observation record that described relevant reading, writing, and language behaviors,[5] and the process of abstracting patterns in the observation record began all over again. The group broke up into two-person teams to identify patterns that cohered in the "reading data," and each team reported its headings and examples of supporting documentation back to the full group. The group reviewed these headings from the observational data together with headings derived from the oral reading samples, in order to construct a set of headings that emcompassed both kinds of data. Headings were then charted through both kinds of data (oral reading descriptions and relevant observations), and necessary revisions of the patterns were made on the basis of the charting results. This revised set of headings constituted the thematic description of the child's *reading record.*

The last procedure in data integration was to review the two sets of themes (one abstracted from the total record and the other from the reading record) and to highlight points of continuity and discontinuity between them. As it turned out, continuities were more prominent than discontinuities for every child.

The outline of data integration sketched above was the basic model followed in the longer integration sessions of 4 to 5 days. Sessions of 2 to 3 days required more preparation in advance of a meeting, foreshortened discussion periods, and modification in the number of thorough chartings that were attempted. (One shortcut was to chart a heading by sampling only portions of the data throughout an observation record.) Whether accomplished in longer or shorter sessions, however, the process was painstaking and time consuming. On the other hand, it was no more painstaking or time consuming than analytic and interpretive procedures used in many naturalistic research investigations. The entire process, in fact, took less time than has been reported for many such studies.

Thus, the most unusual features of the study's data integration process from a methodological standpoint are neither the time involved nor level of detail examined. Rather, the most unusual features are the concept of "headings" and the practice of "charting"; and it is these ideas that deserve closer scrutiny.

---

[5]These portions of the total observation record were later reproduced and filed in a separate notebook, referred to thereafter as the "Reading Record."

"HEADINGS" AND THE PRACTICE OF "CHARTING"[6]

Initially at least, headings are tantamount to impressions gained from the first one or two readings of a child's record. As a heading becomes more firmly grounded in data, it takes on the character of a considered interpretation. Within the theoretical framework described in Chapter 1, headings may be regarded as permeable constructs. The term "heading" is used because it makes sense to most people as an organizing concept (e.g., newspapers have headlines and subheads), yet it avoids the connotations associated with the term "category."

A category system in research usually implies a mutually exclusive system, with each category serving to circumscribe some data and to exclude others. If a decision is made to place a particular datum in category "A," then that same datum cannot also be placed in category "B." The condition of mutual exclusiveness thus creates categorical constructs that force a person to make "either/or" judgments. Although such constructs may be helpful in disentangling certain kinds of phenomena, they are not very useful for discerning recurring patterns of behavior that reflect a person's developing patterns of thought. As described in Chapter 1, constructs are most valid for discerning patterns in life's ongoing events when they are optimally permeable and adaptable, allowing for multiple perspectives on the events of interest. In a very real sense, then, the forging of headings in data integration was an attempt to create permeable constructs that would structure the ongoing events of a child's classroom functioning over an 18-month period into a comprehensive and comprehensible pattern.

As contrasted with category systems, a system of permeable constructs invites the overlap and multiple membership of data. Thus, the procedure of charting is distinct from categorizing to the extent that any given piece of data may be placed under as many headings as seem appropriate. Such a procedure leads to the accrual of related data within headings and to instances of repeated data across headings. In practice, the intersections of a particular piece of data with several headings constitute the most fruitful points for further examination after the first charting has been accomplished.

A piece of data that is charted many times in the matrix of headings may be an episode from the observation record, a quality ascribed to the child by the observer or teacher, or a particular characteristic of the child's work or oral reading. Whatever the nature of the datum, the fact that it intersects many headings signals its importance in capturing several facets of the child's classroom functioning. Such data were sometimes examined analytically, in an attempt to discern elements that made up the episode or that contributed to the

---

[6]The following paragraphs do not attempt to portray Carini's rationale, but derive from the theoretical discussion in Chapter 1. Carini traces her own formulation of these ideas to different philosophical roots. (See, especially, Carini, 1979.)

characteristic or quality. At other times they were examined by means of a reflective conversation, the procedure described previously in conjunction with the descriptive analysis of work samples. Reflective conversations, in this instance, typically focused on some idea suggested by the episode or characteristic in question. Used singly or in tandem, these analytic and reflective procedures often yielded insights about critical pieces of data that led, in turn, to a more adaptable configuration of headings for the second charting.

Adaptability was the criterion for assessing the validity of the final set of headings. Since the documentation for every child included diverse sources of data, and since these data spanned a variety of settings as well as a significant period of time, each charting through the data represented repeated trials of a heading's predictive and construct validity. That is, every interview, observation, work sample, and oral reading selection constituted a single trial of the heading's validity, and the charting of a heading through all the documentation constituted repeated trials. If the final headings encompassed a major portion of the total documentation and adequately anticipated various aspects of the child's behavior over time and across settings, then that set of headings was regarded as reasonably permeable, adaptable, and valid for that particular child.

The cycles of charting, examining intersections of data, and revising headings could theoretically go on forever; and, with each cycle, the headings would presumably capture more subtleties of the child's behavior. But even an infinite number of chartings would not subsume every last piece of data, because there are facets of every individual's thinking and actions that remain surprising, obscure, and ultimately "unknowable." Practically speaking, then, the time spent on data integration depends on one's purposes. Two complete cycles of charting generally proved sufficient for purposes of the reading study.

As a last comment on headings and charting, the phenomenon of "straggling data" deserves mention. The aim of constructing permeable headings means that charting errs on the side of being inclusive rather than exclusive. And this type of error means that the placement of some data under a heading will be debatable and will probably occasion disagreements among the people who are charting. Such disagreements make little difference in the long run, however, for a few instances of questionable data do not significantly alter the overall pattern designated by the heading. They are analogous to data that load with very low weights in a factor analysis and play little if any role in influencing the investigator's interpretation of the factor. In effect, these data simply fall through the cracks and settle with other uncharted data in the documentation.

TECHNICAL AND COMPARATIVE ANALYSES

ETS staff continued data analysis during the third and final year of the operational research. A few individual children's records were reviewed for purposes of abstracting thematic patterns, but the bulk of the work was of a different nature then that described above. One set of activities centered on technical coding and analysis of oral reading samples, and another focused on the comparison of integrative themes across children.

The development of technical coding procedures for analyzing oral reading began in the pilot study and continued throughout the data collection phase of the operational study. For the most part, this work involved minor adaptations of existing schemes for coding and analyzing children's oral reading.[7] Each ETS interviewer was responsible for making a notational record of a child's key reading selections (in preparation for the descriptive analysis), and these notational records also served the purpose of carrying out a standard type of error analysis.

As helpful as standard error analysis is in highlighting major knowledge resources that enter the skill of reading (e.g., semantic, syntactic, and letter-sound knowledge), there was a growing awareness among ETS staff that such schemes are less adequate for handling other systematic differences observed among beginning readers (e.g., differences in patterns of repetition, pausing, skipping ahead). Moreover, the descriptive analyses of oral reading that were accomplished by small groups of collaborators kept suggesting yet other important aspects of a child's reading that might be made amenable to technical coding. Thus, during the final year of the study, concerted efforts were devoted to devising coding procedures that would encompass additional aspects of a child's oral reading performance. The procedures were tried out, revised, and then applied again in recoding two of the standard oral reading selections for every child (*Big Dog, Little Dog* and *Ben Bug*); and they were also used to recode other "key" selections for a sample of children. Some of the major features of this coding scheme are outlined and illustrated in Chapter 7.

Another line of work pursued by ETS staff involved the comparison of integrative themes across children. The first step in this process was to compare themes from the total record (together with summaries of the data supporting each theme) for children in the operational study as well as several children in the pilot study. A similar process was followed in comparing themes from the reading records of individual children. Ultimately, of course, the commonalities discerned among both sets of themes were compared. The most important single outcome of this analysis was the abstraction of stylistic behaviors that characterized the children's functioning in many classroom activities, including the activity of learning how to read. These style characteristics are discussed at length in Part II, which centers on theoretical formulations derived from the study.

---

[7]In particular, we relied on the work of Clay (1979), Goodman and Goodman (1977), and Goodman and Burke (1972).

REFERENCES

Carini, P. F. *Observation and description: An alternative methodology for the investigation of human phenomena.* Monograph of the North Dakota Study Group on Evaluation. Grand Forks: University of North Dakota Press, 1975.

Carini, P. F. *The art of seeing and the visibility of the person.* Monograph of the North Dakota Study Group on Evaluation. Grand Forks: University of North Dakota Press, 1979.

Clay, M. M. *The early detection of reading difficulties: A diagnostic survey with recovery procedures.* Auckland, New Zealand: Heinemann Educational Books, 1979.

Goodman, D. S., & Goodman, Y. M. Learning about psycholinguistic processes by analyzing oral reading. *Harvard Educational Review,* 1977, *47,* 317–333.

Goodman, Y. M., & Burke, C. *Reading miscue inventory manual: Procedures for diagnosis and evaluation.* New York: Macmillan, 1972.

A CHILD-BASED THEORY OF LEARNING HOW TO READ

This section of the report presents a theoretical analysis of reading as it occurs during the circumscribed period of "learning how to." For many children in our culture, this phase occurs within the first 2 or 3 years of school, or roughly between the ages of 6 and 8. For some it occurs earlier and for some later, but the evidence presented here comes from the records of children who were studied during the primary grades (K–3). Most were studied during their first- and second-grade years.

5

Introduction To The Theory

One afternoon early in December, Dana's first-grade teacher held a scheduled interview for the ETS reading study. The frist words she uttered to the interviewer were not the usual greeting, but an announcement—"Dana started to read today!" Excerpts from the opening portion of the write-up of this interview are reproduced below.

> —"Dana started to read today!" Ms. Lichert was going over the *Pig Can Jig* book [the first instructional text in the SRA linguistic reading series] to see if he knew any words. Unlike the last time she tried this, Dana said that he could read the first word list: MAN, DAN, FAN, CAN, RAN, I, and THE. He knew those words in any order and when Ms. Lichert wrote them on paper. He then went on to read the first five pages of simple stories (e.g., "Dan can fan the man")—not one mistake.

> —He said he was going to read 20 pages today. He got to the second word list (NAN, PAN, TAN, VAN) and Ms. Lichert thought sure he could do it; but Dana said he couldn't read them. Ms. Lichert went over them three times, with Dana saying them with her the last time. She asked if he could read them now, but he insisted he couldn't. He said he didn't want to read any more and closed the book.

> —Dana had not taken the *Pig Can Jig* book home over Thanksgiving vacation, but he did take it home this afternoon. When Ms. Lichert asked, "Did you know you can read?" Dana replied, "Yes, I knew." Ms. Lichert asked him how he knew, and Dana said he's been reading at home—a book with Spot and Sally in it that his aunt brought him on Thanksgiving. Dana reported that he "just started reading it." Ms. Lichert is reasonably sure that Dana hasn't been pressured about reading at home, and Dana said no one helped him. He just "knew the words."

—Ms. Lichert is as shocked as anyone. She'd thought Dana would read soon, but hadn't really thought it would be this soon. The last time she went over *Pig Can Jig* with him was about two weeks ago (November 18th). She felt he was interested in the book at that time, and she went over the words to see if he could recognize any after she showed them to him. He couldn't. Ms. Lichert isn't sure why Dana couldn't go on today. Perhaps it was too many words at one time. Or perhaps things were a bit too confusing. It was choice period, and children were coming over to Ms. Lichert to tell her their plans or to ask questions.

—Ms. Lichert has mainly been working on beginning and ending sounds informally with Dana, using material he dictates and then copies in his diary. (See previous interview notes.) It's clear that he has some knowledge of letter-sound correspondences (e.g., he knew that "brother" started with a *b,* and that *p* and *t* were the beginning and ending sounds of "paint"). It's also clear that he understands and enjoys rhyming words. When Ms. Lichert says "quiet" at class meetings, she had heard Dana say "smiet, wyet, piet" softly to himself. But Dana didn't use any observable letter-sound strategy today when he read the word list and the first five pages. Ms. Lichert didn't push it as a strategy, since this is not part of the SRA instructional design. The emphasis is on a child's inducing letter-sound correspondences from spelling patterns, not from direct instruction in phonic rules.

—Afterward, Ms. Lichert gave Dana the SRA workbook and went over it with him. He could do all the exercises related to the first word list and its associated pages.

—As far as his dictionary is concerned, Dana has only asked for words he needs in order to write the entries in his diary (e.g., "I like alligator"). Although he has a handful of words he knows by sight (*brother, like,* and a few animal names), he's shown no burning interest in collecting words per se. Neither has he shown much interest in learning how to read. He has never lingered to watch Ms. Lichert work with other children in the SRA readers or otherwise indicated a particular desire to begin reading.

—Dana was as excited today as Ms. Lichert has ever seen him.

For his own part, Dana announced the day's event to the world with his typical reserve. He wrote in his diary the simple, matter-of-fact sentence, *I can read.*

Dana's reading progress was neither fast nor slow, but steady and methodical. He worked his way systematically through the SRA series, completing half of the level C book by the end of first grade. As in everything else he undertook, Dana demonstrated a firm understanding of what he read and a firm understanding of the workbook requirements. In fact, hindsight led the data collection team to believe that his earlier refusal to read the second word list in *Pig Can Jig* (after he had completed five pages perfectly) was more a matter of "wouldn't" continue than of "couldn't" continue. Dana preferred not to read anything aloud unless he had practiced it to the point of mastery or near mastery. As Ms. Lichert repeatedly observed, it was like pulling teeth to get him to try a word he didn't know—either to try reading it or spelling it. Dana never worked on the SRA reading materials at times other than the required period each day, and he seldom looked at the easy-to-read trade books in the classroom. During free reading time, he almost always selected a TIME/LIFE science book or some other reference book, usually one on animals. Although he couldn't read these books, he would study the pictures.

In the second grade, Dana's preference for information books continued, and his reading ability progressed to the point where he could read books that captured his interest during free reading time—books like *Dinosaurs Do the Strangest Things* (a Step-Up book at the second-grade level). For his last oral reading of the study, taped in February, Dana read a 32-page book about a penguin who leaves the South Pole for the city. In number of words, the text is roughly equivalent to two double-spaced pages of typing. At the end of the reading, Ms Lichert asked him to recount the story without looking back at the book. Not only did he remember all of the several details that occur early in the story, he related them in their proper sequence—"He buys a necktie, and a pair of shoes, an' a umbrella, an' a hat, an'. . ."

Dana's expression of interest in animals was not restricted to his choice of books. Animals appeared in his diary throughout the first grade. Initially, these entries took the simple, repetitive form of "I like ———" ("I like alligator," "I like dogs," "I like peacocks"). Later the entries became more complex: "My baby brother went to the zoo," "Me and Jordie caught a moth Tuesday," "I'm going to catch me some grasshoppers today." Throughout the study, too, Dana observed the animals and insects in the classroom, often assuming major responsibilities for their care. Dana also liked to draw, and his carefully executed efforts revealed an eye for detail even at the beginning of first grade. His drawing capability, and the interest he sustained through books and first-hand experience, came together in the second grade and was expressed in free-hand sketches like those shown in Figure 5.1.

A Praying Mantis

A Grasshopper

FIG. 5.1.   Dana's Free-hand Sketches

Second Prologue: Jenny

Although Ms. Lichert had something decidedly new to report about Dana's reading on that December afternoon, her report about the other child in the study (Jenny) was filled with observations similar to those she had noted in the past. Jenny was still engaging in much quasi reading and quasi writing.

Jenny often elected "to read" during the afternoon choice period. She would completely memorize a book or else fill in part of the story line from pictures and then "read" it to Ms. Lichert, refusing any help with words and insisting that she could actually read. As Ms. Lichert had commented earlier in the fall:

> —She almost gets insulted when I tell her a word she can't read. She'll say "I know"—even when she's just misread it and I've just corrected it. She really . . . is very determined about this.

The earliest books she memorized were books from home. Later, she began to memorize books at the Listening Center by following the text as she listened to the tape recording. When reading these books to Ms. Lichert, she would imitate the tape exactly—even to the point of pausing to hum for the music! In all of this "reading," however, Jenny could never recognize a word when Ms. Lichert wrote it down, or pick out a particular word on a page. She could recognize only two book titles in isolation by December: *The Gingerbread Boy* and *Three Billy Goats Gruff*.

Jenny approached writing in much the same quasi fashion as she approached reading, and she presented similarly striking contrasts with Dana's approach. Dana's writing was always neat; Jenny's was always messy. Dana's spelling throughout the fall of first grade was almost always accurate, because he asked for spellings and copied the words correctly. Jenny's spelling was essentially unreadable. Dana's diary entries through November constitute a record of continuing variation on one sentence structure ("I like _____"). Jenny's diary entries constitute a record of experimentation with spelling and letter/word orientation. Among the mechanical variations represented are letter and number reversals, mirror writing, right-to-left writing, and writing from the back to the front of her diary. Although it was difficult for Ms. Lichert and the study team to decipher Jenny's writing at first, Jenny usually knew what it said and could read it back. The sentence in Figure 5.2, for example, was written on a crayoned design that Jenny handed to Ms. Lichert. When Ms. Lichert asked her what it said, Jenny replied, "Samantha is my favorite friend."

The qualities described above are all mentioned by Ms. Lichert in the following excerpts from the December interview.

> —Lots and lots of writing letters. Her drawings are getting more and more covered with letters. They don't form words for the most part, but sometimes MOM or POP will appear. She did a lot at the beginning of the year, but does even more now.

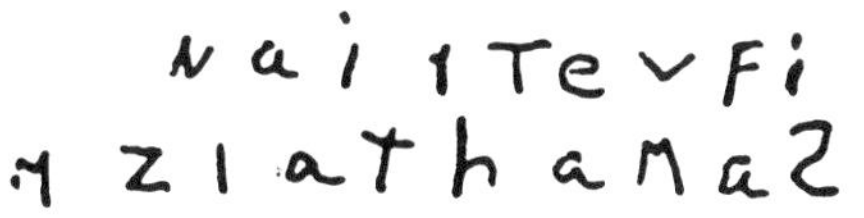

FIG. 5.2. Jenny's Writing

—Her handwriting is still poor and hard to recognize. She will leave no spaces between words, and then at times leave gigantic spaces between letters. But she can read back what it says.

—Doesn't seem to have the sense of what a sentence is in diary writing. She'll write POP POP and call it a sentence. When I ask her if she wants to write something more (approximating a sentence), she'll usually dictate something and I'll write it down. Then she copies it.

—She also continues to copy words from her dictionary into her diary, unattached to anything else. Just words in random order.

—Jenny is very disorganized about paper work in general. It ends up looking a mess. Lots of scribbles, erasures, writing and rewriting all over the paper so you can barely see what's there. Her diary is typical of this—it's a disaster area!

Despite Jenny's eagerness to read, Ms. Lichert did not begin formal reading instruction with her in the fall because of the numerous difficulties in letter and word orientation. In December, she said she would continue to forego formal instruction for a while in order to see how the writing and invented spelling progressed.

It was not until mid-January that Jenny started to "really read," but when she did begin, she did so with a flurry. She learned the first six word lists in *Pig Can Jig* on her own, and she asked to start instruction. By the end of January, Jenny knew all the words in the first linguistic reader and had gone through two-thirds of the accompanying workbook. Unlike Dana, Jenny's early reading in the linguistic books was marked by many word approximations and the consequent production of ungrammatical errors (e.g., *his/hats* for *has*) as well as nonword errors (e.g., *nout/noup* for *not*). She concentrated so much on the words themselves, trying to correct almost every mistake, that she sometimes didn't know the meaning of what she had read. Jenny also read many of the easy-to-read trade books in the classroom during free reading time. When reading these stories, however, her errors were usually grammatically acceptable, and she didn't correct as much.

By early May, Jenny had gone through level D of the SRA series and had exhausted much of the fiction in the room. By June she was able to read from the *Little House on the Prairie* series and understood what she read, though the books themselves were too long for her to read in their entirety. Her proficiency in reading at the end of first grade outstripped her demonstrated progress in other areas, however, including her ability to deal with workbook exercises. An example of her workbook efforts reported by Ms. Lichert in June is as follows: "I have the _____; we need it to fish." The two alternatives given were *wait* and *bait*. Jenny circled *wait* in the workbook, although she knew in discussing the sentence that *bait* was the appropriate word. Ms. Lichert attributed her difficulty to the fact that she was still young and somewhat "scattered." (Jenny was, in fact, the youngest member of Ms. Lichert's combined first- and second-grade class.

> —I don't think she's zeroed in yet on work involving pencil and paper. Everything on paper is still very messy. . . . Also, she's not independent in the sense that she can finish a piece of work and go on to the next thing. She constantly needs a lot of feedback and checking with me.

In addition to reading and writing, other dominant themes that characterized Jenny's activity throughout the first grade were her love of the classroom animals (she would fondle them, talk to them in imaginary play, even read to them) and her intense interest in "messing about" with wax, paint, and weaving. She rarely tried to produce realistic or representational products in these mediums, but would experiment with various processes each medium offered—color mixing, design, and the changing of shapes and textures. As with her writing, the end result of this experimentation usually looked messy and slipshod, failing to reflect the resolve with which she undertook these activities.

Jenny became generally more independent and focused in the second grade, and she showed much improvement in her ability to demonstrate comprehension in workbook exercises. Although her reading did not take the quantum leaps it had in first grade, it continued to thrive. For her last oral reading tape, made in March of second grade, she read a section from *Stuart Little* with considerable expression. When she came to an especially difficult word (like *sarsaparilla*), she simply glossed over it or "swallowed" it without interrupting the flow and intelligibility of her reading.

Diversity and Similarity in Learning How to Read

Children in the study convincingly demonstrated that learning how to read bears the stamp of a person's individuality. The contrast between Dana and Jenny was not unusual in this respect but was typical of differences that occurred between children. Particular points of contrast were unique to specific child pairs, of course, but the fact of contrast held for all pairs of children documented within the same classroom. The children also exhibited continuity in their learning endeavors, displaying the marks of individuality in many aspects of behavior. For this reason, our theoretical analysis necessarily extends beyond a consideration of the knowledge and strategies evident in children's reading to a consideration of their personal styles, approaches to classroom activities, and ways of managing complex tasks. In other words, the theory takes into account the kind of substantive variation among pupils that every teacher faces each day.

Children in the study also exhibited likenesses in their physical, emotional, and intellectual functioning. Although essential likenesses among people are an obvious fact of life, some of the similarities evidenced by the children were surprising. For one thing, they displayed much greater uniformity in what they knew about reading and print than in how they brought their knowledge to bear on text. Many differences exemplified by Dana and Jenny, for instance, turned out to be more a matter of how they used knowledge than of knowledge acquisition or knowing per se. Analysis of the oral reading data also revealed intriguing similarities in the ways children monitored and adjusted their reading efforts.

The combined findings of diversity among children, continuity within children, and similarities across children prompted us to reexamine the literature on skill and skill learning, especially as discussed in the work of Neisser (1967), Polanyi (1958), and Scheffler (1965). Viewed within a context of skill learning, of the theoretical rationale discussed in Chapter 1, and of recent trends in reading research, the study's documentation suggested a comprehensive conception of beginning reading. The remainder of this chapter summarizes the basic thrust of that conception.

READING IS A COMPLEX BUT SINGULAR SKILL

Phonic skills, word-analysis skills, vocabular skills, auditory discrimination skills, and a host of other "skill" terms figure prominently in discussions of reading, in instructional programs designed to teach reading, and in tests intended to assess reading. Yet in each of the instances just listed, the word "skill" actually refers to knowledge (knowledge of letter-sound correspondences, of phonic rules, of word meanings, of word and syllable boundaries, and so on). Important distinctions between skill and knowledge have thus become obscured through casual usage. Occasionally, "knowledge" and "information" are also treated as equivalent words in contexts where they denote quite different concepts. This semantic confounding would rate little more than passing mention if propriety were the only thing at stake, but it is not. The semantic problem in this case tends to create conceptual confusions, and these confusions are especially troublesome when it comes to understanding the skill of reading. Clarifying the terms that delineate central issues of beginning reading and reading instruction therefore seems a warranted exercise.

Information, Knowledge, and Skill

Information refers to just about everything that exists or happens in the world, and it resides in all the available data of the world. Potentially knowable and meaningful information, however, consists only of those events a person actually heeds. But heeding, in and of itself, does not suffice to boost information to the status of knowledge. An individual must discern some unifying pattern in events before information becomes predictable and interpretable. And only when information is interpreted, however tentatively, does it gain the power to influence an individual's thought and action and thereby qualify as personal knowledge. The meaning attributed to information may or may not be shared by others, and it need not be formulated in words (many realms of experience are represented in inarticulate form), but a pattern must be noted and an interpretation made before a person can be said to know something.

The distinction between heeding and knowing implies certain qualifications about an otherwise sensible assumption that pervades many programs of reading instruction. The assumption stems from "time on task" research, and its logic is straightforward—the more time a child spends attending to instructional information (within reasonable bounds), the more he or she will learn. The only problem with this logic is that it doesn't go far enough. A person could conceivably pay attention to a particular kind of information for years without ever discerning a pattern that unifies the information or relates it to other meaningful patterns. Such an outcome is not only theoretically possible, it is quite probable if the information a person heeds consists only of isolated fragments of an event. Although sufficient attention to information is a necessary condition of knowledge acquisition, it guarantees nothing in and of itself. Information must be rich enough to encompass the relevant relationships to be learned. The brain, in effect, is an exquisitely designed pattern detector, but it depends on adequate information to work efficiently.

The data of written language contain information that is crucial to reading, and the beginning reader must figure out what it means. This task involves separating irrelevant data (the size and style of print, for example) from potentially meaningful events, and then detecting patterns that make the potentially meaningful events predictable and interpretable. The word "events" is used advisedly in the last sentence, because most phenomena (including writing) are distinguished by more than one set of relationships. Typically, patterns overlap to produce redundancy in the informational events that comprise and define a particular phenomenon.

As children succeed in detecting the underlying patterns of written language, they acquire more and more knowledge about writing. Knowledge about writing does not add up to the skill of reading, however, and to suppose that it does will distort the concept of reading and lead instruction astray. What many "skill" programs in fact emphasize is not reading skill at all, but articulate knowledge about the information encoded in writing. What many "skill" tests measure is children's ability to demonstrate this knowledge.

A skill is not a knowledge, or a collection of knowledges, or an attitude, or an intent. Skill usually assumes intention, it is effected by attitudes, and it depends on knowledge; but it is something other than these. Skill, by definition, is an act of orchestrating personal resources to achieve a particular result. The greater the level of skill complexity, the more resources (knowledge and capabilities) enter the act. Always, however, the skill is the orchestrated action itself rather than any component knowledge or capability that figures in the action.

Skill is also characterized by certain constraints and demands. Were there no criteria involved in skilled acts, then virtually any action could be called a skill, and the word would lose discriminating power. One obvious constraint follows from the fact that the action is intended to achieve a desired effect. Skill is not an exploratory undertaking but implies effort with a sense of direction. The particular goal or effect to be achieved specifies the purpose of the effort and constitutes an essential definition of the skill. In the case of reading, the defining goal is to construct meaning from text.

Another inherent demand follows from the fact that skill is an action. Because action is motion, it requires a certain degree of momentum to keep going; and the source of momentum in skill is anticipation. If a performer cannot figure out what resources are called for until they are actually needed, the performance necessarily stutters or breaks down altogether. The course of the action must be anticipated and needed resources triggered in advance if they are to be mobilized in time to maintain the flow of the action. Anticipation is therefore a cognitive demand of all skills. The degree to which a person satisfies this demand is manifest in the fluency of the performance.

A third constraint characterizing most skills concerns ground rules for attaining the desired objective. The goal of constructing meaning from text thus entails certain restrictions—namely, that the meaning be accountable to the writing. Although word-perfect accuracy is not the ultimate objective (even proficient readers rarely negotiate text with absolute word-for-word accuracy), the reader must remain faithful to the writer's basic communication.

The nature and constraints of skill suggest a conception of reading that underlies all of our theoretical formulations. Reading is the act of orchestrating diverse knowledge in order to construct meaning from text while maintaining reasonable fluency and reasonable accountability to the information contained in writing. This is the singular skill of reading and the skill that must be acquired in learning how to read. The cognitive ingredients of the act are schematically represented (Fig. 5.3) as an upright triangle. Two sides of the triangle (anticipation and accountability) converge toward the apex of meaning, and the whole is supported by a base of knowledge. The act begins when the knowledge is orchestrated.

Skill Learning

Any skill exercised by a beginner will necessarily be more awkward and less proficient than the same skill performed by an experienced individual. But the only way for a novice to gain the proficiency that comes with experience is to

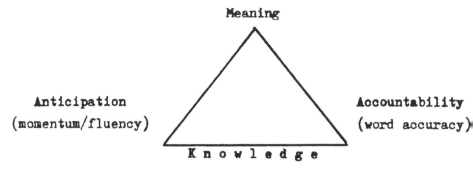

FIG. 5.3   A Schematic Conception of Reading

practice the skill, using whatever relevant resources he or she commands. Nothing else suffices in the long run, because acts of orchestration and coordination are functions of the brain that apparently can be learned only through repeated attempts to perform them. Learners may want to concentrate on different aspects of the action at times (the flow or the accuracy), and they must limit their ambitions at first, but practicing the action is what counts.

The necessity of practice stems from the fact that skilled action takes place in real time and is therefore an irreversible process. In this respect, skill is distinctly different from knowledge and from the reversible mental operations of logical thought. Although reversibility is a key concept in Piaget's theory of intellectual development, the concept has no direct equivalent in skill development. Conversely, practice has no direct counterpart in knowledge acquisition. Knowledge may be refined, transformed, or supplanted by discerning new patterns in information or reinterpreting established patterns, but it makes little sense to talk about "practicing" an interpretation per se. The mobilization and orchestration of resources that take place in skilled action constitute a flow through real time, however, and they need to be practiced as a flow through real time if the learner is to master them. This means that children must practice negotiating text— making their way through sentences and paragraphs—if they are to learn how to read.

The paradox of skill learning is that novices can begin to practice before they control all the requisite knowledge that enters a polished performance. There is, in fact, no other way to begin learning a skill. As long as a person possesses some of the necessary knowledge and understands what the skill is intended to accomplish, practice can start. And once started, the brain picks up additional knowledge in the course of practice efforts. This explains why initial stages of practice are both fumbling and fatiguing. Beginners are operating under the handicap of incomplete and partial knowledge, they are learning the crucial act of orchestration, and they are detecting and interpreting relevant patterns of information along the way. Fortunately, the brain can handle such a complex task, but the task is tiring, and a person needs the encouragement of outside support and of desiring the end result. If appropriate support isn't forthcoming, or if the outcome of a person's efforts continually proves to be dissatisfying and relatively meaningless, the learner may eventually decide the effort isn't worth it.

Whether skills are performed by an experienced individual or a beginner, the action takes place within a larger context of expectation that exerts a profound influence on the performer. In part, this context arises from the performer's own purposes, standards, and stylistic preferences. But many expectations derive from the situational influences of physical reality and social standards. In reading, the most dominant physical reality is the particular text a person is trying to read. Adults mobilize their resources differently, depending on whether they are reading a cookbook, a novel, or a poem. Children need to make such adjustments too, because texts for beginning readers differ just as dramatically as recipes differ from poetry. Social expectations likewise influence a reader, and they are an especially powerful influence on beginning readers. Although explicit standards set by a teacher may or may not be attained by children, the expectations expressed by those standards will almost certainly effect how children practice and what they attempt to achieve in practice—if, indeed, the teacher expects them to practice the act of reading at all. Since our theory views practice as the key to skill acquisition, it follows that the nature of a child's practice will determine the course of learning more than any other single factor.

Technical Facility and Competency

Scheffler (1965) makes a distinction between simpler skills (facilities) and more complex skills (competencies). The distinction is not an either/or proposition, however, for facilities may be nested within a complex skill. Facilities are technical aspects of a performance that are capable of becoming routinized and automatic with practice. Competencies, on the other hand, are always under the guidance of strategic judgment. They may become improved but not routinized with practice.

Although Scheffler doesn't mention reading in his discussion, his distinction is aptly applied to reading. Proficient readers don't struggle over the problem of being accountable to written language, nor do they think about it much at all. Their ability to satisfy this demand is primarily an automated response which no longer requires much conscious attention. Thus, accountability to the information contained in writing (i.e., acknowledging the words printed on a page) is an aspect of reading that can assume the status of a technical facility. The process of anticipating and constructing meaning, however, can never become automated to quite the same degree or in quite the same way. Making sense of text is the competency aspect of reading that necessarily remains under the guidance of judgment.

A STATEMENT OF THE THEORY

Many of the ideas mentioned above will reappear in one form or another in the chapters that follow. The basic conception of reading-as-skill and of skill learning presented here sets the necessary context for summarizing our theory of beginning reading. The theory is stated in the form of four propositions.

1. The several categories of knowledge necessary to support proficient reading are also evident in the beginner's efforts. These knowledge resources include the following: (a) background knowledge of book content; (b) knowledge of grammatical structure; (c) knowledge of literary styles and rhythms of writing; (d) knowledge of the information encoded in writing; and (e) prerequisite understandings about the nature of reading and the conventions of writing and print.

2. Given the opportunity to practice negotiating text, most young children quickly evidence attributes of skilled reading. Not only can they orchestrate knowledge resources (within limits), they are able to build on their own orchestration efforts and to shift knowledge emphases for different kinds of texts.

3. Personal learning styles play a crucial role in learning how to read, determining to a large extent how a child uses knowledge. Styles refer to ways of gaining, organizing, and transforming information.

4. Learning how to read is continuous with other patterns that characterize a child's activity in the classroom. To the extent that children's general classroom activity and functioning also exhibit signs of personal styles and knowledge, such continuity is to be expected.

The next three chapters in this section elaborate on the first three propositions of the theory. Evidence of continuity is presented in the chapter on personal learning styles and is amply illustrated in the child studies that appear in Part III.

In formulating our ideas about how children learn to read, we have obviously been influenced by, and are indebted to, the work and thinking of other researchers and educators. But the primary influence has been the children in the study, and our primary purpose is to present and discuss the evidence from the children. In order to maintain a focus on children in the study, we mention related research and theory only as it seems especially appropriate or necessary in the pages that follow. Although a systematic review of contrasts and similarities between our findings and theory and the findings and theory of others would be useful, such a review is not the intent of this book.

REFERENCES

Neisser, U. *Cognitive psychology.* New York: Appleton-Century-Crofts, 1967.

Polanyi, M. *Personal knowledge: Towards a post-critical philosophy.* Chicago: University of Chicago Press, 1958.

Scheffler, I. *Conditions of knowledge.* Chicago: Scott, Foresman, 1965.

6 Knowledge Resources That Support The Skill Of Reading

In the preceding chapter, we claim that reading is a complex but singular skill that may be defined as follows:

> Reading is the act of orchestrating diverse knowledge in order to construct meaning from text while maintaining reasonable fluency and reasonable accountability to the information contained in writing.

This chapter focuses on the particular kinds of knowledge resources that are orchestrated to support the skill of reading.

Although children in the study obviously did not possess the same content knowledge and level of understanding that mark a mature person, they did draw upon the same range of resources a mature reader employs. In other words, the same categories of knowledge that are hypothesized to support proficient reading were also evident in the documented reading efforts and reading-related activities of the beginners. This array of resources includes the following: (1) background knowledge of book content, (2) knowledge of grammatical structure, (3) knowledge of the styles and rhythms that characterize written language, (4) knowledge of the information directly encoded in writing, and (5) prerequisite knowledge about the nature of the reading task and the conventions of writing and print.

The order in which the knowledge resources are listed and discussed below has nothing to do with their importance. All are important, and their particular significance to the reader may shift from text to text or from moment to moment within a given text. The chapter concludes with some observations about the reciprocal nature of the relationship between knowledge and reading—i.e., not only does knowledge support the skill of reading, reading supports the acquisition of knowledge.

BACKGROUND KNOWLEDGE OF BOOK CONTENT

Evidence from the study suggests that children inevitably mobilize background knowledge in reading if it is at all possible for them to do so (if the text has meaningful substance and if the child possesses the relevant knowledge). This act is not essentially a matter of conscious effort or of being encouraged to do so, but rather a matter of not being able to do otherwise. People spontaneously bring what they know to bear in identifying and interpreting the content of any event, whether it be a tree, a face, a traffic jam, or a book.

Young children possess a respectable store of knowledge about the world by the time they enter school. They understand a great deal about the natural and physical environment (e.g., animals, weather, food, clothing, buildings, vehicles) and about the customs and interdependent activities of the human community. They also grasp the logic of similar and contrasting relationships as well as the humor of incongruity. The following are but a few examples of how such knowledge entered children's attempts to identify words, to anticipate text, to make sense of books, and to relate to what they read in meaningful ways.

—Tanya wrote the word *NO* after one sentence in a workbook exercise. The exercise contained several sentences ostensibly dealing with the subject of cats. When the teacher asked why she wrote what she did, Tanya replied: "I don't think a cat would do that—my cat used to go out at night."

—On another occasion, Tanya read a book entitled *Magic Doors,* which tells of a young boy who wanders away from his big brother to explore the automatic doors at a supermarket. The first page of the text reads as follows:

Johnny's mother asked him to go to the big new store at the corner.

His little brother Howie said, "I want to go too! I want to go too! I'll be good."

So Johnny took his little brother to the big new store.

There were two big doors.
One door had the word IN on it.
The other door had the word OUT.

After reading only through the third sentence ("So Johnny took his little brother"), Tanya began to comment about her anticipations to the teacher—"It's gonna be bad luck!" Several lines later (when Johnny cannot find Howie), her prediction became more specific—"He's gonna be playin' with the doors." She repeated this prediction twice more as she read along, and when it was finally confirmed in writing, she burst out—"See, I told ya!!!"

—Jack read *Jumping Kangaroo* as the title of a book called *Joey Kangaroo,* presumably on the basis of knowing the letter *j* and of his general knowledge about kangaroos. Later in the year, he read a somewhat old-fashioned book about cowboys and, to his teacher's surprise, read the word *wrangler* without any hesitation.

When the teacher asked, "What's a wrangler?" Jack responded, "I guess it's not jeans!" He finally figured out that wranglers must be cowboys.

—Rita sounded out *ladies* in the phrase "Ladies and Gentlemen." Then she told her teacher, "I didn't even have to sound out 'gentlemen,' cause they usually say 'Ladies and gentlemen.' "

—One of the first texts Crystal read was an easy-to-read book for beginners entitled *Go Dog Go*. The book contains no real plot but consists of sentences that describe cartoon-like illustrations. The sentences on one page are as follows:

> A blue dog on a red tree.
> A red dog on a blue tree.

Crystal began to read the first sentence correctly but then hesitated. The ensuing conversation with her teacher revealed that Crystal's logical expectations had been violated. She expected the blue dog to be on the blue tree and the red dog on the red tree, not the other way around.

—As a kindergartner, Carrie's reading and partial improvisation of *The Loose Tooth* was aided considerably by her knowledge of the subject. She also drew heavily on background knowledge to ponder an event in *Blackboard Bear* from many perspectives. One page of the book depicts a boy drawing a bear with chalk on the blackboard. The next page shows the bear walking off the blackboard and following the boy. Highlights of Carrie's discussion with the ETS interviewer about this event are reproduced below; the interviewer's comments appear in parentheses.

> But how can a bear turn to life? If he turn to life he would still be *flat!* He would be a flat bear. (You mean because he was on the blackboard?) Yeah. So how could he get off—how could he stand up? If he stood up, he's supposed to fall down. (I agree with you; I don't know how that could be.) Just like Pinocchio—puppets'll fall down if you don't hold them. I don't know how Pinocchio came to life, he didn't have no strings. [Later] Maybe he could come to life . . . cause maybe he uh uh . . . uh uh he could have just been, you know, like the things, like when the sky makes animals—shapes of animals. (You mean clouds?) Yeah. Maybe he just, uh maybe the air just made him. And when he [the boy] drew him he came to life because the air made him when he was inside the chalk.

—Tim had difficulty with the word "mud," as it appears on the first two pages of a book entitled *Ben Bug*. This book is one of the standard oral reading selections given to children who were in the operational phase of the study. Illustration 6.1 shows the pages in question.

At the first encounter of the word "mud," Tim tried unsuccessfully to sound it out and then omitted it. At the second encounter (page 2), he tried "met" and "make" and then omitted it. Then, looking at the picture on page 2, he suddenly asked, "What melts?" When the ETS interviewer didn't answer this question, he moved on with the reading. On the third encounter ("The hut is a lot of mud"), he finally got it right and repeated the word with enthusiasm:

Ben is a big bug.
Ben has a mud hut.

Ben is sad.
His mud hut got wet.
The hut is a lot of mud.
Ben can not get in it.

FIG. 6.1.   Pages from *Ben Bug*.

Mud! Mud! Mud! Now I got it!!
When the interviewer asked how he got it, Tim continued with his line of thought about melting. He had reasoned that mud is a substance which could "melt" (i.e., diminish, dwindle) in the rain.

The book *Big Dog, Little Dog* is another of the standard oral reading selections that were given to children during the operational phase of research. The first half of this book establishes a theme of contrast between the two canine heroes. Fred is big, Ted is little; Fred always has money, Ted is always broke; Fred plays the flute, Ted plays the tuba; Fred uses green paint, Ted uses red; and so on. Contrasts of this kind continue for several pages preceding the major plot, which finds the two dogs staying at a hotel and assigned to inappropriate bedrooms. Fred gets a little bed, and Ted gets a great big bed. After a sleepless night, they meet a wise little bird who tells them the solution to their problem is to switch bedrooms. Every child in the study quickly grasped the theme of contrast that was being established, and they used this knowledge to anticipate the text.

In fact, the responses of two nonreaders[1] to *Big Dog, Little Dog* were particularly revealing, because they demonstrate the influence of background knowledge in "reading" a story from the pictures alone. Although the illustrations of Fred and Ted are suggestive, we did not expect that they would be very informing of the story text.

---

[1]Actually, three children in the operational study were not yet reading well enough to handle the standard oral reading selections in May of first grade. The third child, Kate, looked at the book but was not pressured to tell the story.

—Louis looked only at the first few pages, but his terse replies clearly indicated an understanding of the theme of contrast. With some prodding, he summarized the pages as follows: "tall-short"; "wet-dry"; "loud-soft"; "got-giving" and "red-green."

—Murray, another nonreader, wanted to go through the entire book. When he got to the end, he turned back and looked through the pages showing the dogs thrashing about in ill-fitting beds, their walk the next morning, their interchange with the bird (who advises them to switch bedrooms), and their dash back to the hotel to plunge into comfortable beds. The fact that they had slept in inappropriately sized beds is clear from the pictures alone, but the bird's role in the plot is not so obvious. Nonetheless, Murray offered the following explanation:

> Murray: (softly) He told em . . . he told em . . . he told em dis his bed and dis his bed (pointing).
> Interviewer: What was that? What did he tell them?
> Murray: (a little louder) The little bird told em this is his bed and this is he bed. And they ran to the house . . . and they went to sleep . . . and the little bird's laughin!

The discussion thus far has illustrated knowledge pertaining to the physical and social world of experience. But people also share an emotional world, and this world has been the source of great literature for children and adults alike throughout the ages. Every age may invent its own creative ways of depicting human motives and emotion, but the dominant themes change very little: themes of love and hate, victory and defeat, separation and reunion, nurturing and being nurtured, trust and betrayal, acquisition and loss, to name but a few. Children and adults have little difficulty recognizing these themes when they are portrayed well, even though they may be portrayed in totally make-believe settings or in settings far removed from a person's own physical and cultural environment.

As far as children's literature is concerned, the most powerful and compelling expressions of emotional life are usually found in books intended to be read to children, rather than in texts that beginning readers can negotiate themselves. When such themes do occur in books intended to be read by children, they generally take somewhat stereotypic forms of good prevailing over evil and of dangerous adventures that end happily. Not only are these thematic forms usually well loved, they are predictable; and their very predictability supports children's anticipation of the text. The research data offer examples of such anticipation in readings unique to individuals, but more uniform evidence comes from the standard selection *Blackboard Bear*.

We chose *Blackboard Bear* as one of the standard oral reading texts, because it seemed likely to elicit knowledge of human themes and also to be "readable" by children whose reading ability was still very limited. The story is carried as much by pictures as by text, opening with two pictures of a little boy watching older boys at play. The remainder of the book intersperses text with pictures and tells the following basic story.

> A little boy, his teddy bear in hand, asks to join the "cops and robbers" and "cowboy and Indian" play of older boys who are bedecked in appropriate costumes. But the older boys reject his pleas, saying he's too little to do the things they do and dismissing him with the taunt to "Go play with your teddy bear."
>
> The young hero goes home, looks at his teddy bear, throws it out the window. He gets chalk and draws a large picture of a real looking bear on his blackboard. The bear then magically comes to life and walks off the board. The little boy goes back outside and parades his "real" bear in front of the older boys who are still in costume playing. They are envious and ask if they can hold the bear's leash, pet the bear, and ride on him. But to each of these requests the little boy retorts "Of course not—he only let's *me*".
>
> The little boy then announces he is going home to feed the bear. Once inside, he proceeds to draw chalk figures of the older boys (complete with their costumes) on the blackboard.
>
> The next to last page of the book shows the older boys outside the little boy's house, talking with him through the window. They ask if he and his bear can go fishing with them. The little boy says he will ask his bear after he (the bear) has finished lunch. The last page shows the bear sitting in front of the blackboard, licking his chops, and getting his mouth wiped by the little boy. The chalk figures of the older boys have disappeared and all that remains on the blackboard are parts of their costumes (a cowboy hat, policeman's cap, Indian headband, and robber's kerchief). Presumably, Blackboard Bear ate the chalk figures for his lunch!

Two pivotal pictures in the story (the bear walking off the blackboard, and the last picture) are shown in Fig. 6.2. The standard procedure adopted with most children was to have them read the text and to tell what was happening on pages that had only a picture. When they had finished, we asked them to go back through the book again and to tell the story in their own words. This procedure was slightly modified with three nonreaders, in that the ETS interviewer read the text lines to the child.

Several interesting things happened with *Blackboard Bear*. First, every single child recognized the theme of rejection and retribution, even though the text does not explicitly state that the little boy is "getting even" with the older boys. The children's comments during the reading as well as in retelling the story indicated that they knew how the boy felt when he threw the teddy bear out the window (hurt, anger, disgust) and why he did not let the older boys hold the bear's leash, pat him, or ride on him. Many children also assumed that the smaller boy was the "little brother" of one or all of the older boys. Interestingly, however, the majority of children did not interpret the last picture as most adults do—i.e., that the bear ate the chalk drawings of the older boys for lunch. They either ignored the last picture's relevance for the plot ("He's finished his lunch now") or else said the little boy had erased the drawings and was now going to erase the bear.

FIG. 6.2. Pages from *Blackboard Bear*. Top: The Blackboard Bear Comes Alive. Bottom: The Bear Has Finished Eating The Chalk Figures Of The Older Boys, Leaving Only Parts of their Costumes Behind On The Blackboard.

Although we were interested in children's understanding of the story we were equally interested in their reading. There is little to say about the children who read accurately and fluently, except that they read with appropriate expression, that most stumbled or hesitated on the words "lasso" and "leash," and that almost all of them read "pet him" for "pat him." The behavior of less proficient readers was more informative, for their understanding of the story seemed to aid their negotiation of the text.

As a rule, the less proficient readers would begin reading an unfamiliar book (which *Blackboard Bear* was for all the children) with some degree of caution, as if they wanted to "feel their way" into the text. Some typically negotiated unfamiliar books at a deliberate, almost word-by-word pace. Yet many of these same children read the first short line of text ("Can I play?") with uncommon ease, and everyone in the group read the line fluently on the second encounter. The children also picked up other phrases during the course of the reading and uttered them with appropriate expression: "Of course not." "You're too little." "You can't." "He only lets me." Although the last page of text does not contain these phrases, the less proficient readers tended to continue reading accurately and with greater fluency than was typical of them.

Our impression that the children's understanding of this story facilitated their actual reading of the text was strengthened by the performance of one of the nonreaders, Kate. Kate started the first grade with an intense enthusiasm for reading, but she had barely begun to learn when she hit a plateau that lasted throughout the rest of the year. As a consequence, she had difficulty reading anything aside from the simplest beginning books that she had practiced over and over. Kate's plateau coincided with a period of stressful events in her life; and by spring, her stress had become manifest in disturbed patterns of classroom behavior. For this reason, the study team decided to present the standard oral reading material to Kate but not to pressure her to read it. When presented with *Blackboard Bear,* however, Kate immediately attended to the text and started reading along as the interviewer read the lines. She also interpreted the last page of the book as most adults do, exclaiming with delight—"Oh, he ate them!" But it was Kate's retelling of the story that was the most impressive aspect of her performance.

> —Kate did not retell the story mainly in her own words, as most of the children did, but gave a fairly faithful rendition of the text. She concentrated on the words, getting much of the text absolutely accurately or with only slight deviations ("You can't shoot guns" for "You can't shoot a gun"). The only line she omitted was "You can't lasso anyone." Her rendition was also nearly perfect on the last page of text, which does not repeat earlier phrases.

Kate's "real reading" and the performance of the less skilled readers in general are provocative. We are convinced that the children's understanding of the rejection and retribution theme was unequivocal. There simply was no doubt in any child's mind about the basic meaning of the story (with the exception of the last page). We are also convinced that their grasp of the material developed almost instantaneously as they went along, much as Tanya immediately grasped the implications of the little brother tagging along to the store and predicted, "It's gonna be bad luck!" Finally, the documentation indicates that Kate and the less proficient readers negotiated *Blackboard Bear* with somewhat greater fluency and accuracy than they typically negotiated unfamiliar texts. Their increased proficiency was only slight in some cases and dramatic in others. In Kate's case, she seemed actually to have memorized the text after her initial exposure to it, though we do not mean to imply the kind of conscious effort usually associated with rote memorization.

Summary Comments

The examples presented above illustrate children using background knowledge in an attempt to support every aspect of the reading process. They grappled with the sense of the content—Tanya's argument with the workbook sentence about cats; Crystal's reluctance to accept the logic of a blue dog on a red tree; Carrie's ruminations about how the bear came to life; Jack's good-natured acknowledgement that (in this case) wranglers could not be jeans. They anticipated themes that carried the story—"He's gonna be playin' with the doors"; the theme of contrast in *Big Dog, Little Dog;* Murray's specific inference about the role of the bird. They identified words and sentences with the conviction of accuracy (though in fact they were not always perfectly accurate)—"gentlemen"; "mud"; "Jumping Kangaroo"; the text of *Blackboard Bear*.

In many of the examples that have been cited, children momentarily halted the act of negotiating text to comment, and their comments provided firsthand evidence of how they were bringing background knowledge to bear on reading. In other examples, we have inferred background knowledge at work on the basis of a child's entire reading performance or on the basis of a particular substitution error (e.g., "Jumping Kangaroo" for "Joey Kangaroo"). The facilitating effects of background knowledge were not evident in every reading performance, however. When children appeared to have no handle on the content of a text, one of two consequences generally followed. Their reading either never got off the ground in any sustained way at all, or it proceeded at the level of technical facility alone. Both of these outcomes are discussed further in Chapter 7.

KNOWLEDGE OF GRAMMATICAL STRUCTURE

Background knowledge of book content pertains to the concepts, characters, objects, events, situations, and settings that are treated in a written work. The knowledge considered here refers to the grammatical form in which content is presented. Although readers obviously need to know the meanings of words, vocabulary knowledge alone does not enable a person to grasp the sense of speech or writing. Two sentences may contain identical words (The cat chased the dog/The dog chased the cat) and yet convey a very different picture of the relationships involved. Grammatical structure shapes the sense of language, and grammatical structure is what young children learn when they develop the capacity to understand and to speak language. By the age of 5 or 6, children have almost as much command over the grammar of their native language as adults have.

Reading research has repeatedly and convincingly demonstrated that beginning readers, like mature readers, rely on their intuitive understanding of language structure as an aid in negotiating text. Evidence of such reliance comes from the examination of oral reading errors.[2] When children misread a word, the errant substitution they produce is often the same part of speech as the word in the text—a noun is substituted for a noun, a verb for a verb, an adjective for an adjective, and so on. This kind of substitution shows sensitivity to the grammatical constraints of language, because it preserves the grammar of the text sentence at least up to the point where the error occurs. And since the grammatical structure of a sentence is central to its communicative function, sensitivity to grammar indicates a sensitivity to meaningful language.

Children in the study displayed sensitivity to the structure of written language from their earliest oral readings on. Not every error honored grammatical constraints, of course, but no child ignored the structural requirements of meaningful language for any prolonged period. Every documentation of the reading process (i.e., every oral reading tape) contains at least some evidence of grammatical sensitivity.

Sometimes, children produced synonym or near-synonym substitutions that maintained syntax (and sense) very well, but showed almost no graphic resemblance to the text word.

> Text: "Who pulled the fire *bell?*" asked the policeman.
> Jenny: "Who pulled the fire *alarm?*" asked the policeman.

> Text: He is going to be *very* bad.
> Dana: He is going to be *real* bad.

> Text: . . . *was caught* in the rain.
> Tommy: . . . *got stuck* in the rain.

> Text: They see our *boat.*
> Crystal: They saw our *ship.*

---

[2]See, for example, Barr (1974), Biemiller, (1970), Clay (1972), Goodman and Burke (1972), Goodman and Goodman (1977), Kolers (1969), and Weber (1970).

> Text: It feels so good when we go fast.
> We like to feel the breeze go *past*.

> Rita: It feels so good when we go fast.
> We like to feel the breeze go *by*.

More often, however, the children's grammatically acceptable substitutions bore greater resemblance to the text. That is, the substitution was graphically similar to the text word in one or more letters, and it often approximated the length of the text word.

> Text: When they *walk* in the rain.
> Alex: When they *went* in the rain.

> Text: Fred ate the *spinach*.
> Debbie: Fred ate the *salad*.

> Text: and Ted ate the *beets*.
> Abby: and Ted ate the *beans*.

> Text: He shut his eyes and let the wind *brush* him.
> Shirley: He shut his eyes and let the wind *blow* him.

> Text: . . . a *tiny* little waist.
> Colin: . . . a *thin* little waist.

The errors just illustrated neither violated grammatical constraints nor grossly distorted the meaning of the text. Other errors clearly did upset both the grammar and meaning of a sentence, although many of these seemed also to have been generated by a child's knowledge of language sense and syntax. Examination of the more blatant errors, and of the child's intonation in committing them, often indicated a strong expectation about where the text was headed. In the example below, for instance, Dana apparently anticipated that the sentence would continue on to the next line, giving more specific information about where the man ran. The sentence itself does not present a grammatical problem or snarl; it is simply rather truncated, and Dana started to lengthen it after the manner of a more ordinary English sentence.

> Text: The sad man ran.
> The sad man ran to Nan.

> Dana: The sad man ran
> to. . . [self correction]

Another common type of mistake entailed children's correct anticipation that a sentence would continue, but incorrect anticipation of how it would continue. Thus, Meg's error below suggests that she expected the sentence to continue with another main clause, presumably one that would express some idea contrary to the thought expressed in the first line.

Text: Policemen go all over the city,
      By day and by night.

Meg: Policemans go all over the city,
      But. . . [teacher correction]

Dana's substitution of *to* for *the* and Meg's of *but* for *by* typify many instances in which a child's error involved the small class of "functor" words and morphemes (i.e., auxiliaries, prepositions, articles, pronouns, conjunctions, and inflections such as *ed, s, ing, al, er, est,* and *ly*). Unlike nouns, verbs, and adjectives, functors convey little content information in and of themselves. Instead, they perform grammatical functions in a sentence. The meanings that functors carry are therefore meanings that accrue to them in context rather than in isolation. Young children's reading of functor words can be so unreliable at times as to seem nothing short of capricious to a teacher. But analysis of such miscues by children in the study suggests that many errant readings are not simply a matter of shaky "decoding" knowledge. As in the examples cited above, mistakes often appeared to spring from well-founded grammatical expectations.[3]

Other mistakes involving functor words seemed to reflect the child's version of reality. As Brown and Bellugi (1964) have stated: "The meanings that are added by functors seem to be nothing less than the basic terms in which we construe reality: the time of an action; whether it is ongoing or completed; whether it is presently relevant or not; the concept of possession; and such relational concepts as are coded by in, on, up, down, and the like." Children in the study frequently changed the tense of verbs, though in no consistent direction. Sometimes they changed a past tense to the present tense and sometimes a present tense to the past, seemingly in accordance with how they viewed the particular situation presented by the text. In many other instances, children also changed the relational concepts specified by text. For example, the story about policemen that Meg read contains the sentence: "Policemen ride in boats." Meg changed it to "on boats." Whether "*in* boats" or "*on* boats" best captures the reality of the situation may seem a trivial matter to adults, but it may not be so trivial to young children, especially if they tend to view language rather literally. The reality/language dilemma that functor words pose for some children is well illustrated in the following excerpt from an observation of Kate.

—Kate's task is to draw pictures that illustrate particular sentences. The sentence in question is: *This is a cat in the tree.* She draws the tree very quickly—two lines for a trunk and a shaded ball for the top. She then draws a cat on top of the ball. The observer asks if the cat is supposed to be in or on the tree. Kate slaps her head and

---

[3]If given the choice, mature readers would probably consider *but* to be a more likely alternative than *by* in the sentence Meg read, particularly in light of the comma that appears after *city.*

smiles: "I was thinking of on!" She erases the cat and draws it by the base of the trunk. The observer continues his questioning.

> Observer: Is she (the cat) in the tree now?
> Kate: Well, I'm not drawing it inside the trunk!!!
> . . . [which she then proceeds to do anyway]

Still other "misreadings" of functor words were not really misreadings at all. They were properly executed translations into the syntax of an ethnic dialect or into the syntax of childhood. An instance of the former kind of translation is represented by Meg's reading of the following sentences.

> Text: A policeman sees it. He calls for help.
> Meg: A policeman see it. He call for help.

The syntax of childhood occasionally reflects a failure on the child's part to distinguish when a particular grammatical rule should be applied. Thus, many children in the study read *slow* for *slowly,* and some read *hisself* for *himself.* More often, however, the syntax of childhood demonstrates children's learning of grammatical rules only too well, for it is basically the syntax of over-generalization. Miscues of this kind reveal the child applying a general rule to words that are an exception to the rule—e.g., *mine's* for *mine, peoples* for *people, drived* for *drove, skieded* for *skied.* When teachers try to point out such errors, their instructional efforts may bear fruit if a child is on the verge of "seeing" the exception to the rule for himself or herself. If a child is not at that point, instruction is often stymied altogether or only temporarily mimicked at best. The following exchange took place after Meg had read a page in which she consistently substituted "policemans" for "policemen."

> Teacher: It's police*men,* not policemans. Can you say that?
> Meg: Uhuh, policemans.
> Teacher: No, there's no "s" in it. It's police. . . *m.* . . *e.* . . *n* (drawn out). Try again.
> Meg: (equally drawn out) police . . . *m* . . . *a* . . . *n.* . . . *s!*

Although Meg was cooperative enough, the teacher might just as well have tried to instruct a native New Englander to say *caught* rather than *cot.*

Errors that upset grammar and meaning also occurred in sentences that featured familiar words used in their less familiar grammatical forms. In the example below, Rita confidently acted on the assumption that *"eat"* was a transitive verb (which it usually is) and would be followed by a direct object (either a noun or noun phrase). The picture accompanying the text showed children eating some ice-cream cones, and perhaps that is what Rita expected the sentence to say.

Whatever her expectation, the teacher wanted to make certain that Rita understood the meaning of the sentence structure.

> Text: We ride and ride
> about a mile
> and then we stop
> and eat a while
> Rita: We ride and ride
> about a mile
> and then we stop
> and eat some . . . eat a. . . a. . . (long pause). . . while.
> Teacher: What does that mean, to stop and eat a while?
> Rita: To eat for a little bit.
> Teacher: A little bit of food?
> Rita: Yeah.
> Teacher: Is that what "while" means?. . . a little bit of food?
> Rita: No. To stop for a while—to stop for a little bit.
> Teacher: Little bit of what?
> Rita: Of time.
> Teacher: Ohhh. Okay, let's go on.

Sometimes, an error involved not only a grammatical variant but also a spelling variant, as in *too* (the less familiar adverb) and *to* (the familiar preposition). Jenny obviously thought the word she encountered was the familiar preposition, although her hesitancy and intonation also signaled puzzlement about what she read.

> Text: "It is good to read. But you must think too. Read and think."
> Jenny: "It is good to read. But you must think to read . . . and think.

The deviant spelling of Jenny's "to" as "too" in the text, the punctuation she skipped, and the peculiar semantics of the sentence she read aloud may all have clued Jenny to the fact that something was wrong. Despite her apparent awareness of a problem, however, she didn't know what the problem was or how to go about finding it. She tried the sentence again and read it exactly as she had the first time.

Whether Jenny had ever before encountered the adverb "too" in writing is unclear, and it is really immaterial to the point we wish to make. In this example, as in the others we have cited in this section, the child's reading error appeared to result from anticipations generated by basically sound grammatical knowledge. That children rely on grammatical knowledge to support their reading is hardly an original conclusion, for it has been reiterated again and again in the literature on children's oral reading errors (see footnote 2).

Anticipation inevitably produces a margin of error, and errors are indigenous to skill learning. Although some children were comparatively cautious in acting on grammatical knowledge early in their reading development, the net result of their self-imposed restraint was usually slower and more methodical reading rather than more error-free reading. In the long run, these children simply postponed reliance on grammatical anticipations as a major resource for reading. No child in the study by-passed such reliance.

KNOWLEDGE OF LITERARY STYLES AND RHYTHMS

Although the spoken and written versions of a language are obviously governed by the same basic grammar, writing is not simply speech written down. Writing is far more stylized than ordinary speech, and its styles vary tremendously. Not only do writing styles differ in such ways as suggestiveness, clarity, and logical persuasion, they differ in aesthetic qualities as well, depending on how an author fashions the sounds and grammar of language. Discussion here centers on children's sensitivity to these aesthetic qualities.

Some beginners' books feature language structures that lack much literary merit but are nonetheless so conventionalized as to be predictable (''Run, Spot, run''). Other children's books of both prose and poetry capitalize on sound sequences and rhythmic structures to the extent that the language literally seems to flow off the page. And still other books deliberately ignore literary qualities in the interest of promoting decoding skills. Most writing falls somewhere between these extremes, of course, but virtually every child's book can be characterized in terms of its literary qualities or lack thereof.

Because the rhythms of writing not only depend on word sounds but are created from the grammatical forms of a language, rhythmic and syntactic (phrase and clause) structures are necessarily related phenomena. Whereas young children's knowledge of language sounds and grammar is well documented, however, their knowledge of writing styles as a support for reading is barely mentioned in the research literature. For this reason, we have chosen to begin the present discussion in something of an historical manner—more or less as we ourselves began to formulate the notion that children rely on knowledge of literary styles and rhythms in their reading. We did not enter the study with this idea but stumbled onto it through an interest in the behavior of prereaders who engaged in ''pretend'' or quasi reading.

The first instance of such behavior that captured our attention occurred early in the pilot study with Jenny's insistence on quasi reading to her teacher, Ms. Lichert. (See the second prologue of Chapter 5 for a brief summary of Jenny's reading progress.)

—One of the books that Jenny brought to school in the fall of first grade was *The Magic Wallpaper,* a story about animals in wallpaper who come to life and talk. Although the plot is readily grasped by young children, the text (which had been read to Jenny many times at home) is reasonably sophisticated. The first page, for example, contains approximately 200 words and includes the following kind of vocabulary and structure:

> and Jimmy asked, "May I see the wallpaper now, before you roll it on?" "No you may not," said father, "because the only way to see it properly is up on the wall."

When Ms. Lichert read the book to the class, Jenny mouthed the words along with her, getting bogged down only toward the middle of the story. Jenny then "read" the first page aloud to Ms. Lichert and gave a near perfect rendition from memory alone. She knew the word that ended the first page and started the next page, but she could not pick out any other word in the text when asked to so do (e.g., "which word is giraffe?").

Our initial reaction to Jenny's feat was in part admiration and in part dismissal. After all, it was neither "real reading" nor an especially unique accomplishment. The example could be multiplied a thousandfold by parents all over the literate world and in all walks of life who have observed their preschool children recite a favorite story verbatim from memory. But as instances of quasi reading were documented again and again in Jenny's record and in the records of other prereaders, we began to wonder. And wonder turned to intrigue as it became clear that this obvious and vigorous memory phenomenon could not be explained by recourse to the mainstream of reading research.[4]

Gibson and Levin (1975), for example, discuss cognitive strategies of memory in their review of the reading research literature. Their introduction to this discussion states that memory for language is primarily a matter of conscious recall and that efficient memorization requires imposing some kind of logical organization on language (as compared with rote memorization or memorizing by a stimulus-response association strategy). According to the studies they cite, however, perfect recall of 20–30 words (grouped by logical category) is considered an achievement, and such capabilities are not evident in young children much before the third-grade level. Results of this kind are difficult to reconcile with Jenny's near perfect reading of 200 words or with any child's verbatim recital of a story. We believe the discrepancy stems from a particular conception of written language implicit in the research. Because the studies reviewed by Gibson and Levin seem to equate writing with "a collection of words" rather than with connected discourse, they overlook the possibility that intentional recall may be facilitated by the inherent grammatical structure of language. Neisser (1967) did not overlook such a possibility, however, and his line of thought is far more provocative as far as quasi reading is concerned.

Neisser's chapter on verbal memory includes a brief but seminal discussion of "Rhythm and Structure in Auditory Memory." He opens this section by observing that most people rely on some kind of rhythmic grouping when they are asked

---

[4]The only extended discussion of quasi reading we have found in the literature appears in Holdaway, 1979.

to learn a series of digits for a memory experiment. In other words, they do not learn the digits as an ordering of individual units (61935827) but as some kind of segmented sequence (e.g., 619–358–27). Neisser then poses two questions. How is the rhythm stored and recalled? Why does it help in remembering the digits? His answer to the first question is based on Lashley's (1951) argument that any temporally integrated series of responses, such as occur in playing the piano or in speaking, must necessarily be learned, anticipated, and performed as holistic sequences. Accordingly, Neisser reasons that the whole rhythmic pattern in the digit recall example (–––/–––/––) is stored and remembered as a single structural unit.

In addressing the second question, Neisser draws on Gestalt Psychology to suggest that the digits themselves are ''integral parts, visible tips, of the entire rhythmic structure.'' After acknowledging obvious limits on the human capacity to organize extended rhythmic sequences in this manner and to recall their content verbatim, he nonetheless concludes that rhythmic structure is a powerful facilitator of verbal memory. He ends the discussion by hypothesizing that the syntactic organization of language is an integrative structure which facilitates speech, much in the same way that a rhythmic pattern facilitates memory for digits.

Although linguistic research has confirmed beyond a reasonable doubt that grammatical structure facilitates speech, the implications of Neisser's hypothesis for reading, for learning how to read, and for the recall of written material remain largely unexamined.[5] Had he pursued his thought further, Neisser may well have hypothesized that the more stylized structures of formal writing serve as an integrative support for remembering text. This is our hypothesis, at least, and it implies the following interpretation. What Jenny and other quasi readers committed to memory were not individual words but the phrase structures of a story. The individual words flowed from the structures.

Support for this hypothesis comes from the records of prereaders who freely improvised text as opposed to memorizing it by heart. In all such improvisations, it was clear that the children were making a pronounced distinction between the language of utterance and the language of writing. Not only was the distinction a structural one, it extended to vocabulary and a ''book voice'' intonation as well. The following paragraphs illustrate two versions of this phenomenon.

Tanya's improvised response to *The Birthday Car* occurred early in January of first grade, when she was on the verge of reading but knew only a few sight words. The book is a simple primer, written in the style and language of a traditional basal text. Tanya had never seen the book before, and she started rather hesitantly, making sure to match each spoken word with a word in the text. She read: ''*Dad said, 'Run fast'* '' for ''*Father said, 'Come here.'* '' The teacher

---

[5]The influence of organizational features of prose on a reader's ability to recall written content has been investigated of late. By and large, however, the implications of these research findings for the problem of learning how to read have not been explored.

then read the first page to her, and Tanya subsequently started over again. This time, she abandoned the word-matching strategy and read the first five pages with several embellishments.

Text	*Tanya*
Father said, "Come here.	Father said, "Come here.
Come here.	Come here.
Run, run, run.	Run fast, run fast.
Come and find something."	Come and find something that you want.
Father said, "Look, look	Dad said, "Hi Ho
Here is something for you."	Do you like it?"
Oh, oh, oh.	Oh, Oh, Father.
A little red car.	A lovely red car you bought.
I can go.	I like the car.
I can go away.	I like the car already.
Away, away, away.	A . . . [away] away.
Oh, my.	It's a lovely car.
Oh, my.	It's a lovely car.
See me.	
It is fun.	

As a prereader, Kate chose two familiar books to "tell about" for her initial oral reading sample of the study. The first selection was a book of rhyming couplets, most of which she proceeded to recite from memory. Her second selection was a rather unusual text entitled *The Popcorn Book*. The children featured in this book are cartoon characters, and the words appear in cartoon-like balloons; but the content is that of an information book, and the structure is complex. Two separate threads of text interweave on most of the pages as follows:

> (a) a little boy reads to a little girl from a technical book about the nature and history of popcorn (e.g., "Popcorn pops because the heart of the kernel is moist and pulpy and surrounded by a hard starch shell"); and

> (b) the boy and girl carry on an informal conversation while she cooks the popcorn (e.g., "Are you sure you didn't put too much popcorn in the pan?" "Of course not, Silly!").

The two threads of text are visually separated by different styles and sizes of typeface. Kate had not memorized this text as she had the rhyming couplets, but she did imitate the dual structure of the book as she looked at the pictures and "read" it. In the following excerpts from her "reading," the indented portions indicate a definite change in her tone and pace.

> They're looking at a Popcorn show (on TV). Then they called to his mother could they make some popcorn.

> *Some Indians made jewelry out of popcorn and discovered it. . . [inaudible].*
> *. . Some of them cooked the popcorn. Some of the Indians popped up popcorn*
> *in a warm fire.*

And the little boy eats some.

> *Then the Indians eat popcorn rice. And then. . . and where. . . where they*
> *give the Pilgrims popcorn and they make it out of butter.*

And now we know. . . The little boy said, "Now we know everthing about how to make popcorn!"

Although Tanya had never seen *The Birthday Car* before, her performance reveals clear ideas about the general structure and vocabulary of basal readers. Similarly, Kate's rendition of *The Popcorn Book* shows dawning sensitivity to the difference between expository and narrative writing. Not every prereader in the study engaged in quasi reading at school to the extent that Jenny, Tanya, and Kate did (memorizing entire texts or freely improvising them). Other prereaders simply talked about books they perused or else, like Dana, were reticent to say anything until they had some degree of elementary skill. As most children entered a stage of "very beginning" reading, however, they also picked up and relied on structural characteristics in writing. For example, we have already mentioned the less proficient children's ease and expressiveness in negotiating the repeated phrases in *Blackboard Bear:* "Can I play?" "Of course not." "He only lets me." Their reading in this instance seemed bolstered not only by understanding and anticipation of the story line, but also by their ability to anticipate the book's simple structures as single, integrated sequences.

Carrie's record (presented in full in Chapter 10) provides an example of a child who displayed sensitivity to literary structures from the time she was in kindergarten throughout the period covered by the research. Her first oral reading (*In the Village*) was taped in January of kindergarten and reflects some combination of sight vocabulary and memory aided by picture clues. What is noteworthy about this rendition is Carrie's faithfulness in representing adverbial and prepositional phrases. She doesn't always read them accurately, and she sometimes inserts them gratuitously, but the structures, as such, seem clearly to exist in her mind. When she reads "now" instead of "another day," for instance, she obviously misreads the words, but she doesn't misread the grammatical intent. Her entire rendition suggests that phrase structures exist as place-holders for words.

Carrie's progress as a reader lends support to this interpretation, for she developed a decided preference for fairy tales and other books of that genre. From a structural standpoint, such stories are distinguished by the many informational and mood-setting details they convey in prepositional and adverbial phrases—the classic favorite being "Once upon a time."

As Carrie and the other children became more skillful readers, they began to encounter more artful forms of writing. There is a touch of irony in such progress, because artful writing entails the creation of truly rhythmic language structures, and rhythmic structures are easier to anticipate than the choppy and stilted prose typical of so many books for beginners. Moreover, rhythm is inherently pleasing. Thrall, Hibbard, and Holman discuss this quality in *A Handbook to Literature* (1960) as follows:

> Man has a seemingly basic need for [rhythm] or for the effect produced by it. . . as anyone can see for himself by watching a crew of men digging a deep ditch or hammering a long stake or by listening to chanteys and worksongs. In both prose and poetry the presence of rhythmic patterns lends both pleasure and heightened emotional response to the listener or reader, for it establishes for him a pattern of expectations and rewards him with the pleasure of a series of fulfillments or gratifications of expectation. (pp. 416–417)

Rhythm lends movement to language through recurring accent or sounds at approximately regular intervals. Although authors of children's prose must work with a relatively limited repertoire of words, this restriction does not necessarily limit the rhythm they can create. McCullagh, for example, achieves considerable rhythm in *The Golden Tree* (1973) with a vocabulary of fewer than 50 words, including prepositions, articles, and conjunctions. The text begins with a melodious sentence ("The sun shone down on the Island of Trees") and maintains a rhythmic quality in unfolding an interesting plot. It ends on the same melodic note with which it began:

> There is a big hill
> on the Island of Trees.
> There is a golden tree
> at the top of the hill.
> And there are three stone pirates
> by the golden tree,
> on the top of the hill
> on the Island of Trees.

In these concluding lines, a rhythmic cadence is reinforced by the repetition of contrasting with the prolonged front vowels in *hill, Island, Trees, tree,* and *three*). Together, the beat of the passage and the recurrent and contrasting vowels impart a musical quality to the text. This quality clearly had an invigorating effect on Mike.

> —It was late in the afternoon, and Mike was obviously tiring and beginning to make mistakes as he neared the end of *The Golden Tree.* But his voice tone perked up on the last page, and the language literally seemed to carry him through an errorless conclusion of the oral reading.

Mike was hardly a child who struck anyone as being especially sensitive to the subtleties of language. He was big, he was frequently naughty in minor ways, and his presence was sometimes overpowering to other children. This over-powering aura arose from the sheer force of physical energy that Mike invested in life and that gave many of his movements and utterances a heavy quality. We mention these characteristics merely to point out that rhythm is appealing and supportive to a wide range of young readers, not just to those with uncommon aesthetic sensitivity.

Another literary use of sound to which every child responded is onomatopoeia. Strictly speaking, onomatopoeia refers to words whose sounds denote their meaning, as in *hiss, buzz,* and *sizzle*. Children invariably understood the imitative intent of such words, even if they could not pronounce them precisely. More generally, onomatopoeia refers to the use of words whose sounds suggest their meaning or suit the sense of the meaning. This intent, too, was something children seemed to understand and to honor, even in their devia-tions from text.

> Text: And downstairs Ted moaned and groaned and crashed and
>   thrashed all over the bed.
> Jack: And downstairs Ted mowled and growled. . .

Meter and sound cooperate to produce poetry, and the sound most frequently associated with poetry is end rhyme. Although there is no doubt about children's enjoyment of rhymes, they are not necessarily the most important sounds in verse, nor are they even essential. Dana read the following poem with more expressiveness than was typical of his early reading, yet the implied rhyme of "*fum*" and "English*man*" completely escaped him. (He pronounced the last syllable of "Englishman" simply as "man.")

> Fee fi fo fum
> I smell the blood
> of an Englishman.
> Be he alive or
> be he dead
> I'll grind his bones
> to make my bread.

What captivated Dana initially was the heavy alliteration and contrasting vowel sounds of "Fee fi fo fum." The other aspect of the poem to which he responded most enthusiastically was the pronounced rhythm, especially on the line with the most pronounced irregular beat ("Be he alive or").

The variation or "roughening" of a rythmic pattern by introducing an irreg-ular beat is a trademark of good prose and poetry, and children other than Dana seemed to respond to this quality. Rita was a child who almost always corrected her mistakes in oral reading. In fact, she had one of the highest self-correction ratios of any child in the study. Nonetheless, at a time when Rita's self-correcting tendency was at its height, she let two miscues go by uncorrected in reading a poem entitled *Summer*. We have already illustrated one of these errors in discussing synonym and near-synonym substitutions.

Text	*Rita*
It feels so good	It feels so good
when we go fast.	when we go fast.
We like to feel	We like to feel
the breeze go *past*.	the breeze go *by*.

Rita gave appropriate stress to the poem's meter, which continues for several pages in the pattern illustrated above (i.e., ___ _____ ___ _____ / ___ _____ ___ _____ // ___ _____ ___ _____ / ___ _____ ___ _____ //). Only twice in the poem are there two-line rather than four-line stanzas, and one of these does inject some irregularity. It reads, ''Summer brings/so many things.'' Rita apparently perceived a possibility in this variation and used it to introduce some irregularity on the next to last page.

Text	*Rita*
Some summer days	*Summer brings days*
we take a ride	we take a ride.
The car gets very	The car gets very
hot inside.	hot inside.

Whether Rita consciously varied the rhythm of the poem is impossible to say with certainty. But the substitution of ''Summer brings days'' for ''Some summer days'' is the most blatant deviation from text that appears in her first-grade reading record. This is not to say that Rita rejected the poem's inherent rhythm, however. She honored the meter more than the rhyme (as seen in her substitution of *by* for *past*) and seemed to count on it as she negotiated the text. Most children, in fact, were responsive to the predictable, steady beat of an unvaried rhythm, and Josh actually entered reading on this type of poem. Moreover, it was a poem that he mastered by himself.

Josh displayed unusual verbal facility for a first-grader. Not only did he talk a lot (occasionally ''too much''), he was capable of expressing sophisticated thoughts in precise language. And when precise language eluded him, he would create metaphors (''distance heat'' for thermometer), coin a phrase (''super uncalm''), or else explicitly point out that he didn't know how to say what was on his mind. Despite this facility, Josh made no ostensible progress in learning how to read during the fall months of school, and he showed no signs of any desire to start reading. His one spark of enthusiasm for written language was apparent when the children thought up rhyming words as a game, and the teacher wrote them on the board. Early in December, Josh surprised both his parents and his teacher by reading *Put Me in the Zoo*, a rhyming book that he had apparently been practicing in private. According to his parents' report to the teacher, he said he had taught himself to read and had been "keeping it a secret." The teacher immediately taped an interview with Josh in which he read from his book and discussed the story with understanding. The book is about a spotted animal of indeterminate species (something of a cross between a leopard and a bear) who tries to find a home for himself in the zoo and eventually wins acceptance. The first three pages illustrate the poem's regular meter, which Josh consistently intoned in his reading.

> I will go into the zoo.
> I want to see it.
> Yes, I do.
>
> I would like to
> live this way.
> This is where
> I want to stay.
>
> Will you keep me
> in the zoo?
>
> I want to stay
> in here with you.

Josh started to make progress in Dr. Seuss books immediately following this sudden display of reading ability, but he soon reached a plateau where he stayed for the rest of the year. No amount of instructional assistance seemed to help him, and he still could barely read in November of second grade. Not until the middle of the year did Josh make a move, and then it was an extremely rapid and dramatic one. His last oral reading sample of the study, taped in March of second grade, contains several selections from stories of his own choosing. One of these stories is *How Perseus and His Mother Came to Seriphos*. It begins as follows:

> Once upon a time there were two princes who were twins. Their names were Acrisius and Proetus, and they lived in the pleasant vale of Argos, far away in Hellas.

The music of this sophisticated prose can hardly be compared with the verse of *Put Me in the Zoo*, and Josh was such an invisible reader that it is impossible to construct a coherent picture of his progress from one text to the other. The only unifying thread that seems clear is Josh's continuing interest in the sounds and rhythms of language.

The sounds and rhythms of language that we have illustrated from children's literature are not evident in beginning stories that are used for phonic and linguistic instruction. Nor are they intended to be. Such texts are designed to foster analytic knowledge of letter-sound correspondences; and to accomplish this aim, they rely on words that feature a high degree of assonance, alliteration, and consonance, with minimal contrast. Because the intent is to focus children's attention on word analysis rather than on language flow, meter is not considered. The result is a peculiar vocabulary, devoid of notable rhythm, that necessitates an almost word-by-word reading of the text. The following two stories from *A Pig Can Jig* (1970) are illustrative.

The Bad Fan	Kit, the Cat
Dan ran to the fan.	Kit, the cat, sat.
Dad had to fan Dan.	Kit sat in a bag of rags.
Dad had to fan Nan.	Tap! Tap! Tap!
Dad had a bad fan.	Kit hit the bag of rags.
Can Dad fan Dan?	Kit bit the bag of rags.
Can Dad fan Nan?	Pam ran to the bag.
Sad Dad!	Pam had Kit, the cat.
Sad Dan!	Kit sat in Pam's lap.
Sad Nan!	Kit, the cat, has a pal.

It is important to make the distinction between different kinds of texts, because many adults assume that a child who likes sounds or who "has an ear for language" is well suited for a reading program that emphasizes letter-sound correspondences and the phonic blending of words. Similarly, many adults assume that children who "sound out" words do so by means of phonic analysis. Neither assumption proved reliable in our research. Josh rarely, if ever, sounded out a word overtly. Dana, who negotiated the "Fee fi fo fum" poem with unusual expressiveness (and who was heard during class meeting to say "wyet, smiet, piet" when his teacher said "quiet"), was not very facile in phonic analysis. Colin, who was not a very expressive reader or speaker, used phonic analysis to good advantage in decoding words. Rita was a very adept decoder but almost never used phonic strategies when she read poetry. Debbie and Tommy both gravitated to books of verse at free reading time, and both were described as frequently "sounding out" words in their oral reading. Yet neither Debbie nor Tommy was exposed to systematic instruction in phonics. These are but a few examples which suggest that knowledge of phonic rules and knowledge of language rhythms exist as two distinct kinds of knowledge about sound, at least for the beginning reader.

Children's enthusiasm for rhythms and rhymes in their everyday activity has been amply documented (Opie & Opie, 1959). Our data indicate that children also recognize and anticipate rhythmic structures in written language when they read texts that possess this literary quality. Many even anticipate the stereotypic and stilted structures that characterize books of lesser literary merit (as illustrated by Tanya's rendition of *The Birthday Car*). Although the children's understanding of literary styles and rhythms seemed to play a significant role in their negotiation of text, we know of only one article in the reading research literature that treats such knowledge as an important consideration for young readers.

Bartlett (1979) compares two programs of beginning reading instruction with respect to the way they define reading for children and the quality of reading materials they provide. She expresses concern over the lack of good writing in one program, not on literary grounds but from a psychological viewpoint. Drawing on Scribner's (1979) work, Bartlett hypothesizes that children may develop cognitive schemas that correspond to literature structures and that enable them to organize and process increasingly complex information within a literary genre. She speculates as follows:

> . . . it seems to me that learning to read must involve the learning of written discourse structures that might, as cognitive organizations, serve to order various aspects of the reading process. . . . it is possible to argue that the very repetitiveness and predictability of some forms may in fact aid the beginner even more than the child with more advanced recognition skills. (Examples of such forms are certain rhyme structures in the Dr. Seuss books or the cumulative narrative structures found in stories like "This Is the House that Jack Built" or "The Gingerbread Man"). (p. 240)

Our research results provide empirical support for Bartlett's speculation.

KNOWLEDGE OF THE INFORMATION ENCODED IN WRITING

Nothing in the graphic marks of the alphabet contains information about the subject matter, syntax, or literary characteristics of a text. These understandings are resources a reader brings to written language and imposes on it. What the graphic marks of writing encode are two kinds of information at the level of individual words: (a) phonetic information, signaled by letter-sound correspondences, and (b) lexical information, signaled by spelling. Both types of information provide vital clues to a reader, and the beginning reader must come to understand what they mean (though it is worth emphasizing that clues about words alone do not suffice to support the skill of reading). Because knowledge of letter-sound relationships has claimed the lion's share of attention among educators in the field of early reading, we consider phonetic information first.

Phonetic Information and Letter-Sound Correspondence

Every child in the study displayed implicit knowledge of some letter-sound correspondences at the very beginning of the documentation process. In a day and age when children are surrounded by familiar forms of writing (words on signs, cereal boxes, TV commercials, and the like), it is hardly surprising that they pick up certain letter sounds. Such rudimentary knowledge was usually evidenced in correct matches for initial consonants and an occasional final consonant, as illustrated by Susan's substitution of "mommy hat" for "mud hut," and Jack's substitution of "Jumping Kangaroo" for "Joey Kangaroo."

By the end of the documentation process, all but one of the children[6] revealed substantial knowledge of letter-sound relationships *in their oral reading behavior*. We underscore the fact that this knowledge was revealed in the process of negotiating text, because not every child could articulate what he or she implicitly knew about the sounds of letters when asked to do so. For some, only a portion of their working knowledge could be formalized in words. The most obvious and overwhelming evidence of the children's knowledge was the fact that they progressed in reading skill, for it is difficult to imagine anyone making headway without also making considerable use of the phonetic information in writing. Obvious as it is, however, such evidence is indirect.

Direct evidence of letter-sound knowledge was most often displayed in three ways.

—A child substituted a word that matched the text word in two or more phonemic segments (e.g., *pat* for *pet, cave* for *cove, cooking* for *coming, looked* for *liked, blond* for *bland, tub* for *tuba*).

—A child substituted a nonword for a text word, usually in an obvious attempt to sound the word (e.g., *het* for *hot, sike* for *sick, bog* for *bag*). These errors occurred most frequently when children were reading texts designed to focus attention on letter-sound relationships.

—A child voiced the initial consonant(s) or syllable(s) of the text word before pronouncing it.

All of these behaviors are well represented in virtually every child's record, and they often coincide with evidence of other knowledge. That is, the child's final response (if errant) showed sensitivity to semantic and/or grammatical constraints of the text, or the child corrected an errant response to conform more with grammatical and/or semantic constraints.

The children's invented spellings also revealed their understanding of letter-sound relationships. We first encountered such spelling in Jenny's writing during the initial weeks of the pilot study, and it did not take long to realize that her inventions resembled the spelling patterns described by Read (1971). An early example of Jenny's invented spelling, embedded in backward writing, is presented in the second prologue to Chapter 5. A later example, taken from her diary in March of first grade, appears below.

JORDON   THIW   HIS   ERREJ   DAWN   THE   SWR
(Jordon threw his orange down the sewer)

---

[6]The one exception was a child studied during his kindergarten and first-grade years in school. Although his record indicates some understanding of phonetic information, the evidence is generally less vigorous in later documentations than in earlier ones.

Analysis of the spelling evidence obtained in the study would constitute a book in and of itself. Moreover, the phenomenon of invented spelling and the knowledge of letter-sound correspondence such spelling reveals have been extensively documented and analyzed in the literature. Because our data are remarkably similar to those presented elsewhere, we will rest with the assertion that the children's spelling does indicate letter-sound knowledge and refer to the work of other investigators for explication (e.g., Bissex, 1980; Clay, 1975; Henderson, 1981; and Read, 1971, 1975).

To say that all of the children drew upon letter-sound knowledge to read is not to imply that all of the children were proficient "decoders" in the most analytic sense of that word. Slightly over half of the group were exposed to systematic instruction in phonics, and most of these children could demonstrate knowledge of phonic rules and principles in their workbook exercises. However, only about 20% of the total group (8 of the 40 children) were able to analyze and then synthesize sounds in a conscious "blending" strategy with reasonably consistent success throughout the documentation period.[7] The blending of sound segments was simply not a very workable strategy for the majority of children, and their problems with it were numerous. Three problems, in particular, stood out.

One problem that plagued many children on occasion was the failure to recognize words that had been sequentially sounded out, even if the blending process resulted in a fair approximation of the word. Tanya, for example, did not try to blend words spontaneously until the second grade, and then her successes were sporadic. She got "whiskers" by this strategy; but when she pieced together "deefinitely," she could not recognize the word well enough to make the necessary adjustment to "definitely."

A second problem was the reversal or transposition of sound sequences. Although the children did not normally transpose sound sequences in their speech, it was not an uncommon problem when they were trying to concentrate on phonic decoding. Dana exhibited a good grasp of letter-sound correspondence principles in the workbooks accompanying the SRA readers, but he was reluctant to apply them when reading aloud, and he sometimes ran into difficulty when he did use them. During one oral reading of a story entitled *Stan's Test,* he had no trouble with the boy's name on the first page but transposed the sounds every time he encountered *Stan* on the second page. When he first tripped over the name, he tried to correct his error and made a conscious effort to attend to the sounds. But the more he tried, the more he came up with *Sant,* occasionally interspersed with *Sans,* After several futile attempts, the teacher pronounced the name for him, and then Dana said it correctly, but he seemed unable to recoup and again reverted to "Sant" or "Sans" on the next few encounters.

---

[7]More children began using sounding out strategies as they gained an understanding of syllabication, and they did so rather naturally.

In some instances, transposition problems appeared to stem from the way in which children deployed visual attention. That is, they seemed to take in broader spans of print rather than focusing more narrowly on a left-to-right, letter-by letter analysis of words. (We discuss this tendency as a cognitive style in Chapter 8.) In other instances, transposed pronunciations seemed to result from the very self-consciousness of the blending exercise. Many adults have had the experience of becoming "tongue twisted" at a time when they were trying to enunciate most carefully, and we believe this happened with the children as well. In fact, self-consciousness seemed to be the root of Dana's problem in the "Stan" episode.

A related factor that may have contributed to errant blending efforts was the articulation difficulties displayed by many children. These difficulties were due in part to missing teeth, but they also reflected a range of idiosyncrasies often found in young children's speech. Whatever the source or nature of these difficulties, they were evident at times other than when a child was trying to blend a word. Tim continued to have such troubles long after he had abandoned all pretenses to a phonic approach to reading. Even in his last tape-recorded reading of second grade (*All About Prehistoric Cavemen*), he tried three times to pronounce "modern" in the sentence, "Prehistoric man, they said, had certainly looked very much like modern man." He seemed unable to form the second syllable correctly, sounding as if he were half swallowing it; and he still didn't enunciate the word perfectly on the last try. Tim's floundering did not reflect semantic uncertainty, for when asked if he knew what the phrase "modern man" meant in the sentence, he replied, "Yeah, more like today, except for their clothes." Tim's articulation problems were so frustrating to him on a few occasions that he resorted to saying "whatever" for the particular word he was trying to pronounce.

A third kind of problem children encountered in using phonic knowledge to decode words was the unreliability of phonic rules when applied to texts that were not controlled for "regular" spelling.[8] Since all of the children read such texts, this problem arose rather frequently. Sometimes, children demonstrated knowledge of the regular letter-sound correspondences they had learned but failed to recognize deviations from the rule that had also been taught in their lessons. The short "u" vowel sound, for instance, is honored in most three- and four-letter words in which "u" is the only vowel: drug, smug, bug, dug, hug, rug, but, cut, hut, nut, rut, and so on. The word "put" is introduced as an exception in phonic lessons. The excerpt below (from an oral reading taped in March of first grade) shows Crystal in command of the regular "ut" sound as well as the sound of the consonant "p." Her actions, however, suggest the following conclusions: she does not recognize the irregular spelling of "put";

---

[8]See Henderson (1981) for a brief and interesting account of how so many irregularities evolved in the English language.

and she is unwilling to act on the letter-sound knowledge she possesses, which would produce the word "putt." Crystal is trying to read the following sentence from a basal reader: *Put your name on your lunch box.*

> Crystal: But your n..n.
> Teacher: I think you're saying it—
> Crystal: name?
> Teacher: (Tells Crystal she is correct, but Crystal continues to hesitate. The teacher then directs Crystal's attention back to the first word, *Put.*)
> OK, what's this? (Spells) p-u-t?
> Crystal: But?
> Teacher: (Spells again) P-u-t. (No response from Crystal)
> That's a "p."
> Crystal: But
> Teacher: You're saying "b-u-t." I want you to say "p" (and she makes a "p" sound)
> Crystal: (Makes the "p" sound the teacher has made. Then. . .) But.
> Teacher: Put
> Crystal: Put your name. . .
> Teacher: Good!
> Crystal: . . . on your lunch box.

A trickier problem for phonics than the comparatively rare exception (like "put") is the rule that may be honored as much in the breach as in the observance. The rule for vowel digraphs exemplifies such a problem. The general rule states that pronunciation should follow the long vowel sound of the first letter in the digraph. (This rule is often presented to children as, "The first vowel says its name," or "When two vowels go walking, the first one does the talking.") Although phonic instruction gradually introduces subordinate rules to cover most of the numerous exceptions to this general rule, the entire network of rules is complicated at best. And if children read traditional literature before they have learned all the exceptions to the vowel digraph rule, they will necessarily make some mistakes in applying the general rule.

Colin, a classmate of Crystal's, adopted decoding strategies more readily than Crystal and was generally successful in his attempts to implement them. At the beginning of second grade, Colin read a sophisticated myth about how the spider got a thin waist. His first attempt at reading the story, which he had not seen before, was tape-recorded for the study. A portion of text is reproduced below.

How Spider Got a Thin Waist

> MANY dry seasons ago, before the oldest man in our village can remember, before the rain and the dry and the rain and the dry that any one of us can talk about to his children, Spider was a very big person. He did not look as he looks today,

> with his fat head and his fat body and his thin
> waist in between. Of course, he had two eyes and
> eight legs and he lived in a web. But none of him
> was thin. He was big and round, and his waistline
> was very fat indeed. Today, he is very different,
> as all of you know, and this is how it came to pass.

Colin committed several miscues in his first reading of this myth, but many of them made sense (e.g., "a thin little waist" for "a tiny little waist"), and he was able to retell several details of the story. Moreover, unlike his earliest oral readings, he kept up momentum and did not stop at every difficult or unknown word. Analysis of his reading reveals both successes and errors on words containing vowel digraphs. Some of these words follow the general rule and some do not. More interesting is the fact that Colin's word identifications did not fall into a neat pattern. He succeeded (and failed) in pronouncing some words that deviate from the general rule; and he failed (and succeeded) on some words that follow the general rule. For example:

	Text	*Colin*
"Regular" Words	waist neither east feast	waist neither east fe-est, fest
"Deviant" Words	sauce eight already caught	sauce eight alreedy coot

Anomalous patterns of success and failure in word identification also characterized children other than Colin who were good decoders. In Rita's first oral reading of the study (*What Will Little Bear Wear*), she wrestled with the difficult medial vowels in "wear" and "around" and finally mastered them to decode both words correctly. A month later (in January of first grade), she read the poem *Summer* with very few mistakes, one of these occurring on the word *does*. She hesitated briefly, voicing "ah. . . dah" and then said "dogs." (The sentence refers to a "pup" and is printed right above a picture of a dog.) When the teacher questioned the presence of a "g" in the word and asked Rita to spell it, the following exchange took place.

Teacher: Is there a "g?" Spell the word, Rita.
Rita: (Spells) D-o-e-s. Then whispering to herself, "dah. . . dahs" (pronouncing the "o" as in "bother"). Then she says aloud— "does?" (correctly pronounced as duz).
Teacher: Right! How did you know?
Rita: I don't know . . . cause I know "o" has an "ah" sound.

Teacher: Sometimes. Actually, that's a hard word, because the "o" and the "e" are together, and usually the first vowel makes its long sound when two vowels are together. But if it made its long sound in this word, the word would be what?

Rita: Does (pronounced correctly as female deers).

Teacher: Right. Now let's hear the whole sentence again.

Rita: "And when we eat, so does our pup."

The episode above ended in success because Rita correctly identified *does* and went on to read the sentence accurately. But the question of how she actually figured out the word was left unanswered by the sounds she made in her decoding efforts and by her subsequent explanation to the teacher. This illustration from Rita's record and the examples drawn from Colin's reading suggest that even children who were the most adept at phonetic analysis did not operate solely on the basis of rules they had learned in phonic instruction.

Lexical Information and Spelling

Information about the sound structure of words is vital to a beginning reader, but it is not the only, or even the dominant, information encoded in writing. The English writing system emphasizes the meaning of words and word parts through consistent spelling more than it emphasizes the sound of words through consistent letter-sound relationships. When the letter *s* is applied at the end of a word, for example, it becomes a meaningful word part—a suffix with a stable semantic (as opposed to sound) representation. Thus, the meaning of plurality is consistently signaled by this suffix, even though the letter itself may take any one of three pronunciations ("s" as in *cats*, "z" as in *cars*, or "ez" as in *houses*). The *ed* suffix is likewise a stable indicator of past tense, even though it also has three phonetic representations ("t" as in *stamped*, "d" as in *hammered*, and *ed*" as in *pounded*). The sound shifts in these letters do not have to be indicated by writing, because they are adjustments every native speaker intuitively predicts and accommodates. Indeed, such patterns of change are the very kind of thing children learn as they learn to speak a language. If the writing system replicated what people already know, there would be three different spellings to indicate plurality and three to indicate action completed in the past (not to mention irregular endings such as occur in man/men and run/ran).

The retention of meaning in English spelling extends far beyond these common inflections, as Chomsky (1970) has illustrated.[9] Semantic regularities are

---

[9]A majority of theorists now seem to agree with the linquistic analysis first presented by Chomsky and Halle (1968) and later summarized in less technical language by Chomsky (1970). English spelling is a morphophenemic system, which means that it places primary emphasis on representing lexical information and secondary emphasis on representing information about the sounds of words.

maintained by stabilizing the spelling of root words as well as of prefixes and suffixes that signal predictable variations in the meaning of root words. The spelling of *national,* for example, retains the root word *nation* and simultaneously indicates that the word is an adjective by the addition of ''al.'' Although adding the suffix creates a phonetic change in the first vowel (from the long ''a'' of *nation* to the short ''a'' of *national*), English speakers make this shift quite unconsciously. The more important information the writing system has emphasized is the intimate bond of meaning between the two words. Similarly, meaning is stabilized but the phonetic realization of the final ''a'' changes in the transformation from *national* to *nationality.* The language abounds with other examples of spelling that may or may not represent phonetic structure faithfully, but that signals both the root meaning of a word and its grammatical function.

The lexical information encoded in writing implies that a person must eventually attend to the visual organization of spelling patterns if he or she is ever to become a proficient reader. This feature of the writing system also suggests a possibility about learning how to read. Some children may attend to the visual organization of spelling more than the sound characteristics of individual letters from the very beginning of their learning. Teachers in the study often alluded to such a possibility in their comments about children who seemed to have a ''visual approach'' to reading as contrasted with an ''auditory approach,'' and teachers in our study are certainly not the first to have commented on such differences among children. The distinction between so-called visual and auditory approaches in learning how to read has long been noted by practitioners, but the theoretical implications of this distinction have not always been apparent or accepted. The implications, in fact, are not very acceptable if they are taken to mean that some children rely primarily on their eyes to learn, whereas other children rely mainly on their ears. Unless one or the other modality is impaired, children clearly use both senses in their everyday learning and living. What is perceived through both senses, however, may be organized more readily in either visual or auditory memory.

As prereaders, all of the children possessed at least a small vocabulary of ''sight words'' that they could reliably identify out of context. Although the phenomenon of sight recognition is probably universal and seems clearly based on visual memory, the phenomenon often ''disappeared'' when children actually began to read. That is, words once identified correctly out of context were suddenly misread in the process of negotiating text. We believe this happened because children were juggling several knowledge resources when they were reading, and their construction of meaning from the text therefore depended on many influences in addition to spelling configurations. But the instability of a child's initial sight vocabulary did not necessarily foreshadow the subsequent influence of spelling configurations in the child's reading history. Evidence that some children drew heavily on their knowledge of spelling per se occurred in the form of immediately recognizing compound words, or ''words within words'' when the teacher covered over certain letters (e.g., ''him-self,'' ''birth-day,'' "class-room," "again/against," "child/children," "right/frighten"). These same children might also look away from the page they were reading, or concentrate on the page without really focusing on it, as if they were trying to visualize a difficult word in their mind's eye.

Children's oral reading errors also provided evidence of attention to spelling, and Tim's record offers numerous examples. The example below is especially interesting, because Tim's errant response is so unexpected.

> —*The King's Shadow* tells the story of a little king who was terribly afraid of his own shadow. In the opening lines of the book, the king asks his three wise men what to do about the shadow, and they respond as follows:
>
> > "Chop off your shadow's head," said one.
> > "Boil it in oil," said another.
> > "Burn it at the stake," said a third.
>
> When Tim came to the third line, he quickly read, "Burn it at the casket."

Substituting *casket* for *stake* seems a very puzzling error when considered in isolation, but it was not untypical of other of Tim's renditions that went astray. The nature of the difficulty becomes clearer when it is seen as part of a pattern in which his substitutions tended to resemble an anagram of the text, containing some or all of the text word letters but in scrambled order. (With the exception of the ''c'' at the beginning, ''casket'' is an anagram of ''stake.'') This type of error was most prominent in Tim's reading from May of first grade through November of second grade, and it is illustrated by the following additional examples from a variety of texts. He read *want* for *what, blump* for *blurp, off* for *for, white* for *while, places* for *palace, last* for *least, still* for *silly, tried* for *tired, screeching* for *searching, left* for *felt,* and *Green Cold Superpie* for *Green Cloud Supreme* (the name of a dessert). These miscues appear to reflect Tim's attention to, and faulty interpretation of, a word's spelling pattern more than attention to (and faulty interpretation of) letter-sound correspondences.

The most convincing single instance of Tim's attention to spelling was not a miscue, however, but a gratuitous remark he made to the teacher during a tape-recorded oral reading session in January of first grade. The following is a summary description of the incident.

> —Tim reads several pages from one book without error until he comes to the word *know,* at which point there is a prolonged interchange with the teacher. She tries several strategies to help Tim analyze the word, but they are all to no avail, so she finally tells him the word. Both Tim and the teacher then agree it is time to start reading another selection. The next passage is one Tim has never seen before, and it is much harder for him. The teacher tries to help him unlock several troublesome words by insisting he sound them out, but this only prompts long and agonizing struggles on Tim's part that inevitably end in failure. His last struggle, near the end of the passage, is over the word *grow.* When the teacher asks him to sound the initial consonant blend, Tim comes out with a whole word—''great.'' After other

attempts, he suddenly makes a comment that sparks the following exchange. (Over 10 minutes have elapsed since his hard work on *know* in the prior selection.)

Tim: If there was an *n* there, I would know.
Teacher: What would it be if there was an *n* there?
Tim: Know
Teacher: I guess I don't know what. . . . Where would the *n* be if it was?
Tim: The *r* wouldn't be there; the *n* would be there.
Teacher: And what would the first letter be?
Tim: A *k*.
Teacher: Oh! So you're talking about the word *know*, huh? Okay, maybe this rhymes with *know*. Could you make it rhyme with *know* but start with *gr?*
Tim: Grow?
Teacher: It certainly would—good job!

It seems unlikely that such an exchange could occur, had Tim not consciously attended to spelling patterns and organized information about spelling in visual memory.

Not all children displayed evidence of visually organizing and recalling whole words in the ways we have just described. But as the children progressed in reading skill, most of them did evidence knowledge of the spelling and grammatical meaning of frequently encountered word parts. By ''word parts,'' we mean common affixes appearing at the beginning or end of a word: *un, in, pre, de, ment, ness, tion, ity, al, able, ful, less, ize, ate, ed, ied, er, est, ly, ier,* and the like. Once children had passed the initial stage of beginning reading and had gained familiarity with a variety of texts, they began to recognize affixes (and their corresponding pronunciations) on sight. Since affixes signal grammatical meanings, the children's knowledge of these orthographic units strengthened their ability to anticipate the grammatical structure of text.

Evidence for this kind of lexical knowledge was found in miscues that we have termed ''word approximation'' errors, in contrast to ''nonword'' errors. Both types of error result in a word that does not exist, but there is a distinct difference between the two end products. A nonword miscue is either an outright nonsense word (''noup'' for not, ''het'' for hot, ''sike'' for sick), or else it is an unlikely word for the child to say and seems to represent a nonsense word from the child's viewpoint (e.g., ''sin'' for sun, ''bog'' for bag). A word approximation, on the other hand, ''sounds'' like a real word, because it has the structural elements of a real word. Jane, for example, came up with the following word approximations while reading a complicated article in *Natural History* magazine—*rammamaxigen, magisterly, properations, universalty, discoveration, parsicles*. The affixes she used to construct these approximations are not the same affixes that actually appear in the text word, but they denote the same grammatical class as the text word. Thus, she said:

rammamax*igen*	for	ramifi*cations*
magister*ly*	for	magister*ial*
universal*ty*	for	univers*al*
discover*ation*	for	discover*y*
pars*icles*	for	perspec*tive*

Jane's errors in reading the article from *Natural History* magazine were more sophisticated than most children's word approximations, just as they were more sophisticated than her own typical errors in other readings. These particular miscues seemed largely a function of the difficult text, which was beyond her ability to comprehend. (See the last section of Chapter 7 for a complete rendering of this text.) Jane made similar types of errors in challenging material that was well within her grasp, however, and so did many other children. Often, these errors occurred when children were reading along rather rapidly and seemed intent on keeping up the pace of their reading.

—Jack selected a book describing how to make puppets for his oral reading in October of second grade. He had used the book the previous spring to construct several puppets, and he was more eager to tell the teacher about the book and his own puppet making than he was to read the text. When the teacher finally pinned him down to read, Jack read quickly and produced the following word approximations. (The actual text word is shown in parentheses.)

most *easable* equipment	(essential)
maniply strips of tagboard	(manipulate)
you can *deoperate* these	(decorate)
and *stape* or glue them	(staple)

Jack's word approximation errors, like those committed by Jane and others, provide convicing evidence that several children recognized the orthographic forms and meaning of affixes and could therefore interchange structures (e.g., eas*able* for essen*tial*).

Overall, the study documentation may be summarized as follows with respect to the lexical information encoded in writing. Some children evidenced attention to spelling patterns from the very beginning of their reading efforts. Although these children also possessed knowledge of letter-sound correspondences, they often had difficulty using this knowledge in a conscious manner when they were trying to negotiate text. The majority of children evidenced attention to the spelling of affixes as they became more proficient readers. They seemed to construct a store of "sight affixes" in somewhat analogous fashion to the way they had constructed a nucleus of "sight words" at an earlier stage of reading.

But there was an important difference in the result of their constructive efforts. The children's knowledge of affixes proved to be a much more versatile and useful resource for negotiating difficult text than their previous sight vocabulary.

PREREQUISITE KNOWLEDGE FOR LEARNING TO READ

Children need to understand basic conventions of writing and print in order to begin learning how to read. They must know that writing progresses from left to right and top to bottom on a page, and from front to back in a book. They must understand the artificial boundaries imposed on writing and realize that every written word has a counterpart in spoken language. Although these conventions delineate areas of challenge and learning for young children,[10] they posed few difficulties for children in the study. The children either knew the conventions or else learned them very quickly. Only in the earliest documentation for a few first-graders and in the records of some kindergarten children does evidence suggest that a child was focusing on the problem of maintaining one-to-one correspondence between written and spoken words. (Carrie's kindergarten record, for instance, contains some clear examples of her trying to make a correct match between the number of words she says and the number she points to in a text.) But such problems did not persist long, nor did they apparently require much effort to resolve.

Children also need to distinguish letters of the alphabet if they are to master the skill of reading. Judging from some of the literature on beginning reading, we anticipated the children would have more difficulty with letter reversals and rotations than they actually did. Although errors that seemed generated by a confusion of letters (e.g., *bad* for *dad*) occurred in almost every child's reading history, these miscues were sporadic and comparatively rare. In no case did they present a serious obstacle to reading progress.

The infrequency of letter-reversal errors in reading was not duplicated in the children's writing. To the contrary, reversed and rotated letters were liberally sprinkled throughout most of the children's writing, and some children had initial difficulties with virtually all the mechanics involved in writing. These mechanical problems (aside from letter formation itself) included maintaining adequate pressure on a pencil, maintaining the appropriate spacing between letters and words, and maintaining appropriate height and width variations among letters. The reading disability literature suggests that writing problems often forecast later reading problems, but such a relationship failed to materialize in the study. Jenny and Josh were among the children who displayed the greatest difficulties

---

[10]See Clay (1975, 1979) for pertinent observations on children's learning of these conventions.

with writing at the beginning of first grade, and their histories are illustrative. Jenny started to read in January of first grade and progressed at a phenomenal rate, though her writing showed only minor improvements through the end of first grade. Josh, on the other hand, began to make marked improvements in his writing during the winter and spring of first grade, but he made almost no observable progress in reading until mid-January of second grade.

Jenny's backward, sometimes mirror-image writing and Josh's scratchy, immature representations in both writing and drawing did not go unnoticed by their respective teachers at the beginning of first grade. Both teachers were concerned, though not alarmed, about the writing, and both took a watchful "wait and see" attitude. Although these children's difficulties would very likely have been flagged by a screening test for perceptual disability (had the school administered one), we have no basis for speculating how Jenny's and Josh's reading would have progressed if they had received special instruction. We can only say that their reading progress seemed unaffected by their writing difficulties under the circumstances in which we did study them. And the same was true of other children who evidenced relatively immature and improperly oriented writing. As far as we can discern from the documentation, there was little connection between the children's reading and the mechanical aspects of their writing.

Another prerequisite for learning how to read is one that seldom appears on any list of educational objectives for beginning reading. This is knowledge of what the skill is supposed to accomplish—the nature of the dynamic constraints that distinguish reading as a skill in the first place. Children in the study appeared to know what reading was "about" from the outset. They didn't offer formal definitions, of course, but their behavior from the very beginning of the documentation process indicated an understanding that reading involves a flow of meaningful language that is somehow beholden to writing.

Jenny, for instance, never uttered memorized stories in the absence of printed matter and called it "reading," though she obviously could have done so. She always had the necessary prop of a book and went through the appropriate motions of looking at it, as did every other child in the study who first approached reading in a "pretend" or "quasi" manner. These children didn't yet know *how* to be accountable to the writing system, but they seemed to understand perfectly well that reading entails such accountability. Other children, like Dana, never approached reading in a pretend fashion, though they could recognize a few sight words. But neither Dana nor any other child acted as if the ability to "read" a sight word was tantamount to negotiating text. They seemed to understand perfectly well that reading involves the meaning of whole thoughts and stories, not the fragmented concepts implied by words in isolation. Dana was a child who tended to focus on the detail of objects and the differences that mark one event from another. (See the first prologue in chapter 5 for a brief history of Dana.) In retrospect, it was probably no coincidence that he marked in his diary the boundary between being able to recognize a few memorized words and his first demonstrated ability to negotiate text. His dictated sentence, "I can read," probably communicated much more implicit understanding than we understood at the time.

The fact that children seemed to know (or easily grasp) the conventions of writing, the differences among letters of the alphabet, and the nature of the reading task raises the question of where they gained such knowledge. The study did not document children's activities outside of school, but evidence of children's and parents' statements to teachers, and of books going back and forth between classroom and home, indicate that some of the children read at home and that their parents read to them. Similar evidence (or lack of it) suggests that such experiences for other children were rare, if they occurred at all. Three facts are clear about the children's classroom experience. Each teacher read to the class every day, the children read or looked at books every day, and they engaged in writing activity several times a week. We conclude that children in the study either came to school with the necessary understandings to begin reading or else they were able to grasp this knowledge very quickly from their school experience. We suspect that most children of entering school age in our culture possess the same qualifications of prior understanding or the ability to acquire it rapidly from exposure to reading and writing in the classroom.

Our speculation as to how children acquired the knowledge prerequisites for reading leads to some concluding (and less speculative) thoughts about the knowledge children gain through reading per se.

READING SUPPORTS THE ACQUISITION OF KNOWLEDGE

Children in the study began to read with two strong knowledge resources at their disposal. They possessed background knowledge to help them understand the content of many books, and they had a firm grasp of the grammatical structure and sound patterns of English. Most of them also possessed rudimentary knowledge of letter-sound relationships, and many understood basic differences between the language of utterance and the language of text. Several children received separate phonic instruction (i.e., instruction outside the context of reading a book), and some who received such instruction profited a great deal from it. Undoubtedly, too, the children picked up knowledge about the rhythmic structures of written language from hearing books read in class. But the bulk of additional knowledge they acquired *about* reading, they acquired *by* reading.

Reading, in fact, is the only way the children could have gained much of the knowledge they evidenced as they became more proficient readers. There were no lessons about the lexical information contained in writing, nor was there direct instruction about stylistic differences among authors or genres of books. Yet these are exactly the kinds of things that children learned as they made progress. For example, one can ''hear'' Debbie's adjustment to the author's style in her reading of the *Little Red Riding Hood* text shown below. (This selection was taped in January of second grade.)

> Many years ago there lived a little girl who, whenever she went out, wore a cape and hood of bright red wool. For this reason she was called Little Red Riding Hood.
>
> One day her grandmother, who lived in a house on the other side of the woods, became ill. Little Red Riding Hood's mother asked her if she would carry a basket of goodies to her, but she warned her daugther not to speak to anyone she might meet on the way.
>
> Off through the green woods went the little girl, singing a happy song to herself as she skipped along.

Debbie had no serious difficulty with any of the words on this page, but her timing and expression were thrown off in the first paragraph by the subordinate clause, ''whenever she went out.'' As Debbie came to the next such clause in the second paragraph (''who lived in a house on the other side of the woods''), she hesitated briefly, as if sizing up the situation, and then proceeded to read the sentence with its appropriate meaning. From this point on, she had the author's style basically under control.

To say that children acquire knowledge that supports reading by practicing the act of reading is really to restate the point we made in Chapter 5. People necessarily begin learning a skill before they have mastered all of the knowledge that enters a polished performance. They discern other relevant information during the course of practice. Skill learning, however, is not primarily a matter of knowledge acquisition. Practice enables the learner to gain control of the orchestration process, and orchestrating knowledge is what reading is all about. This is the essential *skill* aspect of reading that we discuss in the next chapter.

Not only did children in the study learn about reading per se, they frequently expanded or restructured their knowledge of the world on the basis of what they had read. Virtually every child, for instance, read at least one book containing information that he or she applied to ongoing classroom activities: instructional books on how to care for animals; how to plant seeds; how to make puppets; recipes for cooking; directions for simple games. Other incidents in the children's records illustrate the learning of new words for established concepts, new words for new concepts, and sundry information specific to individual interests.

—As mentioned previously, Jack figured out that ''wranglers'' must be cowboys from the context of a book he had chosen to read. On another occasion, he read "autos" in a poem and said (more to himself than anyone else), "What are they?" As he continued reading the full phrase, "autos and taxis and buses," he remarked: "It must be cars . . . must be Spanish or something."

—In reading a book about a school that offered children many different activities, Rita encountered the word "*fence*" used as a verb. She commented that she didn't know what it meant, and after the teacher explained, she moved on with her reading. Her remark in a subsequent discussion about the book indicated that she had learned a new concept.

> Teacher: This [school portrayed in the book] is sort of like our school, isn't it?
> Rita: Yes, 'cept we don't have fencing.

—For his last oral reading sample of the study, Tim read portions from three chapters in *All About Prehistoric Cavemen*. Between his actual readings of the text, he told the ETS interviewer several things he had learned from the book, including the fact that the Cro-Magnons hunted reindeer. The interviewer expressed some skepticism about this fact until Tim proved his point by finding supporting documentation in the text.

Children also learned from illustrations, even those intended primarily for decorative purposes rather than purposes of conveying mood and feeling or elaborating on the text. The more informative the illustrations, of course, the more children were likely to learn from them.

—Several children reasoned that the word "*jig*" (in the title of the instructional text, *A Pig Can Jig*) must mean some kind of dance step, because the pig shown on the cover of the book looks as it if is dancing.

—Dana persisted in choosing science reference books at free reading time throughout his first-grade year. Although he progressed at an average rate in reading his instructional texts, he could not possibly have negotiated all of the complex text in the science books. But judging from his serious perusal of the reference books, his continuing selection of animal books he could read in second grade, and the knowledge of animals and insects he displayed through art, Dana must have enriched his general knowledge of animals from the book illustrations, if not from parts of the text itself. (See the first prologue to Chapter 5 for a sample of Dana's art work.)

The skill of reading is an enabling skill, allowing access to a world of experience far beyond the perceived realities of one's immediate surroundings. Moreover, the method of gaining access to this world is a uniquely reflective process as compared with the access afforded by radio, records, tape recorders, movies, or television. Although the early education literature emphasizes the importance of learning to read more than any other single topic, strangely little is said about the enabling purpose of this skill. Not until the middle primary grades does there begin to be expressed concern about children's ability to learn from reading, and that concern continues to be expressed right up the educational ladder and into the realm of work. Because the study amply documents that beginning readers can and do expand their knowledge from meaningful books, we believe postponing attention to this matter until the middle grades may be a fatal mistake. If children do not encounter meaningful content in books until the third or fourth grade, the major message they may learn in the meantime is that reading lacks purpose.

REFERENCES

Barr, R. Influence of instruction on early reading. *Interchange,* 1974, *5,* 13–22.

Bartlett, E. Curriculum, concepts of literacy, and social class. In L. Resnick & P. Weaver (eds.), *Theory and practice of early reading* (Vol. 2). Hillsdale, NJ: Lawrence Erlbaum Associates, 1979.

Biemiller, A. J. The development of the use of graphic and contextual information as children learn to read. *Reading Research Quarterly,* 1970, *6,* 75–96.

Bissex, G. *Gnys at wrk: A child learns to write and read.* Cambridge, MA.: Harvard University Press, 1980.

Brown, R., & Bellugi, V. Three processes in the child's acquisition of syntax. *Harvard Educational Review,* 1964, *34,* 133–151.

Chomsky, C. Reading, writing, and phonology. *Harvard Educational Review,* 1970, *40,* 287–309.

Chomsky, N., & Halle, M. *The sound pattern of English.* New York: Harper & Row, 1968.

Clay, M. M. Reading: *The patterning of complex behaviour.* Aukland, New Zealand: Heinemann Educational Books, 1972.

Clay, M. M. *What did I write?* Aukland, New Zealand: Heinemann Educational Books, 1975.

Clay, M. Theoretical research and instructional change: A case study. In L. Resnick & P. Weaver (Eds.), *Theory and practice of early reading* (Vol. 2). Hillsdale, NJ: Lawrence Erlbaum Associates, Inc., 1979.

Gibson, E., & Levin, H. *The psychology of reading.* Cambridge, MA: MIT Press, 1975.

Goodman, Y., & Burke, C. *Reading miscue inventory manual: Procedures for diagnosis and evaluation.* New York: Macmillan, 1972.

Goodman, K. S., & Goodman, Y. M. Learning about psycholinguistic processes by analyzing oral reading. *Harvard Educational Review,* 1977, *47,* 317–333.

Henderson, E. H. *Learning to read and spell.* De Kalb, IL.: Northern Illinois University Press, 1981.

Holdaway, D. *The foundations of literacy.* Sidney: Ashton Scholastic, 1979.

Kolers, P. Reading is only incidentally visual. In K. Goodman & J. Fleming (Eds.), *Psycholinguistics and the teaching of reading.* Newark, DE.: International Reading Association, 1969.

Lashley, K. The problem of serial order in behavior. In L. A. Jeffress (Ed.), *Cerebral mechanisms in behavior.* New York: Wiley, 1951.

McCullagh, S. K. *The Golden Tree* (Little Dragon Series). Leeds, Eng.: E. J. Arnold & Sons Ltd., 1973.

Neisser, U. *Cognitive psychology.* New York: Appleton-Century-Crofts, 1967.

Opie, I., & Opie, P. *The lore and language of schoolchildren.* London: Oxford University Press, 1959.

Rasmussen, D. E., & Goldberg, L. "A Pig Can Jig" in *THE BASIC READING SERIES.* Chicago: Science Research Associates, 1970.

Read, C. *Children's categorization of speech sounds in English.* Urbana, IL: National Council of Teachers of English, 1975.

Read, C. Pre-school children's knowledge of English phonology. *Harvard Educational Review,* 1971, *41,* 1–34.

Scribner, S. Modes of thinking and ways of speaking. In R. O. Freedle (Ed.), *New directions in discourse processing* (Vol. II). Norwood, NJ: Ablex, 1979.

Thrall, W., Hibbard, A., & Holman, C. *A handbook to literature.* New York: Odyssey Press, 1960.

Weber, R. M. First graders' use of grammatical context in reading. In H. Levin & J. Williams (Eds.), *Basic studies on reading.* New York: Basic Books, 1970.

7 The Orchestration of Knowledge in Reading

Skill entails the act of orchestrating multiple resources. In effect, every execution of skill is a creative act which produces something more than the sum of its parts. Major resources that enter the skill of reading were discussed in the preceding chapter: knowledge of the content treated in books, of grammar, literary styles and rhythms, letter-sound correspondences, and spelling patterns. Children of entering school age possess much of the requisite knowledge to begin reading, and they acquire additional knowledge as they practice the skill. But learning the skill is not tantamount to acquiring knowledge. Learning how to read is fundamentally a task of learning how to orchestrate knowledge in a skillful manner.

Chapter 5 specifies three defining criteria that reading shares with other skilled acts. First, reading is goal-oriented action, intended to accomplish the purpose of constructing meaning from text. Second, reading shares with other skills the requirement of anticipation, necessary to generate momentum and sustain the flow of action through time. Third, the goal or purpose of the action involves certain constraints, namely, that the meaning be accountable to the text. Together, these essential characteristics of skill led us to define reading as ''the act of constructing meaning from text while maintaining reasonable fluency and reasonable accountability to the information contained in writing.'' We represented this conception in the form of a triangle, as shown in Fig. 7.1, with two sides (anticipation and accountability) converging toward an apex of meaning, and the whole supported by a base of knowledge. We said the act begins when the knowledge is orchestrated.

In focusing on the orchestration process per se, this chapter deals directly with the active nature of reading. We of course do not presume to discuss the neurology of orchestration as it occurs in the brain, for that level of activity was obviously not tapped by the study's methods. Rather, our inferences derive from

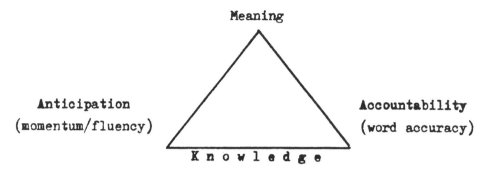

FIG. 7.1.   A Schematic Conception of Reading

observable manifestations of the orchestration process, which are the reader's behaviors in negotiating text. Although the word "reading" can refer to reading individual words out of context, such a feat is not the same as constructing meaning from text, and it may well involve processes that differ slightly or radically from those necessary to construct meaning from text. In order to infer something about the nature of orchestration, we therefore have relied exclusively on documentation of children engaged in the act of negotiating text, as evidenced in the oral reading samples.

Descriptive analysis[1] of oral reading samples took account of the full range of behaviors children displayed in negotiating text and led to several initial hypotheses. For one thing, these analyses made it clear that reading is not the application of knowledge according to some prescribed formula, but is an adaptive interaction between the reader and text. Readers draw on knowledge selectively depending on the text and particular contingencies, and they try to adjust their performance depending on what has transpired. In other words, the action seems to build responsively rather than to proceed in a predetermined fashion. Descriptive analysis also suggested that there is little difference between more and less proficient readers in the adaptive nature of the orchestration process. Although children differed in their preferred strategies of negotiating text, the adjustments that occurred within strategies appeared to be equally responsive to the goal of constructing meaning. Some differences between more and less proficient readers clearly reflected variation in the range or depth of knowledge children were able to bring to bear on text. In the main, however, proficiency differences seemed attributable to differences in the facility with which children were able to perform the act of orchestration. That is, proficiency was largely a matter of controlling the orchestration process—or, as teachers often phrased it, of "getting the act together."

---

[1]See Chapter 4 for discussion of the descriptive analysis procedure.

Descriptive analysis not only led to the hypotheses sketched above, it also suggested more detailed procedures for analyzing children's oral reading. These procedures include the examination of substitution errors but go beyond such errors to consider other deviations from text (e.g., omissions, insertions, pauses, self-correction attempts, repetitions, various kinds of decoding efforts and "noises"). We present data from some of the unique selections children read, but much of the chapter centers on detailed analysis of the standard oral reading selections. The standard selections allowed for comparison between children and (where warranted) the aggregation of data across children. Aggregate data proved especially valuable in this case, because any given reading by a particular child yields relatively few deviations to examine. Group data provided more substantial grounds for checking hypotheses about general patterns in negotiating text.

A description of the standard selections and the sample of children who read them follows. The chapter then presents three formulations about the orchestration process: (a) control of the process, (b) responsiveness to characteristics of different texts, and (c) the balance between momentum and accuracy. The phenomenon of "technical facility" in reading and the related concept of "automaticity" are discussed next, and the chapter ends with a brief comparison of instructional implications that stem from different views of how "automaticity" is achieved.

The Standard Selections and the Sample of Children

Data collection from the operational phase of research included one oral reading session in which children read from a standard set of books. This sample was obtained by ETS staff during April or May of the children's first-grade year. (Two children who were second-graders when the operational study began read the selections in the spring of second grade.) The texts used were not available in any child's classroom, and all but one of the children said they had not seen the books before.

The two texts chosen for detailed analysis exhibit contrasting qualities. *Big Dog, Little Dog* is a conventional storybook that features a varied sample of English spelling. *Ben Bug* is patterned after phonic instructional texts and thus limited mainly to words with regular letter-sound correspondences. *Big Dog* includes some relatively long and/or unusual words (e.g., flute, tuba, spinach, mountains), whereas *Ben Bug* contains no word over three letters. *Big Dog* has a compound sentence and three subordinate clause structures; *Ben Bug* features all simple sentences. The two texts are shown below. Because each selection was divided roughly in half for certain analyses, we have indicated the first- and second-half portions.

Big Dog, Little Dog
(115 words)

First Half (57 words)	*Second Half (58 words)*
Fred and Ted were friends.	When they painted the house,
Fred was big.	Ted used red paint. Fred used green.
Ted was little.	One day Fred and Ted took a trip.
Fred always had money.	Fred went in his green car.
Ted was always broke.	Ted went in his red car.
When they walked in the rain,	Fred drove his car slowly.
Fred got wet but Ted stayed dry.	Ted drove his car fast.
They both liked music.	When they got to the mountains,
Fred played the flute.	Ted skied all day long.
Ted played the tuba.	Fred skated all day long.
When they had dinner, Fred ate the spinach. . .	
and Ted ate the beets.	

Ben Bug
(63 words)

First Half (31 words)	*Second Half (32 words)*
Ben is a big bug.	Ben had to get a hut.
Ben has a mud hut.	It is hot in the sun.
Ben is sad.	Ben met a man.
His mud hut got wet.	The man had a hat.
The hut is a lot of mud.	Ben ran up to the hat.
Ben can not get in it.	It is a big hat.

The standard selections were presented to 21 children who participated in the operational phase of research.[2] Three of these children did not commit even a slight error, nor did they deviate from fluent reading in any way. In other words, they provided no data to analyze and were therefore excluded from the analysis. Another three were excluded because they were not yet reading well enough to do more than respond to the pictures and identify a few words. To make up for this loss of data, we enlisted classmates to read the standard selections, and we enlisted them more or less on a catch-as-catch-can basis. This somewhat unorthodox procedure boosted the sample for analysis back up to 21 children—15 "regulars" from the operational study and 6 "substitutes." As a group, however, the substitute children were indistinguishable from the regular study children in their overall reading behaviors.

---

[2]Twenty-three children from the operational study are included in the total sample of 40 children on whom our theory of beginning reading is based. However, two kindergartners were not followed for a full 2 years and thus were never given the standard selections at the end of first grade.

CONTROL OF THE ORCHESTRATION PROCESS

If skill is viewed as the orchestration of multiple resources, then skill proficiency depends on a person's control of the orchestration process. In reality, of course, skill control is not perfectly stable but can vary slightly or markedly from one performance to the next and even within a given performance. Minor fluctuations in the control of a master performer may be detectable only by other experts, but variations in an amateur's control are often quite evident. Some efforts prove more than adequate; others fall far short of the goal. Performances that start out wobbly may improve, and those that begin with good control may fall apart later on. Indeed, progress in skill development is usually judged by increasing consistency of control under set conditions or similar circumstances, as well as by increasing ability to perform well in unfamiliar and more difficult contexts.

We assume that multiple knowledge resources are being successfully coordinated when a child reads accurately and fluently. The image is of a juggler who, for the moment at least, has the ingredients of the performance clearly under control. Children sometimes ''build up steam'' for a proficient reading, as tentativeness on opening pages gives way to greater confidence and control, and their performance seems to gain momentum through growing familiarity with a book's story line, lexicon, and style. When a reading performance rolls along smoothly in this manner, the reader may deviate slightly from text, but the deviations do not distort meaning and may even support the flow of the action (e.g., inserting a word that suitably connects adjoining phrases). Such deviations often go uncorrected and may well be undetected by the reader. When mistakes of a more consequential nature occur, the reader who is otherwise on top of the task can pause momentarily to remedy the situation without jeopardizing his or her overall control. But if errors occur more frequently, if corrections and adjustments pile up, the juggling performance begins to disintegrate, and the reader becomes involved in detours away from meaning. Control may even decline to the point where particular words that posed no problem within the context of strong control now become major obstacles.

The Control Index

In detailed analyses of oral reading, we defined control as the ratio of words read *correctly AND fluently* to the total number of words in the reading selection. This definition honors both accuracy and momentum as signals of successful orchestration and thus provides a convenient index of the reader's proficiency for the particular text under consideration. The index differs from a straight accuracy score by allowing credit only for words rendered smoothly on first encounter. Self-corrections and words the child correctly identifies after a prolonged pause or overt mediation (such as ''sounding out'') involve significant interruptions of the reader's established pace and therefore do not meet the operational definition of accuracy AND fluency. In fact, only one kind of deviation was allowed by these combined criteria, and that was a simple repetition of a word or phrase read correctly on first encounter. As long as the word/phrase was accurately identified and the repetition did not noticeably alter the reader's pace, it satisfied both demands and was credited.

Figure 7.2 shows the control index for two children, based on the first half of the *Big Dog, Little Dog* selection. Reggie begins the book with strong control.

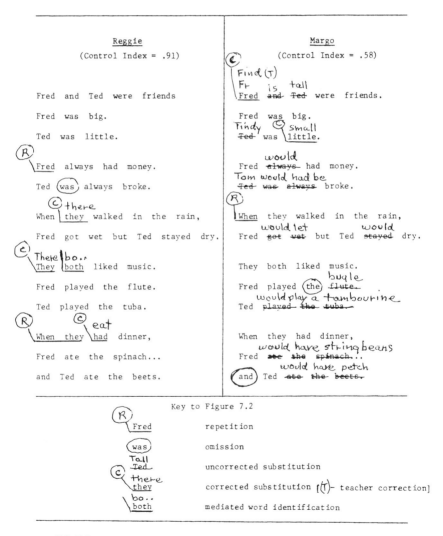

FIG. 7.2.　Notational Records and Control Index of Two Children

Since his repetition of "*Fred*" and "*When they*" do not count as deviations, he receives credit for reading 52 of the 57 words correctly and fluently. (He loses credit only for his omission of "was," his two corrections of the word "they," his mediated identification of "both," and his correction of "had.") Thus, his control ratio is 52/57, yielding an index of .91. By way of contrast, Margo keeps up momentum by plunging ahead but only at tremendous expense to the accountability criterion. She seems to reserve the word "would" as a ready fill-in to insert anywhere in the text, and manages only 33 of the 57 words accurately and fluently for a control index of .58. Margo's was the lowest index of any child on the first half of *Big Dog,* and it clearly demonstrates that a ratio in the .50s (or in the .60s) means "barely reading" by almost anyone's definition.

Two qualifications should be noted about the Control Index as a measure of reading proficiency. Although it is more theoretically compatible with our view of reading-as-skill than a straight accuracy count, it is most valid when applied to the beginner's efforts. Because skillful readers can, under certain circumstances, read accurately and fluently but without much comprehension, they can obtain a high index while falling short of the goal of constructing meaning. (We discuss the circumstances that can produce such readings in a subsequent section of the chapter, but we mention it now as a potential limitation on the validity of the control index.) The second qualification concerns our way of calculating the index. Our theoretical definition of reading assumes only "reasonable accountability" to the information contained in writing rather than perfect accountability to every word, yet we clearly held a child accountable for every word of text in deriving the index. Thus, children were penalized for such minor deviations as omitting an unnecessary word or saying "paint" rather than "painted" and "drived" rather than "drove." We opted for a stringent definition of accuracy simply because it made the bookkeeping of calculation neater and avoided the necessity of judgments that were sometimes difficult to make. For purposes of discerning patterns in a single child's record over time or in group data for a single reading, the strict method of calculating the index proved perfectly satisfactory. Nonetheless, it should be stressed that we do *not* interpret the penalty for a minor deviation (saying "drived" rather than "drove") to mean the child was unsuccessful in orchestrating knowledge about the information encoded in writing.

As a group ($N = 21$), the children displayed similar levels of control on both *Big Dog, Little Dog* and *Ben Bug.* The average index was .86 for the total *Big Dog* text and .87 for the total *Ben Bug* text. Performance on both texts also showed the phenomenon of increasing control as children worked their way into the passages. When an average control index was calculated separately for the two halves of each selection, the second-half index exceeded the first-half by six or seven points. These results are summarized in Table 7.1 below.

Although average figures do not always mirror individual trends, they are a true reflection of individual performance on the two standard selections. No child

TABLE 7.1
Average Control Index
(for 21 children on two standard selections)

	1st Half	2nd Half	Total Text
Big Dog, Little Dog	.82	.89	.86
Ben Bug	.84	.90	.87

declined in control from the first to second half of the texts, most children showed modest increases, and some exhibited dramatic increases. Margo, for example, soared from her infirm .58 on the first half of *Big Dog* (see Figure 7.2) to a more secure .86 on the second half, an increase which produced an overall control index of .72 for the total reading. The notational record of her second half performance is as follows:

> When they ~~painted~~ ^{pAint} the house,
> Ted used red paint
> Fred used green ~~paint~~ ^{paint}
> One day Fred and Ted took a ~~trip.~~ ^{tRAp}
> Fred went in his green car.
> Ted went in his red car.
> Fred drove his car slowly.
> ®Ted drove his car fast
> When they got to the mountains, © meet ? (+)
> Ted ~~skied~~ all day long. ^{SkAte}
> Fred ~~skated~~ all day long. ^{skAte}

As compared with her reading in the first half of the book, Margo's rendition in this second half becomes reasonably well aligned with the actual words in print. Although her overall control of the reading was wobbly (with an index well below the average), Margo nonetheless improved as she settled into the text. So, too, did children at the upper end of the control scale. Reggie, for instance, made only one deviation from a fluent and accurate reading on the second half of *Dog* (stopping to ask for help on the word "mountains"), which gave him an index of .98 on the second half and of .95 for the overall reading.

Improved performance on the standard selections (as measured by a rise in the control index) is a result echoed many times over in analyses of individual reading selections, and the point we wish to make about these results is simple. When children deal with a real book that is reasonably within their grasp (as compared with the very short, two- or three-sentence paragraphs commonly found in reading inventories), they exhibit the capacity to build on growing familiarity with the material. In Chapter 5, we emphasized that reading skill is achieved through practice over time. These data from the standard reading samples indicate that control also typically increases *within* a given reading performance, assuming a text of suitable length and difficulty.

The Control Index and Success in Self-Correction.   To the extent that a reader has command of the orchestration process, multiple knowledge resources not only interact smoothly to produce meaning from text, they also serve as a network of corrective influences to detect and ameliorate error. Indeed, the validity of the control index as an estimate of reading proficiency is partially substantiated by its observed relationship with children's rate of success in self-correction attempts.

Self-corrective attempts indicate a reader's attention to the problem of word accuracy (as opposed to momentum), and they may be classified in one of two categories. A before-the-fact approach to the problem occurs when a child stops or pauses *before* uttering a word and gives evidence of trying to figure it out. Examples are Reggie saying "bo" before coming up with "both" and Margo's brief pause to make the sound "ss" before saying "his." In these two examples, the prior mediation resulted in an accurate identification of the word, but that of course was not always the case. Many prior mediation attempts failed (e.g., "stt" "sta" "sturreid" for "stayed"). An after-the-fact approach to the problem of accuracy is evidenced as an "ooops" kind of corrective attempt. That is, a child utters an inaccurate word and then goes back to try to correct the mistake. Reggie, for instance, confidently said "there" for "they" twice, and on both occasions corrected himself after the fact. Needless to say, not all corrections of this type ended in accuracy either.

Both types of corrective attempt are represented with about equal frequency in the group data for each of the two standard reading selections. Because both approaches also bear the same kind of relationship to the control index, we have combined them for purposes of data presentation. Figure 7.3 shows the children's rate of success in corrective attempts (approaches combined) as a function of their level of skill control for the overall reading of *Big Dog*.[3] Although the three levels of control shown in the table are quite arbitrary (indices in the .90s, the .80s, and the .70s), they are practically useful for making gross proficiency distinctions.

The relationship depicted in Fig. 7.3 means that more proficient readers of *Big Dog* were better able to resolve the accuracy problems they detected than were less proficient readers. (It should be noted that this relationship is not a statistical artifact, since the two scores are based on independent aspects of the reading performance.) Considering the fact that most children improved in control as they read along in the book, the relationship stated in Fig. 7.3 also means that most children were better able to resolve accuracy problems on the second half of *Big Dog* than on the first half. We interpret both manifestations of the relationship as support for the concept of orchestration. Under conditions of greater control, a child's "attack" on a particular word is presumably launched

---

[3]A similar trend holds in *Ben Bug,* but the *Dog* passage is longer and therefore offers a more substantial data base.

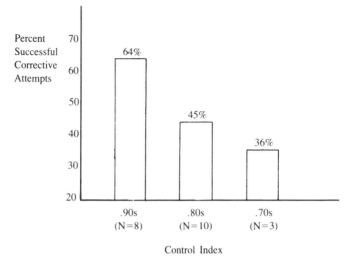

FIG. 7.3.   Control Index and Percentage of Successful Corrective Attempts (for 21 children on *Big Dog*)

from a more integrated base of knowledge about the text content, grammar, style, and vocabulary.

In order to determine the generalizability of this finding from the standard selections, we decided to examine several selections unique to individual readers. Thus, we first chose a subsample of eight children who were part of the *Big Dog* analysis. Three of the children had a control index in the .90s for the overall *Dog* reading, three had an index in the .80s, and two had an index in the .70s. For each child, we then analyzed seven or eight "key" selections that ranged from low-control readings to high-control readings.[4] A total of 58 unique selections was analyzed, and the results were combined on the basis of the control index for a given reading. The number of selections and the percentage of successful corrective attempts at each control level are shown below.

Control Level	# of Selections	% Successful Corrective Attempts
.90s	23	63%
.80s	21	45%
.60s–.70s	14	38%

Although a few individual readings did not follow the general pattern indicated above, the results as a whole are remarkably similar to the *Big Dog*

[4]As described in Chapter 4, "key" selections spanned the period of data collection and were challenging enough to prompt errors. Children included in the subsample were Carrie (7 selections), Colin (7), Crystal (7), Kris (8), Louis (7), Rita (7), Tanya (7), and Tim (8).

analysis. So remarkably similar, in fact, that the relationship appears to warrant a generalization. As a rule of thumb, children are successful with corrective attempts about two-thirds of the time for material they read with control in the .90s, about one-half of the time for material they read with control in the .80s, and about one-third of the time for material in the .60s and .70s. This rule of thumb regarding self-correction suggests interesting implications for teacher intervention, and they are implications the collaborating teachers seemed intuitively to honor much of the time. When children struggle with material that is barely within their ability to control (.60s and .70s), the teacher's assistance is best geared to propping up the performance by providing words quickly and without extraneous remarks or demands. When a child stops to confront a word problem within an otherwise smooth performance, however, the teacher may adopt a more pedantic stance, directing attention to letter-sounds or root words, or reminding the child about the gist of the text. In the context of solid control, children can respond more profitably to cues and coaching than they can when they are floundering. The child who is struggling to keep afloat needs a life-line, not a lecture.

The Control Index and "Readability" Estimates.   The index of control is an inverse measure of text difficulty for a particular child on a particular reading occasion. That is, the higher the index, the lower the difficulty; and the lower the index, the higher the difficulty. But difficulty as measured by the control index is not necessarily the same as difficulty measured by a readability formula. There are actually several ways of estimating "readability," but many popular methods include both sentence length and word length (or number of syllables) as major factors in the computation. Thus, a typical readability formula would rate *Ben Bug* as being easier than *Big Dog,* because the *Bug* test contains much shorter words and sentences than the *Dog* text. Yet *Bug* is not easier than *Dog* when difficulty is determined by children's control of the texts. The average index of control was virtually the same for both books.

Without belaboring the point, we merely wish to note that the rationale underlying readability estimates does not always hold across the entire range of difficulty. The concept carries a great deal of face validity at the middle and upper ranges, since books featuring very long sentences and very long words are generally harder to read than books with moderate or varied sentence and word length. But extension of the concept downward is not nearly so valid. A book filled only with three-letter words combined into five- or six-word sentences cannot help but distort the natural rhythm and grammar of language, making it more difficult for the reader to rely on knowledge of rhythm and grammar in the orchestrated act of reading.

Snags and Problems in Control

We have said the children's control of text frequently increased as they read along in a book. Such increases were observed in the standard reading selections as well as in numerous unique selections. But we also mentioned at the outset of the discussion that control may occasionally deteriorate to the point where relatively easy words and text become problematic. The most obvious factor producing a decline in children's reading performance was fatigue, and no child was immune from its effects. When children had reached their limit for a given reading session, the signs and sounds of weariness in posture and voice were unmistakable, and the slippage in control notable. Adult readers often find it hard to appreciate the mental strain involved in the beginner's efforts, and perhaps the best we can do as adults is recall the strain of fatigue that has accompanied our intense concentration in other mental endeavors. Whether or not adults appreciate the phenomenon, however, it is nonetheless real. Fatigue is an inevitable part of sustained mental or physical exercise, and its effects are predictable.

Whereas fatigue precipitated a decline in control for virtually every child at one time or another, other instances of decline were more or less specific to a particular child reading a particular text on a particular occasion. Examination of these sundry snags and problems uncovered three general circumstances that sometimes—or almost always—led to trouble.

Children sometimes displayed less control of the reading process as their interest in a text appeared to intensify. In these instances, interest seemed to spark imaginative resources which, in turn, prompted inventions of words and phrases. Analysis of one of Tim's readings in June of first grade provides an illustrative sequence of events. (The book is about a frightened little king who has to fight a dragon.) As the story unfolds over the first few pages, Tim's control improves and his interest perks up. Then, as the fight between the king and the dragon is about to materialize, and as Tim anticipates an illustration of the dragon (lowering his voice and saying with some delight, "I'm scared to see the next page"), control begins to deteriorate. The decline starts immediately following his remark about being "scared," when he turns to page 11 and tries the first sentence:

> Text: But there was no getting around it—the dragon had to be fought.
> Tim: But there was no getting around it—the dragon had two beautiful. . . [He stops, and then in a somewhat subdued voice says] . . . fought.

The words "to" and "be" can hardly be construed as a challenge for Tim, since he had read them correctly hundreds of times in the past. Yet in this context he substitutes a blatant invention ("two beautiful") before stopping himself. And problems compound from this point on, dragging Tim's control index from a high of .83 on the previous portion of text to a low of .68 for his reading of pages 11–12. Some of the words he misses on these pages are probably genuinely difficult for him (e.g., "trembling," "ordinary," "slain"), but his plunge in control is mainly due to easy words he trips over in haste (e.g., "but," "he," "sent") and to other whole lines he seems largely to invent. For example:

> Text: He was twice the size of a house, and had a terrible, terrible temper.
>
> Tim: It was twitching to the size of a house, and had a rumble, trumble pumble!

As Tim's inventions suggest, however, the basic import and mood of the story did not entirely elude him as he plowed ahead in the text. This ability to keep the gist of a narrative alive also characterized other performances in which deteriorating control seemed to result from a child getting "carried away" with the story. Such performances were not a common occurrence in the study, but they occurred often enough to deserve mention.

A more common circumstance leading to dips or sudden declines in control was confusion about the structure of one or more sentences. Children often got themselves in such tangles when they missed the period at the end of a sentence and then tried to incorporate the ensuing sentence as a continuation of what they had just read. This strategy inevitably disrupted meaning, and the disorienting effect occasionally carried over to subsequent sentences as well. Although children usually recouped from these entanglements to get back on track, their control index reflected the disarrayed text they left behind.

Overlooked punctuation probably caused the majority of grammatical snags, but there were other problems as well. When children confidently miscalculated the structure within a sentence, they sometimes were unable to reevaluate the sentence despite warning signals from words that failed to fall into place. More often than not, such strong (but inaccurate) anticipation coincided with a slight anomaly in the actual grammar of the sentence. This kind of snarl was evident during Crystal's reading of *Oliver Pig*, a 371-word text she clearly grasped and negotiated with an overall control index in the .80s. Of the 14 errors she made that did real harm to meaning, she attempted to correct 10. The errors she let go by were clustered in the same sentence, and all seemed caused by her incorrect anticipation of where the sentence was headed. The text in question and her rendition are shown below.

Text	*Crystal*
"Are you still hungry as a bear,	"Are you still hungry as a bear,
Grandmother?" asked Oliver.	Grandmother?" asked Oliver.
"No," said Grandmother	"No," said Grandma.
"With cherry pie	"With the cherry pie
and raisin pie to eat	and the raisin pie, it to eat
and you and Amanda to hug,	and you . . said . . Am-a-ly it hug
I am full right up to the top."	I am fell right up . . to the top."

The sentence Crystal stumbles over contains no particularly difficult words (at least none she had not read correctly before), but it does begin with an unusually long prepositional phrase: "With cherry pie and raisin pie to eat and you and Amanda to hug." Moreover, the second half of the phrase (concerning hugging) is not related, on the surface at least, either to the first half of the phrase or to the main clause (which have to do with eating and being full). Crystal's insertions of "the" before "cherry pie" and "raisin pie" do little harm to meaning, but she creates real problems for herself when she injects the word "it" into the sentence. She seems to anticipate that the opening phrase will be relatively short and that the sense of the main clause will be something like, "it is really quite enough." Whatever may have been her exact anticipation, she says "it" following the words "raisin pie," and the sentence falls apart thereafter. She hesitates, goes on, misreads *said* for *and,* hesitates, inserts another gratuitous *it,* substitutes *fell* for *full,* and hesitates some more. All in all, she seems thoroughly confused by what she has read, but she moves on rather than try to rescue the sentence.

Grammatical tangles resulting from overlooked punctuation or faulty predictions obviously lowered a child's average control index for a particular reading. For the most part, however, these were temporary setbacks from which children recovered to regain control of the orchestration process and meaning. As far as overall effect on comprehension is concerned, such instances were generally no more (or less) serious than dips in control resulting from a child's getting "carried away" and inventing portions of text.

Far more serious for comprehension were control problems due to lack of background knowledge about the content of a particular story or passage. In such a circumstance, meaning usually never got off the ground at all. The following description of Meg reading a story called *The Cats and the Cart* is illustrative. Although Meg herself chose the book in which the story appears and gave evidence of enthusiasm about reading it, she seemed to lose interest once she started the story. There is almost no glimmer of understanding in her voice as she labors through the two pages shown in Fig. 7.4.

Meg begins by reading "Tom is a farm head." Assuming she didn't know the expression "farm hand" (the teacher's notes from the reading suggest this probably was the case), then Meg presumably tried to make the first sentence comprehensible, since being the "head" of a farm is more logical than being the "hand" of a farm. On the next sentnce, however, she reads, "Tom was a farm cart," and the following exchange takes place.

> Teacher: Look again. Read that sentence again.
>   Meg: Tom was a farm cart.
> Teacher: Does that make sense, "Tom was a farm cart?" Can a person be a cart?
>   Meg: Uh-uh (indicating "no")
> Teacher: Is there one word that doesn't say what you thought it did? Read it again.
>   Meg: Tom was a farm cart.

The Cats and the Cart

Tom is a farm hand.

Tom has a farm cart.

A card is on the cart.

Tom puts eggs in his cart.

Tom runs off to get a tart.

Tom is far from the cart.

The cats are at the cart.

FIG. 7.4.   Pages from *The Cats and the Cart*

The Cats and the Cart from *Basic Reading, Book B* by Glenn McCracken and Charles C. Walcutt. Copyright © 1975, 1969, 1966, 1963 by J. B. Lippincott Company. Reprinted by permission of the publisher. *DISCLAIMER: J. B. Lippincott has since revised this book and now has a copyright of 1981.

> Teacher: What's the first letter of that word (pointing to *has*)?
> Meg: "h" . . . has. Tom has a farm cart.

Meg reads the next two lines accurately but with hesitation and struggle on the word "card" and with much repeating of words. (The teacher tries to acknowledge her problem by commenting that the "card" is very big and really looks more like a sign.) Turning to page 2, Meg negotiates the first line more smoothly and with reasonable confidence, saying *"Tom runs over to get a truck."* Though two words and the intended meaning are incorrect, her voice tone and fluency indicate she has constructed something meaningful (perhaps because she perceived a correspondence with the picture). But on the very next line, voice tone, hesitancy, and inaccuracy all suggest that the story is going nowhere for her. She reads: *"Tom is for from . . . for from the cart."* Her hesitancy and repetition of "for from" signal distress with this rendition; and when the teacher asks her to read the sentence again, Meg seems relieved and readily obliges by omitting the word "for"—*"Tom is FROM the cart!"* Further analysis of the word "far" (with prompting from the teacher) finally leads to correct identification, but Meg's dispirited reading implies equal dissatisfaction with the phrase ''far from the cart'' as with ''for from the cart.'' At this juncture, the teacher suggests trying another selection, which Meg proceeds to negotiate with much greater control and comprehension.

Our description of Meg's reading highlights the fact that voice tone and expressiveness are often crucial signs of whether a child has constructed sense from text. Thus, they are also crucial signals of whether the orchestration process has fulfilled its purpose. Meg's rendition of the first two lines (''Tom is a farm head. Tom was a farm cart'') and her simultaneous loss of interest in the reading, as evidenced by her perplexed and listness tone, clearly suggest that orchestration missed the mark. Lacking sufficient understanding of a story's characters and setting at the outset, the orchestration process is not likely to result in comprehension. At best, it will limp along as an exercise in word identification. The control index for such a reading (which in Meg's case was .68) will be more or less irrelevant, because the underlying process has not produced comprehension. As illustrated in previous examples, children could usually tolerate jumbled semantics in a portion of text while still keeping the basic story line in tow. But if comprehension never got off the ground, the whole act of reading underwent a qualitative change.

A Summary of the Evidence Concerning Orchestration and Control

We have conceived reading to be a singular skill that entails the orchestration of several knowledge resources. Accordingly, we have said that learning how to read is primarily a matter of learning how to organize and integrate knowledge effectively. By implication, then, it is control of the orchestration process (rather than possession of knowledge per se) that determines the degree of reading skill demonstrated on any given occasion. Evidence from the study that led to these related conceptions may be summarized as follows.

1. Children's reading proficiency often improved as they moved along in a text—even though the general level of text difficulty (as determined by vocabulary, content, and grammar) remained basically constant. This phenomenon was apparent both in descriptive analyses of reading and in analyses based upon a quantitative estimate of proficiency (the index of control). Since a child's knowledge cannot be assumed to improve much within a single reading performance, such a phenomenon is not explained by theories that view reading as the straightforward application of knowledge. The more credible view is that reading involves a dynamic process and that the dynamic itself gains momentum and direction as a reader gains familiarity with text.

2. Children's self-corrective attempts were more likely to be successful under conditions of greater control. By definition, of course, children also made fewer deviations from text when their control was better, but there is no necessary

reason for correction to have been more successful in the context of better control. In fact, one could argue that children performing at a high level of proficiency would err only on words they really didn't know and thus would be relatively unsuccessful in their corrective attempts. By the same logic, it might be expected that children performing at a low level of proficiency would err more often on easy words and therefore be able to correct a greater proportion of their miscues. Certainly, this line of reasoning would not predict a rise in the rate of successful self- correction *within* a given reading performance (as happened when control increased notably from the first to the second half of a text). But a theory that equates reading proficiency with control of the orchestration process does accommodate the obtained results. Under conditions of greater control, the reader has command of a more integrated network of knowledge cues to detect and remedy error.

3. The concept of control is further substantiated by the finding of dips and deterioration in reading proficiency. Four conditions of deterioration were identified as follows:

Fatigue—which usually resulted in a steady decline in control and subsequent loss of meaning.

Inventions—which led to dips in control but not usually to a total loss of the story line.

Entanglements in Grammar—which led to dips in control and the loss of meaning for some sentences, but not usually to a significant loss in overall comprehension of a text.

Lack of Background Knowledge—which was not so much a case of declining control as of a child never attaining understanding in the first place.

We have called these problems of control—rather than problems of text difficulty—because the errors in question did not arise in especially difficult sentences or passages. With only minor exceptions, the miscues involved words and grammatical constructions that the child either had successfully negotiated in other readings or was clearly capable of negotiating. The observed deterioration in these instances thus resulted not so much from lack of knowledge as from a breakdown in the orchestration process. The last circumstance listed above deserves special comment, because it implies a special significance and a qualitatively different situation. It suggests that background knowledge is an essential catalyst of orchestration. Without such understanding, even words correctly identified and sentences accurately rendered fail to produce comprehension and thus represent only a pale facsimile of the normal reading process.

RESPONSIVENESS TO DIFFERENT KINDS OF TEXT

Mature readers generally don't read poetry the way they do newspapers, nor do they negotiate novels in the same manner as tax forms. The properties of written language vary enormously with the communicative intent of the writer, and readers adapt to this variation by shifting gears. Readers may also adjust for changes in their own intentions, of course, but the emphasis here is upon adjustments made to accommodate different properties of text.

Although the children we observed were not reading full-length novels or tax forms, it seemed to us that they did mobilize their efforts somewhat differently when negotiating phonic and linguistic texts as compared with books that feature a more ordinary style of writing. Such differences were noted early in the pilot study among those children who had access to both kinds of reading material.[5] During the pilot study, however, we were able to verify this impression only in cases where a child happened to read both kinds of text at the same oral reading session. The contrasting books used as standard selections in the operational phase of research (*Big Dog* and *Ben Bug*) allowed us to examine these differences more systematically.

In order to detect different strategies in the children's reading, we analyzed substitution errors—i.e., clear instances in which a child substituted some other word for the word that appeared in print. All other deviations from text (omissions, insertions, repetitions, pauses, sound fragments, and self-corrective attempts after an initial substitution) were ignored for purposes of this analysis. We coded each substitution error for its responsiveness to various text constraints, following procedures that have been widely used in previous research. The rationale for such coding is that partially satisfied text constraints imply the kind(s) of knowledge a reader used to generate the error.

Many investigators include semantic constraints in coding, attempting to judge whether a substitution fits the sense of the text. Although an important conceptual distinction needs to be made between the reader's responsiveness to grammatical constraints as compared with semantic constraints, such a distinction proves hard to operationalize when the errors in question have been generated by children reading text material that features a meager story line and may contain unfamiliar words. Several of the children who read *Big Dog*, for example, had never heard of a tuba. Is the child who then says *tub* for *tuba* (in the sentence ''Ted played the tuba'') uttering a ridiculous idea in context? Or might such a child conceive ''tub'' to be the name of some unknown musical instrument? It is impossible to tell. Judgments were even more problematic in *Ben Bug*, because the story line builds so few coherent transitions from one sentence to the next. Thus, we decided not to attempt semantic distinctions in coding and to focus only on two major categories of text constraint: *graphic* and *grammatical*.[6] Criteria for the coding were adapted from miscue procedures reported

---

[5]Every classroom contained conventional children's literature, but phonic and linguistic texts were available in only about half of the classrooms.

[6]Since grammar shapes the meaning of language, errors that honor grammatical constraints also tend to make sense. But that is not always the case, and the sense is sometimes dubious (as in the ''tub'' for ''tuba'' example).

in the literature (see, especially, Goodman & Burke, 1972) and are discussed below.

Graphic Constraints.   A substitution error that corresponds in one or more prominent letters to the text word shows some sensitivity to the phonetic information encoded in writing. Although it is possible to estimate the degree of match between graphic characteristics of the substituted word and the printed word, such a determination was not deemed necessary for this analysis. Our purpose in coding was to establish the fact that a child drew upon letter-sound knowledge rather than to assess how adequately he or she used all the graphic information of the text. Thus, a first-letter correspondence constituted sufficient grounds for coding a substitution in this category. As it turned out, many substitutions represented a much better match than first-letter correspondence alone, and this was especially true of substitutions that reflected sensitivity *only* to graphic information (i.e., those that were not sensitive to grammatical constraints as well). Examples of this latter type of substitution include the following: *much* for *music, the* for *they, blink* for *broke, dry* for *day, hud* (and *hout*) for *hut, made* for *mud, low* for *lot,* and *said* for *sad.*

Grammatical Constraints.   A liberal criterion was also set for this category. To be coded as responsive to grammatical constraints, a substitution needed to be syntactically acceptable in the context of the words preceding the error. It did not necessarily have to be appropriate in the context of the entire sentence. Not surprisingly, the majority of substitutions in this category were semantically acceptable as well, at least up to the point where the error occurred. Examples of substitutions coded for grammatical sensitivity only (they are not graphically responsive) are shown below. Some make sense in the context of the entire sentence, others do not.

>   Text: They both (liked music).
>   Child: They played. . .
>
>   Text: When they walked in the rain, Fred got (wet).
>   Child: When they walked in the rain, Fred could. . .
>
>   Text: Fred played the flute.
>   Child: Fred played the violin.
>
>   Text: Fred used green.
>   Child: Fred painted green.
>
>   Text: Ted was little.
>   Child: Ted was small.

Graphic and Grammatical Constraints.   Children's substitutions often showed sensitivity to both kinds of constraints and were therefore coded in this third category. For example, the words *spinach* and *beets* suitably provoked the names of food beginning with ''s'' (*stringbeans, salad*) and ''b'' (*beans, broccoli*). In many instances, too, the word *tuba* provoked the name of an instrument that accommodated the initial "t" (*trumpet, trombone, tambourine*). Many of the substitutions in this category represented only minor alterations of the text word (e.g., *skate* for *skated, paint* for *painted, drived* for *drove*). Other examples include the following:

>
> Text: Ben has a mud hut.
> Child: Ben has a mud house.
>
> Text: Ben is sad.
> Child: Ben is silly.
>
> Text: Ben met (a man).
> Child: Ben made. . .
>
> Text: Ben can not get in it.
> Child: Ben can not go in it.
>
> Text: When they walked in the rain. . .
> Child: When they went/worked in the rain. . .
>
> Text: Ted skied (all day long).
> Child: Ted stood. . .

Since *Big Dog* was a longer selection than *Ben Bug,* the children's reading of that text yielded a greater number of word substitutions. (It is interesting to note that, for both books, substitutions accounted for slightly over half of all deviations.) The group as a whole made 201 word substitutions in *Dog* and 88 in *Bug.* Analysis of the coding results not only confirmed our observations in the pilot study, it revealed other significant trends that had escaped previous notice. Table 7.2 shows the percentage of substitution errors coded in each constraint category.

The distribution of errors in the Total Text column of Table 7.2 forms a pattern that emerged in earlier analyses of individual children reading phonic material versus a conventional trade book. When the two books are compared, the data indicate that children displayed greater sensitivity to graphic cues in *Bug* (the phonic text) and greater sensitivity to grammatical cues in *Dog* (the trade

TABLE 7.2
Responsiveness of Word Substitutions to Graphic and Grammatical Constraints
(percentage distributions for 21 children on two texts)

	1st Half Text		2nd Half Text		Total Text	
Coding Category	Dog (N = 114)	Bug (N = 47)	Dog (N = 87)	Bug (N = 41)	Dog (N = 201)	Bug (N = 88)
Graphic Only	.19	.42	.16	.22	.18	.33
Grammatical Only	.27	.04	.17	.15	.23	.09
Graphic and Grammatical	.54	.53	.67	.63	.59	.58

χ^2 (2, N = 289) = 9.02, $p < .025$.

book). Comparison of the coding distributions within each text also reveal differences—roughly balanced attention between graphic and grammatical constraints in *Dog* and attention favoring graphic information in *Bug*. Overall, this pattern suggests that children responded to the salient properties of each text with differential attention and use of knowledge.

But the more interesting finding in Table 7.2 comes from an analysis we had not considered in the pilot study: comparing data for each half of the texts. As indicated in Table 7.2, the relationship between text and error category differs significantly when the two halves are compared. Clearly, the pattern apparent in the Total Text column is almost entirely a function of the children's differential strategies in negotiating the opening portion of each text. Every aspect of the pattern (i.e., both between- and within-text comparisons) is exaggerated in the first-half analysis, whereas little evidence of difference remains in the second-half analysis. This finding implies that children immediately sensed the kind of book they were being asked to read and organized their efforts accordingly. They relied more on the grammar and sense of the story line to work their way into *Big Dog,* and they looked almost exclusively to graphic cues for initial support in *Ben Bug.* Once started in each book, however, the children settled into a more balanced allocation of attention and resources.

Considering the brevity of each text (a total of 115 words for *Dog* and 63 for *Bug*), the discrepancy in initial reading patterns and subsequent shift seems rather remarkable. We believe this finding reflects an adaptive capacity of the orchestration process—a capacity which must be truly remarkable in mature readers if it operates with such demonstrable sensitivity in beginning readers. Our interpretation that the pattern was in fact adaptive and worked to the children's advantage rests on two independent trends in the data. First, virtually every child's reading proficiency improved from the first to the second half of the selections, as noted previously and as evidenced by a rise in the control index (which takes into account not just substitution errors but all deviations from text). Second, Table 7.2 shows an increase for each text in the percentage of substitution errors responsive to *both* graphic and grammatical constraints. By implication, such substitutions entail a fuller integration of knowledge than do errors responsive to only one constraint. The pattern revealed in Table 7.2 is thus accompanied by evidence that the children's reading became more accurate and fluent and that their substitution errors got ''better.''

That children respond differently to phonic texts and trade books is probably no news to teachers who have listened to them read both types of material. But we think the finding is of interest from a theoretical standpoint, because it suggests that beginning readers make adaptive adjustments to text variation in much the same manner as mature readers. That is, they display the ability to ''shift gears'' that we alluded to in the opening paragraph of this section. Although the child learning how to read probably makes only a small portion of the adaptive adjustments orchestrated by an expert reader, our data nonetheless indicate that the reading process is responsive and adaptive in nature very early on. Differences between the young child and the mature reader in this respect may well be more of degree than of kind.

THE BALANCE BETWEEN MOMENTUM AND ACCURACY

A third coding procedure devised for the study deals with the balance between momentum and accuracy in children's reading. The basis for the accuracy/momentum distinction hinges on our theoretical conception that anticipation and accountability are the dual requirements for constructing meaning from text. Anticipation sustains the momentum and flow of the action through time, while accountability ensures that the action stays on course. We have portrayed this conception in graphic shorthand by the image of an upright triangle. The apex of the triangle represents the goal of meaning. Supporting this goal on either side are the two essential skill requirements, which rest in turn on a base of knowledge. We present the triangle once more below, but this time with perforated lines. The purpose of the incomplete image is to suggest more clearly that beginning readers are still in the process of learning how to orchestrate the various knowledge components that underlie reading.

Proficient readers, by definition, can orchestrate knowledge smoothly to satisfy both the momentum and accuracy requirements of virtually any text within their conceptual grasp. Beginning readers, by definition, cannot yet do this. Their proficient performances occur sporadically and are gained through considerable practice. The change that takes place as a person progresses from a beginning reader to a truly proficient reader may be envisioned as a consolidation of the lines of the triangle. But for the novice, the perforated lines would seem to convey a more realistic picture of instability and fluctuation.

This graphic depiction of the reading process also underscores the alternatives available to a learner. If something has to "give" in the skill performance of a beginner, it will be either momentum (in deference to accuracy) or accuracy (in

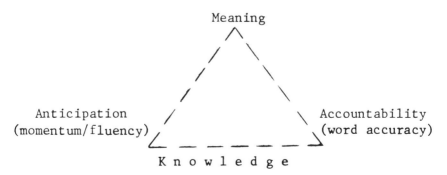

FIG. 7.5.   A Schematic Conception of Reading

deference to momentum). Both alternatives entail the risk of obscuring meaning, depending on how much of the complementary requirement is yielded. Important questions for theory and practice are how beginners typically deal with this option, and whether one alternative is better than the other from the standpoint of learning progress and/or level of proficiency attained after a reasonable period of instruction.

Descriptive analyses of oral reading and the overall reading records for each child contain data relevant to both questions posed above. These pertinent data (together with evidence from the full documentary records) are presented in Chapter 8, where we discuss stylistic aspects of the children's behavior. Here, we maintain the emphasis of the present chapter by focusing on our theory of orchestration and on results obtained from the technical coding of oral reading samples. In order to provide an appropriate context for these coding results, however, it is necessary to summarize some major findings and conclusions in advance of the Chapter 8 discussion.

The full reading documentation indicates that some children in the study did display a decisive preference for attending to either the momentum or the accuracy requirement of reading. Such preferences were most clearly noted in qualitative aspects of observed reading behavior, and it was primarily on the basis of these observational indices that we judged the salience and strength of a child's preference. Typical qualitative behaviors included such things as spontaneous remarks made during reading or about reading, responses to a teacher's assistance or prodding, tendencies to scan ahead in books, and length of pauses while negotiating text.

With respect to the second question posed above, children's preferences were not related in any systematic way either to their rate of learning progress or to the level of reading proficiency they had attained by the end of the study's 18-month documentation period. Rather, each preference was associated with a loosely defined cluster of behaviors, all of which seemed stylistic in nature. We therefore interpret the preferences as a manifestation of style differences in the way children deploy attention and process information in the service of constructing meaning.

The technical coding of oral reading samples clearly confirms the qualitative indications of a preference for one or the other skill requirement. Most important for a theory of orchestration is the finding that the children generally attained greater balance in their attention to both skill requirements over time. These results and the nature of the coding scheme are discussed and illustrated below.

The Coding Scheme

For practical purposes of coding, the requirements of anticipation and accountability translate to considerations of pace and accuracy. A reader's attention to either requirement at the expense of the other is signaled in the coding scheme as "unmodified" and "modified" deviations from text. (Deviations in this coding are conceived exactly as they are for purposes of calculating the control index.)

Unmodified Deviations are defined as any inaccuracy in oral reading, trivial or serious, that does not interrupt the reader's pace. This definition includes omissions, insertions, and word substitutions that are not corrected. Whatever the exact nature of the inaccuracy, the flow of the reading had to continue uninterrupted in order for the error to qualify as an Unmodified Deviation. The child may or may not have been aware of a discrepancy between what was said and the actual text, but he or she moved on regardless. The deviations were thus unmodified, because no overt efforts were made to correct them or otherwise to adjust the reading to coincide more precisely with the printed page.

Modified Deviations are defined as every instance of a child-initiated interruption in the pace of reading. (Adult-initiated interruptions were not counted in the coding.) Thus, all corrective efforts—whether prior mediations or after-the-fact attempts, and whether successful or not—were classified as Modified Deviations, because they necessarily halted the forward progress of the reading. Repetitions that clearly served to smooth over a mispronunciation, inappropriate phrasing, omission, insertion, or other rough spot were also coded as Modified Deviations. So, too, were notable pauses in the reader's established pace for a particular passage. When a pause preceded attempts to sound out a word, then the entire episode (pause and mediation effort) was counted as a single instance of a Modified Deviation.

To summarize, the coding of Unmodified and Modified Deviations was based on evidence of the reader's concern for upholding pace or accuracy. Instances in which pace was maintained at the expense of word-perfect accuracy were coded as Unmodified Deviations. Instances in which the reader's forward movement was interrupted out of an apparent concern for accuracy were coded as Modified Deviations. The types of deviation classified within each category are shown below. (Pace-maintaining repetitions of a word or phrase read accurately were not counted in either category.)

Unmodified Deviations (pace maintained)	*Modified Deviations* (pace interrupted)
Omission	Correction of a Substitution
Insertion	Prior Mediation (Decoding) Attempt
Word Substitution	Corrective Repetitions
	Pauses

The tendency for children to make one or the other type of deviations in any given reading performance was influenced by text characteristics and instructional interactions. Phonic and linguistic books for beginners introduced a bias toward the accuracy requirement of reading (modified deviations), because they proved hard to anticipate and tended to elicit overt decoding responses from children. Such texts are designed to emphasize graphic more than grammatical features of writing, and Table 7.2 shows that they did indeed draw disproportionate attention to graphic constraints. Teacher interventions could also influence a child's demonstration of preference, since children usually tried to oblige a teacher's cues to move on with the reading (''Guess,'' ''Keep going'') or to identify words correctly (''Look at that again''). For these reasons, the present analysis of the Unmodified/Modified coding was limited mainly to occasions where children read a trade book (with more conventional writing), and where they were given reasonable autonomy to follow their own preferences in negotiating text. The analysis also focused on readings that challenged the children's capabilities and thus prompted enough deviations to make the detection of preference possible.

Results of the Coding

The *Big Dog* standard oral reading selection qualified as a good candidate for analysis on all three counts: it is a trade book, it presented some challenge to most children, and it was a reading sample collected under conditions of minimal adult help. Coding results for the 21 children who read *Big Dog* reveal a roughly equal proportion of unmodified and modified deviations over the total text (47% unmodified to 53% modified). Although this finding establishes that the text was relatively free of bias, group data mask the possibility that children may have exhibited opposing preferences—some trying to uphold momentum most often and others trying to honor accuracy most often. As stated previously, signs of momentum/accuracy preferences showed up in the observational records of reading behavior and were associated with other general classroom behaviors that seemed stylistic in nature. The following is a capsule description of characteristics associated with each preference. (These characteristics are discussed more fully in Chapter 8.)

> *Style Cluster A (Momentum):* An observed preference for maintaining momentum in reading tended to cluster with evidence that a child deployed attention broadly, emphasized similarities and continuities among events, and processed diverse information in parallel fashion.
>
> *Style Cluster B (Accuracy):* An observed preference for upholding accuracy in reading was associated with evidence that a child focused attention rather narrowly, emphasized differentiating details and distinctions among events, and processed information in step-by-step linear fashion.

In order to examine the relationship between observational evidence of classroom learning styles and the Unmodified/Modified coding distinction, we selected two subgroups (of seven each) from those who had read *Big Dog*. Children were classified on the basis of observations in their descriptive reading record and overall record as exhibiting either Cluster A or Cluster B tendencies. Results of this subgroup analysis are presented in Table 7.3.

The analysis reveals differential strategies in the anticipated direction. Children in Cluster A tended to err in the direction of unmodified deviations (indicating a strategy that favors momentum), whereas children in Cluster B tended to err in the direction of modified deviations (indicating a strategy that favors

TABLE 7.3
Proportion of Unmodified and Modified Deviations
for Two Style Groups on the *Big Dog*
Standard Oral Reading Selection

	Cluster A (N = 7)		Cluster B (N = 7)		
Error Category	%	No.	%	No.	Total No.
Unmodified Deviations					
(pace maintained)	.59	(71)	.35	(39)	(110)
Modified Deviations	.41	(49)	.65	(74)	(123)
Total Number of Deviations		(120)		(113)	(233)

χ^2 (1, N = 233) = 14.19, $p < .001$.

accuracy). Preferences observed over a wide range of classroom settings and activities thus had counterpart expression in the ways children negotiated the *Big Dog* text.

Although unfamiliar and challenging books (such as *Big Dog*) tended to elicit a child's preferred style of negotiating text, our theory states that proficient reading depends on a balanced act of orchestration. The theory thus implies that progress toward proficiency will be marked by increasing balance between momentum and accuracy among those children who exhibit decisive initial preferences for upholding one or the other requirement. Because this type of progress is visible only over time, additional key selections from the children's longitudinal records were coded and analyzed. Figure 7.6 presents the results of this longitudinal analysis for two children: *Carrie,* designated as a strong and consistent Cluster A child on the basis of observational evidence; and *Rita,* classified as a strong and consistent Cluster B child on the basis of such evidence.

Figure 7.6 shows that Carrie and Rita also exhibited opposing preferences as defined by the unmodified/modified coding. Carrie consistently favored the momentum requirement in her early readings (defined by a preponderance of unmodified deviations), and Rita consistently favored the accuracy requirement (defined by a preponderance of modified deviations). Over time, however, the gap between the unmodified and modified line narrows for each child, and the lines eventually cross over. The crossover cannot be interpreted as an abrupt switch in underlying styles, since both children continued to display behaviors characteristic of Cluster A or Cluster B throughout the period of documentation. In spontaneous remarks, for example, Carrie continued to anticipate narratives and muse about story lines, while Rita continued to be concerned about the accuracy of details or the "fit" between one part of a text and another. The technical coding results nonetheless indicate increasing balance between momentum and accuracy concerns in their reading, and this trend was duplicated in the longitudinal records of a majority of the children who exhibited strong initial preferences.

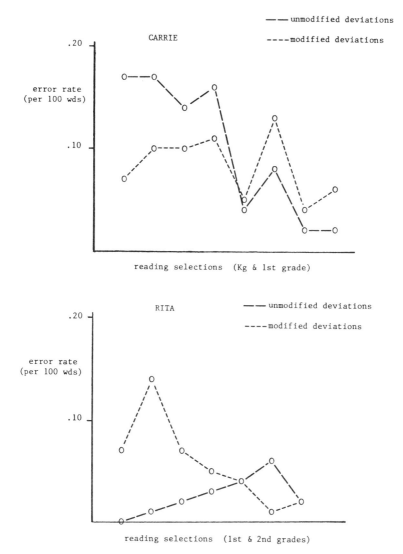

FIG. 7.6.   Longitudinal analysis of modified and unmodified deviations in reading selections spanning 2 school years.

For some children, the redress of balance between accuracy and momentum concerns in reading was equally definitive as that evidenced by Carrie and Rita and illustrated in Fig. 7.6. For others it was less definitive, though some redress was apparent in almost every case. Louis was the one outstanding exception, as his record shows a continuing imbalance (favoring accuracy over momentum) throughout the entire documentation period. This continuing imbalance is also paralleled by comparatively little reading progress during the study. Only toward the end of the documentation period did Louis begin to integrate his considerable resources for reading and start to make real headway. (See Louis's case history in Chapter 12.) Although one exception doesn't necessarily prove the rule, the data generally support the notion that progress toward proficiency is marked by increasingly balanced attention to both the accuracy and momentum requirements of reading.

It is tempting to speculate further about the significance of the observed redress of balance among children with strong style preferences. Such speculation follows the lead of several investigators who have drawn a distinction between cognitive styles and cognitive strategies.[7] Styles are conceptualized as characteristic modes of perceiving, remembering, thinking, and problem solving which tend to be stable, relatively pervasive across diverse activities, and applied without conscious consideration. Strategies, on the other hand, are viewed as reflecting conscious decisions among alternative approaches to a problem, with the particular strategy chosen depending on task requirements, problem content, and situational constraints. Cognitive strategies are also thought to be selected, organized, and controlled in part as a function of broader style characteristics.

If this style/strategy theorizing is essentially sound, then children's initial tendencies to uphold either accuracy or momentum in reading probably reflected some borderline area between unconscious and conscious control. To the extent that all children's unmodified versus modified deviations were influenced by text characteristics and instructional interaction (as mentioned at the outset of the discussion), our data suggest the obvious fact that reading is a conscious effort for beginners and that they can apply conscious strategies to the task. In texts and situations that allowed ample leeway for choice, however, the children's tendency to commit either unmodified or modified errors were probably controlled largely by unconscious style characteristics. Thus, the redress of balance that occurred over time may well reflect increasing control over stylistically determined preferences, to the point where children could suppress them at will and bring the opposite strategy into dominant play. Such a conscious exercise of choice would seem to make a significant turning point in the process of learning to read—perhaps a dramatic point for some children and barely discernible for others, but the point at which style tendencies become genuine cognitive strategies.

The discussion thus far has focused on children whose stylistic preferences were both strong and consistent. Overall, such children account for about one half of the total study sample. The other half presents a more varied picture. One form of variation is represented by Crystal, a child who exhibited strong but vascillating style preferences (as illustrated in Chapter 11). At certain times and in certain contexts, Crystal's classroom behavior resembled characteristics asso-

---

[7]For example, Bruner, Goodnow, & Austin, 1956; Messick, 1983; Pask, 1976; Shouksmith, 1970.

ciated with Cluster A children; whereas at other times and in other contexts, it was more typical of Cluster B children. The coding results for her oral reading selections at different points in time are congruent with this "mixed" style pattern. They reveal about the same proportions of unmodified and modified deviations, indicating roughly equal attention to the momentum and accuracy requirements of reading from the very outset of her learning.

Another form of variation was simply the absence of pronounced style preferences. Generally speaking, the children for whom no distinct preferences could be discerned were also those who displayed relatively little personal investment in learning how to read. Although these children made visible progress in reading and were usually diligent in their efforts, their motivation nonetheless seemed lukewarm. At least it seemed lukewarm for most, if not all, of the period covered by the documentation. Perhaps the surest signal of moderate personal investment in reading was a continuing inclination to "read" the teacher's face and voice for cues. Children who displayed such behavior persisted in looking to external supports to get them through rough spots rather than relying on their own resources. This tendency resulted in many interruptions of reading pace, which in turn produced a predominance of modified deviations that resembled the typical Cluster B reading pattern. But the resemblance was only superficial, since these children were generally less interested in resolving problems on their own or in moving on with the reading once help was received than were children in Cluster B. In some cases, the reasons for a child's modest investment in learning to read was rather clear—e.g., unsettling circumstances in life outside the classroom, or an overriding interest in other aspects of school life (frequently in social interactions). To the extent that a child's investment in reading is not especially strong, it seems reasonable to assume that his or her solution to the problem of juggling momentum/accuracy requirements would be less controlled by underlying personal styles and more responsive to external influences.

TECHNICAL FACILITY IN READING

Readers don't struggle forever with the problem of word identification. As they master the skill of reading, they become able to identify most words automatically. Scheffler (1965) predicts this kind of phenomenon when he makes a distinction between complex skills (competencies) and simpler skills (facilities), asserting that complex skills are guided by judgment, whereas simpler skills become rountinized and automatic with practice. He goes on to say that facilities may also be nested within a competency. That is, certain aspects of a complex performance become automatic in time and thereafter require little conscious effort or monitoring. Many reading theorists use the term "automaticity" in referring to the way word identification becomes an automatic aspect of reading—a technical facility nested within the complex skill of comprehending text.

Although mature readers ordinarily strive for comprehension, they can also make their way through text by relying on technical facility alone. When this happens, they read words fluently and accurately for the most part and yet give little thought to what they are reading or perhaps don't even try to comprehend. Preoccupation and lack of interest often result in such a reading. Another provoking circumstance is text content that goes so far beyond the reader's background knowledge it is virtually impossible to comprehend. We illustrated the effect of insufficient background knowledge on a beginner's efforts with the example of Meg reading *The Cats and the Cart*. Here, we expand an example cited previously (Chapter 6) to show the effect of difficult content on a child much further along in reading progress.

Jane was perhaps the most proficient reader in the study, and the guidelines for obtaining oral reading samples periodically specified the "most difficult" material a child could manage with reasonable proficiency. Accordingly, the data collection team for Jane decided to try a sophisticated book review from *Natural History* magazine as one selection for her oral reading session in September of second grade. Part of the review article appears below.

The Eighth Day of Creation, by Horace Freeland Judson. Simon and Schuster, $15.95; 686 pp. . . .illus.

> The discovery of the structure of the DNA molecule was a unique event in the history of biology, and this book, which takes us from the origins of the discovery into its wider ramifications, is a unique book. From time to time a reviewer will be given a book of such magisterial proportions and quality that it almost defies analysis and criticism. **The Eighth Day of Creation** is such a work, a product of unrivaled devotion to a topic, where scholarship is happily wedded to literary skills.

> Horace Freeland Judson was the European arts and science correspondent of **Time** magazine. Clearly, the discovery of the structure of the gene triggered a consuming passion to record the circumstances leading to and following that discovery, before the people and the documents disappeared into the bland perspective of history.

Jane started out by reading all the identifying information at the beginning of the article. She said "one hundred fifteen and ninety-five" for the price, repeated the letter *p* rather than saying "pages," and correctly pronounced the full word "illustrated." From this point on, her phrasing and intonation were basically appropriate to the content of the article, and her momentary hesitations were only long enough to concoct some ingenious approximations of the words. These behaviors indicate that she believed the material was meaningful—at least meaningful in some way to someone—but she made no apparent effort even to try to comprehend. Although she read with amazing accuracy (rolling off words like *discovery, structure, criticism, science, correspondent,* and *passion* with little difficulty), some of her approximated attempts provide a good index of how well she comprehended the review. She read *rammimaxigen* for "ramifications," *magisterly properations* for "magisterial proportions," *defiles* for "defies,'' *universalty discoveration* for ''unrivaled devotion,'' and *blond parsicles of history* for ''bland perspective of history.''

A moment's reflection suggests most proficient readers are not only capable of reading without comprehending but have probably done so without batting an eye on more than one occasion. Just to test the idea a bit further, we tried it out on ETS employees. We asked a small group of secretaries, editors, and psychologists to read aloud two pages from the middle of one of Piaget's more technical books without any advance study of the pages. They, too, read with appropriate intonation and a great deal of accuracy, yet comprehended little of what they read. Their errors were interesting, though not quite as imaginative as Jane's, consisting mainly of synonym or near-synonym substitutions (e.g., ''expert opinion'' for ''professional opinion''). A few of the adult readers started out as if they were trying to comprehend the text, going back to rephrase something and pausing to ponder a sentence, but they soon abandoned such efforts and just read.

When Jane and these adult readers ''just read,'' they altered their understanding of the reading process for that particular reading occasion. Faced with an impossible task of comprehension, they suspended the idea that reading is the process of constructing *personal* meaning and simply monitored the intelligibility of their reading as best they could. That they did try to monitor intelligibility (by phrasing and intonation) signifies their assumption that the author intended meaning and that the material indeed made sense. In settling for a more abstract and less personal notion of ''meaningfulness,'' however, they modified their goal in reading and negotiated text as a technical facility rather than as a competency under the guidance of judgment.

Theoretical and Instructional Implications of Technical Facility

How does word identification become an automatic process in reading? Researchers have addressed this question over the past few years and will probably continue to do so for some time to come. It is a question of intense theoretical interest, it holds important implications for instruction, and the complex issues involved warrant study from converging perspectives. Results of our reading research offer no answers to the puzzle, but they do suggest some clues. Equally important, they cast serious doubt on one tentative theory concerning the chain of events that precipitate automatic word identification and the kind of instruction that fosters it. Unfortunately, some advocates have translated this tentative theory into fairly ''hard conclusions'' regarding the nature of effective instruction.

The conclusions we question originate in the following line of theoretical argument. There is a fixed amount of conscious attention to be divided between word identification and comprehension. Thus, a reader must make trade-offs: the more attention devoted to word identification, the less is left over for comprehension. When word identification becomes automatic, the reader obviously has more attention to devote to comprehension. The most effective method of fostering automatic word identification (and hence comprehension) is therefore of greatest value to the reader. By implication, the most effective method must be one that focuses the reader's attention on words and emphasizes techniques of word analysis that do not rely on ''extraneous cues'' from grammar or story line. Since phonic instruction focuses on words and emphasizes such techniques, it must be the most effective method of reading instruction. This line of reasoning has led one researcher (Biemiller, 1970) to suggest a phonic approach that prohibits *any* interference from extraneous sources.

> . . . the teacher should do a considerable proportion of early reading training in situations providing no context at all, in order to compel children to use graphic information as much as possible. As they show evidence of doing so (through accurate reading out of context) they would be given contextual material to read. (pp. 94–95)

Although the essence of the argument summarized above is logically consistent, it rests on assumptions that the study challenges. First, word identification and comprehension processes are probably not related in the direct 1:1 manner assumed by the theory of a ''fixed pool'' of attention (i.e., the more attention devoted to one process, the less is left over for the other). The organization of knowledge and attention for purposes of word identification seemed to be handled in similar ways by all children in the study. But the management of knowledge and attention to construct meaning from text (i.e., to uphold momentum and accountability requirements) was handled in different ways. Although resources for these two managerial tasks undoubtedly overlap, they do not appear to be identical. Attention to word identification goes on quite independently of how overall reading requirements are managed.

The notion of a fixed pool of attention implies a second assumption that has to do with the course of reading development—namely, that automatic word recognition is the leading edge of progress toward proficiency. Thus, the argument assumes the following chain of events: ''when and as children learn to identify individual words rapidly and accurately, they become more accurate, fluent, comprehending readers.'' But evidence presented in this chapter runs counter to such an assumption.

> —Children's ability to read words accurately and fluently (as reflected by the index of control) often improved *within* a given reading performance, as they gained familiarity with the text and were better able to orchestrate multiple cues from story line, grammar, vocabulary, and rhythm of the writing. Children were also better able to correct errors in word identification when they had better control of multiple cues.
>
> —Some children struck a rough balance between attention to momentum and word accuracy from the beginning of learning, and they maintained that balance as they

became more proficient. Other children started by investing most of their energy in accurate word identification. Their progress toward proficiency was marked by an increasing concern for momentum in reading.

Finally, our results do not coincide with the assumption that facility in identifying and blending the phonemic elements of words (a phonic emphasis) is the facility underlying automatic word recognition. Several children began to evidence technical facility in identifying words over the course of the study, Jane being one example, But their adeptness (especially as evidenced by their "word approximation" errors[8]) seemed largely a matter of facility in manipulating roots and affixes, not individual letter-sounds. Thus, Jane's approximations of *parsicles* for *perspective* and *rammimaxigen* for *ramifications* are difficult to construe as errors in the rapid blending of letter-sounds. By the same token, her accurate rendering of such words as *passion, criticism,* and *science* seems an unlikely outcome of rapid blending efforts. In short, automatic word identification appears to involve the lexical information encoded in writing more than the phonetic information.

Our last critique is not meant to imply that the promotion of letter-sound knowledge has no place in beginning reading instruction. Children clearly must (and do) acquire and use such knowledge in reading, and instruction can hardly ignore this fact. Rather, we would question beginning reading materials and associated instructional methods that highlight one category of knowledge to the exclusion of others. If learning to read entails learning to orchestrate knowledge from the outset, then gaining control of the reading process clearly depends on ample opportunities to negotiate representative and appropriate texts.

REFERENCES

Biemiller, A. J. The development of the use of graphic and contextual information as children learn to read. *Reading Research Quarterly,* 1970, *6,* 75–96.

Bruner, J. S., Goodnow, J. J., & Austin, G. A. *A study of thinking.* New York: Wiley, 1956.

Goodman, Y., & Burke, C. *Reading miscue inventory manual: Procedures for diagnosis and evaluation.* New York: Macmillan, 1972.

Messick, S. *Developing abilities and knowledge: Style in the interplay of structure and process* (ETS RR-83-2). Princeton, NJ: Educational Testing Service, 1983.

Pask, G. Styles and strategies of learning. *British Journal of Educational Psychology,* 1976, *46,* 128–148.

Scheffler, I. *Conditions of knowledge.* Chicago: Scott Foresman and Company, 1965.

Shouksmith, G. *Intelligence, creativity and cognitive style.* New York: Wiley-Interscience, 1970.

---

[8]See page 104 for the distinction we have drawn between "word approximation" errors and "nonword" errors.

8 Stylistic Influences in Learning How to Read

Although children in the study exhibited many similarities in how they orchestrated knowledge resources as beginning readers, differences surfaced when they encountered text beyond their ability to negotiate smoothly. Some children consistently geared their orchestration efforts to uphold the momentum requirement of reading when the going got tough, whereas other children consistently geared their efforts to uphold the accuracy requirement. Still other children vascillated attention between the two requirements when they could not honor both, and the remainder of the group most often looked to outside sources (teacher or other adult) for suggested strategies of dealing with troublesome text.

In Chapter 7, we presented results of the coding for Unmodified versus Modified deviations from text, which showed clear differences between two groups of children displaying consistent tendencies to uphold either momentum or accuracy in reading. We said the two groups were initially selected on the basis of preference noted in descriptive analyses of their oral reading, and that such preferences were associated with various style characteristics documented in their overall observational records. This chapter presents evidence of the pervasive style differences that marked many children's general classroom functioning as well as their reading behavior.

Styles connote how people typically act and think and express themselves rather than what they accomplish or know. As mentioned in the preceding chapter, styles are often conceptualized in the literature as characteristic ways of perceiving, remembering, thinking, and problem solving. We also mentioned stylistic features of behavior in our summary of Kelly's theory, noting that a person is often unaware of the several "how" characteristics that distinguish his or her individuality.

> Personal construct systems are characterized not only by knowledge (by *what* a person anticipates and understands), but also by stylistic features (by *how* one conducts commerce with the world). Some stylistic features are determined by the way the construct system is organized. Other style characteristics are undoubtedly determined more by biological make-up, coming close to what is implied by the old-fashioned word "temperament.". . . Whatever their origin, these stylistic features are often more salient to others than to the person involved. Unless a particular way of interacting with the world is foiled by external circumstances or specifically brought to an individual's attention, it often remains on the periphery of awareness. . . . Although people are generally oblivious of how they go about things, the how is an integral aspect of personal meaning that pervades every realm of life and learning. (Chapter 1, pp. 14–15)

The study's data integration procedures identified patterns of behavior in the research documentation accumulated for each child. Many of these patterns turned out to be stylistic in nature, highlighting how individual children approached and engaged the people, activities, and materials in the classroom; how they organized and presented their ideas; and, more generally, how they seemed to perceive the world. The overall configuration of patterns for any given child was unique, and it is the uniqueness of individuals that is emphasized in the Child Studies of Part III. Comparisons across children, however, revealed many points of similarity and contrast with respect to specific patterns. Moreover, these points of similarity and contrast were fairly consistently related across children, so that the same subgroups who evidenced similar and opposing tendencies in one aspect of behavior also evidenced similar and opposing tendencies in other aspects of behavior. This finding suggested that we were comparing children in terms of bipolar style characteristics, all of which varied more or less systematically to form two generalized style clusters.

Since we can document the two style clusters only for the 18-month to 2-year period of data collection, when the children were in the early primary grades, we cannot attest to their stability and have therefore refrained from trying to label them. They are referred to throughout the chapter simply as "Cluster A" and "Cluster B." We suspect that the bipolar styles composing the clusters are reasonably stable characteristics, but they may well be manifest at older age levels in more differentiated forms of behavior that are not so systematically related. As evidenced among young children, however, the component bipolar styles and their opposing manifestations may be described as follows:

Preferred Expressions of Meaning (Imaginative and Divergent versus Realistic and Convergent)

Manner of Work (Mobile and Fluid versus Contained and Methodical)
Attentional Scope and Emphasis (Broad and Integrative versus Narrowed and
   Analytic)
Sequencing of Thought Processes (Parallel versus Linear)

Because styles are rarely dealt with in reading research, and because they are quite different from knowledge resources, a few qualifying remarks seem in order. Styles are manifest as tendencies or preferences and are therefore more relative in nature than knowledge. For one thing, style tendencies may vary in intensity from one situation to another in a way that knowledge does not. Knowledge can also be defined by propositional statements in a way that styles cannot. For example, a person's typical pace of action may be described along the style continuum of "fast-slow," but "fast-slow" is a relative idea, not an absolute proposition. The continuum is a contrastive one, in which the meaning of either end (e.g., "fast") derives from its contrast with the opposing tendency ("slow"). Because bipolar styles defy definition in terms of absolute standards or propositions, they must be anchored by behavioral descriptions. And they are most clearly defined at the extremes, by the behavior of individuals who exhibit the most decisive tendencies in either direction.

Approximately half of the children exhibited consistent preferences across a wide variety of classroom contexts on the bipolar styles listed above. The other children exhibited milder and/or more fluctuating preferences. Since our characterization of each style necessarily draws on behaviors that most clearly define opposing tendencies, the summary descriptions that follow are taken from the records of only half of the total sample of 40 children. In particular, we rely on documentation from the records of the following 10 children, who were considered most representative of each style cluster:

Cluster A	Cluster B
Carrie	Colin
Debbie	Dana
Jack	Louis
Jenny	Rita
Tim	Susan

Finally, we should point out that the styles we have posited are not value-laden characteristics. They are neither "good" nor "bad" attributes, although they could be more or less serviceable to an individual, depending on the situation and the extremeness of the particular style. Neither were the styles differentially associated with "more proficient" and "less proficient" readers (as illustrated in the last half of the chapter), or with other obvious classifications of the children such as sex or race.

We describe general classroom manifestations of each style first and then consider how the combined characteristics of each style cluster were evident in the children's efforts to learn how to read.

PREFERRED EXPRESSIONS OF MEANING
(IMAGINATIVE AND DIVERGENT VERSUS REALISTIC
AND CONVERGENT)

Decisive preferences with respect to this style showed up most clearly during periods in the classroom that were specifically designated as a time for choice. That is, children's preferences were manifest by the tendency to express more conventional or personalized meanings in situations where they had a genuine option to do either.

If children could choose from a full range of possibilities, then preferences were sometimes evident in their consistent options for a particular type of activity. By a full range of possibilities, we refer to the range of possible meanings that can be imposed on material or the range of possible directions an activity can take. At one end of the range are natural materials that have no fixed shape and imply no particular use (e.g., sand, clay, water, wood). The shape and meaning of these materials are fashioned entirely by the person who works with them. At the other extreme are structured materials that fit together in prescribed ways and activities that have defined rules or standard procedures and patterns to follow (e.g., commercial games and construction materials such as Lego, Lincoln Logs, and erector sets). There is a wide area in the middle, of course, comprised of such materials as large construction blocks, accoutrements for dramatic play, paints, magic markers, and craft supplies (fabric, colored paper, paste, and so on). The majority of children selected from this middle range of materials quite often and/or sampled across portions of the range; but a few showed marked preference for one extreme or the other. Louis, for example, almost always chose to work with small construction materials (especially Lego) during choice time, ignoring most of the other options in the full range that was available to him.[1]

Since the children did work a lot with middle-range materials, what they chose to do *with* material was usually a more telling indication of preferences than the specific material chosen. Some children rather consistently focused on creating a recognizable or usable product in whatever medium they were working, as if they were trying to reproduce the structures and meanings they found in

---

[1]What children choose is obviously a partial function of what is available to them. Every classroom in the study was well provisioned with materials in the middle and structured end of the range, though fewer had a rich sampling of natural materials. (Louis's classroom offered the full range of possibilities.)

the world around them. Other children seemed more intent on "messing about" and experimenting with different media, or else they would create more idiosyncratic and fanciful expressions of meaning.

Dana and Jenny, the two children introduced in the prologues to Chapter 5, present a striking contrast in how they worked with material. Dana sustained an interest in art (mainly drawing) throughout the 2-year period of documentation, and his intention was clearly a representational one throughout. Although he usually drew freehand, he also liked to trace book covers. Among the major motifs seen in his own artwork are tanks, flags modeled after pictures in the encyclopedia, sharks (a popular motif with many children in the wake of the first *Jaws* movie), boats, and helicopters. Dana also worked frequently with clay and occasionally with wax during the first grade. In these mediums, he almost always produced animal shapes, usually porpoises, sharks, and penguins. Jenny's products in drawing and painting were rarely representational. For the most part, she experimented with colors, mixing them in paints and creating relatively amorphous designs with crayons. She also used painting and drawing as mediums for forming letters and for her experimentation with invented spellings. And Jenny's major concentration when working with wax and clay seemed to be on the process of changing shapes and textures.

Only a few children were as consistent and intense as Jenny in their concern for exploring the characteristics of materials; but differences in style also surfaced when children used materials for representational ends, and these differences were often readily detected in drawing. Dana's realistic bent, for instance, is evident in the insect drawings reproduced in Chapter 5, and it is equally evident in the sample drawings shown in Figures 8.1, 8.2, and 8.3. The first sample is one of the many "Jaw-inspired" drawings that he produced in the spring of first grade, and the third shows an integration of favorite motifs (boats, helicopters, and flags). The second drawing in the series deserves special comment. Dana chose to draw this picture after a class trip to the harbor to see a replica of the Santa Maria. His representation faithfully depicts the many flags that flew from the ship's rigging and the many pennants that decorated its hull. It is also faithful to the reality of the children's experience in other ways. The children were ushered onto the deck of the ship via a gangplank. As shown in the drawing, one member of the crew climbed up to the crow's nest for them. They were then guided down into the body of the ship and saw the hatch through which supplies are loaded on board. The hatch opening in the center of Dana's ship is obvious and clearly distinguished from the surrounding pennants. Not so obvious, but unmistakably there, are steps leading down into the hold. These are the interior stairs which the children descended.

The next three illustrations (Figures 8.4, 8.5 and 8.6) are not so much attempts to represent conventional reality as to express personal and private meanings. They are from a collection of pencil drawings that Tim produced in the

FIG. 8.1. Dana's Shark Drawing (magic marker)

FIG. 8.2.   Dana's Santa Maria Drawing (pen and magic marker)

spring of first grade.[2] All the drawings in the collection reflect the same sort of science fiction themes that pervaded Tim's dramatic play throughout the year, but the drawings capture his own version of the fantasy adventures and heroes in a way that could not be expressed well, if at all, in dramatic play with other children. Both Dana's and Tim's pictures show interesting perspectives, relatively good control over the medium of drawing, and a good use of detail. The contrast they exemplify is not one of skill or conceptual development but of the meanings they chose to emphasize, Dana's preference leaning towards realistic portrayals and Tim's toward privately imagined scenes.

---

[2]A descriptive analysis of the total collection of drawings appears in Chapter 4, pp. 48–49.

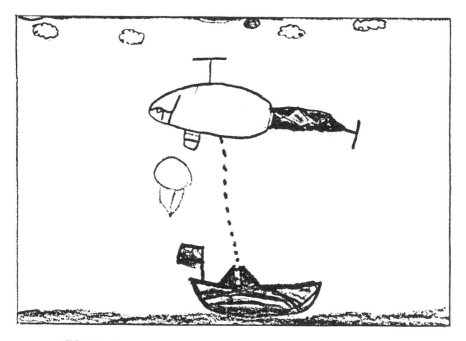

FIG. 8.3. Dana's Helicopter and Boat Drawing (pencil and magic marker)

What children chose to do in the block area was equally revealing of expressive preferences as what they chose to do with art materials. Some children used large blocks to create settings and props for dramatic play, with their major energies going into the drama rather than into the construction per se. Tim's continuing enactments of space fantasies with his friends represent a clear preference for creating imaginative meanings in the block area. Other children invested their main energy in constructing elaborate and realistic buildings (e.g., towers, forts, cities) or in creating structures intended to resemble the form and function of real objects. Mike, for example, spent many hours of his choice time building different versions of a bowling game, and Rita and her friends once built an elaborate representation of an amusement park.

Differences in orientation among children could also be seen in dramatic play, although these differences were rarely evident as "pure" examples of imaginative play versus "pure" example of imitative play. Since fantasies were only more or less real, the distinction was one of emphasis. Thus, Tim's space adventures reflected large doses of imagination, although they were obviously stimulated by the plots and characters of popular movies, TV programs, and comic books. The fantasy productions of some other children, however, were actually episode-by-episode reenactments of well-known fairy tales or stories.

FIG. 8.4. Tim's Pencil Drawing (Sample A)

FIG. 8.5. Tim's Pencil Drawing (Sample B)

FIG. 8.6.   Tim's Pencil Drawing (Sample C)

By the same token, children's attempts to recreate realistic events (e.g., in playing house) involved greater and lesser degrees of poetic license. Whereas children like Rita generally opted for considerable realism in such play, Carrie and Tanya tended to bend reality to suit their own purposes. Tanya, for example, often assumed the baby's role in house play because of her small size, but she rarely portrayed any of a baby's passivity. In one observation, all the "house players" told her to go to sleep. Tanya made a few baby noises and then sat up and said the baby wasn't tired any more and good parents wouldn't make the baby sleep if the baby wasn't tired. The other children immediately yielded and inquired what the baby wished to do next.

Like Tanya, Carrie often engaged in dramatic play in the house corner, and her presence was usually a commanding influence there as well as elsewhere in the classroom. What made Carrie's contributions special was the sense of drama and "story" she imparted to events. Thus, while she rarely instigated fantasy play of the space adventure or superhero variety, she could transform even the most ordinary situation into a dramatic episode by weaving a story line around it. Sometimes, her stories did broach fantasy, as when she once told the class about a dog she had at home and promised that her sister would bring the dog to school. Her story was so convincing that everyone including the teacher believed her at first. When it later became clear that the sister knew nothing about a dog in the house, Carrie "explained" the discrepancy by saying that the dog lived in her closet and only came out at night. And the dog continued to live in Carrie's imaginative narrations for the next few days.

Another way in which preferred expressions of meaning were manifest was in the children's use of structured materials in the classroom. As stated previously, structured materials like Lego have clearly defined shapes, the pieces fit together only in certain ways, and they invite construction that tends toward realism. Lego was a popular construction material with many children in the study, but different children approached the material with noticeably different attitudes toward its intrinsic qualities. Tim's approach was exemplified in a remark he made to a group of boys who were arguing about whether a certain piece of Lego could be used as a "muffler." Tim said it could be a muffler and summarized his thoughts on the matter in the following way—"*You can make it what it is.*" According to Tim's view, then, just about any piece of Lego could take on the qualities one imagines and attributes to it. This tendency to perceive multiple meanings and functions in objects is one defining characteristic of what the psychological literature calls divergent thinking.

Louis, on the other hand, would persist in looking for just the "right" pieces of Lego to build his realistic constructions. The payoff of Louis's persistence and patience is well illustrated in the photograph of one of his crowning achievements—a gas station, with a roof that serves as a landing strip for an airplane, and a nearby control tower. (The photograph is reproduced in black and white in Fig. 8.7.) Louis invested particular care and time in selecting appropriate pieces to create camouflage for the plane in the design of the station's roof and trim. In contrast to Tim, Louis's tendency to narrow in on a single, "most appropriate" meaning and function for the Lego shapes may be construed as convergent thinking.

The opposing tendencies described in this section characterize those children who gave freest reign to their imaginative resources versus those who drew most heavily on ideas and images about the real world. Evidence of stylistic preferences was most apparent in situations where the children could act on either inclination without adverse consequences. In situations that clearly called for the expression of imaginative or realistic meanings, the children were usually able to respond quite appropriately. Thus, to a greater extent than other stylistic differences we will discuss, preferences defining this style appeared subject to moderation by conscious, decision-making processes.

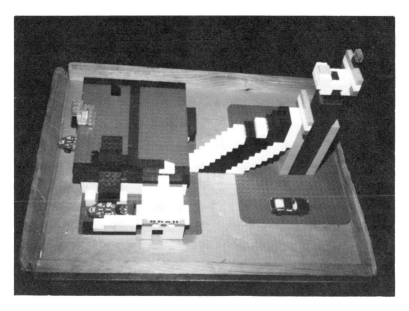

FIG. 8.7.   Louis's Lego Gas Station

MANNER OF WORK (MOBILE AND FLUID VERSUS CONTAINED AND METHODICAL)

One prominent feature of many children's work habits was the creation of "boundaries" to demarcate a working space. Many children habitually delineated a work space as they set about a task, surrounding themselves with the materials they needed and containing their work within that space. The space might be more or less compact, and the lines of demarcation more or less conspicuous, but the designated area itself was usually quite clear. It was that child's "turf." The initial observation of Dana, in September of first grade, describes him working in a very compact space, consisting of his chair, a desk, and the area under the desk. The following is an excerpt from the observation.

> Dana is seated alone at a desk in the back of the room, his legs straddling each side of the chair, concentrating on a drawing he is doing with thin magic markers. . . . Although there is other activity in the science area nearby, he only glances up at it occasionally. Lots of magic markers are under the desk where he is working. He replaces the caps and puts them back one at a time as he finishes with each, then chooses the color he wants next. He finishes one drawing and begins work on another, placing the first drawing under the paper he is now working on.

This initial observation of Dana was also one of the first observations of the study, occurring early in the pilot phase of the research. Though we had no way of knowing it at the time, similar descriptions of working within a contained space (as opposed to ''spreading out'') were to recur often, not only in Dana's record but in the records of several other children as well.

The excerpt above illustrates another characteristic that was strongly associated with the creation of spatial boundaries for work. Dana used the magic markers one at a time, putting each one back before he chose the next color. Replacing the caps on magic markers was an operating procedure emphasized by almost every teacher in order to avoid the waste of markers drying out. But actually using one color at a time was a procedure Dana imposed on himself, as if to delineate discrete units within the work process. The tendency to accentuate separate steps, or units, or parts of the work process lent a methodical quality to the manner in which Dana and other children went about their projects. Rita, for example, was observed systematically ordering the colors in her design from lighter to darker hues. In another observation of a choice activity, she glued cut-out pictures in orderly fashion, turning them over one at a time to glue them and then placing them in rows from left to right, starting at the top of the paper. Louis's incremental, step-by-step manner of building with Lego and of doing virtually everything else in the classroom was so pronounced as to become an overriding theme in his record (see the write-up of Louis in Chapter 12).

Methodical qualities in the children's manner of work also showed up in the form of planning and projecting needs over time. When Dana drew or traced, he always counted out the pages he would need beforehand and then used just that number. Rita would gather all the relevant supplies for her many craft projects and rarely had to interrupt her work to fetch a forgotten item. Susan typically checked all the paint jars to make sure she had the colors she needed before starting a painting. In one observation during her kindergarten year, Susan seemed to have planned 24 hours in advance. In this particular episode, she worked her way over to the piano and began to play the *Happy Birthday* tune, persisting until she caught the teacher's attention. When the teacher came over to the piano, Susan said she was ''practicing'' and then asked if she could play for her friend's birthday, which was to be the following day.

Some children who worked methodically and created boundaries to delineate a working space also paid special attention to various physical aspects of their setting—to having the right chair, the right working surface, the right lighting, and so on. Rita, for example, spent several minutes of one work period trying to locate her proper chair (the one with her name on it) rather than settling down in one of the many chairs that were vacant and available to her. Some children, too, were careful to observe the boundary line that separates working materials from the worker. They seemed to avoid mess as a matter of personal preference more than in response to parental exhortations about not getting clothes dirty. Dana and Colin, for instance, often worked with messy materials such as paints and clay, but they usually managed to keep themselves immaculate in the process.

Other children's manner of work was diametrically opposed to the characteristics just described. These children would work in almost any space or setting, and their trademark was mobility. Although they rarely usurped other children's working space, their own spaces were noticeably "unbounded," as they frequently transported themselves and occasionally their work from one part of the room to another. Moreover, these children displayed no consistent tendency to organize their work procedures into discrete chunks or units. Their manner of working was marked by a certain fluid quality, in contrast to a methodical quality.

When Tim built with Lego, for example, he would often build in his hands and carry the construction with him from place to place. And unlike Rita, who was in the same classroom, he did not go out of his way to find the chair with his name on it—or, for that matter, to find any chair if something else would do. Not only did Tim eschew spatial boundaries for his work (except the designated limits of the large block area), he avoided sharp time boundaries as much as possible. That is, he tended to slur over transitions from one period to the next by gliding from one activity directly into another (e.g., math to writing) without waiting for the teacher's official signal to stop the one and start the other.

Jenny and Carrie also worked in unbounded spaces, and they tended to plunge into their working materials whenever it was possible for them to do so. Thus, both girls were described on more than one occasion as "up to their elbows" in sand, paint, water, clay, or whatever. Jenny also ignored boundaries that many children observed when she spilled her writing over from journals and diaries to drawings and paintings. And since Carrie's preferred medium was "story," she carried the medium with her, using it to connect her diverse activities in various parts of the classroom.

Carrie, Jenny, and Tim all had reasonably well-defined interests that gave direction to their activities. When this was not the case, however, a child's fluid manner of functioning was often one of the most striking characteristics in his or her record. Debbie and Jack are good examples. Debbie frequently opted to work with water or in the house corner during choice time, but whatever she undertook, her diffuse manner of work and tendency to extend spatial boundaries were usually highly visible.

—Water . . . she pours it into bottles, pours bottles into cups . . . it always ends on the floor. [October, 1st grade]

—Debbie turns sideways in her chair and leans back as far as she can, holding onto the table with one hand and the back of the chair with the other. She begins to slip and says, "Help." Then she leans back again. She turns and sits astride the chair with her back to the table. She rests her head on her arm, which is draped across the back of the chair. Then she turns and leans over the table, hands at her side, her mouth resting on the table. [Observation, November, 1st grade]

—Her pictures tend to get mixed up with the other kids', or to fall on the floor. [January, 1st grade]

Jack was perhaps the most "mobile" child in the study. The teacher's descriptions of his behavior, like those of Debbie above, stand in marked contrast to the observation of Dana presented previously.

—He has a long stride and walks back and forth a lot. He goes from one project to another . . . he might get around to each activity within a day's choice period. [November, 1st grade]

In summary, children who displayed opposing preferences on this style characteristic worked in distinctly different ways. We have tried to capture the flavor of the difference by the metaphor of "boundaries." At one extreme, children conceived spatial boundaries that delimited their working area, and they tended to emphasize discrete components in the process of work, using one material or completing one segment at a time. Some paid special attention to physical aspects of the working environment (appropriate conditions, furniture, tools), and many kept themselves free from the mess associated with paints, clay, paste, and the like. At the other extreme, children tended to minimize spatial and process boundaries in their work, just as they tended to minimize distinctions between discrete activities in the classroom. Because individuals comprising this group managed to minimize or blur distinctions in a variety of ways (ranging from smooth transitions to seemingly restless or aimless behavior), the group as a whole appeared much more diverse in their approach to work than the children characterized by a methodical style. The trait that singularly unified the group was mobility.

ATTENTIONAL SCOPE AND EMPHASIS (BROAD AND INTEGRATIVE VERSUS NARROWED AND ANALYTIC)

Most children in the study showed an interest in classroom life and would stop periodically to survey what their friends were doing or what was going on in general. Likewise, most children had the capacity to shut out the world and concentrate on things that intrigued them. But some children did appear to narrow their perceptual attention more consistently than others. The excerpt from the observation of Dana working at his desk describes him as glancing only "occasionally" at the activity in the nearby science area. This tendency to focus in on work with apparent oblivion to surrounding events was noted in the records of several children. Often, teachers described such behavior in words that implied a bomb could be dropped and the child wouldn't know it.

Other children seemed to know what was happening around the room even when they were engaged in an activity and the peripheral event was of relatively minor interest. The following summary from an observation in Tim's record is illustrative.

—The teacher and a parent are conducting eye tests during free activity period, summoning individual children over to the test area in alphabetical order. Tim is across the room from where the eye tests are taking place, engaged in dramatic play in the block corner. He stops in the midst of an exchange with Manuel to call out and alert a friend whose name is next in alphabetical order—"Donald, you're next!" The observer had no idea Tim was even aware of the eye proceedings.

Jack's attention deployment was so broad, he had difficulty choosing and sticking with one activity during choice time. The image his record suggests is that of an explorer on a strange planet, with antennae tuned in all directions. As Jack explored many activities in the classroom, he also looked around a great deal. In fact, he displayed more evidence of visually scanning the classroom than any other child. The following are but two of many similar descriptions contained in his record.

—He was the only person in the room who noticed that the alphabet chart was up wrong. He'll be sitting on the rug and just say something he observes. Once he said the title of a book that was across the room on a shelf; he read it as *Jumping Kangaroo* rather than *Joey Kangaroo*. [Teacher interview, November, 1st grade]

—As he works at Lego, he is also checking to see what the others are doing and offering commentary either on his own work or on their work. [Observation, October, 2nd grade]

Although behaviors of the kind just described reveal tendencies toward broad or narrowed attention deployment, it is only by chance that naturalistic observations can pinpoint exactly *what* a child is attending to and the cognitive intent or emphasis of the attention. Dana presumably could have been daydreaming as he focused and worked on his drawings. That Jack wasn't daydreaming as he looked around the room was signaled only by his voluntary comments about what he observed. Similarly, Tim's awareness of the alphabetic arrangement for the eye tests would not have been noted by the observer except for his gratuitous remark to Donald.

By definition, attention means that a person "takes hold" of the world cognitively as well as perceptually. But since cognitive manifestations of attention are often impossible to discern from observations alone, one must look elsewhere for them. We believe such manifestations may be inferred from two other sources of data. One source just mentioned is the comments children happen to volunteer. A more reliable and universal source is the work they produce. The study's analysis of children's work products revealed contrasts in their representational emphasis that seemed to reflect underlying differences in attentional emphasis. Moreover, such differences were directly related to evidence concerning the scope of a child's attention deployment. Children who displayed a narrowed scope of attention also tended to accentuate distinctions among the events and objects they represented. In other words, their representational emphasis suggested an analytic perspective on the world. Children who displayed a broad scope of attention deployment tended to emphasize connections and continuities among objects and events, suggesting an integrative or synthesizing outlook.

The metaphor of "boundaries" used to describe children's manner of work is also remarkably valid for describing their work products. This is true because the presence or absence of boundaries and borders is a conventional way to indicate either discreteness or unity among parts of a work. Thus, Dana's proclivity for drawing flags was, at one and the same time, a proclivity for drawing designs marked by especially sharp boundaries. But the boundaries he often created within his representational artwork were more interesting because of their subtlety. In every single one of his many shark pictures, for instance, he drew a distinct outline around the fish (see Fig. 8.1).

Although few children drew flags per se, several created distinct designs. That is, they fashioned patterns that had clearly differentiated sections—in contrast to the color mixtures that children like Jenny produced and called "designs." Rita, for example, drew many intricate and symmetrical patterns throughout the fall and winter months of first grade, eventually elaborating this work in the creation of layered collages. And Susan, even as a kindergartner, became something of an expert in making cut-out designs. To emphasize these cut-out shapes, Susan often bordered them with a dark color, using crayon or magic marker. The effect was usually a striking frame for her work, as shown in Figure 8.8.

The children's tendency to emphasize boundaries in their own artistic creations was sometimes evident in the tendency to comment on contrasts and differentiating detail in pictures appearing in books. The following excerpt from an interview with Susan's first-grade teacher provides an especially clear example.

> —Susan gets very involved with the pictures in the Bank Street series. There was one picture of a girl with a white headband on, and she stopped reading completely and said, "Oh, she has a headband like mine." Then she went through all the ways that it was different—"But hers is white, mine is pink . . . hers is wider . . . mine has a design on it, hers doesn't."

Both Colin and Louis accentuated boundaries and borders in their construction work. Louis's most elaborate representation of border detail (for his Lego gas station) has already been illustrated. Colin's emphasis could be seen in his work both with large blocks and with smaller construction materials and figures for creating "miniature worlds." With large blocks, he often built contained spaces for himself and his fantasy play—"I'm making a wall so nobody ain't getting in here." Similarly, walls tended to be the most prominent feature in the forts and castles he built with smaller construction materials.

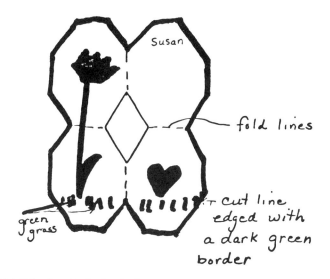

FIG. 8.8.   Susan's Cut-Out Design

In contrast to the work of children like Dana, Rita, Susan, Louis, and Colin, other children tended to minimize distinctions between objects and events in their concrete representations. Thus, Jenny's color mixture type of design was echoed in the design efforts of others as well. One of Carrie's typical paintings, for example, was the subject of descriptive analysis by the data integration team. At the level of overall impression, the composition reminded everyone of a surrealistic painting of the Manhattan skyline. Carrie almost certainly did not intend such an impression, but it was nonetheless an overwhelming one. Her light pastels at the bottom of the paper (suggesting water) merged into blobs of smoky grays, pinks, and browns across the middle portion (suggesting buildings and skyscrapers), and then gradually transformed to lighter color blends again at the top of the paper (suggesting the horizon).

A second picture of Carrie's that was analyzed for purposes of data integration differed in content and medium from her ''Manhattan skyline.'' This was an outline drawing of her family, done with red magic marker, that Carrie produced when she was in kindergarten. Part of the drawing (which actually took up both sides of her drawing paper) is reproduced in Fig. 8.9. One of the most notable features about this drawing is the way in which all the family members are connected. Since Carrie was not observed in the process of drawing this picture, it may be that some of her connections were accidentally produced by a lack of complete control over the medium. For the most part, however, the connecting lines appear to be quite deliberate strokes. Family drawings were certainly not unique among the children. But unlike many family portraits, in which all the persons are represented in a horizontal line across the paper and clearly separated

FIG. 8.9.   Carrie's Family Drawing

by space, Carrie represented her family as physically and concretely related to one another.

Observations of children in the process of drawing or painting can reveal a great deal about their representational intentions and priorities. One such observation of Tim points up two additional ways in which some children tended to minimize boundaries—even boundary lines that they themselves had created. Tim painted three pictures during the course of this particular observation, all of them representative of space themes, but only the last one being a straightforward depiction of space heroes. Tim transformed the first painting by obliterating boundaries, and he transformed the second by invading them. His actions are described in the abridged excerpts below. (Full texts of the original observations and photographs of both paintings appear in the write-up of Tim in Chapter 13).

—Tim begins the first picture by painting the outline of a space ship and what he calls a "planet" in blue. Then he announces, "I'm gonna do the space," and starts to overhaul the painting. He adds horizontal blue strokes across the top that finally obscure the planet altogether. He cleans his brush and begins painting the interior of the spaceship white; then scrubs white across the ship until all that remains of the original outline are two white, cloudish spots. Next, he goes back to blue and brushes it back and forth across the painting, leaving only the blurs of white where the ship was. When a friend expresses skepticism, saying that the spaceship Galactica doesn't look like that, Tim explains—"It's in light speed." [The observation continues with further conversation between the boys and another revision of the painting by Tim.]

—As he begins the second picture, Tim tells his friend that he plans to paint "Starbuck shooting." He paints a blimp-like shape with red in the center of the paper and then adds horizontal and vertical crossbars inside the shape. He changes to blue and paints a broad band around the red shape, saying that this addition is Starbuck's "jail." Then, becoming less careful, he takes green paint and makes a squiggly circle in the lower left corner. He imitates shooting noises to accompany the green then suddenly draws the green brush upward into the red area, exclaiming: "Look, look! P-ugh, P-ugh!!!" He next scrubs orange paint over that area of the central red shape that has been invaded by the green line. This creates a vivid, fiery look within the blimp shape, as if molten lava were pouring out of a gaping hole. He is apparently satisfied with this effect and gives the painting to the paraprofessional, saying it is finished.

Another type of boundary that some children typically included in their drawings, and others typically left out, is the line that separates ground from horizon. Dana almost always represented such a demarcation, whereas Tim almost always omitted it. These respective tendencies can be seen in the examples of both boys' drawings (Figures 8.1 through 8.6).

In summary, the most obvious evidence of children's preferences to accentuate contrasts or connections in the world they perceived was found in their most common forms of representation—paintings, drawings, designs, and three-dimensional constructions. We have interpreted these opposing preferences as cognitive manifestations of a child's style of attention deployment. Broad attention deployment implies not only perceptually scanning the environment but the tendency to minimize boundaries and to accentuate continuities between objects and events. In effect, this style seems indicative of an integrative emphasis in attention. A narrowed attentional scope implies not only the narrowing of perceptual attention but the analytic tendency to emphasize distinctions that set one object or event apart from another.

SEQUENCING OF THOUGHT PROCESSES (PARALLEL VERSUS LINEAR)

The contrasting poles of this style imply two distinct ways of processing information and creating meaningful structure. A preference for parallel sequencing was suggested by evidence that children entertained a wide range of associations and juggled diverse ideas, made apparent leaps in connections to new meanings, and frequently short-circuited the linear structures inherent in many classroom materials and procedures. Occasionally, parallel sequencing was evident in the unmistakable form of dual processing—i.e., of monitoring diverse sources of incoming information simultaneously. Both Jack's and Tim's records contain evidence of this latter type.

Indications of dual processing appear several times in observations and the teacher's reports of Jack's behavior. Often, for example, he worked on two or more Lego projects at the same time.

—Building and concentrating on his own Lego construction, Jack reaches over and adds pieces to another child's building nearby. [Observation, October, 1st grade]

He was also observed doing writing assignments and completing workbook assignments while simultaneously carrying on one or more coherent conversations. In one instance, Jack skimmed through a book while monitoring his own previous reading in another section of the book. This episode happened in the spring of first grade, when he wanted to hear a passage he had just taped for an oral reading sample. He listened to the tape and also looked at the book, but he was looking to find something several pages beyond the actual passage he had recorded. While leafing ahead with all the outward appearances of purposefulness, he simultaneously commented on the tape and, at one point, anticipated and filled in an upcoming word that he had had difficulty with during the taping. Jack's teacher summed up this particular incident, as well as many others, in the following way: "He can do two things at one time—he does it like you'd expect a grown-up to do it."

The clearest evidence of dual processing in Tim's record is found in observations of his dramatic play activity in the block corner. By early March of first grade, Tim's domination of the space fantasy play at choice time had become an obvious yet puzzling fact to the data collection team. On the one hand, it was clear that Tim managed to engage his friends in plots of his own choosing and basically of his direction. Moreover, he led and directed the dramatic activities without ever engendering strife or recrimination among the boys. On the other hand, it was equally clear that his friends had other ideas for block play that they enacted in Tim's absence. The puzzle of how Tim got his way without creating antagonisms motivated the decision to focus a series of observations on the block corner. These observations revealed Tim's ability to orchestrate a complex social undertaking. He interacted with different friends in ways that showed sensitivity to their differing characteristics (which served to minimize conflict) while simultaneously keeping his several interactions directed toward a flexible but definitive plot which presumably served to enhance his own purposes. In Tim's case, then, the dual processing involved monitoring social interactions as well as ongoing possibilities for an interesting story line.

A more common indication of parallel sequencing occurred in the form of comments evoked by books. Some children's comments typically revealed rather obvious and immediate connections to events portrayed in a book, whereas other children's comments often revealed more remote connections. Carrie's reaction to the bear walking off the blackboard (in *Blackboard Bear*) provides a classic example of far-reaching associations. She first related the bear's two-dimensional existence on the blackboard to its ability to walk in a three-dimensional world; she next made the connection between Pinocchio and the bear both being magically infused with life; and she then drew upon her knowledge about clouds to hypothesize how the bear might have come to life. Although her response was cited previously, it seems worth repeating here.

> But how can a bear turn to life? If he turn to life he would still be *flat!* He would be a flat bear. (You mean because he was on the blackboard?) Yeah. So how could he get off—how could he stand up? If he stood up, he's supposed to fall down. (I agree with you; I don't know how that could be.) Just like Pinocchio—puppets'll fall down if you don't hold them. I don't know how Pinocchio came to life, he didn't have no strings. [later] Maybe he could come to life . . . cause maybe he uh uh . . . uh uh he could have just been, you know, like the things, like when the sky makes animals—shapes of animals. (You mean clouds?) Yeah. Maybe he just, uh maybe the air just made him. And when he [the boy] drew him, he came to life because the air made him when he was inside the chalk.

In telling stories, too, some children ranged much further afield than others to encompass diverse characters and events in their fiction. Debbie was perhaps the most extreme in this respect, as her stories often sidestepped from one event to another, without ever falling into the more conventional pattern of a beginning, middle, and end.

Perhaps the most obvious behavior differentiating opposing style preferences among the children was their reaction to the linear structures inherent in books and in various reading-related activities. Certain kinds of implied structure seem quite natural and even essential for reading (e.g., progressing from the front to the back of a book), whereas other kinds seem rather arbitrary (e.g., the particular ordering of problems in a workbook). Regardless of the apparent "naturalness," "essentialness," or "arbitrariness" of such linear structures, some children typically managed to work around them, at least to some extent.

When observed doing workbook assignments in math and reading, for example, Tim, Jack, Carrie, Debbie, Jenny, and others rarely did problems in the order presented but would skip around within a page and go back and forth between pages. This same group of children also tended to flip through books at free reading time, looking over the entire book before they read it, sampling parts of the book, or else periodically looking beyond the page they were reading. It seemed as if they wanted to get a sense of the whole book before or as they tackled parts of it. Thus, Jenny often started a book by carefully thumbing her way from the back to the front. When she had perused it in this manner and finally arrived at the front, she would begin to read. Jack usually skipped from place to place while previewing a book, frequently verbalizing his intentions to find out what the book was "like" or "about." He also tended to pose questions to himself or others as he was reading and then would flip ahead in the book to find his own answers.

Some children tried to predict what would happen in stories they were reading for the first time, though they didn't necessarily flip ahead. Whether or not a child's predictions were accurate, the mere fact of predicting signaled a cognitive leap ahead in the book's structure. Tanya liked to predict outcomes, even at the very beginning of books. In an example cited previously, she correctly predicted that the little boy (in *The Magic Doors*) would get into trouble before she had finished the first page. She said, "It's gonna be bad luck," as soon as she read that the boy was going to be taken to the store by his big brother. Her predictions about the nature of the trouble, or "bad luck," became more specific as she read along; and in this instance, they were eventually confirmed. Needless to say, faulty predictions by the children called for backtracking and adjustments.

Some of the most unusual instances of bypassing the conventional structure of classroom materials and activities come from Debbie's record. Especially conspicuous was her tendency to transform assignments involving sequence cards. Rather than putting the cards in their more obvious sequential order and then telling a story to match the sequence, she often seemed to ignore the intended structure of the cards altogether. The first instance of her scrambled sequences and stories occurred in October of first grade. She was working with four pictures representing a Halloween theme that were supposed to be ordered in the following way:

Picture 1: A pumpkin in a field.
Picture 2: A pumpkin in the market.
Picture 3: A half-carved pumpkin.
Picture 4: A full carved pumpkin sitting in a window.

Debbie interchanged the third and fourth cards of the intended order and then dictated the story below.

One time a pumpkin grew in a window. One time it fell out. It rolled down the hill. The mother pumpkin was crying. The father pumpkin was mad. The baby was hungry. The father said, "Let's buy the baby some paint so she should stop crying.'' Then the baby stopped crying cause her brother came back and the mother made a pumpkin for dinner. He took pictures, cut it up, and made a drawing of this.

Debbie's story about the pumpkin family relates back to the sequence cards only in the last sentence. It seems as if someone in the family, presumably the brother, drew and/or cut up pictures to make the set of sequence cards. If this interpretation is essentially correct, then Debbie used an interesting literary device (a sophisticated one by adult standards) to deal with the ultimate demands of the situation. But however one interprets the rather strange ending of her story, Debbie's failure to follow the expected ordinal logic of the task is obvious.

Since Debbie's manner of work was generally ''unfocused'' and ''unbounded,'' the teacher was not sure how she perceived most tasks or if she really understood their requirements. The teacher had had Debbie as a student in kindergarten; and, on the basis of that experience, had recommended she be retained on the school's official records as a kindergartner. In part, the teacher's reasoning in making such a recommendation was to allow Debbie time to mature. As the year progressed, Debbie did become somewhat more focused in her work habits and better able to deal with conventional requirements in conventional ways. But it also became clear that her own style of logic was a relatively enduring characteristic, and that she could learn the academic essentials with it. By the end of the year, she was reclassified and promoted on to second grade with her classmates.

Although Debbie's many stories lacked coherent organization by conventional standards, they were not unstructured as far as she was concerned. She remembered them almost perfectly. If the teacher or aide missed writing down a part of her dictation, Debbie always pointed out the omission when the story was read back. Like Jenny, she also knew what her writing said even when others could not read it. Her writing was sometimes difficult to follow because she typically wrote in columns starting down the middle of the page and then moving to a column at the right or left. Once, when copying from a book, she got several words out of order. She copied as follows:

> If you are a
> crocodile you will
> flot alon(g) with
> the water the other
> But if your way
> a log you will go

When she was finished, she read her writing aloud in the following way (as the sentences actually appear in the book from which she had copied them):

> If you are a crocodile,
> you will float along with the water.

> But if you're a log,
> you will go the other way.

Despite the unorthodox organization of Debbie's writing, it was her writing more than anything else that first signaled one of the ways in which she apparently structured her thought. For a child her age, Debbie had an unusual ability to engage in genuine dialogue with others, and her dictated stories frequently contained bits of dialogue. As she began to rely less on dictation and wrote more on her own in the spring of first grade, the dialogue mode intensified. Virtually all of her diary entries contain at least some dialogue, and many are extended dialogues that continue over several days. The back and forth of dialogue, whether in conversation with others or oneself, is an effective means by which people often clarify and structure their thoughts. It is also worth noting that dialogue usually proceeds and diverges along many fronts, in parallel fashion, rather than progressing in an unbroken line of thought from one point to the next.

In contrast to the group of children just discussed, other children rarely deviated from the requirements implied or imposed by structured tasks and materials. They usually followed directions in proper sequence and tackled workbook problems in the order designated. They typically progressed page by page through books at free reading time, whether they were actually reading text or looking at pictures. Often, teachers would remark on the persistence of these children in working their way to the bitter end of a task, even when it was not necessary to do so. The children who most clearly represent these tendencies to accept and follow linear structure are Louis, Rita, Colin, Susan, and Dana.

Since standardized tests usually require a linear style of working and thinking, this group of children had something of a head start in understanding how to take tests. Louis's teacher commented on the benefits of this kind of know-how after she had observed Louis taking the standardized test given to all first-graders in the school.

> The test is a good indicator of the children's ability to tune in to what the nature of the task is—in what order to read and how to follow along. They can get a lot of it right, even if they can't read the actual words, if they have those orienting skills. Louis does have them. [February, 1st grade]

Attention to the ordering of details in books and stories also indicated a linear sequencing style. It was not so much a matter that children either could or couldn't retell a story in correct sequence when asked to do so, for most children could satisfy such a request reasonably well. The more significant forms of evidence were spontaneous comments that signaled a child's attention to sequential detail and/or the manner in which he or she chose to summarize a story. Rita's remark to her teacher while reading *Monster Looks for a Friend* illustrates the kind of spontaneous comment we mean. She pointed out a discrepancy between the sentence she was reading, which said Monster "goes out of the house,'' and a picture at the beginning of the book that depicts Monster standing outside his house. She wondered aloud how in the world Monster got back inside when he was already outside before.

For his last oral reading sample of the study, Dana read a long story about a penguin named Willie who left the South Pole to live in the city. When the teacher asked Dana to recount the story without looking back at the book, he could have responded with a capsule summary. In fact, Dana's general tendency toward sparse communication would lead one to predict that he might summarize only the gist of the story. Instead, however, he told why Willie left the South Pole (because he wanted ''to be different'') and then briefly related the details of the penguin's city adventures in their proper sequence—''He buys a necktie, and a pair of shoes, an' a umbrella, an' a hat''

The most remarkable recounting of a story on record occurred in connection with one of Colin's oral readings, taped in January of second grade. If there was a child in the study who was less talkative than Dana, it was Colin. As an introduction to Colin's reading (of a book called *Henry Huggins*), his teacher asked him a few general questions about the book. Colin's general taciturn nature comes through clearly in his response to these more ''chatty'' kinds of questions. When the teacher then asked hom to ''tell a little bit'' about what had happened, however, Colin launched into a minutely detailed account. He seemed to understand the story perfectly well, yet the transcript of his response shows why the teacher sometimes wondered if he missed the forest for the trees. Although the transcription is long, we have reproduced it in its entirety below.

> Teacher: What's the name of this book?
> Colin: *Henry Huggins*
> Teacher: How did you get this book?
> Colin: (sigh)
> Teacher: Where did you get this book?
> Colin: I got it uhh. . .
> Teacher: Where? Where did you get it?
> Colin: Off the shelf . . . in the library.
> Teacher: Did you pick it yourself?
> Colin: Yes.
> Teacher: Have you ever read it before?
> Colin: No.
> Teacher: You just started reading it, didn't you? What page are you up to?
> Colin: Nineteen.
> Teacher: Page nineteen. Do you like it?
> Colin: Yes.
> Teacher: Want to tell me a little bit about it?
> Colin: Ummm. A little boy named Henry had hurried home from school and had three nickels 'n a dime. And then he went to a store and bought an ice-cream cone with one of his nickels.

And then when he went out the door of the store he saw a dog at the corner by the street. Then he went down there to see the dog. Then . . . And then the dog started to wiggle his tail and then he said, "You're not going to get none of my ice cream cone. And then the dog started to bark and then Henry said—

Teacher: You don't have to remember every single thing that people said or did, you can skip parts of it. What did he finally do with the dog?

Colin: Ummm. Tried to take him home on the bus. And then the bus driver said, "You can't take the dog home on the bus." And then he said, "Why?"

"You gotta have him in a box."

And then Henry went to the store and asked the man for a box. And then the man said, "A cardboard box?"

And Henry said, "Yes."

And then the man looked at the dog (pauses).

Teacher: Did he get the dog home?

Colin: No.

Teacher: Why not?

Colin: Because when he tried to get on the bus, the bus driver said he meant a box with holes in it so the dog could breathe and with string tied around.

Teacher: So—did the dog ever get home?

Colin: Yeah, because when Henry had went back to the store to get some string and to get some holes in the box, he had got on the bus when it started to rain. And then when he had took the dime out of his pocket and put it in the slot, he had went to the back of the bus and sat down. And then when the bus had stopped a lady with a bag of apples and a man with a garden hose had fell onto the floor of the bus. And then the bus driver had looked in back and had told Henry to get him off the bus and his dog. And. . .

And then a man that was sitting beside Henry said, "You can't put that boy and that dog off of the bus in the rain."

So a police car came to the bus and he said, "Is there a boy named Henry Huggins here?"

And then Henry said, "Yes."

And then he got into the police car and said, "Are—am I going to get arrest?"

And then the driver of the police car asked his partner and then his partner said, "He's already late for dinner."

And then they had took him home and his mother and father was waiting on the porch and his neighbors was looking out the window.

Teacher: What do you think his parents thought when they saw him coing in a police car?

Colin: He was going to go to jail.

The above account of *Henry Huggins,* which is accurate in its ordering of detail as far as it goes, took Colin only through a few of the 18 pages he had read. At this point, however, the teacher understandably asked that he start reading on page 19, which he proceeded to do rapidly and with very few errors.

THE RELEVANCE OF STYLES IN LEARNING HOW TO READ

As mentioned at the outset of this chapter, the four styles discussed above tended to be pronounced in the records of approximately half the children in the study. And where they were pronounced, they were interrelated. Evidence of parallel sequencing of thought processes was associated with broad attention deployment and an integrative perspective, with a mobile and fluid manner of work, and with the expression of imaginative and divergent meanings. Evidence of linear sequencing was associated with narrowed attention deployment and an analytic perspective, with a contained and methodical manner of work, and with the expression of realistic and convergent meanings. A capsule summary of the styles, of the preferences defining each style cluster, and of the children who most consistently exhibited the preferences appear in Table 8.1.

A clear manifestation of each style cluster could be seen in qualitative differences between children's preferred approach to reading. By "preferred approach," we mean the tendency to uphold either the momentum or accuracy requirement of reading skill when a child could not orchestrate knowledge profi-

TABLE 8.1
A Summary of Style Clusters

	Preferences	
Style	Cluster A	Cluster B
Preferred Expressions of Meaning	Imaginative & Divergent	Realistic & Convergent
Manner of Work	Mobile & Fluid	Contained & Methodical
Attentional Scope and Emphasis	Broad & Integrative	Narrowed & Analytic
Sequencing of Thought Processes	Parallel Sequencing	Linear Sequencing
Children most representative of each style cluster	Carrie Debbie Jack Jenny Tim	Colin Dana Louis Rita Susan

ciently enough to honor both requirements (see Chapter 7). Not surprisingly, children with strong Cluster A preferences chose most consistently in favor of upholding momentum, whereas children with strong Cluster B preferences chose in favor of upholding accuracy.

The remainder of the chapter expands and elaborates on this important finding of the study. Although the quantitative data presented in Chapter 7 show clear differences between the two groups of children, our focus here is on qualitative contrasts in the children's style and priorities. These qualitative differences were captured primarily in descriptive analyses of the children's oral reading behaviors, and to a lesser extent in the teacher interviews and outside observers' accounts.

The discussion begins with a summary of the evidence and of our theoretical formulations concerning stylistic variation in the children's initial approach to reading. Illustrative documentation is then presented from the records of the 10 children considered most representative of the two style clusters. To bolster our interpretation of *stylistic* differences in reading (as opposed to differences in knowledge or ability), we next examine relationships between children's preferred approach to reading, evidence that they possessed knowledge relevant to their nonpreferred approach, and their overall reading progress by the end of the documentation period. We conclude with some further theoretical speculation about the significance of styles and their implications for classroom practice.

Overview and Theoretical Conception of the Children's Preferred Approach to Reading

Children who displayed Cluster A preferences tended to put their primary energies to the task of upholding momentum in reading. They might skip over words or phrases and move right on, or else skip ahead and then circle back to an unknown word. Some invented portions of the text. As the children progressed in reading skill, tendencies to omit and/or invent portions of text generally gave way to the strategy of approximating a troublesome word or slurring over it. Every child in the group freely offered word substitutions based on memory of the story line, picture clues, partial word analysis, grammatical knowledge, background knowledge, or some combination of these resources. The majority of children gave indication in one form or another that they took in relatively broad spans of print. The most common indication was a tendency to repeat "easy" words or phrases that occurred two or three (or more) words before a segment of text that proved to be genuinely difficult. Since the repetitions involved no corrective attempt (the word or phrase had been read correctly and smoothly on first encounter), there appeared to be an effort on the child's part to gain time before hitting the real trouble spot. Each one of the tactics just described enabled a child to say something when faced with uncertainty and thus to keep the reading performance moving.

The corrective adjustments in reading made by Cluster A children were predominantly of the after-the-fact variety. Sometimes they erred with great confidence and then suddenly seemed to realize the word they had said was wrong. An ensuing corrective attempt in this case was often rendered with some sense of surprise or apologetic humor—a quality we characterized previously as an "oops" correction. At other times, the children's substitutions and subsequent corrective attempts were offered almost in the same breath, as if they were ticking off likely possibilities in a search for the correct identification of the word in question. But the defining characteristic of this group (as compared with "Cluster B") was the tendency to move on and make no corrective attempt at all.

Children who displayed Cluster B preferences gave top priority to accuracy in their early reading. They usually attended to every word on a page and seemed determined to get each one correctly. They rarely showed signs of reading ahead. If they didn't know a word, they tended to wait or ask for help, to remain silent while they tried to figure it out for themselves, or to engage in a head-on struggle of phonic analysis. Pauses and/or decoding attempts lasting as long as 30 to 60 seconds are common in the records of several children. Despite such prolonged interruptions of their reading pace, some children retained the meaning of what they had read perfectly well. The children did not by-pass words or offer guesses spontaneously, nor would many of them skip or guess even with considerable urging from the teacher ("It's like pulling teeth"). This tendency to balk at adult requests to guess extended to all forms of proffered support, whether the suggested grounds for making a guess were context clues, letter-sound clues, or a supplied rhyming word. The whole thrust of the Cluster B approach was to maintain accuracy and thus to make before-the-fact corrective adjustments. Whatever strategy the children used (pausing to figure out a word, asking for help, or phonic analysis), they recognized a problem and sought a remedy *before* committing themselves to reading the problematic word.

These portrayals of the two stylistic approaches to reading highlight the most typical ways in which the children coped with words or phrases they couldn't negotiate proficiently. We stress the typicalness of the behavior to reemphasize the fact that styles denote preferred ways of doing things rather than an ability or inability to do something. We stress the coping nature of the behavior to emphasize that the children knew a problem existed. When their reading was moving along smoothly, without much apparent effort, the children were more likely to evidence hints of both approaches. Cluster A children might pause briefly to voice an initial consonant, and Cluster B children might skip an inconsequential word. They hardly seemed aware of such minor deviations in the midst of an otherwise proficient performance. The coding of Unmodified/Modified deviations presented in Chapter 7 takes into account all deviations from text except the repetition of words read correctly and fluently on first encounter (a behavior most strongly associated with the approach of Cluster A children). Because the coding ignores such repetitions and because it confounds minor deviations with obvious coping strategies, results of the coding analysis (though statistically significant) somewhat underplay the differences children exhibited when they knew they were facing a problem. Here, our discussion of the two groups focuses primarily on their problem-solving behavior, especially during the early stages of learning how to read.

Theoretical Discussion.   Phenomena that appear particularly obstinate often claim quick attention in research, and the obstinacy that first caught our eye was a characteristic of the Cluster B approach. We were intrigued by the stubborn refusal of some children to guess at words, even with urging and clues from the teacher, and even though the word seemed well within their ability to figure out. Our initial reaction in the pilot study was to interpret such reluctance as somehow associated with risk taking. As is true of many initial reactions, however, the risk-taking hypothesis soon proved inadequate. Dana, for instance, was not reluctant to state the meaning of what he had read when the teacher asked questions, to recount the details of what he had read when a summary would have sufficed, or to commit himself to a detailed representation of reality in his drawings and other work. Neither were other children reluctant to do these things. Although fear of risking failure may have prompted some of the more cautious approach of Cluster B children, the avoidance of risk per se was certainly not a pervasive characteristic of their behavior.

A more powerful explanation of refusing to guess at words is found in the children's generalized preference for realistic meanings and their tendency to converge on a single, "best" interpretation of reality (the *realistic and convergent* pole of the style we have called *Preferred Expressions of Meanings*). If one views written words more or less as literal objects, each having a singular pronunciation and meaning, then the act of reading becomes something of an either/or proposition. Either you know the words or you don't. And if you don't know a particular word, anything less than the accurate rendition may seem superfluous. There is, of course, the possibility of arriving at a correct rendition through phonic analysis, and some Cluster B children engaged in this strategy frequently. But as discussed in Chapter 6, comparatively few children were skillful in blending phonetic segments even though they could sound out component segments of a word quite well. Dana was a case in point. And in retrospect, it was Dana's teacher who first suggested a stylistic interpretation of the reluctance to guess when she gave the following report:

> Dana can use a sounding out strategy in trying to identify words, but often he simply stops dead when he comes to a word he doesn't know, and you have to press him to sound it out. Sometimes I press him, but it usually goes nowhere and he'll just say, "I don't know." So usually I tell him right away, because I know it won't go anywhere. . . I really think it's a practical thing with him. If he doesn't know, he really doesn't know—and I might as well tell him.

The general proclivity for realism expressed by Cluster B children thus seemed to extend to their view of written language. Although they would occasionally guess at words in their early reading, their whole demeanor suggested dissatisfaction and even discomfort with such an approach. At the other extreme, children who exhibited imaginative and divergent preferences appeared to regard text more as guidelines than prescriptions for the construction of meaning. Though necessary in pointing the way, guidelines leave room for deviation. And Cluster A children seemed perfectly comfortable in straying from a literal translation of each and every word. On the face of it, one might expect that the *Preferred Expressions of Meaning* style would have been manifest in the kinds of books the children chose to read (i.e., nonfiction versus fiction). That did not happen. As the children became more proficient readers and could choose from a wider range of books, their choices often reflected interests evident in other activities (space, animals, sports, fairy tales, adventure, people, humor, rhythm and rhyme, and so on). But their choices also reflected interests and curiosity not previously noted, and they typically included a sampling of both nonfiction and fiction (ranging from biographies, information books, how-to books, and books depicting different times and cultures in the nonfiction category to prose, poetry, fables, and myths in the fiction category). In summary, the children's different styles of expressing meaning were evident in contrasting views of the constraints imposed by written language, not contrasting interests in particular types of books.

The behavior of Cluster B children not only captured our first theoretical attention, it also posed an initial theoretical puzzle. How could children construct *any* coherent meaning from text when they interrupted their reading so frequently and for such prolonged periods (20, 30, even 60 seconds)? The role of short-term memory is central to many models and theories of the reading process, and the evidence concerning this functional characteristic can scarcely be ignored. In brief, short-term memory acts as a receiving station for the brain, processing incoming information into meaningful units and passing them on to long-term memory for storage and future retrieval. Moreover, it does this work in the span of a few seconds. From a theoretical standpoint, the exceedingly slow pace Cluster B children evidenced in many readings should have disrupted information processing to the extent that little if any meaning could be constructed from the text. Some children did lose meaning on occasion. But it was clear in several instances that the children indeed understood what they had read, as evidenced by their ability to discuss the passage and answer questions.

We could infer only one explanation of such behavior from the research literature, and that was the strategy of rehearsal. People can beat the limits of short-term memory for a little while by continually rehearsing information, much in the way a person repeats an unfamiliar phone number on the way to the telephone or to a place where the information can be written down. (Retention is further facilitated by chunking the digits into some kind of rhythmic sequence.) Remembering telephone numbers is one thing, however; constructing meaning from text is quite another. It seemed unlikely that children could keep mentally rehearsing words already read while at the same time struggling to identify a new word, and it seemed even more unlikely that they could sustain frequent interruptions using such a strategy. The puzzle was tabled for many months.

The notion of a rehearsal strategy was revived after the data for individual children were finally integrated and comparisons across children revealed a picture of contrasting styles. The children who paused most often in reading also tended to work in a step-by-step, methodical manner. More importantly, they seemed to organize their thinking in a linear fashion, linking one detail or inference with the next so as to cumulate meaning each step of the way. If a person constructs meaning in this kind of incremental manner, then each individual step assumes importance and should be construed as meaningful. And if this is true, it is perhaps not so difficult to remember and repeat the steps of the sequence, arriving at a similar conceptual end each time. We think the Cluster B children retained meaning as well as they did because they were able to cycle back through a single chain of ordered relationships. Had these children skipped steps (words or phrases) in the process, they probably could not have retained meaning so well, nor would skipping have allowed them to build meaning cumulatively in the first place. Certainly the children's actions gave every indication that skipping was not a sensible strategy from their viewpoint.

We are aware of no experimental data that support our hypothesis, but all the available study data suggest its credibility. The children's records include numerous instances of their ability to reconstruct the successive details of events. Susan's early reading, for example, was primarily a recital of memorized text. Louis could remember exactly where or how he had come across a particular word before. And much of the documentation for linear sequencing provided earlier in this chapter concerns the children's ordering of details in commenting on books or in recounting the plot of a story (see especially Colin's retelling of *Henry Huggins,* pp. 171–172).

The process of constructing meaning incrementally implies that component steps in the process must be differentiated and each one attended to. The narrowed and analytic attention manifest by Cluster B children was ideally suited to such a task. Initially at least, the children focused on word units or segments of words and gave virtually no indication of reading ahead in text. The implicit logic of this thinking style would seem to demand narrowed and analytic attention if meaning is to be constructed at all. For that matter, a methodical approach to work and the tendency to make singular interpretations of events may also be construed as logical correlates of linear sequencing. Whether one of these styles "causes" or developmentally precedes another, or whether all of them stem from some other more pervasive style characteristic, is impossible to say on the basis of present knowledge. What we do claim is that these styles influenced the way in which Cluster B children perceived written language and the way they conceived and went about the task of learning to read.

Since the two style clusters represent contrasting preferences and tendencies, our conception of the one approach to reading necessarily mirrors our conception of the other. A person who typically juggles ideas and entertains several interpretations in the process of constructing meaning (a *parallel* style of sequencing thought) must be able to see what possibilities exist. Cognitively speaking, such a person needs all the relevant information he or she can get. The tendency of Cluster A children to uphold momentum in their early reading was probably not just a by-product of their general manner of work, but a facilitating strategy that allowed them to sample as much information as possible from text. Both the attentional and cognitive styles that marked this group's classroom functioning were geared to searching out multiple information cues and weaving them into a meaningful pattern. Reading entails the skill of orchestration, and these children came to reading with orchestrating skill as one of their strong suits. It seemed as if they led from their strength, using whatever knowledge resources were at their command (background knowledge, grammatical knowledge, picture cues, and so on).

As our conception suggests, we believe the children's preferred approach to reading was commensurate with their preferred approach to virtually everything else in the classroom. They went about this new learning task in the way that made the most sense to them, each of the two groups taking the approach that resulted in the clearest meaning. Although they chose to uphold opposing requirements of the skill of reading (momentum versus accuracy), both groups of children were striving to construct meaning from text.

A Redress of Balance to Varying Degrees.   Some redress of balance in these initial approaches to text was necessary in order to progress beyond the entry point of formal reading, and such shifts occurred as the children became more proficient readers. Those who initially stopped and balked at guessing became less intent on figuring out every individual word and would sometimes skip or approximate text in the interest of moving on. Similarly, children who were initially intent on upholding momentum became more attentive to the accountability concerns of word accuracy. When confronted with unfamiliar and challenging text later on, however, most children returned to their initial preference. In this respect, their behavior was reminiscent of stylistic differences in adult approaches to difficult text. Some adults read such text quickly, extracting what meaning they can, and then go back as many times as necessary to fill in the details. Others take a much slower initial pace, attempting to construct (and often arguing with) the author's meaning at every step of the way. We suspect that the "reverting behavior" observed in many children portends their future strategies of dealing with difficult material.

Of the children whose reading histories are discussed below, Jenny showed the quickest and most pronounced redress of balance. She went from quasi reading in the fall, to a strategy of stabbing at words and offering numerous substitutions when she began real reading (January), to a preoccupation with word accuracy for the remainder of first grade. Jenny also exhibited a quick return to her original approach of upholding momentum once she had gained reasonable proficiency in reading. Although other children also evidenced distinct turnabouts in their approach to reading, some displayed only a minimal redress of balance. This was especially true of Louis, Colin, and Tim. For these children, initial approaches to reading became less pronounced but nonetheless remained dominant throughout the period of learning covered by the study.

Documentation from the Children's Reading Records

The following illustrative data are taken from the reading records of children judged to be most representative of the two style clusters.

Upholding Momentum: The Approach of Cluster A.   The earliest version of this approach took the form of prereaders engaging in quasi reading. By this we mean "reading" books from some combination of memory, invention, and fragmentary knowledge. Both Jenny and Carrie persisted in such reading for a long period of time, Jenny throughout the fall of first grade, and Carrie throughout the winter and spring of kindergarten. Both girls offered their renditions in the spirit of real reading, posturing the actions of a reader, reading in a book-like voice, and even (in Jenny's case) insisting to the teacher that the performance was real. Where the two children differed was in the nature of their respective transitions to real reading. For Jenny, the transition was sharp. In Carrie's case, one would be hard pressed to say where quasi reading left off and actual reading began.

Jenny's first oral reading sample (In October of first grade) documents one of her impromptu quasi readings to the teacher during the afternoon choice period. She is reading a rhythmic book that keeps repeating the refrain, *"ears, ears, ears."* Despite a great deal of background noise and several interruptions from other children asking the teacher questions, Jenny maintains a steady pace, distinctly enunciating each word. The sound of her voice would convince almost anyone that she was really reading, but she was not. She was saying some of the words printed on the particular page she had turned to, but she was also inventing words and repeating phrases that appear elsewhere in the book. As the noise level increases on the tape and various children interrupt, Jenny does not halt her reading. She maintains her measured pace and simply reads louder and more emphatically—*"EARS . . . EARS . . . EARS!"*

In January, Jenny suddenly learned the first six word lists and accompanying stories in the beginning book of the SRA linguistic series (*A Pig Can Jig*), and she never looked back at quasi reading. Her second oral reading sample (taped in late January) reveals her preference for maintaining momentum in a conventional storybook and shows how she also tries to sustain this approach in the linguistic reader. The conventional text is a book from the *Breakthrough* series entitled *Dressing Up*. Although she doesn't know several words in this text, she guesses without hesitation. Her guesses are based either on a partial analysis of the graphic cues (e.g., *cap* for *cup, play* for *party*) or on picture clues that lead her far afield from the actual text word (e.g., *grandmother* for *teachers, desk* for *chair, nurses* for *doctors, wedding* for *bride*). Her steady march through the text in this manner is interrupted on many occasions, but it is interrupted by the teacher, who either corrects Jenny's substitution by quickly providing the right word or else tries to direct her attention back to the error and help her figure it out. Occasionally, Jenny herself attempts a self-correction (*plays,* then *plats* for *puts*). Only twice, however, does Jenny spontaneously halt her pace and try to sound out a word before offering a substitution.

Jenny also stops but twice (to sound out) in reading for selections from the linguistic text. These are pages she has practiced several times, and her reading is accurate for the most part. But the fifth selection chosen by the teacher presents more of a challenge, for it is one Jenny has not practiced. Although she stops to sound out some words, her dominant strategy is to substitute and then attempt after-the-fact corrections. She reads at her typical deliberate pace and says a word on every beat. If the word is incorrect, however, she offers rapid-fire corrections, in a tone conveying urgency, until she either hits on the right word or the teacher provides it for her. Then she continues on at the same pace. The following three lines are illustrative.

Text	*Jenny*
Tim can dig.	Tim can bag/dig.
Tim can dig a pit.	Tim can dig a pig/pit.
Can Tim dig a big pit?	Can Tim dig a pit/dig/big pit?

The remainder of Jenny's oral reading samples in first grade reveal her increasing concern with word accuracy, to the point where she is self-correcting or attempting to self-correct virtually every mistake she makes. She also stops more often in anticipation of a difficult word, either sounding it out or trying to figure it out in her head. As Jenny becomes more preoccupied with accuracy, her teacher also notes that she often loses the overall meaning of what she is reading. When Jenny reaches a level of reasonable proficiency, however, her reading takes on many aspects of her original approach. She reads more rapidly than she did as a beginner, and she rarely halts to self-correct or to decode a word. In fact, she doesn't seem to hear minor mistakes in the way she once did. In one of her later reading samples, for instance, she says "*ust*" for the text word *used,* and then indicates puzzlement when the teacher implies something was wrong with the way she read the sentence. By the middle of second grade, her main strategy for dealing with unusually difficult words (e.g., *sarsaparilla*) is simply to slur over them.

In Carrie's record, quasi reading and real reading intermingle in virtually all of her kindergarten efforts to negotiate text. Her first tape-recorded reading sample illustrates this mixture well. She read *In the Village,* one of her favorite books that had been read to her often. She frequently pointed to the words as she went along and read many of them accurately. But she also inserted phrases and in other ways changed the text according to her memory of the story line. For

Carrie, the overriding purpose of reading was to tell a story; and that is precisely what she managed to do, no matter what. The teacher summarized Carrie's early reading in the following way: "If she doesn't know the words, she will make them up. Nothing gets in the way."

Unlike Jenny, Carrie's reading history contains no dramatic points of transition. Her inventions simply diminish to the point where there is no doubt that she is really reading. Unlike Jenny, too, Carrie never attended to accuracy at the expense of meaning. Although her reading became more and more accurate, her prime concern was always for keeping the story line moving. When she did stop her momentum, it was not usually to struggle over a particular word but to reflect on the story, much in the way she verbalized her thought about the bear walking off the blackboard in *Blackboard Bear*. In this respect, Carrie's oral reading never changed. Her last tape of the study (in May of first grade) shows no let-up in the tendencies to relate her own experience to stories, to embellish them, and to speculate about them. This last tape-recorded reading is a fairy tale about three brothers whose wishes are granted by an old woman. One brother's wish is for a river to be turned into wine, and this stimulates a series of comments from Carrie about the wine at church and about being baptized. The second brother in the story sees a flock of doves and wishes that they could be changed into cows. When the old woman produces this magical transformation, Carrie observes that the picture still shows a few remaining doves. She comments about this observation to the teacher and then proceeds to embellish the story—from the doves' perspective!

> You know what? She missed some doves. [That's right, she missed two doves.] Three doves, three doves! Probably they were hiding behind this rock and they saw half of their family changed into cows. They came out of the rock and they said, "OH, I'M OUT OF MY MIND!"

Jenny and Carrie sustained momentum in their early quasi-reading efforts mainly by relying on picture clues and their memory of the story. Debbie also relied on memory to some extent, but in a different manner from either Jenny or Carrie. The differences was the energy she expended. For a long time, Debbie seemed content to "tell a story" and did not go out of her way to posture reading by concentrating on the text or pointing to words. Although she turned pages, her storytelling was sometimes not synchronized with either the text or the pictures. Even after she began to read in February of first grade (her second year of being officially classified as a kindergartner), she continued to "tell a book" on occasion, apparently reserving this strategy for texts she judged too difficult to read.

As Debbie actually began to negotiate text, however, she used several tactics to maintain momentum. She omitted, she repeated, she substituted, she relied on her intuitive sense of rhythm, and she refused to fuss or worry much about mistakes. The overall flavor of these tactics comes through in the following excerpts from descriptive analyses of her performance on the standard oral readings.

> *Big Dog, Little Dog.* She seems to react to the whole context, takes in whole experience, not just mechanical reading. . . . She picked up on the interviewer's suggestion that she skip the word she could not read. . . . She had several ways of dealing with words she didn't know, and in each case was able to go on. There is a forward pull to her reading, she does not let getting stuck on a word hold her up. . . . She reads with good intonation, phrasing correctly even when she comes to words she does not read well. . . . There were instances when she tried hard to get a word, other times did not. She may have tried when she "almost knew." . . . When a word was completely unfamiliar, she skipped, did not work on it. Debbie's general mood in reading seems happy, comfortable, eager. She wanted to read the whole book, not to stop when the interviewer gave her the chance.

> *Ben Bug.* Starts out omitting words, then going back and filling them in—e.g., "Ben is a bug . . . Ben is a big bug." Seems to take different approach to this text than last by going back to fill in words. . . . Attacks with a lot of confidence. . . . Relaxed about trying out, experimenting. Does not get upset when she gets it wrong, happy when she is even "close." . . . Does not make ordeal out of reading.

> *Blackboard Bear.* Read this story with most expression of all the selections, sentences articulated, rising and falling inflection. Teacher pointed out that this story resembles her own diary writing, which often contains dialogue, short back-and-forth interchanges. . . . Clearly invested in meaning of story, particularly the dialogue. Uses the pictures to enrich story.

In many of her oral reading tapes, Debbie frequently repeats words or phrases that she has already negotiated correctly. Since many of these repetitions precede a portion of text that is difficult for her, they suggest she is scanning ahead. But the clearest evidence of scanning ahead in text comes from Debbie's last reading sample of the study, taped in January of second grade. The initial selection on the tape is *Little Red Riding Hood.* Although the text itself is easy for Debbie, some of the embedded clauses are tricky to read with appropriate expression, and the first such clause trips up her rhythm. After that, however, she is able to anticipate the embedded clauses and to adjust her rhythm accordingly. (See page 109.)

The second selection on the tape, *A Child's Swiss Family Robinson,* is unfamiliar (it was selected by the teacher) and much more conceptually difficult for her. Debbie reads most of the words correctly, making only a few mispronunciations, but she had trouble understanding what the story is about, and her reading is more tentative. The portion of the text she read is shown below.

> For many days, we had been tempest tossed. The raging storm increased in fury until, on the seventh day, all hope was lost.

> Our ship, which was sailing from Switzerland to Philadelphia, was driven completely off course. Neither the captain nor any of the crew had the slightest idea as to our whereabouts.
>
> I stood on deck with my good wife, Elizabeth, and our four sons, fifteen-year-old Fritz, thirteen-year-old Ernest, twelve-year-old Jack, and eight-year-old Franz. Leaks had sprung all over the ship. We watched in great dismay, as the water rushed in over the deck.

The one word in this entire passage that Debbie read with great expression and enthusiasm (as if she had seen an oasis in a desert) was a word she knew well: *Philadelphia*. She must have spotted this word right away, for she started to say it at the beginning of the third sentence:

> Phila . . . Our ship, which was sailing from Switzerland to PHILADELPHIA(!!), was driven completely off course.

Jack's record contains the most conspicuous instances of skipping and reading ahead to the end of a sentence to try to figure out words. The following two excerpts from observations of his early reading suggest that he learned how to employ the technique to good advantage.

> —(Jack is reading a story called *The Fox and His Bag*.) He reads until he comes to a word he doesn't know. Then he . . . reads the whole sentence from start to end, as if to establish a clear context, and tries to sound out the unknown word when he gets to it. He repeats through the whole process several times and finally, still not having figured out the word, moves on to the rest of the story. [January, 1st grade]

> —He read up to the word he didn't know, jumped over the word and read the rest of the sentence, then went back again and jumped over again. He seemed to be waiting for his brain to fill in the word, and most of the time he got it that way. It was very effective. He knew all the comprehension questions. [March, 1st grade]

Another strategy for maintaining momentum appears in the last half of Jack's record, and this tactic allows him to continue forward motion without circling back to fill in gaps. He simply approximates difficult words and moves on. A sample of these word approximations was illustrated previously (p. 105): *maniply* for *manipulate, deoperate* for *decorate, easable* for *essential*.

Tim's record contains some of the most unusual evidence of attention to perceptual units broader than a single word. One indication is the fact that he occasionally juxtaposed words. This tendency is captured on two oral reading tapes as follows:

Text	*Tim*
you look just like . . .	you just look like . . .
suit of shiny armor . . .	suit of armor shiny . . .

Another indication of broad attention deployment is a type of error that occurred very infrequently in the study—reading two words as one word. The first instance of Tim's compressing two words into one occurs in his initial tape-recorded reading sample of the study (December of 1st grade). The second instance occurs 18 months later in his final oral reading sample (June of 2nd grade). On the initial tape, Tim reads a relatively simple book (*Hand, Hand, Fingers, Thumb*) at a steady pace and with very few errors through the first several pages. The pages at the end of the book are ones he had not practiced, however, and they are tougher sledding for him. One of these pages contains four lines, each beginning with the phrase, "Many more." The heroes of the story are a band of monkeys, and Tim substitutes the word *monkeys* (for the phrase *Many more*) at the beginning of each sentence. On his final tape, he reads very rapidly from an information book about prehistoric cavemen that he had chosen to study during the year. As Tim swiftly negotiates this text, he again commits an error of compressing two words into one.

> Text: Now many scientists all over Europe. . .
> Tim: Memory scientists all over Europe. . .

Tim's strategies of skipping and approximating words to sustain momentum are amply illustrated in Chapter 13. What remains to be said here is that Tim, more than any child we have discussed thus far, was to some extent a victim of his own stylistic tendencies. That is, he seemed paralyzed when asked to process words by sounding out component segments and then blending them. When he tried, he usually came out with a whole word or else reversed sound sequences. Ultimately, he would give up.

Upholding Accuracy: The Approach of Cluster B.   The outstanding characteristic of Cluster B children was their tendency to stop at every unknown word and attempt to figure it out or to seek help elsewhere. It never seemed to occur to these children that they could omit anything in their early reading attempts. They appeared to construct meaning in incremental steps and to retain what they had read while struggling with new words. This capacity to retain meaning despite frequent and extended pauses was first evident in the pilot study in Dana's initial oral reading tape (January, 1st grade). All the selections on this tape are from his beginning instructional text (*A Pig Can Jig*). The incident in question occurred during his reading of the last story, which is reproduced below.

The Nap
Nan ran to a mat.
Nan had a nap.
Dan ran to Nan.
Dan had a bat.

> Tap! Tap! Tap!
> Dan can tap the bat.
>   Nan sat.
> Nan ran at Dan.
> Dan ran.

Dana read this story word-by word, stopping for long periods to wait for help. Not counting his reading of the title, it took him a total of 2 minutes and 32 seconds to finish. According to information-processing theory, it would be virtually impossible to read that slowly and maintain the sense of the story. And according to most standards, there is scant "meaning" in the story to begin with. Nevertheless, the teacher asked a comprehension question at the end of the reading: *"Why do you think Nan ran at Dan?"* (We have asked numerous adults this same question, and most have not come up with an answer.) Not only did Dana answer the question correctly, he answered it instantaneously.

> Teacher: Why do you think Nan ran at Dan?
> Dana: 'Cause he woke her up.

Although this is the most extreme incident of its kind in Dana's first-grade reading tapes, it is by no means the only incident. He continues to read slowly and to pause frequently, yet he is able to answer any question the teacher puts to him, even about stories that he has just read for the first time. The teacher underscores this characteristic in her comments about Dana at the end of his first-grade year:

> He definitely expects meaning in what he reads . . . always knows the questions I ask him about a story.

Colin became a proficient reader (upholding both accuracy and momentum) by the early spring of his first-grade year. But his preferences are clear in the October and January samples of his oral reading. He was just beginning to read his instructional phonic text in October, and one taped selection is from this book. The other selection is a trade book (*Hot Rods*), which he cannot read. The January tape finds him struggling with a trade book entitled *Go Dog Go*. The following excerpts from descriptive analyses of these three selections illustrate his style.

> *Fat Nat (October).* Colin reads it word for word. There are a few lengthy pauses as he seems to be figuring out the next word. His only errors are to read *in* for *on*, and to insert the word *cat*, which he immediately self-corrects. His pace is slow at the beginning. It picks up at the end, but remains essentially very slow, punctuated with sighs and hesitations.

Hot Rods (October). Colin can read the title and a few other words. He sighs and says, "mmmmmm" a great deal. He finally uses the picture on the first page and says a sentence which describes it. Then, at the teacher's suggestion, he continues to tell the story from the pictures.

Go Dog Go (January). He never asks for help in the hard spots. Rather, he stops reading and remains silent as he figures a word out for himself, or else whispers some of the sounds of the word. At one point the teacher asks, "Are you ready for help or do you want to keep trying?" Colin answers, "Keep trying." Typical pauses are 30–60 seconds.

Rita's initial approach to reading differed from Colin's and Dana's in one noteworthy respect. Rita rarely engaged in long pauses. She would work on decoding a word phonetically until she had reasonable command of the sounds, and she almost always managed a final pronunciation that was either correct or very close. Her elapsed working time was occasionally as long as Dana's or Colin's pauses, but it was time filled with sounds that only a phonetic notation could recreate. There are two instances in her first oral reading sample (*What Will Little Bear Wear?*) where she works interminably, without the least signs of discouragement, to unravel the diphthongs in *wear* and *around*. And when she finally gets them right, there is no sense of an "aha!" or "finally!" experience in her tone of voice. Rather, she seems to take it for granted that she would unlock the words, and she continues on as if nothing had happened. At other places in the *Little Bear* text, she decodes words very quickly and with a minimum of struggle. Never in this first reading sample, however, does Rita substitute a word on the basis of picture clues, slur over a word, or omit a word.

Prolonged work in sounding out a word would seem to interfere with the retention of meaning more than prolonged periods of silence. Yet Rita, too, retained meaning. More to the point, she always seemed to know the meaning of the particular word she was trying to decode. Her record thus suggests not just rehearsal strategies to retain the meaning of text already read, but the projection of a line of thought to guide her ongoing efforts. The data integration team summarized the evidence in the following way: "She seems to know where she's heading in the decoding process, as opposed to sounding out something in the hope that it will ring a familiar chord and make sense."

Louis's style was so extreme that it actually seemed to hinder his reading progress in first grade. Although he also paused for long periods, he couldn't negotiate enough of the text to infer much meaning at all. His most profound difficulties appeared to stem from his narrowed attentional focus. As described and documented in Chapter 12, Louis gave every indication that he focused on discrete and fragmentary elements of information (a letter, a single word, a single aspect of a picture), one at a time. If not literally one at a time, then almost so.

One of the manifestations of narrowed and analytic attention deployment is the tendency to emphasize boundaries that distinguish one event from another. An incident in Louis's record illustrates how his accentuated sensitivity to boundaries interfered with his "pulling things together" to make sense of reading. The incident occurred in April of first grade, while he was reading a book entitled *Mr. Pine's Signs*. The text page in question is shown in Fig. 8.10. Louis read each line correctly up to the sign boundary, but he did not cross those demarcations to read the words inside the signs. When the teacher asked if his reading made sense and pointed to the words inside the signs, he then read the lines as they were intended.

Although Louis's persistence in practicing his instructional texts led to gradual progress in those books, he did not make equal progress in his ability to negotiate other books. Only toward the end of the documentation period in second grade were there indications that he was starting to make real headway in integrating what he knew about reading. And only when that happened was he able to make real progress in negotiating unfamiliar books.

Susan's reading history is something of a puzzle. As a kindergartner, she was enthusiastic about books and worked hard at memorizing several texts virtually word for word. She also memorized other things well and quickly. For example, she was the first in the incoming class to memorize everyone's name, and she committed the classroom rules to memory sooner than most everyone else. All of her kindergarten reading tapes except one find her either reciting a text accurately from memory (e.g., *The Very Hungry Caterpillar*) or else telling the story of a book. By the first grade, however, she was definitely reading, and she read with enough accuracy and momentum to make the detection of a clear preference impossible.

Only one oral reading sample in kindergarten reveals anything about Susan's preferred approach to reading, and this sample is interesting because of its ambiguity. Although the standard oral reading selections (*Big Dog, Little Dog,*

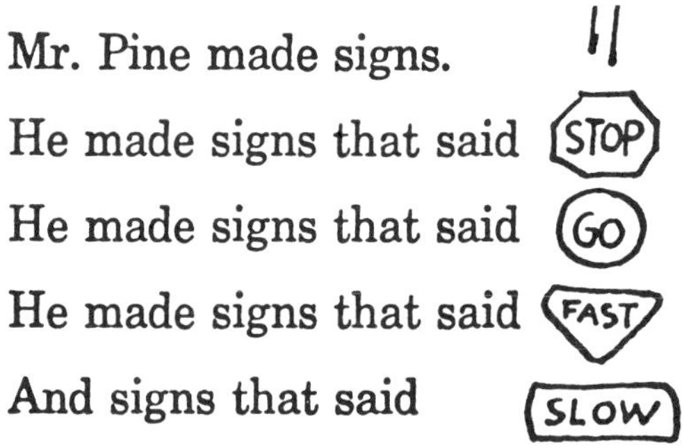

Mr. Pine made signs.

He made signs that said (STOP)

He made signs that said (GO)

He made signs that said (FAST)

And signs that said (SLOW)

FIG. 8.10   Text from *Mr. Pine's Signs*

Ben Bug, and *Blackboard Bear*) were intended for first-graders, the data collection team decided to administer them to Susan in her kindergarten year. The interviewer taped the first two selections with her at the end of one afternoon, but time ran out and she did not finish. Accordingly, the interviewer asked the observer to finish up. When the observer came to the classroom about 3 weeks later, she repeated the *Ben Bug* selection with Susan and then went on to *Blackboard Bear*. What is so interesting about the two tapes (one obtained by the interviewer and the other by the observer) is that they differ notably. And they differ for only one reason we can discern.

Because Susan was among the children in the study who displayed the greatest concern for classroom rules (one manifestation of her general preference for realism), the interviewer told her at the outset of the standard oral reading session that no help would be provided and that she (Susan) should simply "read" as best she could. Susan does just that on the tape, omitting some lines and offering many substitutions based on picture clues or beginning consonant sounds (e.g., "*mommy hat*" for *mud hut*). On this first tape, then, she displays an approach characteristic of children in Cluster A. The observer, however, said nothing about the "rules" of the reading session, and Susan stops many more times in anticipation of a difficult word. She either asks the observer for help with a word; or (in the case of *Ben Bug*, which she had read previously with the interviewer) she engages in a conversation with herself, trying to remember what she said for the word "the last time." Susan's reading on this second tape thus resembles the characteristic approach of other children who displayed Cluster B preferences in their general classroom activity. It would seem that her sensitivity to rules and the differing constraints actually placed on the reading context by the two adults resulted in two very different performances. In the first instance, she complied as best she could with the instruction to read "as best she could." In the second instance, she tended to stop and ask for the correct word or to rely on her memory to supply what she had said before and presumably thought was correct.

The Relationship of Styles to Reading Knowledge and Progress

Little has been said thus far about the children's knowledge relevant to their nonpreferred approach—that is, to the inherent obligation of reading they most often let slide when something had to give. A closer look at this evidence supports the idea that style differences reflect differences in how the children organized and used information rather than differences in knowledge per se or in the ability to acquire knowledge.

The evidence is most straightforward in the case of Cluster B children. Although these children tended to honor accuracy, they clearly possessed the knowledge to uphold momentum. And, as far as we can tell, they possessed it in almost equal measure as Cluster A children. The observational data indicate no systematic differences between the two groups in their language competence, in their general familiarity with book content, in their general background knowledge, or in their ability to understand the relationship of pictures to text. Moreover, when children in Cluster B did make substitution errors in reading, their errors showed as much sensitivity to grammatical and semantic constraints (indicating relevant language knowledge) as the substitution errors of children in Cluster A. The only detectable differences between the two groups concerned knowledge of the rhythmic structures of language, and this difference was accounted for entirely by the three boys in Cluster B (Colin, Dana, and Louis). All three were relatively unexpressive speakers and readers, and their oral reading tapes contain relatively little evidence of rhythmic phrasing. Whether they latched on to rhythmic structures to anticipate text and sustain momentum in their silent reading is a question that cannot be answered from the data. On the whole, however, the evidence suggests that Cluster B children possessed ample knowledge relevant to the task of upholding momentum in their early reading attempts.

The picture for Cluster A children is somewhat more complex. The knowledge most relevant to their nonpreferred approach was knowledge of the information encoded in writing; and that, of course, is the knowledge all the children understood least, and all were in the process of acquiring. The complexity arises because there are two distinct kinds of information encoded in writing (see Chapter 6). English writing encodes information both at the phonemic level of letter-sound correspondences and at the morphemic, or meaning-bearing, level of stable spelling configurations (word roots and affixes). Although the two kinds of information are directly related in some words, there is no one-to-one link for a large portion of the English vocabulary. Thus, knowledge of letter-sound correspondence must be supported by a network of rules (concerning consonant clusters, diphthongs, blending, and so on) in order to transpose many spellings into a sequence of blended sounds that correspond to meaningful words.

The evidence for Cluster A children regarding knowledge of information encoded in writing may be summarized as follows. All the children exhibited considerable knowledge of discrete letter-sound correspondences (as did every child in the study), but evidence of phonic rule knowledge varied greatly. Only Jack and Jenny demonstrated a clear command of rules necessary to "sound out" words in the manner of phonic blending. Whether Carrie and Debbie possessed the relevant knowledge to do this remains a question. If they did, they didn't exhibit that knowledge to any great extent (though both girls exhibited keen sensitivity to the "sounds of language" at a more basic level). Tim may also have possessed some relevant knowledge of phonic rules, but his record indicates that he could *not* put such knowledge to use effectively in oral reading. All of the children in Cluster A, however, evidenced attention to spelling patterns very early in their respective reading careers. Although virtually every child paid attention to this kind of information eventually, Cluster A children exhibited a greater awareness of spelling earlier than did children in Cluster B. The evidence thus suggests the two groups differed primarily in *what* encoded information they attended to most judiciously in written language.

As far as reading progress is concerned, there was variation in both groups. In Cluster A, Jenny made very rapid progress from January through June of first grade and then settled into a pattern of more gradual advance. Debbie made little ostensible progress until the very end of first grade but then continued at a rapid pace thereafter. Tim, Carrie, and Jack showed steady progress but no ''leaps'' throughout the period of data collection. In Cluster B, Susan's transformation to a stage of proficient reading occurred mainly during the summer between kindergarten and first grade. Colin and Rita both progressed at a fairly rapid rate throughout the study. Dana worked his way methodically through the first-grade instructional texts but was able to branch out more on his own during second grade. Louis's progress was the slowest in either group, for not until the end of second grade was he able to venture much beyond the familiar territory of instructional books. The excerpts shown in Figures 8.11 to 8.14 below illustrate the kind of reading material the children were handling toward the end of data collection.

Some Theoretical and Practical Implications

This chapter has illustrated pervasive style differences in children's general classroom functioning that were also manifest in how they went about the task of learning to read. We have suggested theoretical links between two clusters of stylistic preferences and two initial approaches to reading, and have further claimed that the approaches were not inconsequential by-products of the children's styles. Rather, we have argued that each approach enabled the children who used it to construct the most coherent meaning they could from text. Our concluding thoughts of the chapter raise theoretical and practical implications of this argument.

A theoretical extension of the argument leads to some basic considerations about the nature of skills and skill learning that were discussed in Chapter 5. We made a distinction there between simpler skills (facilities) and more complex skills (competencies), noting that facilities are often nested within a complex skill. Nested facilities refer to technical aspects of a complex skill that are capable of becoming routinized and automatic with practice. The complex skill itself, however, is not subject to such routinization. Competencies enable people to deal with new situations and are therefore applied to ever-changing configurations of events. Competencies may improve with practice, but they never become automated responses. They must be guided by strategic judgment.

A translation of this facility/competency distinction to the act of reading is fairly straightforward up to a point. The construction of meaning from text is a complex skill that necessarily remains under the guidance of judgment. As the

CARRIE: *The Three Brothers*

The old woman ate one of the pears and put the other one carefully in her pocket. She said, "You have been kind to an old woman and now I shall be kind to you. Come with me."

So Peter and Stevan and Marko followed the old woman through the wood.

TIM: *All About Prehistoric Cavemen*

What did prehistoric man look like?

That was the question some people had been asking even before the Paris Exhibition of 1867.

Now many scientists all over Europe, including those who had once argued against De Perthes's whole theory, were eager to find the answer to that question. But they couldn't find the answer without first studying some of the clues which to this day are very rare—the actual bones of prehistoric man.

Already several such clues had been discovered.

FIG. 8.11. Materials Read by *"Cluster A"* Children Toward the End of the Study. Top: A page from *The Three Brothers*, read by Carrie in May of 1st grade. Bottom: Excerpt from *All About Prehistoric Cavemen*, read by Tim in June of 2nd grade.

Rod Puppets

Similar to a stick puppet, a rod puppet allows more movement and also more realism. A wooden dowel glued to the tagboard body forms the main support, while you manipulate strips of tagboard up and down to move the puppet's arms and legs.

Illus. 19. Rear view of a rod puppet.

Brass paper fasteners at the joints let each limb move independently of any other. The little boy on the back cover is a rod puppet whose right limbs and left limbs are fastened to two rods. You can move your puppet into comic positions with this arrangement.

Illus. 18. Brass paper fasteners make movable joints, allowing rod puppets to dance around the stage.

DEBBIE: *A Child's Swiss Family Robinson*

For many days, we had been tempest tossed. The raging storm increased in fury until, on the seventh day, all hope was lost.

Our ship, which was sailing from Switzerland to Philadelphia, was driven completely off course. Neither the captain nor any of the crew had the slightest idea as to our whereabouts.

I stood on deck with my good wife, Elizabeth, and our four sons, fifteen-year-old Fritz, thirteen-year-old Ernest, twelve-year-old Jack, and eight-year-old Franz. Leaks had sprung all over the ship. We watched, in great dismay, as the water rushed in over the deck.

"Children," I said. "We must trust in God," and we knelt down together to pray.

Amid the roar of the thundering waves, I suddenly heard the cry of "Land! Land!" At the same instant, the ship struck bottom with a frightful shock. The captain cried, "Lower the boats!"

FIG. 8.12. Materials Read by *"Cluster A"* Children Toward the End of the Study. Top: A page from *Puppet Making*, read by Jack in September of 2nd grade. Bottom: A page from *A Child's Swiss Family Robinson*, read by Debbie in January of 2nd grade.

I wish something exciting would happen, Henry often thought.

But nothing very interesting ever happened to Henry, at least not until one Wednesday afternoon in March. Every Wednesday after school Henry rode downtown on the bus to go swimming at the Y.M.C.A. After he swam for an hour, he got on the bus again and rode home just in time for dinner. It was fun but not really exciting.

When Henry left the Y.M.C.A. on this particular Wednesday, he stopped to watch a man tear down a circus poster. Then, with three nickels and one dime in his pocket, he went to the corner drugstore to buy a chocolate ice cream cone. He thought he would eat the ice cream cone, get on the bus, drop his dime in the slot, and ride home.

That is not what happened.

He bought the ice cream cone and paid for it with one of his nickels. On his way out of the drugstore he stopped to look at funny books. It was a free look, because he had only two nickels left.

LOUIS: *Adventures of a Whale*

WALTER was a whale. He was young, but big. He lived in the ocean with his mother.

He splashed in the salty, blue-green water. And his mother told him everything a whale needs to know — how to dive to the bottom to get nice fresh squids for dinner; how to come up and blow a spout in the air; how to sleep in the water, rocking gently on the waves.

Walter was very curious, and he asked lots of questions.

"What are those?" he asked his mother.

FIG. 8.13. Materials Read by *"Cluster B"* Children Toward the End of the Study. Top: Excerpt from *Henry Huggins*, read by Colin in January of 2nd grade. Bottom: A page from *Adventures of a Whale*, read by Louis in June of 2nd grade.

RITA: *A Child's Garden of Verses*

MOON SONG

MILDRED PLEW MEIGS

Zoon, zoon, cuddle and croon—
  Over the crinkling sea,
The moon man flings him a silvered net
  Fashioned of moonbeams three.

And some folk say when the net lies long
  And the midnight hour is ripe;
The moon man fishes for some old song
  That fell from a sailor's pipe.

And some folk say that he fishes the bars
  Down where the dead ships lie,
Looking for lost little baby stars
  That slid from the slippery sky.

And the waves roll out and the waves roll in
  And the nodding night wind blows,
But why the moon man fishes the sea
  Only the moon man knows.

Zoon, zoon, net of the moon
  Rides on the wrinkling sea;
Bright is the fret and shining wet,
  Fashioned of moonbeams three.

And some folk say when the great net gleams
  And the waves are dusky blue,
The moon man fishes for two little dreams
  He lost when the world was new

And some folk say in the late night hours,
  While the long fin-shadows slide,
The moon man fishes for cold sea flowers
  Under the tumbling tide.

And the waves roll out and the waves roll in
  And the gray gulls dip and doze,
But why the moon man fishes the sea
  Only the moon man knows.

Zoon, zoon, cuddle and croon—
  Over the crinkling sea,
The moon man flings him a silvered net
  Fashioned of moonbeams three.

And some folk say that he follows the flecks
  Down where the last light flows,
Fishing for two round gold-rimmed "specs"
  That blew from his button-like nose.

And some folk say while the salt sea foams
  And the silver net lines snare,
The moon man fishes for carven combs
  That float from the mermaids' hair.

And the waves roll out and the waves roll in
  And the nodding night wind blows,
But why the moon man fishes the sea
  Only the moon man knows.

SUSAN: *The Wizard of Oz*

man sitting down by the window, engaged in deep thought.

"I have come for my brains," remarked the Scarecrow a little uneasily.

"Oh, yes; sit down in that chair, please," replied Oz. "You must excuse me for taking your head off, but I shall have to do it in order to put your brains in their proper place."

"That's all right," said the Scarecrow. "You are quite welcome to take my head off, as long as it will be a better one when you put it on again."

So the Wizard unfastened his head and emptied out the straw. Then he entered the back room and took up a measure of bran, which he mixed with a great many pins and needles. Having shaken them together thoroughly, he filled the top of the Scarecrow's head with the mixture and stuffed the rest of the space with straw, to hold it in place. When he had fastened the Scarecrow's head on his body again he said to him,

FIG. 8.14.   Materials Read by "*Cluster B*" Children Toward the End of the Study. Top: The poem "Moon Song" from *A Child's Garden of Verses*, read by Rita in February of 2nd grade. Bottom: Excerpt from *The Wizard of Oz*, read by Susan in May of 1st grade.

skill is practiced and improved, however, certain aspects of the performance assume the status of a technical facility and no longer require much conscious attention. What becomes routinized is the ability to interpret the squiggles of writing and rapidly reconstruct the author's message. When this level of proficiency is attained, then the strategic judgment involved in reading is clearly a matter of *appreciating* and *appraising* the author's message. Such evaluative judgments may be made on the basis of several criteria—the relationship of the message to what the reader already knows, the relevance of the message to the reader's concerns, the apparent validity or logic of the message, its aesthetic or suggestive value, and so on. These are the kinds of conscious judgments that guide the act of proficient reading; an awareness of the message per se seems to happen automatically.

But what about the person who is learning to read? By what judgmental standard is the novice guided in his or her efforts to reconstruct the author's message? The only reasonable standard for the novice would seem to be the standard of sense. For the beginner, then, the act of constructing meaning from text may be thought of as the act of constructing a message that makes sense. And judgments about how best to make sense of the world are rooted in stylistic preferences of the kind we have discussed.

The children's styles were manifest as preferred ways of expressing (interpreting and representing) meaning, of working, of deploying attention, and of thinking. Such preferences necessarily play a guiding role in the way people make sense of the world, and they are not of an ephemeral nature. Particular manifestations of these styles may change as individuals mature and their social interactions and intentions change, but the preferences tend to endure and would seem to account for much of the continuity that marks human development. Evidence of such continuity was observed in the fact that children's initial approaches to reading resurfaced when they were faced with challenging text later on. In mentioning this observation, we noted the similarity between the children's handling of such text and adult tendencies to handle difficult material in different ways, either skimming and going back for details, or else taking it paragraph by paragraph. Adults who struggle with difficult material in one of these two ways are engaged in a task analogous to that of the beginner. That is, they are trying to reconstruct the sense of the author's message. Once the sense has been reconstructed, then other judgments will be brought to bear. But for the adult, as for the child, making sense of the message in the first place is an act that appears guided by stylistic judgment.

One practical implication of our theoretical view seems obvious. If you want people to make sense of something in the most efficient manner possible, let them rely in large part on their stylistic strengths. Or to state the principle conversely, don't cut them off from the seat of their best judgment. Though obvious in a certain respect, ramifications of this idea are far from simple or self-evident when it comes to the everyday instructional task of helping children learn how to read.

Perhaps the most complex aspect of the instructional task hinges on the distinction between knowledge and styles. Reading depends on knowledge, and a teacher must help children acquire knowledge by providing them with relevant information. Offering children clues, filling in unknown words as they read, pointing out mistakes, discussing the background or context of a story, teaching them rules—all of these are important and legitimate ways of helping children acquire knowledge. The trick is in sensing when to provide information, what to provide, how much to provide, and how long to keep on providing it. From what we have been able to observe, important clues for making these decisions come from the children. We have also observed that children are neither fragile nor prone to give up too easily. They will keep on signaling what information they need in one way or another and will generally overlook those instances when unhelpful information is provided or needed information withheld. In other words, children don't appear to be put off or terribly harmed by a teacher's miscalculations in offering information (and there are bound to be miscalculations when any one person is trying to help 30 or more other people). But such benign consequences may not be the case if instruction deliberately or inadvertently focuses on children's styles. Instructional materials, direction, and intervention that in effect try to change or otherwise predetermine how children orchestrate knowledge will most likely be self-defeating. In the long run, such efforts may sever children's access to the very judgments that best enable them to make sense of text. The distinction between providing information to foster knowledge and trying to direct how children make sense of written language will certainly not be as clear in practice as it is in theory. Nonetheless, it is a difference worthy of the teacher's most discriminating attention and thought.

Another aspect of instruction that obviously demands thought is planning and providing for differences in the way children approach reading. One essential feature of such provisioning is selecting a variety of books for the classroom. (Books are also a necessity from the standpoint of fostering knowledge, since they are children's most important source of information about written language.) Above and beyond supplying books, however, there would appear to be no absolutes. Teaching is not so complex as to verge on the impossible or to defy conception at an abstract level, but it does defy concrete prescriptions for action. It, too, is a complex skill that must be guided by judgment.

Where reading instruction does reduce to a particular method that involves a set of prescriptive actions, it will almost certainly work to the benefit of one stylistic approach and to the detriment of the other. This, in fact, is what the research literature on teaching methods reveals time and time again. This or that method seems to help some children but not others. Where a method claims universal success, it invariably emphasizes a particular type of knowledge, and its success is almost always gauged by tests that assess the knowledge taught.

Teachers need information about children's knowledge, just as they need information about how children engage books and approach reading. Much of this information will have to be observed firsthand, though telling behaviors will vary from child to child just as they varied among children in the study. To say that stylistic preferences were clear in many children's behavior is not to say that the behaviors were identical. In short, there are neither prescriptions for action nor checklists for observation to assure intelligent and responsive teaching. All that *can* be offered are a guiding theory and abundant examples.

We have sought to provide such a theory along with pertinent examples of children's behavior in this section of the book. Part III of the book focuses in greater detail on the classroom functioning of four children in the study: Carrie, Crystal, Louis, and Tim. In doing so, it also provides many explicit as well as implicit examples of teaching behavior. We do not claim that the teachers are "models" in the sense in which that word is often used in education, because we do not believe there is such a thing—any more than there are model chess players, model pianists, model surgeons, model quarterbacks, or (for that matter) model readers. Anyone who literally tries to model a skill performance after someone else will end up being mediocre at best. On the other hand, we do believe the examples are informing. Sometimes they provide glimpses of "miscalculations." Overall, they suggest a variety of ways in which it is possible to create a responsive and intelligent approach to reading instruction.

STUDIES OF CHILDREN
LEARNING HOW TO READ

9 Introduction to the Child Studies

The studies in Part III portray the unique constellation of styles, interests, and reading accomplishments that marked the classroom lives of four children during the time when each of them was learning how to read. These are but four of several such studies resulting from the ETS Collaborative Research Project on Reading. Collectively, the studies constitute the basis for a general theory of learning how to read that is presented in Part II of this book. The purpose of Part III is to document a fundamental proposition of the theory—a proposition which states that learning how to read is continuous with patterns that characterize the child's learning and functioning in other areas of the classroom.

A BRIEF OVERVIEW OF THE RESEARCH[1]

The ETS reading study was a collaborative venture by researchers and educational practitioners to observe, document, and analyze the ordinary classroom activities and interactions of individual children. The emphasis was on "ordinary" behavior, because such a record of events was thought to hold the most important clues to the meanings children derive from an instructional environment and, therefore, to the nature of their learning. Data collection was carried out by collaborative teams that followed two children in a classroom. Each team consisted of the classroom teacher, an outside observer (usually an advisor associated with a teacher center), and an ETS researcher. For purposes of data

---

[1]Chapters 2–4 describe details of the research design and procedures.

integration, these teams were expanded to include additional teachers and researchers who were not personally acquainted with the child in question.

The research proceeded in two distinct stages: a pilot stage and an operational stage. During the 3-year pilot study, collaborators concentrated on the development, field-testing, and refinement of all procedures. Then the project entered a 3-year operational phase of work in which the refined procedures were used to follow a small sample of kindergarten and first-grade children. All of the case studies presented in Part III are of children who were studied during the operational phase of the research.

This second stage of work focused on 26 children from 13 classrooms. The classrooms are located in four public schools, two in New York City, and two in Philadelphia. Approximately two-thirds of the children who comprised the sample are black and one-third white, and they represent a range of low- to middle-income families. Children for whom English was a second language were excluded from the study, as were children who showed signs of being precocious readers or of being severely handicapped either intellectually or emotionally. Thus, the sample consisted of a reasonably "normal" group of young children who had spoken English from birth and who were in the process of learning how to read their native language. One child from each classroom was selected by the teacher for study, and the other child was selected at random.

The educational environments of the children had several features in common. All of the classes were heterogeneously grouped, and some were mainstream classes that included individuals with special problems. More importantly, the children's teachers valued observational information, since they considered such information an important basis for making instructional decisions. The teachers were also quite similar in five aspects of their reading instruction.

—They provided a range of reading material in the classroom and encouraged children to select from this range, either all of the time or during specified times each day.

—They had a "free reading period" each day when children were expected to be engaged with books on their own, either reading them or looking at pictures.

—They worked at least some of the time on an individual basis with children, hearing each child read and/or discussing what the child had read.

—They read to the class each day and usually followed up with a brief group discussion of the book or story.

—They expected children to write, either every day or two or three times a week. Some teachers spent more time on writing than others, but all supported it to some extent, both as an expressive medium in its own right and as an approach to reading.

Beyond the commonalities just described, however, the teachers' reading programs varied greatly. Five of the 13 teachers used a structured program of phonic instruction as a core approach to reading; a sixth teacher used the Bank Street basal readers as core materials; and a seventh teacher built her instruction around a program that reflected a language experience approach to reading. The remaining group of six teachers relied on easy-to-read trade books and several beginning reading series as entry points for the children, and they varied in the emphasis they gave to supplementary phonic instruction. Three of the group systematically taught phonic lessons to subgroups of children, whereas the other three supplied such instruction on an individual basis, as needed. A detailed account of the instructional practice of individual teachers appears in each one of the case studies.

Data collection on each child continued for a period of 18 months to 2 years and included the following kinds of documentation.

Teacher Interviews: At regular intervals throughout the year, the research member of the team interviewed the teacher in order to gain access to the teacher's observations of the child over the preceding weeks. Guidelines for the interview directed the teacher's attention to general areas of the child's functioning as well as to aspects of behavior more specifically related to reading and writing.

Observer's Narrative Records: Systematic observations of each child were also made by the observer member of the data collection team. These observations took the form of a narrative record of the child's activity (for periods of approximately 20 minutes) in various classroom settings and contexts.

Work Samples: Samples of work that were judged to be typical or particularly illustrative of some aspect of the child's functioning were collected by teachers throughout the period of data collection. These were primarily examples of writing, drawing, painting, and worksheets, but also included photographs of three-dimensional craft work and block constructions.

Oral Reading Samples: Tape-recorded samples of the child reading aloud were obtained by the teacher and interviewer at specified intervals. Most of the taped samples contained from two to four reading selections. The child chose some of the texts, and the teacher chose others. The interviewer member of the team tape-recorded the child's reading of a standard set of texts.

Selected samples of the children's work were analyzed by small groups of collaborators, following descriptive procedures developed by Patricia Carini and staff at the Prospect School and Center for Education and Research. These descriptive analyses were then incorporated into each child's record. Similar group procedures were adapted to analyze key selections from the oral reading tapes, and results of these analyses likewise became part of the documentation. Thus, a child's total documentary record consisted of all the interview transcripts and narrative observation accounts, together with the descriptive analyses of selected pieces of work and selected oral readings.[2]

The total record for each child was then examined by a team of six collaborators for purposes of data integration. The task of the data integration team was to identify recurring patterns in the documentation record that characterized the child's functioning over time and across various classroom settings. The patterns were labeled as descriptively as possible, and specific data falling within each pattern were "charted"—i.e., each piece of defining data was actually written down on a chart. The charted data were then reexamined, and patterns revised, refined, and relabeled as necessary. The final patterns resulting from this process were called "themes." Ultimately, the data integration teams produced two sets of themes for each child: themes abstracted from the total record of documentation; and themes abstracted from the subset of the record that pertained specifically to the child's reading and writing activities.

ORGANIZATION AND FORMAT OF THE CHILD STUDIES

The portrayals of individual children that follow are based directly on the outcomes of the data integration process. Thus, they are organized according to themes abstracted from the total documentary record ("Report from the Total Record") and themes abstracted from that portion of the documentation concerned specifically with reading, writing, and relevant language behaviors ("Report from the Reading Record"). The discussion of each theme interweaves narrative description with illustrative data taken directly from the documentation for each child. All concrete data illustrations are identified as to the month and grade in which the incident occurred (e.g., May/1st grade); and, in most instances where several illustrations are presented consecutively, the data are listed in chronological order.

Because "themes" reflect patterns of behavior rather than mutually exclusive categories of behavior, it was possible for discrete behavioral events to be classified under more than one thematic heading. (The rationale for using overlapping categories in data integration is explained in Chapter 4.) In reality, then, some data were considered as defining instances of two or more behavioral patterns. And, by the logic of the data integration procedure, some data were also coinci-

---

[2]Oral reading samples were also analyzed by ETS staff, using technical coding procedures developed especially for the study.

dent with themes abstracted from both the total record and the reading record. For practical reasons, however, the repetition of illustrative data was reduced to a minimum in writing the child studies. Thus, only in rare instances are specific behavioral instances repeated in the portrayals of the children.

Each portrayal follows the standard format shown below.

> *Synopsis:* A thumbnail sketch of the child and of general issues highlighted by the child's learning patterns and progress.
>
> *Instructional Environment and Reading Program:* A description of the child's classroom, the organization of activities during a typical day, and details of the teacher's reading program.
>
> *Report from the Total Record:* An expanded account of the child's functioning, based on themes abstracted from the total record of documentation.
>
> *Report from the Reading Record:* An account of the child-as-reader, based on themes abstracted from evidence pertaining specifically to reading, writing, and language behaviors.

The introductory paragraphs to the last part of each portrayal (''Report from the Reading Record'') point out specific continuities between the child's more general functioning in the classroom and those patterns that characterize the child-as-reader.

Each study was written by the ETS staff member whose name appears first in the by-line. The other two authors indicated in the by-line are the other two members of the data collection team for the child. In the actual write-ups, however, the name of the child, the child's classmates, and the child's teacher are pseudonyms.

THE CHILDREN PORTRAYED IN THE STUDIES

The four children included in Part III were selected primarily because they represent well the range and variety of the stylistic qualities that form the basis of theoretical formulations reported in Chapter 8. CARRIE and TIM are among the nucleus of children defining one of the interrelated style clusters discussed in that Chapter, and LOUIS is among the nucleus defining the polar cluster. CRYSTAL is a child who functioned very much within the middle ground of styles, exhibiting behaviors characteristic of each cluster.

Secondary considerations in selecting the four children reflect an effort to balance the sample along several lines. Boys and girls are equally represented. Two children are black (Carrie and Crystal) and two are white (Tim and Louis). Two are from the Philadelphia sample and two from New York. Although we did not consider how children initially were selected for the research, three of the children (CARRIE, CRYSTAL and TIM) happen to be among those chosen for the study via a table of random numbers. Only LOUIS was among that half of the total sample selected by the teacher.

10 Carrie

Edward A. Chittenden, Pamela Cushing, Vivian Wallace
Teacher: Norma Pollack
Grades covered by the study: Kindergarten and First

SYNOPSIS

Carrie, one of the youngest and smallest children in her class (a combination kindergarten and first grade), is also one of its most influential members. Whatever the activity may be—group discussion, block building, or caring for the animals—she makes her presence felt. She is confident in her opinions and voices them with authority. Her manner of speaking is lively and expressive, and her approach to any project is animated by a flair for the dramatic. Although she obviously effects what others are engaged in, her classmates usually welcome the ideas and excitement she introjects. The level of her energy is high and the range of her undertakings is broad, but at no point in the record do Carrie's efforts seem random or purposeless. She knows what she wants, whether making a pie at the sand table or selecting a book for quiet reading time.

Midway in the kindergarten year, Carrie initiates her first attempts to read. As with most undertakings, she approaches reading with confidence and resourcefulness and apparently sees the task to be not so much a question of "learning to read" as of "starting to read." She plunges directly into the matter, insisting that her teacher, parents, others, read to and with her. In her first "readings" to the teacher, she relies principally upon memory for the story, aided by picture clues and a willingness to ad-lib. Although she soon begins to draw reliably on information encoded in print, acquiring word analysis skills along the way, her confidence in reading and her allegiance to the story line remain firm throughout the record. She never goes through a phase of word calling or of attending excessively to letter sounds. Her progress is steady, with no evidence that learning leaps forward or is suddenly transformed. By the conclusion of first grade, she is a competent young reader, firmly in control of the reading process and able to branch out into a variety of books.

If there is a single question that Carrie's record raises, it is how she smoothly acquires a working knowledge of print without ever abandoning her adherence to story and her confidence that she is a reader of stories. Several themes emerge in the total record, with counterparts in the reading record, that shed light on this question. One such theme is her engagement in story and drama. In the total record, this is manifest in the drama and narrative comment she brings to her play with friends and to various school activities; in the reading record, it is reflected in her strong memory for story line and her love of books with substantial tales. Another connection between the records is found in the expressiveness of her speech and her keen sense of the literary style and rhythm of the books that she becomes involved in.

The analysis of her record indicates that these resources of memory, anticipation for story, and sense of style are the underlying supports for learning to read. Her reading record therefore presents a case study of how information in print is gradually acquired and brought into alignment with the deeper grasp of narrative.

INSTRUCTIONAL ENVIRONMENT AND READING PROGRAM

Carrie begins her school career in a full-day kindergarten program as a member of Norma Pollack's K–1 class. Although Ms. Pollack and other members of the educational staff are experienced practitioners, the school itself is only in its fourth year of operation when Carrie enrolls. Part of a district network of "magnet" alternative schools, Carrie's school is open to children throughout the city as well as those who live in the immediate neighborhood. The school is relatively small, with seven classroom teachers and a student population of 200 children in grades K–6. Because it operates entirely on normal tax-levy funds, however, the average class size is about the same as in other city schools. The building that houses the school is fairly old and large, serving as the home of two other schools as well—a regular neighborhood elementary school (with about 350 pupils), and an alternative junior high school with a population approximating 200 students. Carrie's alternative school occupies one wing of the four-story building, but all three schools share the use of common facilities such as the lunchroom, auditorium, gymnasium, and library. In addition to the seven classroom teachers, the school employs a full-time music teacher and several (part-time or full-time) staff members who are available to provide special support services to children.

Physical Arrangement, Provisions, Schedule of Activities

The classroom is divided into major activity areas—e.g., block building, painting, a house corner, sand table, science area, cooking area, a spacious loft for quiet reading or "escape." The reading area, which contains a rug, couch, and a display rack of books, also serves as the site for class meetings. Children do not have assigned desks and chairs, although each child does have a bin in the cubby area for storing personal items. (See diagram, Fig. 10.1.)

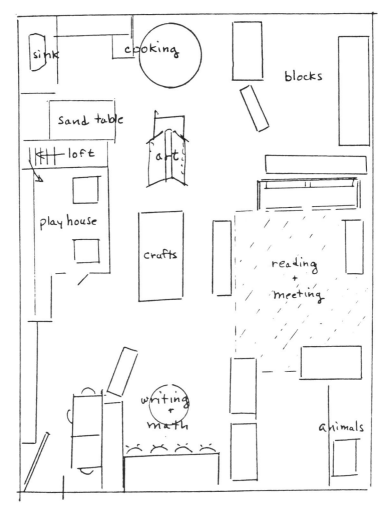

FIG. 10.1.   Sketch of Carrie's Classroom

The room is well stocked with provisions that the various activity areas imply—paints, clay, costumes for the house corner, enough blocks to enable two or three children to construct elaborate buildings, and so on. Aside from the insects and fish, which remain in their respective containers, the animals in the room are regarded as pets. They have "home" cages, but are normally allowed the free run of the room. There is always such a pet animal or two in residence.

The schedule for the morning is typically made up of two activity periods. The first occurs as children enter the room and resume ongoing projects or perhaps start something new. This is followed by a whole class meeting during which the happenings of the day are discussed. A second work period ensues. In either period, activities are initiated or chosen by the children themselves or selected by children in consultation with the teacher. Sometimes, they are assigned directly by the teacher. Following lunch and a music period (a whole school "sing" in the auditorium), there is a quiet reading time when every child selects some book(s) to read or otherwise peruse. At the conclusion of this time, the teacher reads to the class. The remainder of the afternoon is taken up with journal writing, another work period, recess, clean-up, and a final class meeting. This schedule is flexible and may be altered to meet requirements of class trips, special projects, and holiday happenings. As the year advances, the quiet reading period becomes longer, and journal writing includes more children.

The various ongoing activities usually center around a theme or topic that encompasses all areas of the room and all major academic subjects: mathematics, reading, social studies, and science. In the fall of Carrie's kindergarten year, the thematic topic of study was the neighborhood and its apartment buildings, tenements, stores, a park, and major hospital. During January, the class moved from a study of the neighborhood to a study of bridges. In the spring, a visit to the Tutankhamen exhibit at the museum stimulated a study of ancient Egypt and of King Tut specifically. The final thematic topic of the year was the study of different transportation vehicles.

The Reading Program

Reading and writing of some form occur in association with most all activity areas and at any time during the day. However, as the schedule indicates, there are aspects of the program that can clearly be designated as central components of reading instruction. One such component is the teacher's daily practice of reading aloud to the class and discussing the book with them. A second regularly scheduled component is the quiet reading period when each child must read or look at books, individually, and with reasonable silence. Children can select among picture books, trade books, reading series, and books that classmates have produced. This is also a time when the teacher circulates, listens to children read, or talks with them about their reading. The opportunity to read is also always an option during the activity periods. At such times it often takes the form of two or three friends sharing a book, reading to and with each other.

The amount of time that Ms. Pollack spends listening to or reading with an individual child depends very much upon the nature of the child's progress. Thus, she may meet three or four times a week with individual children who are clearly engaged in beginning attempts, whereas such individual meetings occur less frequently with young pre-readers and with proficient readers. In the case of the latter, the teacher's purpose is to review with them what they have been reading and to provide guidance in the selection of new materials. Listening to their actual reading becomes less important. Records of meetings are maintained that note the date of the meeting and the books involved.

Although the reading program depends upon the full range of literature available for children, special use is made of several series of instructional "little books" that have been designed for beginners. (Many of these series were originally published in England and only recently have become more broadly available in the U.S.) In particular, the series associated with *Breakthrough to Literacy* is used by Ms. Pollack with children at some point in their beginning efforts. Depending upon each child's responsiveness, some may eventually work with all aspects of these materials, including the word cards and sentence makers as well as the little books. Other children spend less time with the word and sentence materials and move to other series more quickly. One assumption of the Breakthrough program is that beginning books should be close to children's own language and experiences. It pays relatively little attention to specific instruction in letter-sound correspondence. Other series that share the assumptions of *Breakthrough to Literacy* and that Ms. Pollack uses with children who are in the initial stages of reading include: *One Two Three and Away, Reading with Rhythm* (Carrie's selection of *The Woo-Wind* is drawn from this series), the *Monster* books, *Little Nippers,* the *Holt Basic Reading System,* the *Scott Foresman* series, *Tarzan and the Tortoise* series, and the *Mollie Clarke* books (*The Three Brothers* tale that figures prominently in Carrie's reading record is a *Mollie Clarke* book).

REPORT FROM THE TOTAL RECORD

Overall, the record of Carrie yields impressions of liveliness, humor, and of much social activity. It is a record of a highly visible child who expresses her thoughts and feelings clearly and directly. Although her sociableness is striking, she is also very much involved in the substance of classroom learning, as when she observes the animals, paints with her fingers, or listens to or reads a good story.

One of the strongest initial impressions has to do with Carrie's influence on her classmates. Her skills at manipulating a situation are part of this impression, but her influence also stems from magnetic qualities associated with self-confidence and a sense of drama. In the following report, the first four headings deal primarily with aspects of Carrie's style that are prominent in her relationship with others. The fifth heading points up another side of her learning, and the sixth identifies a thematic interest.

1. Authoritative, influential
2. Narration: play and story
3. Awareness of agenda and presence
4. Expressiveness in speech: meter and articulation
5. Exploration through hands: diffuseness and directness
6. Familial, inclusive

1. Authoritative, Influential

Carrie tends to be at the center of action and to affect directly and indirectly what others will do, whether these "others" are children or adults. There is a manipulative quality to her behavior at times, but her influence depends upon much more than mere assertiveness. (In the first year of the study she is, after all, one of the youngest and smallest members of the class.) As is evident in episodes cited below, she imparts a forward motion to activities through providing direction and offering substantial suggestions; moreover, she does this in a manner that usually engages her peers and often captivates adults. She is authoritative in the sense of almost always holding an idea or opinion, and of manifesting confidence (warranted or not) that she knows what the situation requires.

Carrie's leadership among her friends is apparent in the fact that they seek her out and that she often becomes the central, "directing" figure in their group play or projects.

—She is part of a group of little girls who often cling together and tell stories to each other. She takes the role of a sort of leader. For example, one of her friends will ask me, "Can Carrie read this book to me?" A few times they have played school and Carrie will be the teacher or the boss . . . the one who gives the directions. [Interview: January, kindergarten]

The broader scope of her influence is apparent in class meetings when she can set the pattern of reaction during a discussion, or when others pick up and use her expressions.

—One day she was using the word, "boring." Everything was described as "boring." . . recess, school, etc. A few days later a parent told me that her daughter had picked up a new word . . . the girl had told her mother that praying in church was "boring." [Interview: October, 1st grade]

Also skillful at engaging adults, Carrie characteristically seeks out anyone who visits. On one occasion, she was more successful than the teacher in making a visitor feel comfortable and welcomed in the classroom.

—One of the parents stopped by the other day, a mother who prefers not to become involved in the classroom. Despite my invitation, she remained outside the room. Carrie, on her own, asked if she could read a book to the mother. She left the room and somehow eventually managed to get the woman into the classroom, where she subsequently visited for the rest of the day. [Interview: October, 1st grade]

Carrie assumes authoritative knowledge on a whole range of topics; her opinions are accepted and only occasionally challenged.

—Carrie is watching some spiders that the children have collected in a jar. Carrie: "They're crawling. They're crawling up the mother's web." Then, to Jake: "Don't you see the baby spiders?" (whose existence is highly questionable.) [Observation, October, 1st grade]

—The student teacher and a boy are looking at a dinosaur book. When he doesn't respond to a question the teacher poses, Carrie, who has been listening in, provides an unsolicited comment: "And look at his body and his head. His head is soooo little, that's why his head is so little cause his brain is inside and it's so little." [Observation: March, 1st grade]

Her authority among the children regarding classroom pets is so firm that, in one episode, her defense of the hamster's behavior is accepted over the principal's verdict that the animal was guilty of biting someone.

—Some children protested that the hamster had only scratched, not bitten. When I asked if they had actually seen it happen they said "No, but Carrie told us." [Interview: October, 1st grade]

When she speaks to the entire class, she provides much detail and elaboration and is unhesitating in formulating her opinions.

—One day Carrie brought in an oil truck. She had it in a bag and let me peek at it but didn't show it to the children until group time. She knew everything you could possibly know about that truck . . . little things such as the part that the steam comes out of. She said her father "bought it for her for free" at a gas station. She had a long story about going to visit a particular relative, about needing gas, about stopping at the station. She had long answers to everything whether or not she was really answering the question, like a politician at a press conference. [Interview: April, kindergarten]

Carrie's effectiveness in influencing others is well illustrated in the extended excerpt below. She joins Geoff at the sand table and very soon imparts a new direction and excitement to the activity, one that he goes along with. While she is obviously assertive, it is important to note that Geoff, who is not an especially compliant child, readily and agreeably responds to her ideas and commands. In effect, she transforms the sand table from a "graveyard" in which Geoff was burying people to a "kitchen" where the two children eventually produce a whole line of cakes, pies, and ice creams.

Carrie walks to the sand table, neatly rolling up her sleeves, first the left, then the right. Geoff is already there working by himself. Carrie begins working, both hands in the sand, opening and shutting her fingers.

> Geoff: Watch it! A lady is buried in the sand there.
> Carrie: I don't see no lady. You don't have to keep all the sand and don't say I can't come around here.

After brushing off her hands, she digs both hands in again, precisely where the "lady" is buried. Geoff continues working, looking at Carrie. He selects a pie plate to put sand in.

Carrie builds a sand hill, then takes three handfuls from the top and delicately puts the sand on Geoff's building in the pie plate; she spills the sand slowly from her hands.

> Geoff: We need water. (He takes a cup and walks toward the sink but stops when Carrie speaks to him.)
> Carrie: You can't get water if you don't ask the teacher.

Geoff comes back to the table, returns the cup, brushes his hands on top of Carrie's hill, and goes off to ask the teacher. After a few moments he comes back with the information that the teacher "said yeah."

Carrie finds a tin cup, goes to the sink, and then fills the cup at the drinking fountain. (She can't reach the sink faucet.) She uses her right hand to hold the fountain lever down, left hand to hold the cup, and brings her head down to her right hand to scratch her nose. She returns to dribble the water into the pie plate.

> Carrie: OK. I'm mixing it up. (Geoff takes a fork she had found) OOOOOH, let me . . . you get some more water . . . let me mix it up.
> Geoff: OK. What are we making?
> Carrie: This is a goooood cake. Don't dump it (water) all out. We're making this gooood cake for the teacher, don't make it a water cake (as Geoff adds more water.)
> Geoff: It's a sand cake.
> - later -
> Geoff: Let's make some hot chocolate milk.
> Carrie: (purses lips, hands on hips, mock anger?) But we didn't finish the cake (giggles.) [Observation: January, kindergarten]

2. Narration: Play and Story

Observational records of the dramatic play of Carrie and her friends show Carrie to be a central figure in establishing the pace of these dramas and in providing momentum. She seems to be both principal actress and "directress." Her social skills and the force of her opinions, outlined in the previous section, are obviously part of this pattern of influence, but by themselves they do not explain why she is sought out by children or how she contributes excitement and a sense of forward motion. A closer analysis of these records indicates that the nature of Carrie's participation is that of "narrator," the one who brings out a story line. As the story teller, she articulates connections in what is happening and keeps the thread of the action in focus, while at the same time providing embellishment. For example, in the observation (above) of Carrie and Geoff at the sand table, she is the one who states a purpose for their cooking (making a cake for the teacher), who describes what they are doing ("I'm mixing it up"), and who keeps the activity more or less on course. Geoff's comments are more prosaic, or they provoke from Carrie a reminder of the boundaries of their imaginative activity. In activities that include several children, Carrie's function as narrator often seems critical to the group's cohesion and to the maintenance of interest and momentum. Within the total record, the theme of narration is equally evident in contexts that are quite different from group play. It is particularly strong in her love for books with well-told tales. She reads and listens to the classic form of "once upon a time" with absorption and anticipation of what may unfold.

There are many instances in dramatic play episodes in which Carrie acts out one role while simultaneously shaping the roles of others. The teacher reports that Carrie "is a pivotal part" of such play.

—Carrie is in the play house with Marlene. She says "I'm a baby" and begins to imitate a baby crawling and climbing on the furniture. Marlene, who was previously just sitting in the playhouse, now becomes actively involved in the role of "Mamma."

> Carrie: Now, make believe I'm scared of the dark. . . . Now, Mama could I sleep with you in your room. [Observation: May, kindergarten]

Her theatricality and ability to dramatize her feelings add an important dimension to her effectiveness in engaging and holding the attention of others.

—Carrie walks into the play house with a half-eaten strawberry in her hand. She holds it up in her right hand and waves it in front of Charles' face, singing, "Me and my strawberry." Carrie eats her strawberry with incredibly tiny bites, grinning, squinching up her eyes and nodding her head, yes. [Observation: May, kindergarten]

In another instance, when her friends seem to be losing interest in playing with the guinea pig, Carrie dramatically reminds them of its presence and is successful in restoring the original focus to the activity.

> Carrie: Let's go back to the guinea pig.
> Nicole: No, let's stay here.
> Carrie: Please
> Nicole: No.
> Carrie: Ooooooh, the guinea pig is squeaking. Ooooooh. (And Nicole
> and Linda quickly follow Carrie to the cage.) [Observation:
> October, 1st grade]

On one occasion, Carrie's facility with story and drama take her further than she had perhaps anticipated. She tells the class about a puppy she has just "received," embellishing her account of its behavior with such elaborate and convincing detail that the children and the teacher fully expect her sister to bring the dog to school that afternoon, as Carrie claims she will do. When the sister arrives, her surprised response to inquiries about the dog is, "What dog?" For two or three weeks thereafter, Carrie continues to claim that the dog was real, explaining that no one knew about it at home because it lived in the closet and she only played with it in the middle of the night. Finally, after some joshing, she whispers an acknowledgment to the teacher that indeed she did not have the puppy.

When looking at books or magazines, Carrie can find stories where perhaps none exist. She goes beyond the surface of the pictures or the text and speculates upon what might be going on or what might have happened to the characters. Thus, in the examples below she infers that a boy might have lost his mother, and that the dinosaurs might live together.

> —(Carrie and Vanessa are cutting out faces from a magazine.) Carrie: "You just passed a face. Why don't you cut out this little face. . . . I found the face of a little boy . . . lost his mama, sad little face." (Makes her voice sound sad.) [Observation: September, 1st grade]

> —(Looking at a picture of two dinosaurs, tyrannosaurus and brontosaurus): "I don't think he gonna eat him cause they live together and have a family."

Carrie's feeling for story comes out clearly in her response to books that the teacher reads to the class. Her comments about a new book reflect anticipation of a story to come, and her remarks at the conclusion of a reading are elaborations on its content. In this regard, the teacher notes that she is unusually perceptive in detecting connections between a particular story and some other book, or between the story and an event at school. Such connections are subtle. They are not ones that occur to Carrie's classmates; but once she expresses them, they engage the attention of others and their validity seems recognized.

Carrie's speculations around story, and her ability to identify connections are well illustrated in her remarks about "Blackboard Bear." In this tale, a child's chalk drawing of a bear comes to life, an episode that prompts Carrie to examine

FIG. 10.2.   Page from *Blackboard Bear*

the parallel between this happening and the adventures of Pinocchio. (Comments in parentheses are those of the ETS interviewer; the picture to which Carrie is responding is reproduced in Fig. 10.2.)

> —"But how can a bear turn to life? If he turn to life he would still be flat! He would be a flat bear. (You mean because he was on the blackboard?) Yeah. So how could he get off—how could he stand up? If he stood up, he's supposed to fall down. (I agree with you—I don't know how that could be.) Just like Pinocchio—puppets'll fall down if you don't hold them. I don't know how Pinocchio came to life, he didn't have no strings. [Pause] Maybe it was because his father said he was going to do the strings tomorrow and it was too late because he was already alive. So may be this bear . . . came to life before he [the boy] could make the leash. Maybe he could come to life before he could write [draw?] him. [Oral Reading Tape: May, kindergarten]

3. Awareness of Agenda and Presence

Early in the record, the teacher notes that Carrie rarely wants to be babied or cuddled despite being one of the littlest members of the class. Instead, her classroom posture reflects a sureness about what she wants to do and a confidence that she will be able to use the resources of the classroom to achieve her ends. She readily becomes involved in many kinds of activities and projects, but she does this with an awareness of what she is doing, as evident in her comments about her own behavior. In the same vein, she is aware of her effects upon others and of how they must perceive her.

Carrie is selective in what she does and in how she goes about it. She is generally a cooperative child but will balk on occasion when the suggestions from the teacher or someone else do not seem to fit her plans. For these reasons, she cannot easily be hurried when in the midst of something that interests her.

> —When reading with her the other day, time was running out so I had to decide whether to stop or rush her. I tried rushing, but this is not something you can do with Carrie. She continued to elaborate and comment and pretty much keep the same reading pace. [Interview: June, kindergarten]

There is also evidence that she plans ahead and anticipates her needs.

> —At quiet reading time she usually takes a stack of books to read, otherwise she would have to get up each time she finished one, to get the next. [Interview: October, 1st grade]

Her awareness of her agenda and her ability to adjust it comes through clearly in her reaction to an event that must have been a disappointment. For about one month the class had been practicing a dance and making costumes for a school performance. A few days before this event is to take place, Carrie learns that she will be unable to participate because of a previously scheduled doctor appointment. When asked if she wouldn't at least like to perform in the dress rehearsal, she responds, "What do I have to practice for? I'm not going to be in it anyway."

Her awareness of her learning extends to her physical self. For example, when the teacher suggests that she do some cutting and pasting, Carrie, responds, "Oh no, not me!" as if reminding Ms. Pollack that such activity is not her forte. She does, however, become involved in this project and at a later point again remarks upon her facility: "I got to sit down to cut." Other comments about her own abilities and physical status appear throughout the record.

> —"I'm skinny. I'll never be fat."

> —"If my heart wasn't alive, I'd die."

> —"I'm not a baby."

> —While reading the book, *The Loose Tooth* she notes the "gap" (her term) in the boy's mouth and points to a corresponding gap in her own mouth.

Carrie is also aware of the effect she has on others and will comment on how they might be expected to perceive her. When she and some friends are making kites, she remarks, "Don't you know I love to make kites?" as if chiding them to remember. But perhaps the clearest example that sums up awareness of her own style and of its impact on others comes toward the end of the record when the teacher asks some of the children to consider carefully whether, as individuals, they would be appropriate persons for the school council. Ms. Pollack reminds them that they will need to be able to speak up in the presence of "big kids." When she gets to Carrie with this question, the response is:

—"You don't need to ask me if I get shy! You know I won't be!" [Interview: May, 1st grade]

4. Expressiveness in Speech: Meter and Articulation

Because of her loquacity, the observational record is replete with samples of Carrie's speech. In sheer amount of talking, this record confirms the teacher's global impressions reported early in the study.

—She can talk and talk and talk. She might be saying something about her brother spitting out food and then abruptly turn around and talk about something else. The topics don't have to connect, but that's not to imply that Carrie is spacey. She can chew your ear off. [February, kindergarten]

—At discussion time, even if she doesn't have some idea to offer, she will say clearly, "I don't know," or "I forgot" instead of shrugging or mumbling. There is even language in her non-answers. [January, kindergarten]

She has an interest in words and will inquire about their meaning; throughout the record she chooses words that are apt, that fit. For example, when the teacher becomes somewhat annoyed and reminds her to help Nina put the blocks away, Carrie responds with a grin, "I am. We are *sharing putting* them back."

Carrie's speech is often poetic. There are qualities of rhythm and meter evident:

—You don't put meatballs in carrot cake. you don't put beer in carrot cake. we need carrots, carrots, carrots.

—Cause I made it before and I ate it before.

—A mess. A real mess. We'll get it. We'll clean it up.

—You gotta be fast, make it in a hurry, you only have a second.

—I found the face of little boy . . . Lost his mama, sad little face.

There is rhyme on occasion:

—Should we look? Where should we look? You and your bear book.

—Yeah. You getting the weasles, the measles, the peasles.

—Relief! Good grief!

There is also repetition of words, phrases and sentences.

—Fold it up. Fold it up. I know. . . . I know. . . . I know.

—But it'll fall. I've been saying that over and over and over again.

—Get this off, get this off, get this off.

—Oh, forget it, forget it. You act like it's true, true.

In some of her explanations or proclamations, she attains a dramatic effect by emphasizing contrasting elements.

—Lillian, that is a guinea pig, that is a hamster. And (pause) that is a her, and that is a him.

—That one (a dinosaur) is bigger than twenty buildings, but his brain is in his ear.

—The yellow costs 50 cents, the blue costs 25 cents, and the red one is free.

—I can't even clean up my room, in my own house, so how can I clean out the cage?

Finally, Carrie is aware of words and of their effects on others. This is the sort of linguistic sophistication that enables her to trap Dominick in a tangle of words.

Carrie:	(to Dominick) You like Renee? She's a friend? She's a girl? That makes girlfriend. She's a girl and she's your friend, so she's a girlfriend . . . you love her!
Dominick:	No. You made a mistake. She's a friend . . . friend . . . friend!
Carrie:	Girlfriend.
Dominick:	Friend. . . . I'm going to tell (teacher) that you are telling stories about me.
Carrie:	Not stories. The truth. Billy told me. [Observation: March, 1st grade]

5. Exploration Through Hands: Diffuseness and Directness

If speech can be regarded as a dominant mode of expression, another side of Carrie is conveyed through her use of hands. Sometimes hands accompany and punctuate language, but often her contact through hands suggests a different form of exploration. She gets into things directly, up to her elbows, often creating messes in the process. This messiness gives the impression that her use of hands is diffuse, less differentiated, less under control when compared to the versatility and precision of language.

Reference to the movement of hands and fingers occur regularly throughout the record. In some instances her hands accompany and accentuate her speech.

—When she tells people what to do, she puts her hand to her hip.

—"Look. I want to sweep the house." (She makes a sweeping motion with her arms and hands.) "Look, how dirty."

In other instances her hands serve as counterpoint to other gestures, as when she is apparently trying to appear demure for the benefit of the student teacher.

—Carrie sits on the edge of the couch, kicking her legs together, hands folded neatly in lap, feet dancing.

She is aware of her hands, as though she observes them:

—I got to wipe these hands.

—"When you knead it (dough) it gets your fingerprints in it."

A number of observations show that she does not hesitate to become involved through her hands, and that she indeed thoroughly enjoys the contact.

—(Sand table) Carrie has begun working, both her hands in the sand, . . . opening and shutting her fingers.

—(kneading dough) Carrie picks her hands up slowly; the batter sticks, and she alternates giggling with "yeech's." She stands up and pounds the dough with her fist.

—(reading) While reading a book for the taping of an oral reading sample, she becomes involved in showing the interviewer how pages sometimes stick together, and how she licks her fingers in order to separate the pages.

The use of her hands may be considered diffuse in two senses. First, it is often associated with messing and with lack of precision or neatness. Letters are scrunched together in her writing, paint is smeared, fabric is torn with scissors, dough sticks to her fingers. Second, she does not work well with implements such as brushes, scissors, and pencils. They appear to get in her way and almost to come between herself and her intended product. In the examples below she impatiently discards the implement, whether cutting or painting.

—She first uses her right hand to cut with, puts the scissors in her left hand and begins to cut (they are right-handed scissors). Then back to her right hand, then back to her left. She begins to move her feet around and starts ripping the picture out with the scissors.

—With a paint block, she prints on the other side of her painting, singing: ''I don't even need a brush. I don't even need a brush, but I better wipe some of the water off.''

—She became involved in string painting, but she ended up smearing with her hands.

She plunges into the task of writing, but the mess of her notebook suggests that here, too, her attention is not on the implement but on the content.

—Her writing is messy. She erases, and crosses out, but she will write anything. Nothing stops her from guessing the spelling [Interview: June, 1st grade]

6. Familial, Inclusive

The theme of family is strong and persistent in the record. In its more obvious forms, the data consist of Carrie's comments about her immediate family: her parents, siblings, and grandmother. There are also the teacher's reports that the family is definitely interested in school and in Carrie's reading. More subtle, but equally prominent, is the way in which Carrie extends the notion of family. Thus, there is family in dramatic play and in mothering of the animals; there is Carrie's attentiveness to visiting parents and children; there are her claims of familial relationship to other children (''my niece,'' ''my cousin,'' etc.)

Carrie often talks about her family while in school. She ''brings'' them into the classroom, into the playhouse, into the block area, or wherever she is working. She makes a point of mentioning them specifically.

—''My brother thinks he's never going to die and he acts like he can't get hit.''

—''My mother didn't want anything for Mother's Day. I guess she didn't want me to waste my money, my allowance, so I'm making this.''

—Carrie is in the playhouse and telephones her father at work. She has a telephone number and assumes that he is willing to speak with her. She ''tells'' him that she is busy and ''tells'' the other kids that he will come and cook for them.

—''I was picking peas and my grandma was washing dishes, and she said, 'Carrie, stop picking peas, and I said, 'How do you know I'm picking peas?' and she said, 'Cause I got eyes in back of my head.' ''

In first grade, the theme of family is prominent in her journal writing. Some representative entries are:

(Approximations To Carrie's spelling)	(''translation'')
IeAt CANDY BUT do I hae to tel mymom	I eat candy but do I have to tell my mom
I likei Pattyann bcas sHe is my find and i lek her ais a lttl sata	I like Pattyann because she is my friend and I like her as a little sister

Animals are also part of family. Carrie is mother to the guinea pig and asserts that it needs her.

—''I have a comfortable lap. Oh precious honey baby. Oh, look at my baby'' (rocking him in her arms.)

Even dinosaurs have familial relationships.

—(looking at a book) ''I don't think he (tyrannosaurus) gonna eat him (brontosaurus) because they live together and have a family.''

In addition to referring to her own family, she extends the relationship to others within the classroom community. One time, for example, she claims that a visiting child (daughter of a friend of the teacher) is her niece. On another occasion she explains that since she and a classmate live in the same building, they must be cousins. In the following observation she welcomes some visitors to the classroom with the spirit of including them in the ''family.''

—A visiting mother and two-year-old child have come to observe the classroom. Carrie stops working at the art table and watches for a minute or so. She stands up, walks to the mother and asks how old the baby is. The mother says that she is two. Carrie goes to the baby, kneels down (so they are on the same level) and asks her her name. The baby doesn't answer. The mother smiles. Carrie asks if the baby talks yet. The mother says yes, but that she doesn't like to talk very much. Carrie smiles again at the baby, and returns to the art table. [Observation: May, 1st grade]

Although the theme of family is a strong one, there is no sense of immaturity on Carrie's part or of wanting to be babied. Indeed, very early in kindergarten, when Carrie is one of the youngest and smallest members of the classroom, Ms. Pollack notes her independence.

—There is a littleness about her when you see her or are with her, yet her ''being'' isn't young. She is very very capable of taking care of herself. She's not babylike. Sometimes I want to cuddle her, but I can feel that she doesn't want that. She is not a baby. [Interview: January, kindergarten]

As a theme, family has less to do with nurturance than it does with inclusiveness, with being related and being connected. The fact that this is not an inward-looking preoccupation but rather one of openness and inclusion is well conveyed by a magic marker drawing that Carrie made in the fall of kindergarten. The descriptive analysis of this drawing points up its humor and its spirit of connecting and including people. The drawing (Figure 10.3) shows Carrie and various child members of her family; on the reverse side of the paper, she depicted her parents.

Analysis of this drawing (as well as one of Carrie's paintings) was undertaken by a group of collaborators after the first year of the study, one year prior to the

FIG. 10.3.   Carrie's Family Drawing

full-scale integration of data that forms the basis of this report. (Similar analyses of the art work of several study children were carried out during the same time period.) The group analysis was led by Patricia Carini and conducted according to guidelines developed by Carini. The purpose of independently analyzing children's art was to focus on such work samples as statements in their own right—as a child's direct expression of thematic interests and styles. The excerpts below are taken from Carini's summary report on the group's analysis of Carrie's "family" drawing.

> The simplicity of the forms of the figures is qualified by variety in line and detail, particularly of mouths and feet, that lends an individual expressiveness to each of the siblings. The sister has a big open mouth, eyelashes, and what is probably an earring; the brother has long spindly legs, a wide grin, and what may be teeth; "Me" has a Lucy, Charlie Brown-style smile; and all the figures have active, interesting feet. The cousin is not as detailed and the portrayal suggests a baby lying down. The brother and "Me" have bodies (although no arms, ears, or hands), but the sister is less clear, and she has more of the little broken, extra lines than the brother or "Me." The variety of line and the mouth expressions convey a remarkable subtlety and range of humor: belly laugh, chuckle, satire, wryness.

> The page is full, and the compositional tightness is increased by the connecting line that goes around the figures and the turning of the page to fit them in. The visual arrangement suggests a jig saw puzzle. Liveliness, humor and contact/relationship pervade the drawing. While two sides of the paper are used, the composition "fit" of the figures, the connectedness of line, and the humorous range of the expressions make it one piece, and definitely one family—a totality.

> The portrayal of family is of the organic, original, secure, and sustaining relationship of belonging and place. The connecting lines, overlapping figures, and the jigsaw fit of the figures are the visible certainty present in the drawer that the drawing will work, that everyone will be in it.

REPORT FROM THE READING RECORD

Carrie approaches reading with the same air of confidence and authority that she brings to most classroom activities. About midway through kindergarten, she voices her intent to begin reading and plunges ahead with a determination that suggests she indeed views the task as one of "starting to read" rather than of "learning to read." She involves many people in her early efforts (parents, teachers, classmates, visitors to the classroom) and works her way through books by drawing upon a varied array of resources and strategies. Notable among these resources is her memory for the story content and style of books she has heard. She is especially enamored of books with a substantial narrative, such as folk tales and stories of adventure or family life—a genre of book that has a counter-part in her general interest in narrating plays and stories (as described in the total record). Other resources and strategies evident in her early attempts to negotiate text include a reliance on picture clues, a fragmentary knowledge of beginning letter sounds, soliciting help from others, and, when all else fails, inventing phrases and sentences.

By the end of the record, Carrie is a proficient and independent young reader. The analysis that follows addresses the question of how her sensitivity to the style of a book and her memory and anticipation of story act as the central resources for her learning. These resources appear to guide her discovery and use of infomation encoded in print, and they underlie her preferred patterns of practice. Her allegiance to story also means that she rarely is concerned with word-perfect reading or with practicing skills in isolation.

The major themes in Carrie's reading record are organized and documented under the following headings:

1. Confidence and Persistence in Beginning Reading
2. Familiarization and Rereading
3. Memory and Anticipation of Narrative
4. Capitalizing Upon Contexts for Reading: People and Settings

1. Confidence and Persistence in Beginning Reading

At every point in the record, Carrie's approach to reading is marked by self-confidence and determination. In her first attempts in kindergarten, she tackles the task as if, in essence, she already knows how to do it—as if it is simply a matter of getting the ''technical'' aspects under control. Ms. Pollack's descrip-tion of Carrie's initial reading is indicative.

—If she doesn't know the words she will make them up. Nothing gets in the way.

On the oral reading tapes there is never a tone of discouragement in Carrie's voice, and she is rarely at a loss for words even when grappling with very difficult selections. Her general determination to read is reflected in the verbs, ''grab,'' ''pester,'' ''bother,'' ''insist,'' that appear in the record with reference to her desire to read to and with other people.

Carrie's persistent involvement in learning to read was obviously encouraged by adults, but her efforts from the outset seem self-initiated. Her energy and flair in going about reading bear the stamp of her own style of work; and when she seeks a parent, teacher, or friend to read with, it is she who usually determines what the book will be and how she will proceed. Thus early in the kindergarten year, her father ''complains'' to the teacher that Carrie continually wants him to read.

—He told me that she is after him all the time to read . . . and after he reads, she says to read it again. And then the next day, she'll want him to read the same book yet again.

Her interest in reading in the classroom comes to the surface in midyear of kindergarten when she and a few of her friends ask the teacher for "reading work." They want to "read" (tell) books to the teacher; they want her to "make some homework." Ms. Pollack also notes at this period that Carrie is spending increasing amounts of time with books, even when there are other options available.

—She is in the reading area a lot of the time, looking at books, looking at pictures. If she knows the book she points to the words and tells the story on her own. If she doesn't know the book she just looks at the pictures. [February, Kindergarten]

By June of kindergarten, reading in the company of others has become a strong interest, one that will persist well into the first grade year.

—I cannot keep track of Carrie because she reads so much. She finds books to read with whomever comes into the room. . . . It is her favorite activity.

This social expression of her interest in reading continues through first grade although it becomes somewhat more subdued and less flamboyant. She still likes to read with others, but eventually she does not pester as much to do this and begins to read more often by herself. Although the evidence suggests that she still reads at home, she no longer insists on taking as many books home.

—She is probably not as conscious of reading now as she was last year. She still likes the attention, but does not seek out people to read to. Sometimes at quiet reading time, she becomes really engrossed in a book. She will be lying on the floor, her feet up in the air, and the world could collapse around her. [May, 1st grade]

Her confidence in her abilities and her determination to read are evident from the beginning, but equally evident is an awareness on her part that the words she utters—her version of the text—must in some way be accountable to the print. Thus, the teacher notes her early efforts to point to each word at the same time she is retelling a story from memory. On occasions, Carrie detects a discrepancy between how many words she has uttered and how many she has pointed to, but this does not impede the performance.

—She will make finger pointing coincide with her "reading" and may point to words more than once to make it come out right.

In April of kindergarten, she is reading a *Breakthrough* beginner book to the teacher, one that she has been working on for several days. She knows the story well so that on some pages she recites from memory, but on others she is clearly attending to the print. Characteristically, when she can't recall a line or recognize a word, she is not deterred. On one line, for instance, she ad-libs *came* for *got*, and *out* for the phrase *looser and looser*.

> Text: My tooth got looser and looser.
> Carrie: My tooth came . . (pauses, looks at words and picture) . . out.

Confidence and persistence are well exemplified in an oral reading sample recorded in May of kindergarten with the interviewer. The book is an unfamiliar one and although Carrie does not know its story and can recognize only a few words at first encounter, she nevertheless plunges into the task, undeterred and unembarrassed by her many mistakes and by her need for assistance. When asked at the start of the reading whether she want to guess or to be told a word, she unhesitatingly opts for "guess." (The words in brackets below indicate the unsolicited help supplied by the interviewer.)

	Text	*Carrie*
Page 1	Fred and Ted were friends	First [Fred] and the [Ted] Fred and Ted are friends.
	Fred was big.	Fred were . . . was big.
	Ted was little.	Ted were . . . was little.
Page 2	Fred always had money.	Fred . . . and [always] always has money.
	Ted was always broke.	Ted was always broke.
Page 3	When they walked in the rain	Fred [When] When the . . . it . . . when it was . . . was rainy, in the rain . . .
	Fred got wet but Ted stayed dry.	Fred goes with [Fred got wet] but Ted . . . always has a umbrella.

She controls none of the conventional decoding skills at this point in time, but by building upon anticipation of structure, she gets maximum mileage from the few words that she can recognize and from those supplied by the interviewer or those guessed from the pictures. Particularly noticeable is her reliance upon redundancy of the text's style and words. Thus, she starts out on page 3 by trying "Fred" for "When," undoubtedly because the two preceding pages had started with "Fred." As another example, on the first line of page 2 she is given help with "always." She subsequently reads "always" smoothly on the next line and then

FIG. 10.4.   Page from *Big Dog, Little Dog*.

seems to expect it again on page 3, when she inserts the phrase "always has a umbrella" as a parallel structure to the earlier phrase, "always has money."

Her confidence in reading the "Ted and Fred" book is also manifest in remarks that embellish the story. At one point, when she apparently is aware that she has misread a line, she repeats her version and instead of correcting or seeking help, justifies her rendition by pointing to the picture and explaining why "they wrote it that way."

Text	*Carrie*
Ted skied all day long.	Ted skied long . . . but slow. (Pause) Long, but slow. (Points to the skier's zigzag tracks.) You see, the reason why they put "long but slow" is . . . etc.

Carrie's confidence in her reading is not based on blind belief that she is reading the words accurately. In fact, the intonational patterns of phrases such as "always has a umbrella" or her glance at the teacher when reading "out" for "looser and looser" are acknowledgments that her version may not be exactly like the one in the book. Her confidence rests instead upon the firm belief that she knows what the book is about. Her reading tapes, whether recorded early in kindergarten or late in first grade, are sprinkled with remarks about the meaning of a particular word, why something was written in a particular fashion, what the author intended, and what is probably going to happen. A prime example of engagement with the story can be found in her comments about *Blackboard Bear*, cited in the Report from the Total Record. She sees a resemblance between the story of the bear and the tale of Pinocchio, and speculates about how the bear, like the marionette, became animate. In the example below she is reading *The Woo-Wind* and explains the author's intentions to the teacher, imitating in her explanation the repetitive phrasing style of the book.

Text	*Carrie*
At last the wind got tired	It [At] At last the wind got tired
. . .	. . .
Down came the hat,	Down came the hat,
the balloon, the umbrella and the	down came the balloon, down came
newspaper.	the umbrella, down came the
	newspaper.

Teacher: How come they all fell down?

Carrie: Well you know when its windy and you go outside. . . . You go out and your hair blows, right? You know how the wind stops and then it keeps going? . . . That's what they mean in the story. [What do they mean?] They mean the wind blew and then it stopped and then the wind blew and then it stopped and then it blew and then it stopped and then it blew and then it stopped and then it blew and then it stopped . . . and then it stopped. [June, Kindergarten]

2. Familiarization and Rereading

Carrie becomes familiar with a book ("read this to me") and then will often want to read it again immediately, with or without assistance but always with an audience. She assumes the initiative in creating and sustaining this pattern, beginning as it does with her insistence (in kindergarten) that her parents read particular books over and over to her. As noted in the following section, she involves a great many of her classmates and many of the school staff and visitors in this pattern, pursuing visitors to read to or with. The desire to reread never seems to serve purposes of showing off for its own sake (much as she likes an audience) nor does it ever take the form of repeating some particular book to the point of word-perfect performance. Rather, reading familiar materials to others creates the arena in which Carrie can practice and develop her competencies. Expressed another way, rereading becomes the principal learning context for

Carrie's beginning reading—the context in which she expands and consolidates her abilities.

The pattern of becoming familiar with books appears early in the record, before Carrie can read words. She borrows books to take home that the teacher has read to the class.

—For a time, she took books home every day and insisted that her father read them to her over and over. Despite his suggestions of a different book, she would insist on repeating some certain book. [January, Kindergarten]

—She has been picking out very simple repetitive books to read with me. . . . Usually she chooses books she can read, or thinks she can read. [June, Kindergarten]

When the teacher introduced the *Breakthrough* series to Carrie in kindergarten, she printed some of the basic words of the series on cards in sentence form (e.g., "I can play," "Can you play"). Carrie read them aloud as Ms. Pollack was printing and then immediately wanted to read the whole page of such sentences to the principal, to another teacher, to her parents, and so on. The pattern of rereading remains prominent in first grade. In reading to her friends she continues to select material that she has gone through at least once.

—She will read with a friend more or less on her level or to one of the new kindergarten kids. She selects books she can read or almost read [October, 1st grade]

—The other day she read a *Little Bear* book to me. When I asked her how she could read it so well, she told me that her mother read the book to her and then she read it to her mother. [January, 1st grade]

—She has been reading a number of these Bear books lately. She will read a story the first time, struggling a bit, and then want to read it again. She will read a chapter with me and then later read it again to someone else . . . rather than moving on to the next story right away. [January, 1st grade]

The evidence that rereading represents a form of substantial practice for Carrie comes from several sources. First, although she reads material to others that is familiar, she nevertheless selects books that are still quite challenging for her. Thus, her rereading is not restricted to overpracticed books. It is also characteristic of her to wish to read something she had heard or been helped with immediately and without further rehearsal. Second, although rereading is extremely important, the total record shows that she is continually moving along to new materials, to new books within a reading series and to the trade books in the classroom library.

—I think she's touched every book in the room. [October, 1st grade]

—When reading to others, she usually takes a stack of books, not just one. She reads one, then the next, and so on. [October, 1st grade]

These facts, coupled with the fact that she is never concerned with word-perfect renditions, suggest that much of Carrie's rereading has the supportive function of offering an opportunity to orchestrate her abilities. By the end of first grade, when she can branch out comfortably into new reading matter, the pattern of rereading diminishes and takes the form of occasional returns to old favorites.

3. Memory and Anticipation of Narrative

Carrie's orientation to a book's story and style not only underlies her confidence as a beginner, it constitutes the principal resource that guides her attempts to figure out print. Although she draws upon a wide variety of cues in a text, as manifest in oral reading samples, her memory for story and her feeling for structure are always central to her efforts.

Evidence of Carrie's memory for story appears early and often in the observational records. She is attentive to the books that the teacher reads with her or to the class. She remembers them.

—If you read her a story, she will "read" (tell) the story back to you. . . . I think she can retell a story from only hearing it once. [April, Kindergarten]

—She has a fabulous memory. The other day I couldn't remember which book she had read onto the tape recorder earlier in the fall. When I asked Carrie she promptly (and accurately) told me. [October, 1st grade]

Evidence from the first oral reading tape (January of Kindergarten) illustrates her early use of memory and also forecasts her sensitivity to the structure of writing. The excerpts below are from Carrie's reading of a book that is one of her favorites (*In the Village*), one she takes home often. Ms. Pollack has just read it to her, and she in turn reads it back. Carrie's "reading" flows smoothly and her rendition is faithful to the story. Her many deviations from the text are not so much single word replacements as they are transformations of phrasing and style. Significantly, these transformations are not necessarily ones that fit natural speech patterns but are literary alterations; they contain structures ("Tommy is at the window"; "now is at night") that might be found in such a book.

Text	*Carrie*
p. 1 This is Tom's village	Tommy's village.
p. 2 That's Tom at the window.	Tommy is at the window.
p. 3 Each morning	Each morning
he plays with his brown dog.	Tommy plays with his brown dog.

p. 4	Then he gives the hens their breakfast.	Then he goes to feed the chickens their breakfast.
...	...	...
p. 13	It is night. Tom is asleep.	Now is at night. Tommy is asleep.

Although this first oral reading on tape essentially stems from memory, aided by the pictures, there are signs of attention to the information in print. In one instance there is a puzzling and unique self-correction.

p. 9	This morning Tom climbed the pear tree and picked the ripe pears to put in his basket.	Now Tommy is . . . is pig . . . is picking ripe pears to put in his basket.

Carrie apparently starts to say "pig," but then pauses and switches to the correct word "picking." The "error" did not fit the syntax nor did it make sense (there are no pigs on this farm). Whether it represents an accoustic confusion in recall or attention to initial letter is unclear.

Much stronger evidence of attempts to attend to print is found in the teacher's observations that Carrie was often pointing to the words while she read this book. She was aware that the number of words recited should correspond to those in print even though she was "reading" from recall. For example, on the page with the longest text (16 words) her version is correct, but she completes her recitation two lines in advance of her finger pointing. Carrie's solution to this discrepancy is to repeat the last phrase, so that her finger "catches up." As she begins to pay more attention to print, her oral reading efforts reveal corresponding attention to the problem of matching the text with her own rendition, which seems mainly generated by story and a sense of writing style.

—As she was pointing the other day, she was sometimes saying something else because of the story she was trying to tell. She stopped a few times and started over from the beginning, trying to read the actual words rather than telling. She knew something was not right. [April, Kindergarten]

In this respect her reading of one of her first "beginning" books (in April of kindergarten) is indicative. She vascillates between focus on print and recall of the story and its style of phrasing.

	Text	*Carrie*
p. 14	I showed the money to my dad. He said The tooth fairy put it under your pillow.	I showed it to my dad. He said "Told you it will come out soon."

p. 15	My mother said	I showed it . . . My mom said
	A big tooth will grow	A . . . a . . . [big] big
	in the same place.	tooth . . . will . . . grow
		in . . . the . . . same . . . place.

On page 14 she recites from memory and even ad-libs a line that aptly suits the story but obviously ignores the actual text. On page 15, however, after mistakenly starting with a thematic phrase of the book ("I showed it") she shifts to the correct phrasing ("My mom said") and then haltingly but accurately focuses on each word, one at a time, exhibiting no sign of frustration or discomfort. (Her intonation on both pages is one of a "reading voice," and without the evidence of text, the listener would presume that in both cases she was "really" reading.)

The central problem for Carrie at this point in her reading is one of somehow creating an alignment between the story she can construct from memory (assited by picture clues and repetitive grammatical structures) and the actual words on the page. On page 15, above, she is carefully pointing with her finger, as if simultaneously trying to match what she sees with what she recalls.

Her sensitivity to style and patterns in writing is evident not only in her recall of familiar books, but it also surfaces as a principal resource when she is dealing with new material. The example below is from a tape made in May of kindergarten (other excerpts from this tape are reported in previous sections). The book is built around a parallel construction that emphasizes contrast, whereby one character always does things one way and the second character always does them differently. Carrie has great difficulty with the first line of a pair (page 8), trying "beat" for "drove" in an apparent confusion of "b" for "d." She then substitutes "home" for "his" and eventually gets the rest of the sentence with substantial help from the adult and with recourse to the initial sound of "slow." In sharp contrast, she reads the companion sentence on page 9 with sureness and accuracy. Her reading of this pair of sentences illustrates her ability to build cumulatively upon text itself, so that a reading performance becomes progressively stronger as she tunes into the pattern and cadence.

Text	*Carrie*
p. 8 Fred drove his car slowly.	Fred beat [drove] drove home [Fred drove his] car s–s–s–slow.
p. 9 Ted drove his car fast.	Ted drove his car fast.

In these and other early readings there is no evidence that Carrie ever tried to fabricate stories that have little to do with the actual text. Instead, her versions, whatever the degree of their accuracy at the word level, adhere to the narrative that she knows the book contains.

Carrie's responsiveness to the narrative and to writing styles, noted in these first attempts to read, remains characteristic of her reading throughout. Even as she becomes more accurate, the nature of the mistakes she makes and her manner of dealing with them indicate that she rarely reads word for word; her performance relies instead on the larger chunks of phrasing, rhythm and anticipated patterns of words. As the following examples illustrate, there is an inexactness about her reading in the sense that she rarely corrects (or detects?) insignificant substitutions (*will* for *shall*, *the* for *a*); she readily omits words or inserts words; and she occasionally substitutes words that have no graphic resemblance to the word in the text, a miscue generated entirely by syntax and her train of thought. The samples below, covering the span from end of kindergarten to end of first grade, point up the continuity of these qualities in her reading.

Text	*Carrie*
"Come back, come back," but the hat could not stop. It went higher over the house-tops.	Come back, come back, but the hat can not come back. It blew higher and higher, up so high.
	[June, Kindergarten]

Note: The phrase "up so high" appears throughout the book.

Text	*Carrie*
When this little girl was going to school	One time there was this little girl who was walking to school
	[October, 1st grade]

Text	*Carrie*
A bird came down	A bird came by
. . .	. . .
Here is someone to play with you.	Here is someone to play with . . . you?
	[October, 1st grade]

Note: Carrie's initial reading of the second sentence above terminates after the word "with." She pauses, repeats the line, then adds "you" quizzically, as if this addition makes little sense.

Text	*Carrie*
But it looks a little like the box the cat sleeps in.	But it looks a little like a box. . . but it . . . the cat is sleeping in.
	[January/1st grade]

Text	*Carrie*
I'll cook you with my hot breath! I'll fry you! Then I'll eat you!	I'll cook you with my hot breath I'll fry you with my . . . I'll . . . I'll fry you. Then I will eat you.
	[May/1st grade]

Errors such as those above which maintain or anticipate the narrative are more prominent in Carrie's reading of books that she likes and/or knows fairly well. Although she may skip over or change words, she corrects herself or seeks help when the passage begins to make little sense. Her ability to monitor her performance is noted by Ms. Pollack.

—She skips words, adds words, changes words, but they make sense and show she is not reading word for word. Sometimes she skips lines, and when it doesn't make sense she will go back. If she does not know a word and I tell her, or if she has had to think about it a lot, she will go back to the beginning of the sentence as if trying to keep the train of thought. [May, 1st grade]

Although the teacher's observations and the analysis of tapes point to Carrie's reliance on story and structure, it should be emphasized that she can and does resort to phonic mediation on occasion. Attention to letter sounds and other word properties appears in the early tapes and continues as part of the record. Evidence of reliance on graphic/phonic cues (in the form of ''sounding out'' attempts and the construction of nonwords) is more likely to appear when she is reading unfamiliar material or material that offers meager context. For example, such evidence comes to the fore as she tackles the following lines from a rhyming book that is unfamiliar and contains no story line.

> Text: Pairs of bears with chairs
> going up the stairs

On the first line she needs help with the word ''Pairs'' (She tries ''People'') and she then says something that sounds like ''clast'' for ''chairs.'' Undaunted, she struggles on to the second line, producing ''g–g–g–garring'' for ''going.'' When the interviewer provides the word, Carrie responds by remarking ''I almost had it.'' She repeats a gargling sound and talks about the g's at the beginning and end of the word.

> Interviewer: ''You were close''
> Carrie: ''A *lot* close!''
> [May, Kindergarten]

In summary, within the space of about a year and a half, Carrie moves from a phase when her reading is almost entirely a matter of story recall to a level of proficiency that enables her to branch out independently into a wide variety of books. Throughout this record of change there is consistency in her primary orientation to story content and style of writing. Memory for narrative and anticipation of what a book should say and what it should sound like are the resources that seem to generate her performance. In retrospect, her pattern of becoming familiar with books and then rereading them seems aptly suited to these fundamental strengths. When reading a book she has previously encountered, her extra-print knowledge resources guide prediction of the text and enable her to practice the orchestrating skill of reading. Overt evidence of attention to graphic information is also present throughout the record, but letter-sound knowledge and a focus upon words as units surface mainly when the material offers meager context or when her major strengths prove inadequate.

The degree of proficiency Carrie attains by the end of first grade is illustrated by her near perfect renditions of *The Lost Dog* and *The Three Brothers*. (Excerpts shown in Figures 10.5 and 10.6). She read several pages from both books during one of her last oral tapings (in May of first grade), although only a few pages are reproduced here. In reading *The Lost Dog*, she at first says "Rip is finished" for "Rip is frightened" but then immediately corrects to "frightened" (p. 3); and she says "The water runs so" for "The water rushes so" (p. 3). Otherwise, there are no errors except for two trivial omissions (*to* and *the*), and she treats page 4 with some dramatic flair ("The sky was black"). Her reading of *The Three Brothers* is similarly faithful to the text, with only minor omissions and one change that does no damage to meaning. (Her one alteration occurs on p. 5, where she says "I know I shall be kind to you" for "now I shall be kind to you.") Typical of the connections she makes between stories, or between a narrative and real life, Carrie launches into a discussion of "wine at church" and "being baptized" after she finishes reading page 6.

4. Capitalizing Upon Contexts for Reading: People and Settings

Reading to and with others is a preferred activity for Carrie during most of the record. In pursuing this interest, she is not selective about whom she reads with, nor is she choosy about when or where. Her posture too, is variable—standing, sitting, wiggling, leaning over in order to listen in. However, as noted in previous sections, there is a definite pattern to her choice of books and there is clear consistency in how she goes about reading.

People. A total of 24 different persons are mentioned in the record as participants, one way or another, in Carrie's reading. In addition, some unspecified "little girls," "kindergarten kids," and adult visitors are each mentioned in several places. About half (11) of the people are classmates. The fact that there is no one child who figures more prominently than the others is evidence that Carrie distributes her attentions. References to Carrie's family (father, mother, siblings) appear regularly through the reading history. The remaining people consist of her teacher, other teachers and school staff, the research team, and a visiting parent.

She is skilled at creating situations so that opportunities for reading will materialize:

—She takes the role of sort of a leader. For example, one of her friends will ask me, "Can Carrie read this book to me? [January, Kindergarten]

Jennifer and Johnny went out into the road.

It seemed very dark outside, after the bright light in the house.

The sky was black, and there was no moon.

The Red-hats' house was not far from the bridge, and they could hear the river rushing by in the dark.

4

Rip ran out of the open door into the road.

"Come back, Rip," called Roger.

Rip ran back into the house.

"Rip is frightened of the river now," said Roger. "The water rushes so, and the river is very high."

3

FIG. 10.5.   Pages from *The Lost Dog.*

The old woman ate one of the pears and put the other one carefully in her pocket.

She said, "You have been kind to an old woman and now I shall be kind to you. Come with me."

So Peter and Stevan and Marko followed the old woman through the wood.

5

Soon they came to a deep, wide river. The old woman said to Peter, "Make a wish and it shall be granted."

Peter looked at the deep, wide river. He said, "I wish that all this water could be changed into wine and that all the wine belonged to me."

6

FIG. 10.6. Pages from *The Three Brothers*

—The student teacher is busy reading with Billy and, in response to Carrie's request to read with her, she says, "Later." Nevertheless, Carrie proceeds to work her way into the interaction and eventually begins answering questions put to Billy. [Observation summary, March, Kindergarten]

—Carrie brings a book to the observer. "I'm DYING to read this. Can I read it to you?" [Observation: March, kindergarten]

Setting.   Much of Carrie's reading takes place in the designated "reading" area where she reads on the couch or on the rug near the book shelves. This is an area where she reads with Ms. Pollack, with the student teacher, and with other children. In addition, she also avails herself of reading opportunities at one time or another in almost every section of the classroom, as well as the hallway, closet, and the school library. There are references, too, to Carrie's reading at home. She transports books back and forth between home and school, suggesting that home reading is an extension of the classroom, and vice versa.

—For a time, she borrowed books to take home every day and insisted that her father read them to her over and over.

Carrie's posture while reading ranges from lying on the floor (engrossed), snuggling up to others on a couch, and reading while engaged in such activities as cutting or cooking. She rarely stays still for very long. Thus she fidgets while listening, moves about, and maneuvers herself into better positions. For example, her behavior around the student teacher is designed to get her attention and eventual agreement to read to her.

—Andrea begins to read the book . . . to Billy. Carrie without another word climbs on to the couch—hands, then body, then feet, then twists around so that she is sitting properly with just the heels off the couch, plops the book on top of the book Andrea is reading, and says, "Can you read this book?" [March, Kindergarten]

Affection as well as intensity of interest is expressed in her postures around reading. She sits close to people, touching; she cuddles books.

—While Ms. Pollack is reading, Carrie and Renee hold hands. Carrie looks down, fiddles with plaster, glancing up once in a while. She puts the piece of plaster under her leg, stares with absorption at Ms. P. then picks up tiny bits from the rug.

Reading with others is a very strong theme through the record, but a change occurs toward the end of first grade when Carrie begins to read alone. Her interest in reading with adults decreases.

—She does not grab visitors to read to, the way she did.

And in May of first grade, for the first time, Carrie is observed to be absorbed in a book totally on her own.

> —Sometimes, at quiet reading time, she becomes really engrossed in a book. The world could collapse around her and she would continue to read.

> —Actually, the only things she does by herself are reading, and maybe writing.

Along with this shift comes a shift in times when she reads. In the spring of kindergarten and fall of first grade she reads during activity periods, which enables her to read to and with people; correspondingly, at "quiet" reading time she tends to socialize, again to be able to involve people in her reading. Whereas in the spring of first grade, the pattern is reversed.

Finally, it should be noted that when reading with others, the "others" provide an audience for Carrie's practice but do not necessarily give her much specific assistance. Indeed, the "little kids" are less proficient readers than she. Carrie seeks out children and adults to read to but in either case she generally insists on doing the reading in her own way, even in those sections where she senses she is going off course. Generally she does not want correction from the adult, although she does seek help at those junctures that pose major problems for her. The practice with people is under her own direction.

11 Crystal

Edith Klausner, Lynne Y. Strieb, Rosalea Courtney
Teacher: Leah Sein
Grades Covered in the Study: First and Second

SYNOPSIS

Crystal invests energy and interest in the life and tasks of the classroom. Of average height and build, she moves with ease among the children, adults, and material provisions in school. She is expressive with a full range of emotions—smiling, playful, pouting, affectionate, thoughtful, sometimes shy. Although Crystal makes herself personally noticed by the teacher, she also typifies many school children who, by virtue of their very normalcy, escape more general notice. She melts into the mainstream of classroom life, maintaining a balance between ease and struggle, avoidance and involvement. She is serious, but not overwhelmed by school concerns. She does not overstep boundaries excessively, but neither is she always in full compliance with classroom expectations. Her sense of privacy and of her own needs and purposes enliven the record with incidents of fun, secrets, and teasing.

Indeed, the theme of balance between personal intentions and external expectations is one that pervades the entire record. Crystal is usually attentive, she checks in regularly with the teacher and other available adults in order to get help and to inform them of her progress. At the same time, her standards for the content and quality of a piece of work, as well as for its completion, include a healthy chunk of her own ideas about what makes sense.

Crystal is a careful observer, good at combining her own knowledge with what she takes to be other major classroom resources—books and people. She integrates her knowledge and understanding of these resources with the design and pursuit of her own agenda. An interesting complement to the evidence of personal standards is the considerable detouring and distractability Crystal man-

241

ifests, either before she begins or in the midst of an activity or assignment. She is extremely attentive to what is happening around her and takes the time she needs to observe and react.

Crystal arrives in first grade with a feeling for books, some memorized sight words and the expectation that she will become a reader. She learns how to read gradually. There is neither extreme difficulty (except for a short period with writing) nor unusual leap. She appears to choose her own path of instruction, rejecting the school's mandated instructional program in phonics. Instead, she selects other kinds of reading material from books available in the classroom, and she takes full advantage of her teacher as tutor and model. Throughout the record, she seems to prefer to use picture and content clues rather than the "sounding out" strategies taught during periods of instruction in her reading group. Crystal also sets her own pace in reading. She practices and often rereads familiar books, at the same time that she gradually expands her capabilities by persisting at the next level of difficulty. Her path is thus one of plateau, consolidation, and expansion, rather than of step-by-step linear progress.

INSTRUCTIONAL ENVIRONMENT AND READING PROGRAM

Crystal spends her first and second grade with the same teacher, Leah Sein, and with basically the same group of classmates. Although the school does not have classes of mixed age groups (K–1, or 1–2), many teachers in the school's open classroom track keep the same group of children for 2 years. Alternative tracks are available, and parents are encouraged to choose the approach they feel best meets their child's needs. Crystal began in the open track as a kindergartner.

The class represents a balance of boys and girls; the group is defined as academically heterogeneous in a statistical sense, meaning that half of the children scored below the 50th percentile on a standardized achievement test. The class size remains constant at 33 throughout the record, with only occasional shifts in composition. As part of a mainstreaming effort, some children with special needs have been placed in the class, and Leah has to give these children a significant amount of extra time and attention.

Adult help over the 2 study years is provided by parent aides, school aides, student teachers, and parent volunteers. Aside from free reading time, however, this help is not available according to any regular pattern. During the first grade, there is usually an extra adult for one-third of each day. Occasionally, both an aide and a student teacher are present, with the student teacher there a full day. During the second year of the study, regular school aides spend less time in the classroom. Parent aides are assigned to the room for three 10-week periods, and two student teachers are assigned for 8 weeks each.

Physical Setting, Classroom Provisions, and Schedule of Activities

The school is a large and relatively modern structure that houses 1,000 students in grades K–4. The building is designed to provide individually enclosed classrooms as well as several huge open pods set around a central, circular core. Each pod is subdivided into four classroom spaces, and teachers have placed bookcases and other furniture to mark boundaries between the classrooms. Leah Sein's room is at the end of one of these pods.

The space is divided into designated areas for writing, block building, and craft or scrap construction, with an open area serving for group meetings, quiet games, reading, and various floor work. An alcove off the main room houses a library where books are organized according to type of content and level of difficulty. Books of current interest, favorite picture books, and teacher-made books are displayed on racks. Additional shelves in the room contain sets of instructional reading texts, easy-to-read science and social studies books, and supplementary books for several reading series. This reading material is organized so that children may easily find and replace the books they want.

Games, math materials, and craft and scrap supplies are stocked near the areas appropriate for their use. The building area is generously supplied with blocks of all sizes as well as accessories to support dramatic play. Four to six children can occupy this area comfortably; other children may take small blocks or Lego to use on tabletops. In addition to the block building, activities regularly available during choice time include drawing, painting, sand, clay, and collage. Sewing, weaving, cooking, and other crafts are available when there is another adult helper in the classroom. Animal care, planting, and other natural science activities are also frequent and popular.

Although many specific activities reflect the ebb and flow of seasons, interests, and events, basic elements and priorities remain central to the daily schedule. There is always a free reading time, a writing period, a choice time, and a group meeting. Approximately 45 minutes are devoted to each of these activities every day. The format of group meetings may vary (one long period or two shorter ones), but the content predictably includes a discussion among the children and a story read by the teacher. Math is scheduled 4 days a week during 30-minute periods, and children frequently engage in math-related activities at choice time as well. Reading instruction in phonics is mandated and takes place in formally constituted groups during a 30-minute time slot; but there are some days when Leah decides not to schedule this period in order to allow more time for free reading or writing. A daily teacher preparation period is the time children go to art, music, gym, or other special subjects. An outdoor play period usually is scheduled during the fall and spring months, and there are occasional neighborhood walks as well as one or two longer trips per year. Because drama, puppets, and masks represent special interests of Crystal's class, impromptu plays and puppet shows are frequent events. During each of the study years, Ms. Sein and an aide also help the children prepare and present a brief performance for the whole school.

The Writing and Reading Program

Aside from creating opportunities for thoughtful discussion among children, the classroom instruction that bears most directly on reading has four distinct facets: the writing program (with both a group and an individual emphasis); free reading; a mandated program of formal instruction in phonics; and reading to children. This last facet (reading to children) is also construed as an integral part of the writing program.

The Writing Program.   Leah Sein is herself a person who enjoys writing and does a lot of it. She places a high priority on creative writing in her classroom. When she and the children discuss books that have been read at group meeting, she lets the children know what she values in the literature and relates that to ways they might try to write for themselves. Meeting is also a time when contributions for a class book are composed and written down. Sample titles of these composite efforts include: *What I Will Be On Halloween, When It Rains, Dreams, When I Was Sick, True Stories, Animal Tales,* and *Superheroes.* The children come to expect the tradition of this writing, they regard many of their creations as "classics," and they especially love to read books that children in classes before them have written.

Ms. Sein begins the writing program for individuals by making each child a blank book to be used for drawing pictures that tell a story. When the children bring her their books to dictate a sentence about the picture(s), they also bring a card on which she writes one word that they wish to keep. In addition to noting interests that spark the children's writing and drawing, she also begins to assess each child's language and early recognition of sight words and beginning sounds.

Some children write more, some less, and abilities vary markedly, but all are supported and encouraged to write. Ms. Sein especially encourages the children not to worry about spelling and to write their best guess, though she will write words for those who find guessing too frustrating. When she reads the writing with individual children, she doesn't point out errors of spelling, punctuation, or writing conventions until each child seems reasonably confident. Then she may choose to note only one or two things in a story which she feels the child is ready to see and correct. Eventually, the children begin to use small writing books with lines. Some prefer to continue drawing in these books, whereas others forego the drawing in order to concentrate fully on their writing. The metamorphosis is gradual but dramatic if one compares the earliest phrases children write with the tales of home and school, fantasy, adventure, and personal narrative that are written at the end of 2 years.

Quite apart from creative writing, Ms. Sein begins to give weekly spelling tests in the second grade, using the common words children need for their writing. They get the words as homework on Mondays and are tested on Fridays.

Free Reading.   The most crucial apsect of Ms. Sein's reading program is the "free reading" time, so named because the children may choose the book they want to read at this time, may change books as often as they wish, and may read (quietly) with anyone they choose. Each child is expected to be involved with a book; and those who are not yet readers may look at pictures, discuss a book with a friend, or listen to someone else read. Books in the room are color-coded according to difficulty and content area in order to facilitate the children's selection of reading material.

Ms. Sein listens to three or four children read to her during free reading each day. This is the time when she assesses the children's progress, observes their strategies and preferences, and makes suggestions. She might listen to some children read several days in a row, but others might be heard much less often. For some children, she might assign a particular book she wants them to try. There are certain books in the classroom that Ms. Sein considers "watershed" books. As she listens to children read them, she can observe a great deal about a child's strengths and difficulties. These books are *Look Out For Pirates, The King's Wish, Around the City* (a Bank Street basal reader), and *Little Black, A Pony.*

Formal Instruction in Phonics.   The Lippincott Phonic Program is mandated by the school, and Ms. Sein is responsible for seeing that the children are familiar with it. She teaches phonics to the children in either three or four groups that are constituted on the basis of the children's ability to hear separate sounds. Children who have difficulty with phonics are instructed in the Ginn readiness program.

The distinction between a phonics approach and a linguistic approach is important to note, for it is a distinction that figures prominently in Crystal's record. The phonics program teaches individual letter-to-sound correspondences, whereas the linguistic approach teaches groups of whole words that are related by the nature of their spelling patterns. The "rules" taught in phonics imply that reading proceeds from individual letters or letter clusters to whole words. In a linguistic approach, controlled patterns of word "families" are presented (e.g., "can/fan/man" "cat/fat/sat"), and the reader is encouraged to see the relationships of one pattern to the next. Although some children progress well in the Lippincott program and seem to enjoy it, Ms. Sein notes that in her experience many other children are able to use phonics only after they learn to read, not before. Crystal's record appears to bear out this observation.

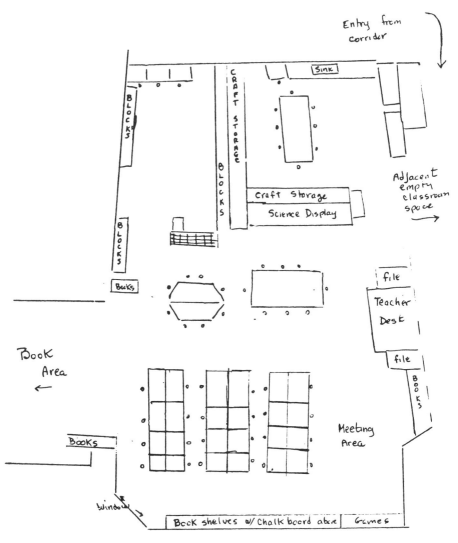

FIG. 11.1   Sketch of Crystal's Classroom

REPORT FROM THE TOTAL RECORD

Initial impressions of Crystal as an intense observer of classroom life are supported throughout the record by instances that highlight her broad awareness of other people, resources, and events. Typically, she interacts with liveliness and good humor as she circles through the room and settles into various activities. Occasionally, she displays marked shyness as well as a tendency to seek privacy when accomplishing her own goals. Her interest in establishing intimate contact with others is apparent from the beginning of the record, but changes in character as she seeks a close relationship first with the teacher and then with classmates.

Her approach to learning is one of confidence and resilience. Although she adopts many classroom standards, she also appears to possess her own set of standards for the execution and completion of work. And she pursues her own agenda with determination, expending particular effort upon learning how to read. In terms of classroom expectations, Crystal is compliant but also has many unfocused moments of "wandering." Over the course of the study, however, it becomes clear that once she has completed a detour, checking on other activity and persons in the classroom, she usually returns to focus with competence on the task at hand.

These patterns of Crystal's functioning are reflected in the following headings:

1. Observant and Aware
2. Cheerful, Playful, Teasing
3. Hiding, Privacy, Intimate Contact
4. Quality and Completion
5. Focus and Detour

1. Observant and Aware

In one of her earliest interview statements, the teacher describes Crystal as an observer: "She is aware of what is going on in the room, will go over to look at something special, then go back to what she is doing." This initial impression is verified and elaborated throughout the record, revealing a significant pattern in Crystal's functioning. Her awareness of activity, persons, and materials serves to expand the range of classroom resources available to her. She uses the knowledge she gleans from observing to further her own learning and participation.

—When I taught chip trading to a group of children, I wasn't even aware of the fact that Crystal was watching. And the next time I asked who wanted to play, she said, "I know how to play that game—I watched." [January, 1st grade]

—The other day, I was showing a child who is a fine reader several books that she could read over a period of time, as an alternative to the simple ones she now reads in one swoop. . . . Crystal was there and later she came to me with *Look Out For Pirates*, one of the books I had been showing the other child. I would never have suggested that book to Crystal, but she read it to me, and I wrote in my notes that she had figured out a lot. [January, 1st grade]

—Often, wherever I am and whoever I'm with, she likes to look over my shoulder and see what they're reading. She reads along sometimes. [January, 1st grade]

—Crystal knows a lot about what's going on in other parts of the room. She will come over and join in conversations, stop and listen to people read books. She checks in at various areas. [April, 1st grade]

—Crystal rotates in her chair to watch Colin retell the story he was reading to Ms. Sein. Crystal holds her book with the binding turned back and looks over the top of it. [Observation: May, 1st grade]

—She holds the paper and scissors at eye level; when I saw her, she was simultaneously watching and talking to other people. [October, 2nd grade]

—Wherever she's sitting, she knows what's happening. [February, 2nd grade]

An incident observed in March of first grade captures Crystal's ability to observe and draw upon several resources.

—Crystal has drawn a picture and is writing a sentence beneath it. She tells a friend that she needs the word *school* for her sentence. She looks through cards in her spelling file box but doesn't find the word. She then picks up a pencil that has "school pencil" printed on the side. She begins to copy *school* from the pencil.

Crystal observes other children with special interest. Her teacher comments on this interest throughout the study and summarizes the evidence in the final interview: "Even sewing, which is something she likes to do, doesn't seem as exciting to her as watching everyone else." Often, Crystal's interaction with other children is highly differentiated. She likes to watch a child who is particularly difficult in the classroom and to engage his attention by showing him things she has done. She is fond of another youngster and watches him but hides her face when he is near her. For a period of several days, Crystal works on some colored block designs with Leila, a child whose balanced and delicate designs contribute significantly to Crystal's own efforts. And in several instances when she has difficulty deciding what to write about, she borrows ideas from someone else's story. She makes the distinction of not copying another person's story, just the characters or general theme.

Included in Crystal's view of other children as prime resources in the classroom is a view of herself as helper and resource to others. She often helps classmates with problems in which she has expertise. In one observation, for instance, she notices that another child's sewing pattern is too small to work and helps her to adjust it. She reminds others (as well as herself) to "stop talking and finish." She also frequently observes others who are less able readers than she is and gives assistance she considers appropriate. Indeed, as Crystal learns to read, the record is full of instances of her observing other children, the teacher, and other children together with the teacher. (Further documentation of this pattern as it specifically relates to reading appears in the report on the reading record.)

2. Cheerful, Playful, Teasing

In two interviews, Ms. Sein says she can tell when Crystal is not feeling well, because ''she is cranky and restless;'' she ''hangs back and is not her usual self.'' Usually, Crystal is cheerful of disposition and bouncy in gestures.

—She stands up and walks away with a swinging step, hand on hip. [Observation: October, 1st grade]

—Her lower teeth show when she smiles. She smiles often, and when I think of her, I think of those little teeth. [November, 1st grade]

—Crystal gets a twinkly look and immediately skips to the sewing table. [Observation: May, 1st grade]

Crystal enjoys sharing her accomplishments with the teacher and with friends. An early observation catches her smiling as she dictates and reads back her story during a class lesson. During the first interview, Ms. Sein describes Crystal's pleasure in her work as well as her ease and cheerful confidence when reading aloud.

—She likes to show me what she's done. She doesn't seem to be asking for praise. . . . When she reads to me and gets to a word she doesn't know, she says, ''I don't know that word.'' There is no distress, almost a surprise that she doesn't know it. Her voice seems to question, ''How could that be?'' [November, 1st grade]

Elements of playfulness and teasing are evident in conversations with other children and with adults. Sometimes she makes rather outrageous statements in tones that underline her playful intent. Sometimes her good humor comes through in ''serious'' situations such as testing. And there are occasions when she is involved in typical boy-girl teasing.

—When a friend says that she can't jump double dutch, Crystal responds: ''My sister is four and she knows how to jump double dutch. But you have to turn *real fast* for her.'' [Observation: May, 1st grade]

—When the teacher's aide asks Crystal if she is going to make tiny stitches, appropriate to the sewing task, Crystal says, ''Yeah, tiny stitches.'' Then, smiling—''I'm going to make *big, fat* stitches.'' [Observation: October, 1st grade]

—She's been talking during the California Achievement testing, making a lot of good-natured but annoying comments. [February, 2nd grade]

—There is a lot of giggly, giddy, boy-girl stuff. And there's a lot of gossiping. Crystal does a lot of flirting with Teddy and John. She told me she likes Paul. She tore up a valentine one of the boys gave her. [February, 2nd grade-

On one occasion in the record, Crystal gets significant help with catching up on her math by copying from a friend's completed workbook. Her excited exclamations about this progress are overlaid with playful innuendo.

> —"Look at this, look at this, Elsie." (Crystal turns back in the workbook to show completed pages.) "Now I'm getting somewhere." [Observation: October, 2nd grade]

3. Hiding, Privacy, Intimate Contact

Crystal's sensitivity to the environment is particularly evident in the kinds of connections she seeks with other persons. As described in the two previous headings, she often reaches out to interact with others. But as counterpoint, there are moments when she seeks anonymity within the group or privacy with individuals.

There are some outstanding instances, particularly during first grade, when Crystal appears shy and embarrassed. She hides her face and does not want to be noticed.

> —Sometimes when I call on her, even when she's raised her hand, she will cover her face with her hands and won't be able to talk. [November, 1st grade]

> —Crystal has a real thing with Colin. When he comes near, she covers her eyes. [January, 1st grade]

> —I observed her extreme shyness. Once she seemed really afraid to come in late— she comes late often. . . she walked behind her mother and held on her mother's back. [March, 1st grade]

> —When we went down to K–1 (the classroom where she spent kindergarten last year), I was stunned to see her hide behind me, hold onto my skirt, hide her face in my back. [March, 1st grade]

> —She looked away embarrassed when I read her story to the group. [March, 1st grade]

> —On the first day this year, when Crystal came in with the line, she was as shy as could be, hanging on her mother, hiding behind her mother's back, leaning against her. . . But it was just an initial reaction. She isn't shy. [October, 2nd grade]

In the last example cited above, the teacher clearly recognizes Crystal's shyness at the beginning of second grade as "shyness in context." Crystal has often been shy on entering a situation, but Ms. Sein recognizes that Crystal is not shy in general. Another context of shyness noted by the teacher is Crystal's uncertainty about knowledge. In the beginning of first grade, Crystal seems more comfortable at group reading instruction if she is not called upon directly to read or answer questions. (Though she is observed more than once reading quietly under her breath.) Conversely, when Crystal seems sure of herself, she is not in the least shy about sharing her knowledge.

—I don't feel that her shyness is a barrier at all in the classroom. When the time comes to give an answer, she gives it. She doesn't hide her knowledge. She seems more comfortable in the reading group with regard to answering than she was earlier. [January, 1st grade]

—She is very active during the instructional reading time. She calls out the words and really knows them. She doesn't hesitate to call out and to be the teacher. She told Leila she would tell her what to do today. [March, 1st grade]

—Crystal was working independently at the same table where Genine and Mary were working with the aide. Crystal pulled the book out of Genine's hand and said, ''That's not right. This is how you do it.'' She was . . . being the teacher. [February, 2nd grade]

Another facet of this heading has more to do with anonymity than with shyness. Crystal turns her propensity to become ''lost in the crowd'' to advantage as she quietly but determinedly pursues her own agenda. She does not make obvious her alternative strategies or her deviations from expected behaviors; she simply does what she thinks she needs to do. When confronted with wrongdoing, she defends herself matter-of-factly. On two occasions, Crystal quietly violates firmly established rules of the classroom: she rips a page out of her writing book, and she takes unfinished work home from school. When Ms. Sein discovers the latter infraction and questions Crystal about it, Crystal replies, ''I just wanted to show my mother.''

Other examples of Crystal's seeking anonymity, or ''hiding,'' in order to pursue her own agenda do not involve the infraction of well-known rules, but they do entail an overstepping of boundaries. For instance, her intense observation of the teacher and other children sometimes reaches the point of being annoying.

—Crystal sits across the table from Leila, who is next to Ms. Sein, and leans forward with her elbows on the table, watching. . . Ms. Sein sends Leila away and calls Elsie to read. Crystal continues to watch. Ms. Sein says, ''Crystal, it's really bothering me that you're sitting here watching.'' Crystal stares back at the teacher, but does not answer. Then she hides behind her book, her face disappearing for a short time and then reappearing again over the top of the book. [Observation: May, 1st grade]

On another occasion, delivery of Crystal's math book is delayed by several days. When Ms. Sein is finally able to give Crystal the book, she ''works hard'' to catch up with her friends.

—She looks in the desk, pulls out another math workbook and opens the book to the same page that she is working on. She leans back and reads the answers, copying them into her workbook. Crystal turns both books to page 46, referring frequently to the one inside the desk. Ms. Sein walks by and she hastily shoves the book back inside the desk, watching until Leah is across the room. She takes the book to another table to show two other girls how many pages she has completed— "Look! We're all three almost together!" [Observation: October, 2nd grade]

The quality of hidden activity in group situations, described above as shyness and anonymity, also has a private expression. Crystal's intention appears to be intimacy—the intimacy of close contact and shared secrets. These personal interactions involve both adults (especially Ms. Sein) and other children.

Crystal frequently shares confidences with Ms. Sein, as she divulges bits of information about home and her life outside of school. She often enhances the effect by touching or leaning close, thus underlining the importance of the exchange and focusing private attention upon herself. Ms. Sein cites many specific instances, expecially early in the first grade.

—If she doesn't have a chance to say what she wants to in the group, she'll come up and whisper it to me. [November, 1st grade]

—At least once a day she'll come over, touch my arm, and whisper something in my ear. This week it was something about the Halloween party she was going to. . . . Another day it was something she had made at home and wanted to show me. It is a little personal interchange. [November, 1st grade]

—When we went for a walk to the park, she came up and took my hand and said, "I want to be your partner." It's not clinging. It's pleasant, not a dire need for attention, just a quiet thing, almost like a friend. [November, 1st grade]

—She enjoys sewing. Part of it is the contact with an adult. [November, 1st grade]

—Often she is leaning on an adult, or pulling down an adult from the shoulder. . . . She's still a touching child when she wants to tell you something. She whispers in your ear. . . . She likes to tell secrets. [June, 1st grade]

Throughout the first grade, Crystal increasingly enjoys secrecy and the reciprocal quality of shared confidences with friends. As she continues into second grade, her need for intimacy with the teacher seems to decrease, and she invests greater energy and interest in sharing fun with peers.

—There is a group of friends that she is often with. . . . Every morning there is a fight about who gets to sit at a particular table. . . . They crowd in there, about eight kids . . . and Crystal is involved in that. [June, 1st grade]

4. Quality and Completion

Much of what Crystal does seems to be guided by high standards for the quality of her products and by an expectation that completion of work is important. Data for this heading intersect the heading of "Observant and Aware," in that existing school standards are immediately recognized by Crystal. Early in the record, she asserts her interpretation of one such standard:

—"If Ms. Sein makes you do it, you have to do it!"

By her own account, Crystal loves to sew. She invests herself fully in the planning and execution of several highly attractive and useful items—a purse, a book bag, a skirt. As she sews, she is careful to plan ahead, to adjust her pattern, to smooth her work, to take small stitches. She is invariably pleased with her finished products. In spelling also, she is most unwilling to make a guess and goes to great lengths to write words correctly.

Along with quality, a commitment to completion is integral to Crystal's standards. The necessity to rework or struggle in order to achieve a high quality product or performance does not often deter Crystal from the eventual completion of a task. She sometimes surprises her teacher by working through to the end of a difficult job. She persists in the perfect completion of a complex pattern block design and of some math tile problems. She often talks about finishing; she counts the number of pages left to do. Crystal is tenacious when she has chosen to read books that seem beyond her ability. She says she wants to complete these books even when she seems obviously tired, and she indicates by several comments that she expects to derive meaning from her efforts—she expects to find out what happens at the end of the story.

Crystal doesn't apply standards of perfection and completion in a rigid, across-the-board manner, however. She can also find ways to "disappear into the crowd" and to avoid distasteful, less interesting tasks. On the whole, she goes about the business of school in a balanced and realistic manner. She is the measure of her own achievement. The key to her attention to quality and her decisions to persist seem to be her own evolving sense of what she can reasonably accomplish. In this respect, it is interesting to note that Crystal often selects activities at choice time that provide continuous feedback about the correctness or quality of her performance—information that can be used along the way in monitoring and guiding an effort to successful completion. These activities include sewing, pattern blocks, paper snowflake cut-outs, cooking, and the like. She rarely chooses more open-ended activities such as clay or painting. Crystal's concern for monitoring a performance along the way and for achieving a finished product which meets her standards are illustrated in the following observation.

—Crystal is sewing a purse and has told her friends, "If I finish today, I can put my money in it to bring in tomorrow." She makes helpful suggestions about her friends' sewing and then notices that her own work needs attention. She pulls out the overlapping stitches with scissors and begins the top part again. After sewing about a quarter of the width, she puts the purse flat on the table and inspects it carefully. She pulls the stitches out again and starts over. "I want to finish and I'm not finished and I have to finish it." [Observation summary: May, 1st grade]

FIG. 11.2   Crystals Purse

The finished purse, one of Crystal's several sewing projects, is pictured here.

Crystal's standards seem to emerge from her own image of the purposes of school and of how to accomplish them, as well as from influences at home. In formal parent conferences, in notes to school, and in informal conversations with Ms. Sein, Crystal's mother makes it clear that she has high expectations for Crystal's learning and activity in school.

Among other things, Crystal's mother reports that Crystal herself has wanted to learn to read since she was four. Crystal's seriousness of purpose about reading bear out that she continues to have this desire and that she expects to accomplish the job. Thus, she tries hard to adopt what she perceives to be the teacher's standards. She especially tries to implement phonic reading lessons, even when it appears that she cannot synthesize separate sounds into words. In March of first grade, after a successful reading of a particularly difficult selection, Ms. Sein asks Crystal: "How did you read all that? Did someone help you (at home)?" Crystal asserts, "I sounded it out," although there is no audible evidence of such a strategy on the tape. There are also moments on tape when Crystal makes valiant efforts to respond to the specific "phonic advice" offered by Ms. Sein. One of those moments is reproduced below. Crystal is trying to read the sentence: *Put your name on your lunch box.*

Crystal: But your n. . n.
Teacher: I think you're saying it.
Crystal: name?
Teacher: (Tells Crystal she is correct, but Crystal continues to hesitate. Ms. Sein then directs Crystal's attention back to the first word, *Put*.) OK, what's this? (spells) p-u-t?
Crystal: But?
Teacher: (spells again) p-u-t. (No response from Crystal) That's a "p."
Crystal: But
Teacher: You're saying "b-u-t." I want you to say "p" (she makes a "p" sound).
Crystal: (makes the "p" sound Ms. Sein has made; then. . .) But.
Teacher: Put
Crystal: Put your name.
Teacher: Good!
Crystal: on your lunch box.

As Crystal gains in reading ability, both she and Ms. Sein abandon efforts with phonics. Crystal's personal standard—her own understanding of what she reads—appears to be her major guide as she approaches print.

—She doesn't know all the words in the books she's read, but she is satisfied that she is understanding and she is reading. [March, 1st grade]

—Crystal has asked another child to help her with a word in a book she has chosen for free reading time. The child tells Crystal the word is "cookies." Crystal points to the word again and gets the same response. With that, she goes back to the beginning of the page and rereads up to the point of the unknown word. She hesitates, apparently dissatisfied with "cookies." This time, she turns the book toward Ms. Sein and shows her the word. Ms. Sein tells her the word is "sandwiches." Crystal, now satisfied, continues to read. [Observation summary: May, 1st grade]

—Crystal reads two lines of a book she has chosen for free reading time. Then she turns ahead several pages. Elsie has been watching her and reaches over to turn the book back to the first page saying, "You haven't read all these pages." Crystal reads aloud, skipping some words but reading most of the text. She carefully studies the picutres. Elsie again leans over and flips back several pages saying, "You skipped these." Crystal responds, "No I didn't." She counts the remaining pages and announces to Elsie, "Look at all these pages; I got three more pages (to finish)." Elsie answers, "You should have read these." Crystal retorts: "I read *ALL* of it!" [Observation summary: October, 2nd grade]

5. Focus and Detour

This heading closely intersects those previously discussed. Crystal's standards and expectations of school support her ability to focus. Her observation and awareness, along with her interest in "hiding" and intimate contact, contribute to the detours. Evidence of Crystal's focus on tasks is at first hard to see, for she typically balances attention to the quality of her work with her more visible attention to observing the classroom scene and social interactions. In this respect, it is notable that sewing is her favorite choice time activity. Sewing projects invite both a focus on the quality of the product and the possibility of detour to events and persons in the setting. In the following observation, Crystal keeps two strands of attention going. One is toward the setting and her friends within it, the other is toward the satisfactory completion of her project.

—Crystal gets a twinkly look and immediately skips to the sewing table. . . . "I like to sew every day. I can sew on this bag all day till I finish—right?" Crystal has sewed the seams on the wrong side and now she turns the material and begins basting the outside. She sews in a confident, capable manner although she usually stops when she is talking. She watches the other children around the table.

There follows some singing and joking, then a girl in the block area says the caterpillar has laid eggs and Crystal leans over the divider to see. The aide has to call Crystal's attention back to her sewing. Later, her friend crawls under the table apparently looking for her needle. Crystal watches, drops her scissors, then laughs and crawls under the table too. Talking and whispering ensue. Finally Crystal is heard to say, "Ohhh! Stop talking or we'll never get done today." They sew quietly for several minutes. Then Crystal teases her friend about jumping rope "double dutch." Her friend's sewing is not working out and Crystal shows her how to sew an overlap stitch. Then Crystal asks, "Is that easy for you now? It should be easy". Crystal watches another girl who is just beginning a purse. She tells the girl the allowance for the flap at the top is not enough and takes the fabric to demonstrate the correct way to construct the purse. She then announces, "I'm going to finish today."

Next, Crystal notices that her own work needs attention. She pulls out the overlapping stitches with scissors and begins the top part again. After sewing about a quarter of the width, she puts the purse flat on the table and inspects it carefully. She pulls the stitches out again and starts over. "I want to finish and I'm not finished and I have to finish it." [Observation summary: May, 1st grade]

Crystal seems to have her own rhythm for settling into (or not settling into) activities and assigned tasks. The extent of her "wandering" occasionally troubles Ms. Sein, who also often asserts that Crystal is "hard to see."

—She wanders. . . . She has only been watching other children, watching them use rods to write numbers . . . watching rod trading . . . spending a lot of time watching and not doing her own work. [March, 1st grade]

—She tends to circle around till she gets to her friends. She makes a point of sitting and working next to them, which isn't so great in terms of getting her work done. [April, 1st grade]

On one occasion, Crystal's detours were caputred by the observer who documented the following behavior.

9:30   Crystal takes her writing book out of her drawer and sits at a table. She moves with her book to a set of desks across the room. She stands by a chair there for a minute and then returns to the first table. She finally settles at another table and begins to write.

9:35   Crystal walks around the room into the block area, checks on the rabbit, circles around the two tables by the drawers and stops at teacher's desk for a pencil.

9:37   Crystal returns to her desk by way of the art area, weaving around the two tables again. She opens her writing book and erases two words.

9:40   Crystal goes over to a shelf and brings back a picture dictionary. As she stands by her chair, she leans over and whispers to a girl. She circles around the room again and stands next to Ms. Sein. Crystal gets a second pencil and returns to her seat (by a direct route).

But the side of Crystal that includes standards and expectations is also well documented. These seemingly opposite strands of focus and persistence woven into wandering and distraction are further evidence of the balance Crystal manages to achieve in the classroom. Her teacher states this directly in several interviews.

—She moves around, but she can also stay with an activity for a long time. She's been sewing a pocketbook and has stayed with it, working the whole choice time of almost an hour. She waits her turn to get her needle threaded. She plays in the blocks for a long time too. [November, 1st grade]

—Today she was reading *Little Bear*. She was serious and didn't get involved with some of the kids near her who were stretching a lot and talking about books. She looked at them sometimes, but then always went back to what she was reading. [May, 1st grade]

During the final interview, Ms. Sein continues to express some concern about Crystal's need to watch others. But she also acknowledges that Crystal usually does complete her work.

—She had to check in with all the kids who were making valentines and see who was doing what. Then she finally made a nice valentine. But all the time she was also watching what everyone else was doing, and she had an interchange with John and Lewis about the valentine she didn't want to get from them. And the same is true for reading—she is talking and getting that work done at the same time. [February, 2nd grade]

REPORT FROM THE READING RECORD

The patterns of balance described in Crystal's total record are also evident in the reading record. Although she regards school as a place where she will learn how to read, and her teacher as an authority, she also brings confidence in her own agenda to the learning process. She relies on a broad range of human and material resources in the classroom, using them in ways that make sense to her in order to further her own learning purposes. She finds the balance point between persistence and frustration, and seems relaxed and able to live with her best efforts. She makes steady progress as a reader, placing primary emphasis on story and contextual meaning as she gradually gains control of knowledge about print and text structure.

When Crystal enters first grade, the stage is well set for her to learn how to read. She is familiar with books. She loves to hear stories read and to tell them herself (later, to write them herself). She has memorized some sight words. She likes to make books and to copy words. She loves to read to the teacher. And, according to her mother, she has wanted to learn to read since the age of four.

On early oral reading tapes, Crystal's major supports seem to be pictures and anticipation of the story line. She learns some letter sounds but does not use them spontaneously when trying to figure out words. She seems uncomfortable during group phonic instruction and prefers to learn when it is her turn for one-to-one instruction, or by "listening in" as Ms. Sein reads individually with other children. Early in the record, Crystal creates occasions for getting extra individual attention in reading. Later, as her ability to read grows stronger, she relies less on this kind of help, and she also appears less reticent during phonic instruction. Ms. Sein suggests that Crystal "knows the phonic lessons before they are taught."

Crystal practices and consolidates her learning by frequently rereading familiar books. At first she rereads books with controlled linguistic spelling patterns. Later she chooses more traditional basal texts and easy-to-read trade books. When reading aloud, she is often satisfied to guess at words or phrases; she plows ahead without breaking rhythm or expression, thus allowing a certain level of error and ambiguity to go by unmarked. She seems to "play the percentages" by sacrificing some accuracy for the advantage of getting a sufficient quantity of information. Only rarely does she stop and try to sound out a word. Her retelling indicates that she can make sense of what she reads by gathering the essentials, if not the full details. The final oral reading tape at the end of Crystal's second-grade year shows that her interest in the story, her attention to pictures, and her ability to grasp meaning (as indicated by her comments and retelling of the story) continue as major elements of the performance.

The reading record is organized according to the following themes:

1. The Teacher and Peers as Resources
2. Physical Contact with the Teacher

3. Persistence
4. Awareness of Own Knowledge and Resources
5. Balance of Attention to Words and Stories
6. Attention to Pictures
7. Self-Selected Pathways

1. The Teacher and Peers as Resources

Crystal's expectation that she will learn to read in school appears to include an understanding that the teacher will, in fact, teach her. On the very first day of school, she responds to Ms. Sein's introductory lesson on how to use a picture dictionary. As Crystal draws and writes later in the day, she uses the dictionary to find the word *boat,* which she then copies into her book. She is attentive to stories read to the class, she participates in group discussions, and she asserts her general belief in Ms. Sein as ultimate authority in the classroom ("If Ms. Sein makes you do it, you have to do it").

Crystal is never far from Ms. Sein at free reading time. She places herself so that she can both see and hear Leah's instruction of other children. Sometimes, Crystal inserts herself into the situation as participant as well as observer.

—She sits across from me while she is reading every day at free reading time. There I am, and there is the child who is reading to me . . . and there is Crystal sitting across from me. [January, 1st grade]

—Ms. Sein is reading with Dora. Crystal is across from them leaning on the table, reading the words in Dora's book and sometimes also reading in her own book. [Observation: March, 1st grade]

—Ms. Sein calls Elsie over to read and Crystal follows, sitting across the table from the two of them. She leans forward with her elbows on the table, watching. Elsie is trying to read the title on the cover. Ms. Sein puts her finger over the *B* in *Bus* and asks, "What's this word?" Elsie: "us." Ms. Sein (removing her finger from the *B*): "And what's this?" Crystal (chiming in): "It rhymes with it!" Crystal continues to read a page in her book, pointing to the words one by one. Then she watches Elsie again, leaning forward and peering over the top of her book. [Observation summary: May, 1st grade]

—Crystal rotates in her chair to watch Colin retell the story he was reading to Ms. Sein. She holds her book with the binding turned back and looks over the top of it. [Observation: May, 1st grade]

—I was working with a child who is new in the class and just learning to read. We were reading *Little Bear.* Crystal pulled a chair up and sat directly across from us and began reading from her book (*City Sidewalks*). She seemed to want to make sure I noticed her, and she looked up every once in a while to check if the other child was reading the words right. She would comment, "Oh, I like that book. . . . I read that book." If the child got stuck, Crystal would say, "I know what that word is." [February, 2nd grade]

For a few weeks during the spring of first grade, Ms. Sein decides to change the arrangements for free reading and to experiment with a strictly "silent reading" period. She no longer allows the children to share books and talk with one another or with her about their books as had been permitted before. Crystal becomes upset and seems to lose interest in reading during this change.

—When I was really enforcing silent reading, Crystal was very cold. I assigned seats and insisted upon silence. Her seat was far away from me. During this time, she would hardly read at all, only just flip through books. She would get in trouble talking. She'd take a book or two, but not stay with it. Then, sometime in April, I changed back to free reading, and there she was the first day of the change next to me again. [April, 1st grade]

Crystal frequently receives individual help from the teacher by managing to find the appropriate moments and methods of approach to ask for it. As her ability to read increases over the year, these bids for individual assistance in reading diminish.

—She comes and waits 'til I'm finished. Or, if I'm not busy, she'll take me by the arm, might even sit me down, and say "I'll read to you," or "Will you read to me?" She also likes to show me what she's done. [November, 1st grade]

—She comes to me with a book and asks to read to me alone. [November, 1st grade]

—She's often around me when she's reading. And I also take the time with her. She gets to read to me a lot, even when it's not her regular turn. [January, 1st grade]

—Crystal now knows she can read, so she doesn't sit next to me as much. But the contact is still there in the form of "What's this word?" or "I like this story." And she'll tell me about the story. [April, 1st grade]

In addition to her teacher, Crystal also regards her peers as resources for learning. She borrows ideas for composing stories from other children. In reading, other children are a major influence upon her choice of books. She notices what Ms. Sein recommends to others and what interests her classmates when they are reading on their own. She then reads these same books.

—She saw some children reading the Lippincott Superbooks and stayed with that group for a while. She is enough aware of what's going on in the room that if I tell someone about a book, she will go to it. [January, 1st grade]

—She came to me with *Look Out For Pirates,* which I had been showing another child. I would never have suggested that book to Crystal, but she read it to me. [January, 1st grade]

—She likes to look over my shoulder and see what others are reading. She reads along and sometimes I have to tell her to be quiet, because the child who is reading with me will get the words from her. She did that with a book about the rain that I made. She doesn't go to books that I've made very often by herself, but when another child is reading one to me, she comes over. [March, 1st grade]

—Today during free reading, they were supposed to keep the same book. Crystal, however, changed books with the boy next to her. She held his book sideways and was actually reading it sideways. Later, Crystal and another girl sat on the rug and read together. It was a Merrill Linguistic reader, and they were reading loudly and in unison, very slowly and rhythmically. [March, 1st grade]

—Alice read *Johnny Lion's New Book,* and then Crystal read it. [April, 1st grade]

—Crystal stands by a table flipping through a copy of *Jack and the Beanstalk.* She looks at the front cover and sees Bert's name. Crystal asks Bert if she can read his book. He nods, and she returns to her place with the book. [Observation summary: October, 2nd grade]

2. Physical Contact with the Teacher

Enjoyment of privacy and physical contact, described in the Total Record, is particularly evident in physical contact with the teacher which accompanies Crystal's early reading efforts. Ms. Sein thinks that lack of such contact may contribute to Crystal's discomfort in the group reading situation.

—There is a lot of physical contact when she talks to you, pushing herself to your lap, holding your hand or arm, putting her arm around you. When she reads, she likes to be physically close to you. She does not like reading group, and I think it has a lot to do with the lack of physical contact at that time—because when I asked her about it, she said she didn't like it and liked it better when she worked just with me. [November, 1st grade]

—She's fascinated with the book *Ann Likes Red.* She read it to the student teacher, then she brought it to me, snuggled up on my lap and said, "I can read this book." [November, 1st grade]

—She sits across from me while she's reading every day at free reading time. She makes herself noticed in a very nice way. She gets the conversation and the help that she needs from me. [January, 1st grade]

—The physical contact is definitely continuing. When she wanted to show me a book (the other day), she took my hand in both her hands. And a few times recently she has slid into my lap. [January, 1st grade]

—She sat on my lap while Billy was reading to me, and she was commenting to him, "That was good! That was good!" [January, 1st grade]

3. Persistence

Crystal takes reading to be a serious business. Her persistence with reading is an interesting contrast to the periods of inattention and wandering described in the total record. Ms. Sein frequently mentions her suprise at Crystal's determination with difficult texts. In addition to the *Look Out For Pirates* incident, when Crystal surprised Ms. Sein by persisting in a choice that seemed much harder than Leah imagined she could manage, there are other instances of Crystal's persistence.

—Today she was reading *Little Bear*. She was serious and didn't get involved with some children near her who were talking about books. She looked at them sometimes, but then always went back to what she was reading. [March, 1st grade]

—Mostly she sits alone when she reads. Today she was reading the Merrill books; she plows through them. I think she's reading the third one now. She took that book home and didn't bring it back today, so she got mine and sat down with it. [April, 1st grade]

—She spent a lot of time reading *My City*. I have the feeling it was too hard for her, but she is very persistent. [October, 2nd grade]

—Last weekend she took home *Around the City*, the Bank Street primer. She had asked to take it. She came back Monday and announced, "Well, I finished!" [March, 1st grade]

—Her mother reports that she reads when she gets her hair combed in the morning and when she goes to bed; she also reads to her father when he comes home . . . . her mother is really happy. [March, 1st grade]

Acquisition of writing is harder for Crystal. She resists writing often, but there are other times when she is notably diligent and patient. The extended observations below are illustrative.

—Crystal has written *Y* on a page in her writing book. She takes a picture dictionary from the shelf and looks through it. Then she writes *yes* in her book. Resting her head in her hand with her elbow on the desk, she looks around the room. She writes *a,* then gets a *Little Bear* book from her file drawer. She copies *Littl* from the cover of the book, hunts in her pencil bag for an eraser, erases *Littl* and then rewrites it.
  Beginning in the back of the book, Crystal looks through the picture dictionary page by page, stopping at *Gg*. She scans all the words on the *Gg* page and then closes the book. Leaving her desk, she goes over to a shelf and opens a small file box of index cards with words printed on them. She flips through the cards as she stands by the shelf. She looks annoyed, puts the cards away and swears quietly. She returns to her desk and looks at the words on the *Gg* page again. She erases *girl*. She finds *man* in the dictionary and writes *man is*. She goes to the shelf, gets the card box and brings it back to her desk.
  A girl claims that Crystal is sitting in her (the girl's) seat, and Crystal moves to another desk with her writing book and cards. She flips through the cards several times but doesn't find what she's looking for. The cards are spread out on the desk out of order. Crystal selects *mother* from the array and puts it to one side. Ms. Sein asks her what she is looking for, and Crystal responds, "going."

Ms. Sein: Did you have it?

Crystal: I know I had it but I lost it.

Ms. Sein then asks Crystal if she can write *go*. Crystal says "yes" and writes it in her book. It is time for the class to go to gym. [Observation: January, 1st grade]

—Crystal takes her writing book and stands next to the teacher, who sends her for a tissue to blow her nose. When she repositions herself next to Ms. Sein, Leah tells her to get in line. She stands at the end of the line, but as the line moves forward, she leaves momentarily and loses her place. Each time she tries to return to the line, the children tell her to go to the end. After the third time, Crystal stays in line and gets to show her picture to the teacher and to dictate her sentence. [Observation summary: 1st grade]

Toward the end of first grade, Crystal seems to enjoy writing more. She occasionally elects to write during choice time, and she frequently comes to Ms. Sein for help with spelling.

Outstanding samples of Crystal's persistence in reading can be heard on the oral reading tapes. Her first experience with taping is lengthy and she has to work very hard. The session continues for over 15 minutes, and Ms. Sein asks several times if Crystal is ready to stop. Crystal finally replies impatiently, "I keep telling you no."

There is a similar example during a taping session in November of second grade. Crystal has inadvertently chosen to read to the interviewer from a very difficult library book, one she has not seen before. When asked if she wants to stop, she asserts, "I'll read two more pages."

There are other times on oral reading tapes when Crystal indicates fatigue by tone or pace. Once when Ms. Sein leaves her to read into the tape recorder on her own, Crystal reads along for a while. Then she sighs "I'm tired"—but she continues to read, though only the tape is listening.

4. Awareness of Own Knowledge and Resources

Crystal's general awareness of human resources in the classroom extends to her own knowledge and capabilities. She is good at estimating what she can and cannot do. As one selection for her first oral reading tape in the fall of first grade, she seeks out the book *Ann Likes Red*, saying that she knows how to read it. When Ms. Sein has her try it, she reads the book very well. In January, Ms. Sein relates that Crystal often says, "I can't read that," especially with respect to the Lippincott Phonic Program. *Look Out For Pirates*, however, does not elicit such a comment, even though Ms. Sein expects it to be hard for Crystal. As it turns out, Crystal reads much more competently in the pirate book than Ms. Sein had thought possible.

The record also suggests that Crystal is aware of her own growth in reading. In the fall and winter of first grade, she is never far from the teacher at reading time. She seems to rely on a significant number of individual contacts with Ms. Sein, both for direct instruction and for only slightly less direct observation. But by April of first grade, Ms. Sein says that Crystal now "knows she can read, so she doesn't sit next to me as much." At about the same time, Crystal masters the sounds and words in the Lippincott Program Book A. After an original reticence, she is now aggressive in group reading instruction.

—She's always the first one with her hand up. We're moving quickly with the phonic things that are part of the program, but she really doesn't need phonics any more. Sometimes I have to ask her not to call out. She also likes the workbook; she understands the directions and has no problems. [April, 1st grade]

Just as she estimates her strengths in reading, Crystal also predicts what will be hard for her. She often seems to know when she will need adult support; if such support is not forthcoming, she switches to something she can read independently. When a book is really over her head, she doesn't attempt it.

—She says about the writing, "Oh, that's too hard," or, "I can't do that." And she always goes and finds an adult to write the story for her or tell her the letters while she writes them down. [January, 1st grade]

—Today I told her I simply could not help her. Then she put that (book) away and got *A Pig Can Jig*, which she knew she could read. [January, 1st grade]

—She's not trying to read *Charlotte's Web*, which I'm currently reading to the class. Several of the children do take copies of that book and try to read it. When I read a book about insects, she was fascinated, so I asked her if she wanted to read it at free reading. She took it and put it in her drawer, but she never attempted to read it and later she gave it to Sally. [October, 2nd grade]

Examples of Crystal's questions and miscues in oral reading point up her awareness of what she is doing as she reads. In one selection on her first oral reading tape (October of first grade), she reads two pages of *Go Dog Go*, drawing upon what appears to be a combination of clues from the pictures and from her memory of the book's story line. Her rendition is quite similar to the actual text words.

Text	Crystal
"Hello!" "Hello!"	Hello . . . Hello . . . Hello.
"Do you like my hat?"	You like my hat?
"I do not."	No.
"Good-bye, Good-bye.	Bye! Bye!

But after this close approximation, Crystal is not ready to continue. Without any outside signal, she seems aware of the discrepancy between the print and what she has said. She acknowledges this as she points to the word *good-bye* and asks, "What's that?" Ms. Sein responds by telling her the word is "good-bye." Crystal says, "Oh" and continues reading.

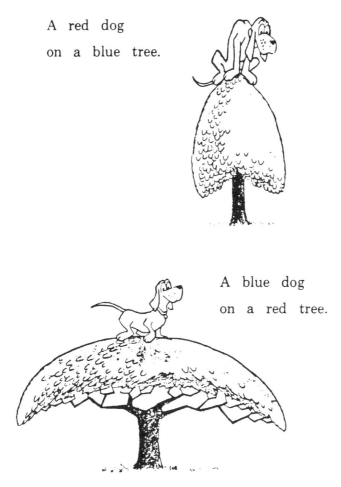

A red dog
on a blue tree.

A blue dog
on a red tree.

FIG. 11.3   Page from *Go Dog Go*

In another instance later in the same book, Crystal spontaneously identifies the cause of her confusion. She knows how to read color words, but she is confused when the colors in the pictures do not match her idea of a proper arrangement. The page in question is shown in Figure 11.3. Crystal begins to read at the bottom of the page, as follows:

> Crystal: A blue dog top on. . .
> top of the . . on th. .
> I don't know what it says.
> I don't know what it says.

Ms. Sein: Which word do you want? (Crystal points to *blue*.) You were
right, read it.

Crystal: A dog

Ms. Sein: No, you were right the first time. It's one of the words that's up
in the room.

Crystal: Blue . . . dog . . . top . . . a . . . red tree.

Ms. Sein: Very nice. (Points to top of page) Can you read this one?

Crystal: A red dog top a blue tree . . . I thought this one supposed to be
on this one. (Points to blue dog and blue tree.) And this dog
supposed to be on this one. (Points to red dog and red tree.)

Ms. Sein: Oh, you mean the blue one (dog) should be on the . . .

Crystal: Blue tree.

Ms. Sein: And the red (dog)?

Crystal: Supposed to be on the red tree.

During the fall of second grade, Crystal volunteers to read a difficult book to
the interviewer. Impressed with Crystal's ability to work out some hard passages, the interviewer remarks, "You're terrific!" Crystal explains: "I didn't
know all these words, but I just put them together."

Later, on this same tape, Crystal comes to the phrase, *along the railroad
tracks*. She has had difficulty with some earlier sentences and is quite tangled as
she substitutes "tellroad" for *railroad*. The interviewer asks her to try again.

Crystal: trainroad?

Interviewer: Pretty close!

Crystal: trackroad!

Interviewer: Well, this (word) is tracks. What kind of tracks are they?

Crystal: Train tracks.

Interviewer: They are train tracks, yes. How did you know that? There isn't
even any picture of that.

Crystal: Cause I saw the word *tracks*, so just has to be something
like . . . something that goes with tracks.

5. Balance of Attention to Words and Stories

As Crystal approaches reading in first grade, she is well aware of words as
separate units. She knows some sight words. She likes to copy sentences from
books and sometimes inserts a large dot in the space between each word. She
uses the phrases, "I know that word" or "I forgot that word" in several
different contexts. She uses all of the word resources in the classroom—the word
cards for spelling, picture dictionary, charts on the walls, and individual words
which she finds in books and copies as she needs them. When reading aloud to
the teacher (or other adult), she asks for words, pointing out the ones she knows
and those she doesn't know. Crystal is also interested in stories. She tells personal anecdotes to the teacher in whispered communications. When she gains in

writing ability, stories appear. And her work on separate words when she is reading does not seem to interfere with her interest in the events and the story line.

This balance of attention to word and story is expressed during an exchange with another child over two word cards. Crystal responds to the first card with an analytic observation about word relationships and then immediately shifts at the second card to a story response.

> —Maryann has the word *drug* on a card. Crystal shows her another card with the word *rug* on it and points out, "You already got that one." As they look at the next word, *drag,* Crystal tells a story about a mother who drags her two-year-old into the house. [Observation: March, 1st grade]

The observation also captures Crystal's focus on words as total entities. Her analytic inclination is to discern wholes within wholes (drug/rug). It is not her inclination to analyze words into letter-sound segments.

Crystal's oral reading tapes show that her interest and focus on words does not include a spontaneous ability to deal with the separate sounds of words that are taught in the phonic reading program. Her early reluctance in phonic instructional sessions and her outright statement to Ms. Sein ("I don't like to sound out words") further support this fact. With the exception of some of her earliest reading tapes, when she tries to use beginning sounds and repeats them many times over, Crystal is not heard spontaneously attempting fragmented sounds. She either substitutes another whole word for a text word, or she approximates a nonword in place of the text word. When asked specifically to blend individual sounds, she appears unable to do so, even though she can reproduce (upon request) some or all of the sounds in question. In the following example Ms. Sein asks Crystal to apply phonic knowledge at a word level. Although Crystal can say the separate sound that "two e's make," she is unable to incorporate that knowledge as she grapples for the whole word in the text. Crystal is trying to read the phrase: "*Don't cry, my sweet potato.*" She substitutes *swet* for *sweet* and repeats this nonword approximation three times over. Finally, the following exchange takes place.

> Ms. Sein: What sound do two "e"'s make?
> Crystal: ee?
> Ms. Sein: Yes.
> Crystal: Swet
> Ms. Sein: What sound do "e"'s make?
> Crystal: ee
> Ms. Sein: Okay.
> Crystal: Sh . . shrunk?
> Ms. Sein: You said two 'e's make the sound ee.
> Crystal: Sweep?

> Ms. Sein: Okay, try again.
> Crystal: Don't cry, my shrump? potato?
> Ms. Sein: Did you ever hear of a shrump potato?
> Crystal: No.
> Ms. Sein: What kind of potato starts like that?
> Crystal: Shrunk?
> Ms. Sein: No. You're not saying the sounds that you know. Let's go on.

Given her whole-word emphasis, Crystal displays a balance between possible responses to word difficulty within a text. At times she attempts to rework a false start or correct a misread word. At other times she simply moves on without a backward glance. In first grade, despite considerable effort, most of her oral reading correction attempts fail. In second grade, Crystal begins to succeed with certain kinds of correction, but she also continues to skip over many substitutions. Examination of oral reading performances in the second grade suggests that her particular response to text at the word level is related to (or cued by) her overall anticipation of text at the sentence and/or story level. The following analysis of an oral reading tape made in January of second grade is illustrative.

The text in question is *Oliver Pig*. There are 371 words in the selection, and Crystal reads with about 90% accuracy (i.e., 326 words read correctly on first attempt.) Crystal's differentiated attention to her inaccuracies would seem to indicate that she makes distinctions among several types of miscues as she reads. The 37 word-substitution miscues in *Oliver Pig* provide an opportunity for description of these distinctions as follows:

Insignificant Changes and Mispronunciations (23 instances).   These are inaccuracies that do not affect the contextual meaning of the sentence, or that represent a translation of text into the child's typical grammar and/or pronunciation. For example, Crystal says "a" for "the," "climb" for "climbed," "cocoa" for "chocolate," and "psgetti" for "spaghetti." She also mispronounces the name Amanda each time it appears, usually saying something like "Amally." In each of these instances of substitution, meaning of the sentence or story is not altered. Crystal makes the miscue and reads on without skipping a beat.

Significant Changes (14 instances).   These inaccuracies do make a syntactic or semantic difference in the text. If left uncorrected, sentence structure is in disarray and meaning is confused. Following 10 of these significant changes, Crystal stops and makes an attempt to rework the miscue. But there are 4 instances of significant change where Crystal does not stop or rework. These instances are all embedded in a single sentence, and Crystal seems to have difficulty anticipating most of the sentence structure.

Text	Crystal
"Are you still hungry as a bear, Grandmother?" asked Oliver.	"Are you still hungry as a bear, Grandmother?" asked Oliver.
"No," said Grandmother	"No," said Grandma.
"With cherry pie	"With the cherry pie
and raisin pie to eat	and the raisin pie, it to eat
and you and Amanda to hug,	and you . . said . . Am-a-ly it hug
I am full right up to the top."	I am fell right up . . to the top."

The structure of the text sentence that contains the 4 significant changes is a bit awkward. Its long opening phrase includes the line, *and you and Amanda to hug*. Crystal appears to anticipate a shorter opening phrase and therefore a totally different structure—perhaps "With the cherry pie, and the raisin pie, it was a good dinner," or "it would be silly to eat more." Crystal's insertion of *it* into the phrase disrupts the sentence structure. Once her original anticipation proves incorrect, she seems confused. She reads *you said* for *you and*, she persists with another wrong *it*, says *fell* for *full*, and never goes back to try to correct anything. She moves along with the story rather than returning to rescue the sentence. In other oral readings, there are similar instances of Crystal moving on rather than attempting to correct.

The analysis thus far suggests the following ideas about Crystal's balance of attention to word and story. When she makes a miscue by substituting a word that neither violates text meaning significantly nor upsets her anticipation of the story line (the 23 insignificant changes), she doesn't bother to correct. She appears to choose semantic integrity rather than literal word accuracy. She also does not attempt correction under the opposite conditions—that is, when her substitution both changes the text meaning and upsets her anticipation of sentence structure (4 of the significant changes). In that circumstance, it appears that she does not have a sufficient baseline from which to approach correction. When the miscue occurs, she can anticipate neither structural relationships nor meaning within the sentence; she does not stop to rework.

There remain for description 10 instances of significant change in Crystal's word substitution miscues in *Oliver Pig*. In each of these, her initial substitutions do not show evidence of faulty anticipation of text structure on her part. She responds differently to these miscues than she did to those just described. She *does* stop to attend to the words and she *does* attempt correction. In five of these instances, Crystal initially substitutes a word that is graphically similar to the text word; this substitution is a relatively isolated event within the sentence, and the surrounding text is well within her grasp. She seems to understand where the sentence is headed. Her anticipation remains intact. In all of these instances, she is able to correct herself successfully and move on with dispatch. For example:

Text: "Supper is ready," said Mother.
Crystal: "Super/supper is ready," said Mother.

Text: Oliver saw the snow coming down.
Crystal: Oliver see/saw a snow coming down.

Text: Oliver got out his pail and shovel
and his dump truck
and his steam shovel.
Crystal: Oliver got out his pail and sh-shovel
and his dump truck
and his steep. . . .steep. . . .steep. [Ms. sein: un-hmmmmp
steam? [Ms. sein: Yes] steam shovel.

In the other five instances of significant change, Crystal also retains her anticipation, but her correction attempts fail. In these cases, she has produced a nonword substitution in her effort to approximate the sound of the text word. Her vigorous attempts at correction are unsuccessful. And she does not move on until Ms. Sein tells her to do so. For example:

Text	*Crystal*
She sat at his table	She sat at his table
and ate spaghetti and meatballs	and ate psgetti and meatballs
and cinnamon toast	and crimmin . . . crispen . . . crispen?
	[go on] crispin toast
and chocolate pudding	and cocoa but . . . bunning . . . bunnied?
	[go on]
and apple juice and raisin pie.	and apple juice and raisin pie.

Another oral reading sample from the book *Snapping Turtle's All Wrong Day* was taped at the end of second grade. It shows Crystal's continued reliance on anticipation of structure and meaning to guide her reading and to support her through interrupted moments while she attempts word corrections.

Text	*Crystal*
"It would make a good bear trap.	"It would make a good bear trap.
That's what I'll do.	That was . . . (starts over) It would make a good bear trap.
	Th . . . That . . . That's what I wi. . . . (sigh) [That's right] I will do.
I will trap a bear and get its skin.	I will trap a bear and get his . . . its skin.
Mama Indian will like that."	Mama Indian will like that."
Snapping Turtle	Trapping . . Snapping Turtle
gathered a lot of branches.	gather a lot of branches . . branches.
"I'll cover this hole.	"I will cover this hole.
Then the bear won't see it.	Then the bear won't see it

He'll fall right through the branches.''

He fall right through the branches.''
[what's he going to do?]
He makin a trap for a bear so he
could get the bearskin and I
think he make his mother a shirt
or a coat. Then he fall in hisself.

In this excerpt, the graphic and grammatical forms of contractions seem to contribute to Crystal's difficulty. She has substituted, inserted, omitted, and repeated words in her attempt to give an accurate rendition of the text. But it seems clear that she has the passage straight. She not only answers Ms. Sein's question at the end, she further enriches the story with her thought of what the Indian boy plans to do with the bearskin and with her anticipation of what will happen next. Her comments are evidence that she keeps the story in mind even though her major attention seems to be on the words.

On the next page in this same book, Crystal's anticipation of the story takes precedence over correction attempts. Her substitutions alter the text to some degree, but she reads with expression and flies past them. She does not acknowledge the discrepancies at all.

Text	*Crystal*
Suddenly, down, down, he went.	Suddenly, down, down he went.
Snapping Turtle dropped right	Snapping Turtle dropped right
out of sight.	into the sight.
"Oh, no!" he said,	"Oh, no!" he said.
"I meant to trap a bear	"I might to trap the bear
And now I've trapped me.	And now I've trapped me.
This is my all wrong day."	This is my own wrong day."

At the end of this page, a volunteered comment to Ms. Sein indicates that Crystal has kept track of the meaning of the text. She says, ''He forgot all about it (the trap) too.'' (It is also interesting that Crystal sweeps right past the contraction *I've* with no difficulty on this page.)

This heading (balance of attention to words and stories) has focused thus far on Crystal's reading, but it is appropriate to take note of her writing as well. Crystal loves stories and is herself a storyteller. But writing is very hard for her, much more difficult than reading, and she goes to considerable lengths to find alternatives to sounding out the words she needs. Despite her difficulties and her long searches for words, even her earliest brief efforts tell stories. Many children in the class simply label their drawings or write a description of their pictures in their drawing-writing books, but Crystal's first-grade writing implies relationships, activity, and sequence.

—A little girl is going to the friend's house.

—Mommy is cooking lunch. I play in the snow. Yes, my mommy and me.

—The girl is looking at the mail and opened the package and dad and mom are at the door.

—I moved in the morning and we unpacked the clothes and my grandmother came. I'm in the house.

—I go to the candy store. No, said mommy.

In September of second grade, Crystal has a mishap, and for the very first time she becomes excited about writing. She bursts into school on a Monday morning, telling Ms. Sein she knows what she is going to write about. And she writes it.

> My sister pushed me . . . and my eye was bleeding and I cried and cried and cried. My mother took me to the bathroom and she took a piece of toilet paper and wet the toilet paper and she put the cold ice on my eye. Today my eye is getting better and my eye did feel much better too. And the swelling went down (and) the cut went down.

As Crystal brings writing activity under greater control, she produces longer stories. In the following story written in November of second grade she is at one moment the storyteller writing in the third person; the next moment she is the central character writing in the first person.

> One day a little girl was lost in the park. She cried and cried and cried. And one day her mother called the park. She was still there. Her and my father was happy to see me, said my father.

She soon settles into the storyteller role and writes consistently in the third person. Her stories also become longer, often continuing from one day to the next like continuous chapters in a book. In March of second grade, Crystal writes a story called "Wonder Girl" over a period of 4 weeks. In this story she incorporates many familiar themes of home, an actual accident that happened to her father, and her love of good times and of pretty clothes. She writes her story in "soap opera" genre, weaving fantasy and reality into a form which places her at some literary distance from the events. The following are some excerpts from "Wonder Girl."

> A girl's name was Wonder Girl. Wonder Girl's mother's name was Betsy. Betsy was a good mother. Wonder Girl loves her mother so much that she goes to school every day and she goes to the store for her mother.

> One day she was jumping rope. She fell down and broke her leg. . . . She had crutches for a week and she went to the doctor's office. The doctor said she had to keep the crutches on for ten weeks. She came back Monday, April 1980. She started walking again at her birthday.

She had a nice party. I went to her birthday party. (It) was outside in the back yard. She played hide-and-go-seek, and she played with her cat. The cake was upside-down cake. It tasted good.

She spent four dollars on her mother's party present. She said, ''I like the dress.'' The dress had a red shirt and a red skirt to it. . . . The next day she wore her birthday skirt and shirt.

6. Pictures

Crystal expects pictures to help her find out what's happening in a book. Sometimes she makes direct reference to the support a picture has given her. When reading *Go Dog Go* (October, 1st grade), for example, Crystal reads the word *tree*. Then she says, ''I knew this was *tree* because I saw it up there,'' referring to a previous page where the word accompanies a picture of a tree. On the particular page she is reading when she makes this comment, there is no picture of a tree, but Crystal explains to Ms. Sein how she originally figured out the word and how she now remembers it.

Crystal is able to scan picture and text without losing the flow of her oral reading, even though she is obviously substituting a word derived from the picture rather than from the print. Her anticipation of word from picture is clearly evident in the two instances reproduced here. Relevant pages from the book *Mouse Soup* are shown in Fig. 11.4 together with a notation of Crystal's version of the text (June, 1st grade). Except for a minor hesitation at her first encounter of the word *up*, she reads fluently. Her two notable substitutions, derived from picture information, are *elbows* for *waist* and *neck* for *chin*.

A provocative miscue involving a picture also occurs on Crystal's last oral taping. She is reading from *Snapping Turtle's All Wrong Day* in June of second grade. Crystal appears to try to resolve her difficulty with the phrase, *he cried*, by taking a cue from the picture (Fig. 11.5), which shows the Indian boy, Snapping Turtle, crawling on his hands and knees. By substituting *he crawled* for *he cried*, she is attending to the print as well as to the picture since crawled and cried each have the same letters at the beginning and the end of the word. In addition, and perhaps contributing to Crystal's miscue, the actual text which says that Snapping Turtle stood up, and which Crystal reads correctly, is contradicted by the picture which shows him crawling.

Text	*Crystal*
Snapping Turtle stood up.	Snapping Turtle stood up.
''I'll never get out of here!''	''I'll never get out of here!''
he cried.	He crawled.

7. Self-Selected Pathway

This heading emerges from the similarities and changes evident in Crystal's choice of books, and of her reading-related activities over time, especially over

The mouse

stepped into the mud
up to his ~~waist.~~ *elbows*

"Here is my living room,"

said the mouse.

"Oh yes," said the bees.

The mouse

stepped into the mud
up to his ~~chin.~~ *neck*

"Here is my bedroom,"

said the mouse.

"Oh yes," said the bees.

FIG. 11.4   Crystal's Substitutions in *Mouse Soup.*

FIG. 11.5   Page from *Snapping Turtle's All Wrong Day*

the period of the first-grade record. As has been mentioned, she enters first grade with the expectancy that she will learn how to read in school. She settles into a classroom environment that provides opportunities and resources for several kinds of encounters with reading, writing, and books. Among those opportunities are two periods set aside each day for learning how to read: the school's required program of phonic instruction, and the free reading time. Throughout most of first grade, Crystal reacts negatively to the phonic instruction and gives little evidence that she has been able to learn or to use the phonic rules. Even after she catches on to the instruction and begins to participate spontaneously and knowledgeably in the group lessons, she continues to be unable to apply phonic rules in her actual reading. All available data indicate that the use of phonic analysis in learning how to read is not the pathway Crystal follows. Although it is impossible to know exactly what pathway she does take, the record suggests her general direction and major resources.

Crystal's seriousness about reading, her persistence, and her ability to locate and to use classroom resources are evident from the beginning of the record. She even spots help that most people would overlook—as when she sees a needed word (*school*) on the side of a pencil and copies it. She is attentive when Ms. Sein reads books to the class. Early in first grade, Crystal joins a popular classroom activity—she copies the words from books that she cannot even read yet.

—There's a lot of bookmaking going on in the class. Some of the children began copying words out of books and Crystal's been doing that. She really loves it. She drew the pictures and copied the words of *Sleeping Beauty*. . . . They are practicing handwriting and noticing punctuation. Crystal has put a large dot in the space between each word. [November, 1st grade]

A sample of Crystal's copying efforts, from a book entitled *Snip Snap,* appears in Fig. 11.6.

When writing on her own, Crystal invariably finds ways (use of dictionaries, wall charts, and so on) to avoid the teacher's recommendation of "sounding out" spelling words.

—She used to say, "I don't like to sound out words," when she read them; she says that now about the writing. [January, 1st grade]

Crystal's specific use of the teacher as a resource for her learning is documented in a previous heading. She seeks Ms. Sein out and manages to get instructional help on her own terms. Those terms are reading to the teacher on a one-to-one basis, or having the teacher read to her. For a long time, Crystal also observes Ms. Sein's individual instruction of other children. Both the seeking-out and the observing behavior diminish only after Crystal gains some proficiency as a reader herself.

FIG. 11.6   Crystal's Copying from the Book *Snip Snaps*

In all of the ways just described, Crystal chooses an approach to books, to writing, and to reading instruction that by-passes phonics. But perhaps her most important direction and pathway is evident in the books she selects for herself at free reading time. Ms. Sein mentions these selections often in interviews.

—From the array of books in my classroom, Crystal does not choose to look at picture books or insect books. She chooses the books that teach her to read. She's aware enough of what's going on in the room that if I tell someone about a book, she'll go to it. Generally when she comes to me for help, she has the Merrill reader, or she'll see someone with the SRA reader, so she'll get that. They're essentially the same, and she's learning both of them. [January, 1st grade]

The SRA and Merrill linguistic readers that Crystal chooses are, in fact, designed to teach children to read short words with similar letter combinations at first. These two linguistic approaches rely on children inferring the letter-sound correspondences from the controlled and phonetically regular vocabulary presented in lists of whole word "families" (e.g., man, Dan, can, fan, van) and in the associated stories (e.g., "Dan can fan the man"). In contrast, the Lippincott Phonic Program teaches phonic rules directly by presenting separate letter sounds and rules (i.e., that *ar* makes an *are* sound). It also presents lists of words (e.g., car, arm, cart, bar) and associated stories (e.g., "Dan has a farm cart."). Because of the controlled vocabulary common to both phonic and linguistic programs, the story content of these readers is necessarily limited. Crystal's choice of the SRA and Merrill readers indicates her option to stick with books that emphasize inference of letter-sound relationships, rhyming whole word patterns and controlled vocabulary. Although Crystal has great difficulty working with phonic rules, she does know many letter sounds and can use rhyming cues in figuring out unknown words.

—She knows all the consonant sounds in reading. . . . She always knows the initial sounds. . . . I'm not sure yet about a style, what way she likes to read. I know she wouldn't choose sounding out. [January, 1st grade]

—During a reading lesson, Crystal attempts to sound out the word *mid*. She says all the parts separately, but she is unable to put the word together. Ms. Sein says the word *did* and Crystal is then able to read *mid*. [Observation summary: January, 1st grade]

By March of first grade, Crystal is better at "sounding out." When Ms. Sein asks her how she learned to read so much of *Look Out for Pirates*, Crystal responds, "I sounded it out" (though the oral reading tape contains no evidence of this strategy). During the March interview, Ms. Sein observes that Crystal has memorized a lot. "She can read the words that she knows upside down and right side up." Ms. Sein also describes the phonic instruction as "irrelevant" since she observes that Crystal manages to memorize the words on the phonic lists.

—I think it's almost irrelevant for her. She's learning it. She takes home lists to read, brings them back and tells me she knows them. She's practicing a lot at home. [March, 1st grade]

In March also, a change is noted in Crystal's selections of books. She begins to choose basals and trade books with increasing frequency. And her reading changes.

—There has been a big change in Crystal's reading (since) she began going over the Bank Street Unit Readers and bringing them to me. Crystal was learning the words in them, and on weekends or when she finished a book, I would let her take it home. There was a great difference in the way she could read those books with stories in them and the way she was reading the Merrill or the SRA readers. [March, 1st grade]

The change to which Ms. Sein refers in the above statement is Crystal's expanding ability (evident on tape) which develops as she begins to read the more traditional language and stories in the basal series in contrast to patterned text structure in the linguistic readers. Ms. Sein concludes this particular thought by quoting Crystal's mother who has told her that Crystal is "reading, reading, reading" at home.

Ms. Sein continues the interview by reviewing the history of Crystal's choices during free reading time.

—Thinking back over Crystal's choices, she began to read in Merrill then got SRA, then added the Bank Street and *Little Bear*. These are all books she chose, not that I told her to read. . . . Now she reads all four of these. She doesn't give up the books that she read before. On the other hand, she doesn't read the same books over and over every day. Now she has *Look Out For Pirates*. And today she read the Merrill again. She also went back to *Ann Likes Red*. [March, 1st grade]

Ms. Sein goes on to comment on Crystal's attention to words and her understanding of story.

—She comes to me for words she doesn't know. She's doing a lot of practicing. When she reads to me, she doesn't know all the words in the books, but she is satisfied that she is understanding, and she is reading. [March, 1st grade]

Evidence on oral reading tapes in the spring of first grade show that Crystal is able to handle unfamiliar books that are relatively simple; but she also continues to reread the old familiar easier ones. Crystal's choice of the easy and familiar along with her persistence in the new and difficult is a pattern that holds throughout the study.

12 Louis

Marianne Amarel, Jessie Agre, and Gibson Henderson
Teacher: Ellen Green
Grades Covered by the Study: First and Second

SYNOPSIS

Louis is a slightly built child, measured in voice, pace, and temperament. He exemplifies moderation in manner and mien.

An even, gradual pace marks his progress in school. He learns to read much the same way he learns everything else in the classroom—incrementally. He augments his skills and knowledge by consecutive addition, through the accrual of discrete elements. He shows a marked preference for modular materials and often segments the tasks he undertakes. He typically begins with the familiar and predictable, moving on a step at a time only when he is reasonably certain of his ground.

Louis's preferred style of work and distinct approach to learning have considerable integrity across settings and over time. Necessarily, these preferences prove to be more compatible with some of Louis's classroom endeavors than with others. For example, he gains competence, even expertise, as an architect and builder in construction activities, but his beginning reading retains a somewhat plodding quality well into second grade.

He begins reading with a few sight words and some letter sounds, steadily accumulating more sight words and learning to use initial consonants. He slowly enlarges his repertoire of strategies for deciphering words by adding context and picture clues. The resources he brings to learning to read are impressive. His language and conceptual capacities include a rich vocabulary, the ability to use language for various purposes, a good grasp of task requirements, and an exceptional ability to understand directions. Other attributes also support his learning: he can sustain engagement and interests, and he has a serious and responsive attitude toward school learning and the demands of the classroom setting.

His overall approach to learning, however, does not serve Louis equally well. The segmented, linear approach, marked by a singularity of focus and a reluctance to guess, to leap, or to ''mess about'' is poorly aligned with those aspects of reading that call for integrative processes. These qualities keep him engaged with the surface structure of text for an extended period, since he treats single words as the salient unit for reading. He is thus slow to gain access to the content, the meaning of text; reading, as a result, is a difficult, and not altogether rewarding experience for him. However, other features of his style, combined with his other resources, support the steady accumulation of knowledge and skills, and Louis becomes a fairly competent, if not enthusiastic, reader by the end of the second grade.

INSTRUCTIONAL ENVIRONMENT AND
READING PROGRAM

The Children's School, where Louis spent his first primary grades, has some uncommon features for an inner city school. It serves upwards of 35 children and spans kindergarten through second grade. The class is jointly taught by two teachers who work as a team, dividing responsibility for all major aspects of the instructional program.

The school is housed in a three-story row house, a short distance from the main school building. Although under the administrative jurisdiction of this nearby district school, the Children's School retains vestiges of its origin in a parent cooperative nursery program. The nursery program was extended to include the early primary grades through the efforts of an active group of parents who created an Educational Fund to purchase the building that now houses the school. The nursery no longer exists, and the district rents the building from the Fund, but the tradition of parent involvement continues. As a result, the teachers have among their students a sizable group whose parents requested that they be assigned there.

Physical Arrangement

The three-story house has a full kitchen and a playyard; the two lower floors are used as classroom space, and the top floor serves as combined office and teachers' room.

The first floor of the house is reserved for activities that need considerable space and are likely to produce noise, such as block building and housekeeping. The two rooms are provisioned with a large collection of blocks, a set of woodworking tools, and a ''big house'' and ''little house'' with a rich supply of dramatic play accessories. Painting and other activities requiring water and freedom to spread out usually take place here. The kitchen, used for communal cooking activities, is also on this floor.

The rooms on the second floor are reserved for more traditional academic activities. Several areas are delineated by work tables or the provisions related to an activity. The math area contains a large selection of manipulatives, games, and other math-related materials; the science area is the home of the classroom menagerie, which may include at any one time the ubiquitous guinea pigs and gerbils, as well as spiders, caterpillars, crabs, turtles, and praying mantises. Rocks, leaves and other natural materials collected during field trips are also sorted and displayed in this area. Arts and crafts supplies, small construction materials, and other provisions for the students' self-selected projects are stored about the rooms.

The reading area is set apart by a rug and surrounding bookcases that hold an extensive class library. An adjacent area is used for writing and for many of the more formal aspects of reading instruction.

Daily Schedule

The schedule of a typical day reveals a balance between assigned or teacher-directed work and self-selected activities. The school day begins at 9:00 a.m. with a whole-class meeting that lasts about 15 minutes. This is the time when the calendar is marked, various announcements made, and birthdays, lost teeth, and other events noted.

The first work period of the day is devoted to reading and writing. The first hour, mainly devoted to reading, is followed by a brief recess from which the children return to spend about half an hour writing. The reading program is discussed in some detail below.

The second work period begins about 10:45, when, on various days of the week, the children might work on science or social studies, or have gym or music with a visiting teacher. This 45-minute period takes the class up to lunch, which is supervised by a lunch aide, thus enabling the teachers to have their lunch at the same time.

At 12:30, the class reassembles for a group meeting, which may involve a discussion, games, or storytelling. At 1:00, the children have a 45-minute math period.

Following the math period, the children go on to the last work period, which permits an opportunity for activities and projects of their own choosing. Many of these activities remain constant over the year, but others change in response to seasonal changes and children's expanding interests. Materials such as paint, chalk, and glue are constantly provided and replenished, as are construction materials and supplies for the housekeeping corner. Other activities, such as working with wood or sand, are usually opened up later in the year, when the children have learned to handle the tools responsibly. Provisioning is also based on common experiences. For example, the children in Louis's class made puppets after a visit to a puppet theater; and weaving was introduced when a parent volunteered to teach it to the class.

The school day ends with another group meeting and, most often, with one of the teachers reading a story.

The Reading Program

The year Louis entered first grade, Ms. Green took charge of the beginning readers. Both teachers, however, are responsible for the conceptual cohesiveness of the reading program, which they view as having four facets: (a) formal instruction, supplemented by reading-related tasks and activities; (b) reading at "quiet reading time"; (c) listening to stories read by the teacher; and (d) writing.

Formal instruction follows a standard "Directed Reading Approach" that uses basal readers (principally, the Bank Street reading series). The children are introduced to new vocabulary words in each story prior to reading it, and they are assigned follow-up activities that involve using or identifying the new words. Other reading activities include teacher-made and commercial word games that the children can play with each other and that require sorting, categorizing, or other forms of word recognition.

The formal aspect of reading instruction is conducted in small groups. Before forming these groups, the teachers observe the children in a variety of reading-related activities (e.g., making "I like" and "I hate" books), in order to gain as much relevant information as possible. They also administer an individual reading inventory to children who are already reading. In Louis's first year, four reading groups were formed initially and later changed in response to the children's progress. Regardless of the number of groupings that may exist at any one time, the groups represent variation within three general levels of reading proficiency. Basically, instruction at these three different levels may be described as follows:

Beginning Readers. Before actually reading a story, the teacher discusses the story's theme with the children and goes over the words contained in the selection. The story is then read together, with the children either taking turns or reading in unison. After the group reading, the story is discussed again and the children are given some independent assignment—worksheets, games, or other activities involving reading, writing, or drawing.

Intermediate Readers. The teacher assigns a story and related work pages and the children meet with her as a group to discuss the story. But they generally read the story on their own and not out loud in the group setting. The children write down words they don't know and ask either a friend or the teacher to read the words. Later, the teacher collects these words and they become part of individualized homework assignments that she makes for each child. Typically, the homework involves copying the word several times and using it in a sentence.

Independent Readers.   The teacher usually meets with these children twice a week, discussing what they've read and assigning work related to the readings—e.g., book reports or activity cards. The books each child reads are of his or her own choosing, selected from the class or school library.

Several opportunities to read or otherwise engage books occur during the day. In addition to the period before class begins, the first work period and the last are times when reading is encouraged. The children have access to the extensive class library, which contains over 200 books, and they also make weekly visits to the main school library.

The class library contains several basal series in addition to the Bank Street readers and supplementary books. (The Merrill Linguistic series, the American Book Company series, and the Scott Foresman Series are among those on the shelves.) There are books without words, picture dictionaries, and a large selection of easy readers to encourage independent reading. The Monster books are very popular, as are books on Star Wars and Superman. Books that can be rearranged, such as the pop-up and flip books are likewise much in demand. The shelves also hold books on special themes: a section devoted to animal books; another, to books about vehicles and machinery. There is a good collection of fairy stories and folk tales from different countries, as well as stories depicting lives of children in different countries and cultures. The library also has audio tapes, recorded by the teacher, for the children to listen to as they follow along in a book.

The teachers read to the whole class daily. The readings often center on a theme, drawn from fiction, biography or history, that continues for several days. Usually, the reading is followed by a general discussion. The children are encouraged to take books home, as well as to bring books to class.

Writing is also an integral part of the reading program, and a period is set aside at least 3 days a week for this activity. Beginners may start by dictating stories or commentaries for their drawings. Ms. Green often meets with the more advanced writers to discuss specific ideas about writing—e.g., the use of descriptive words and similes. Sometimes, class projects documenting a special event are undertaken, such as the "Spaghetti Book" that commemorated the day when the class cooked and feasted on pasta. These group efforts, along with individual projects such as the "I Like" and "I Hate" books that all the children make become part of the instructional materials in the room.

REPORT FROM THE TOTAL RECORD

Louis enters the first grade unobtrusively. He is not a strongly felt presence in the classroom during the beginning months of the school year, tending to remain at the periphery of the group of his classmates and not reaching out to anybody for a while. As the year goes on, he gradually becomes an integral member of the class. He makes his preferences known, exercises choice, and engages productively in both assigned and self-selected tasks and projects. He establishes working and social relations with several members of the class. In all these areas, Louis's progress is marked by a gradual, cumulative sequence of steps, a way of proceeding that proves to be his stylistic hallmark.

The case report spanning the first two grades in Louis's school experience is organized according to the following thematic headings and subheadings.

1. Incremental Manner
   —Preference for materials with multiple units
   —Relating parts to the whole
   —Modification and elaboration
   —Directionality
   —Incremental progress
   —Lego service station
2. Concrete Beginnings, Reality Orientation
   —Summary of drawings
3. Sensitive to Situational Specifics, Rule-Bound
4. Knowledgeable Expert
5. Fantasy, Imagination, Whimsy
6. Cautious, Unwilling to Venture

1. Incremental Manner

Louis's predominant approach to learning and doing is incremental. He typically proceeds and progresses by the consecutive addition and accrual of parts, in a step-by-step fashion. The knowledge and skills he acquires this way are consolidated and made coherent by a set of related capacities that are also reflected in Louis's manner of working. He exhibits considerable understanding of the relationship of parts to the whole, a sense of how things fit together. Equally important, he has a grasp of temporal sequences—a working knowledge not only of what goes with what, but of what comes before what. Proceeding by successive steps, he modifies, elaborates, and reformulates, using to good advantage the evolutionary nature of an incremental approach. Louis also gives evidence of directionality, of moving toward certain aims and ends. These ends, however, seem neither prematurely nor precisely formulated; they evolve during the course of their gradual implementation.

Throughout the record, there is a remarkable congruence between Louis's way of doing things and his choice of things to do. The activity he most frequently elects in the classroom is some form of construction, and his choice of building materials is singularly suited to a step-by-step process. Typified by his most frequent choice, Lego, the materials consist of small, multiple units that require piecemeal assembly. When dealing with assignments or tasks not of his own choosing, Louis tends to segment these into relatively small and distinct units.

Louis's ability to identify the activities and materials most compatible with his way of operating contribute in no small measure to his characteristically purposeful air. There are other indications of purposefulness as well. His projects tend to evolve from concrete beginnings, and to move forward by trial and error—or more accurately, by trial-and-trial, as he modifies, adds, and consolidates along the way.

As a whole, the record speaks more to the way Louis works and learns and does, than to the way he relates and feels. His affective qualities are submerged in the record, whereas his style and manner of work are highly visible. For this reason, it seems appropriate to introduce Louis through excerpts from the first observation in the record, which shows him building with Lego:

> Louis lies on the rug with his construction next to the dishpan of Lego pieces. He props himself on one elbow. He begins to work on his vehicle. Takes parts from the pan. He attempts to separate two thin pieces with his mouth. Continues. Starts to give up and put the pieces back. Immediately picks piece up again, tries again, gets the piece he wants.

> Louis moves off by himself to get space to push his vehicle. He pushes it back over to the pan and takes out more pieces. He begins attaching them to the sides of the vehicle to form extensions. He looks at a boy and says, "I don't got no driver. I need somebody to drive."

> One of the others says, "Let's go to snack." Others go. Louis stays; lies beside the Lego pan. Another boy comes over to him. Louis holds up a piece and says to the boy, "That's the daddy." Pawing through the pieces in the pan, he selects one and adds it to the side of his vehicle. He lies down next to the pan and says to no one in particular, "Look what I'm making." [October, 1st grade]

This observation illustrates qualities of Louis's ways that are elaborated in the sections that follow.

Preference for materials with Multiple Units. Louis's partiality to materials that consist of parts and pieces comes to light early and proves lasting. During the first observation he is found building with Lego, his favorite material and almost exclusive activity during choice time for the entire 2-year period. His teacher describes these constructions:

> His Lego constructions are quite intricate, elaborate, they have an inside to them . . . structures look like tractors, buildings, police cars. Starts new one every day—kids have a chance to put things away if they want to continue working on

them—he doesn't do that. Very organized around Lego, knows what pieces he needs, fishes them out of the box. [October, 1st grade]

When not building with Lego, Louis turns to blocks, to Multi-Rollaway and, occasionally, to Lincoln Logs. During math, he will use cuisinnaire rods, when available, to build elaborate constructions. All these materials consist of small, discrete components, having hard-edged, mostly geometrical shapes that come in multiples but in a limited variety of shapes. They are found in good supply in Louis's classroom.

His affinity for objects that have parts is reflected in Louis's choice of books during quiet reading time. He begins the first year by selecting a series of books depicting heavy machinery and vehicles, such as trucks and tractors, in rich and realistic detail. He pores over these diagram-like pictures, unable to read the compact and rather technical text that accompanies them. He is also drawn to the one type of book that can be said to have parts, the pop-up and mix-and-match books with segmented pages that can be permuted and arranged in many configurations.

The inclination to segment is also revealed in the way Louis learns to read. He treats letters and words as discrete units, acquiring them one at a time. As a result, his teacher is aware of his progress in uncommon detail. At the beginning of the first year, he knows all except four lowercase letters. By October, he acquires 5 sight words. In January, he is able to use initial consonants and has accumulated 23 sight words. Similarly, in his writing, letter follows letter in the early months of the school year; later, Louis proceeds to writing one word at a time, using a fair bit of erasing and reworking.

Similar predispositions come to light in Louis's drawings. Many are composed of carefully outlined areas, frequently geometrical in shape, that seem attached one to the other, not unlike Lego constructions. In another type of drawing, Louis uses the grouping of similar elements to good advantage—such as a phalanx of bees to suggest an oncoming menace, or a grouping of ice-cream cones on a page to create a lighthearted atmosphere.

To sum up, Louis shows a marked preference for modular materials and constructions, to the point where he transforms materials and activities not commonly structured that way into segmented units. Just how highly differentiated these preferences are is revealed by the activities Louis does not participate in, by the materials he does not engage. During the 2 years he spends in the room, he rarely paints, does not cook or play in the housekeeping or dress-up areas and seldom reads or writes spontaneously. He does not work in clay or in wood. Even more interesting, there are available several other construction materials that he does not choose to use: Tinker Toys, table blocks, Rig-a-Jig, plastic straws, and Stickle-Stacks. Most of these materials diverge from his favorite Lego in that the units are somewhat more flexible and fluid, have more rounded shapes, and do not fit into one another as closely.

Relating Parts to the Whole.   Louis's understanding of connections is sum-marized by his teacher: "He has a good sense of how things fit, how they relate." More specific evidence comes from several sources. Observations of Louis building with Lego show him rummaging long and purposefully for just the right piece. He knows the specific color and shape he needs for a particular place or function. He also recognizes how pieces were previously used.

In constructing with the Multi-Rollaway, which consists of wooden blocks with a marble track, he creates rather complex paths for the marble to traverse "underground," joining the pieces to make a path he can't see.

Doing classroom assignments, Louis shows an aptitude for understanding and following directions, whether given by the teacher, in workbooks, or in more formal test situations. He understands that by drawing a line between a picture and a number, a relationship is indicated. He does things in correct sequence; when he is asked to do something last, he does so. In a workbook exercise, where the task suddenly shifts from identifying the beginning sounds of words (represented by pictures) to identifying the ending sounds, he figures out the nature of the task, and does the page correctly (May, 1st grade).

In math, he can handle relational problems—those that require inserting a symbol ($+$, $-$, or $=$) to indicate the relationship between a set of numbers (May, 1st grade).

An analogous task involving words is embedded in the *What's Missing?* books that Louis both likes and reads well. Yet another example of his interest in fitting things together comes to light in the way he handles a common classroom assignment—composing a sentnece with newly learned words. Louis likes to put all his new words in one sentence, taking considerable satisfaction from being able to do so (October, 2nd grade).

Louis also discerns the fit of classroom routines. He knows that the teacher will distribute cards that show pictures of objects whose names start with the letter that was introduced in his reading group. In class discussion, Louis's comments are usually to the point, well related to the ongoing discussion (January, 1st grade).

Modification and Elaboration.   The clearest evidence for this aspect of the incremental approach comes from Louis's work in construction. In an observa-tion recording a segment of the work on a Lego gas station, which was being constructed by Louis and a small group of boys over several weeks during the fall of second grade, he is seen to remove and replace the roof three times in order to modify the structure underneath. This episode is also illustrative of Louis's trial-and-error approach. Earlier in the record he is described modifying a ship he has built. In fact, many of the smaller Lego structures he makes during the school year are versions of ones built previously.

Around Halloween of first grade, Louis makes a series of "shape books," books in the form of a ghost, which he has cut out from a template. Each of his books represents some modification or elaboration of the template; his Dracula book, for example, sports a cape-like attachment to the ghost shape.

Directionality. The purposeful air that is communicated by Louis is most apparent when he is well invested in the activity—as in building with Lego. The record does not clearly indicate at what point the image guiding the selection of components becomes formulated in Louis's mind. Some of the evidence, the working and reworking, suggests that the image evolves and consolidates during the construction process itself, at the same time that there are indications of Louis's moving toward closure and completeness, of his having a strong sense of the whole.

His sense of the "right piece" for his construction is illustrated by the previous as well as the following segment from an observation of Louis building:

> Louis moves over to a group that has now returned from snack and reaches for a Lego piece: "I need that." A boy in the group says, "No, don't take that." Louis leaves the piece, returns to his place by the Lego pan and hits his fist on his knee to express his disappointment. [October, 1st grade]

Louis has, in his teacher's words, "a definite sense of a final, finished product," which he achieves after considerable modification and elaboration.

Another sign of directionality is Louis's tendency to continue with what he has started, through interruptions or in the face of attractive alternatives. He resists an invitation to snack with a group of boys and continues working on a construction. He also stays with academic tasks. He insists on finishing his assignment of making four cards with pattern block shapes, even when his teacher is willing to settle for three. "I did not finish," he says (October, 1st grade).

In reading, his persistence is most evident in the oral reading tapes, where he keeps going in the face of a difficult and, during the first year, apparently joyless task. When reading something of interest, he will return to it after several interruptions. Looking with a friend at Richard Scarry's *The Best Word Book Ever,* he waits out an invasion from a group of older boys, who take control of the book for a while, and overcomes assorted interruptions to return to the book and the discussion of it (March, 1st grade).

There is stability in Louis's interest over long periods. His construction continues over 2 years with no sign of slacking. At the same time, the activities and materials that do not engage him also remain the same. He does not paint, work in clay, water, sand, or other fluid materials, does not participate in housekeeping or dramatic activities.

An understanding of the underlying structure and sequence of activities is also in evidence. Louis grasps instruction easily, does things in the correct sequence. His teacher observes him taking the California Achievement Test:

> He picked out the words that he knew, like *city* and *street,* putting those in his answers more than words he didn't know. The CAT is a good indicator of the

children's ability to tune in to what the nature of the task is, in what order to read it in, how to follow along. They can get a lot of it right, even if they can't read the actual words, if they have those orienting skills. Louis does have them. [February, 1st grade]

Incremental Progress.   The choice of modular construction materials necessarily implies gradual, incremental progress. This way of advancing, however, is evident in other, seemingly unrelated domains, such as the development of a circle of friends. Louis starts out the year with no friends in the classroom. In the middle of first grade, a neighbor, Billy, joins the class as a kindergartner, and the two of them are seen reading, talking, working together. In March of first grade, during an episode involving Lincoln Logs, Louis is observed taking intermittent steps to join the group activity by making suggestions, building a small addition to another boy's barn, and finally succeeding with an attention-getting variation on a stockade fence around the barnyard. At the end of the first year, his teacher finds Louis "much more friendly, playing with many children—it took him a long time to get comfortable, but he is now" (May, 1st grade).

Although evident even in his social relations, progress by increments is most clearly visible in Louis's preferred free-choice activity, Lego construction. He begins first grade by choosing Lego every day, working alone. Later in the year, his teacher reports:

> Louis does not work with Lego every day, but when he does, he will complete three or more constructions, which may have had several earlier versions.
>
> He builds without the benefit of models. His structures are usually of a real object, mostly vehicles. A six-wheeled vehicle that was precisely, carefully constructed, looked very much as if a model was used. After finishing these Louis usually takes them apart, occasionally keeping one for sharing time. He now enjoys sharing, is less hesitant about this than he was at beginning of year. Although there is provision made in the room for keeping work in progress, or even finished work, for more than one day, he does not take advantage of it. [January, 1st grade]

Toward the end of the school year:

> He continues to work with Lego a lot. Occasionally he collaborates with other kids on a project. Recently he built an airplane for a hangar that one of the kids constructed. [May, 1st grade]

Louis's involvement with Lego continues into second grade. By the middle of that school year, he works on construction projects over extended periods of time, in collaboration with classmates. The following is a detailed description of his culminating project.

Lego Service Station.   The structure is primarily a gas station—a low, flat building with a roof that doubles as an airstrip for small planes. An adjacent, independently standing tall structure is a control tower. The structures cover an area of about 15 × 17 inches, the highest point of the tower reaching 9 inches. The whole complex was built over a period of about 3 weeks by Louis and a small group of his friends. Although this was a joint project, Louis is its major architect. Photographs taken by the teacher during this period show the extensive modification that marked its gradual development.

The design is complex and elaborated, its detail accurately resembling that of real gas stations. An observation of the work in progress testifies to the deliberateness of its design and the care taken with the details of the construction. The building is finished on all sides, as well as on the inside. One observation records Louis's removing the roof three times to make modifications on the interior.

The structure features color in a functional as well as decorative role, the red and white pattern of the roof blending with the colors of the plane so as to create a camouflage effect from the top view. The alternating strips of black and white elements for stairs leading to the control tower, and the single inversion in the expected order of the colors at the top of the stairs, create a powerful, and purely decorative effect. The stairs themselves are somewhat disproportionate in size to the rest of the structure; consequently, they appear as the concrete metaphor that expresses Louis's salient characteristic—his incremental style.

For all its close resemblance to a real service station, the presence of an airstrip on top of the building, with a control tower next to it, brings an element of fantasy to the structure. There are rich, imaginative elements in the elaboration of the stairs leading to the tower and in the design of the tower itself.

An outstanding example of the meticulous detail that characterizes the structure is the way in which the airplane parked on the roof matches the roof in color and line. The main axis of the airplane is red, and it is aligned with the red border of the gas station. This is ensured by the placement of the hook-up block under the wing of the airplane. The blending of the colors of airplane and roof give the effect of camouflage as does the white tail of the airplane, which similarly continues the white line formed by the office part of the gas station.

Color thus becomes a structural element in the design, both in demarcating a major structural dimension (i.e., the roof) and in establishing a relationship with an element extraneous to the structure (i.e., the airplane). On the whole, color is used sectionally and symmetrically.

The adjacent control tower, the element of fantasy in the composition, is not structurally realistic. It is composed of three vertical columns that are not securely connected. With an elaborate staircase leaning against them, the somewhat precarious structure tends to separate along vertical lines.

The process of construction and the reality and refinement of detail reveal the knowledgeable expert at work. Though realistic in detail, it is not a specific gas station; rather, it is an archetypal one that Louis and his friends have built.

The pictures in Figures 12.1–12.4 illustrate the construction from several angles.

FIG. 12.1   Louis's Lego Service Station: Front View (ground level)

FIG. 12.2   Louis's Lego Service Station: Side View (ground level)

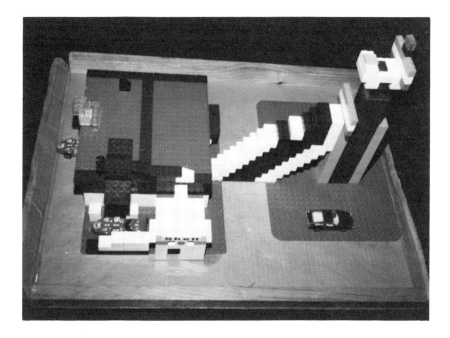

FIG. 12.3   Louis's Lego Service Station: Front Aerial View

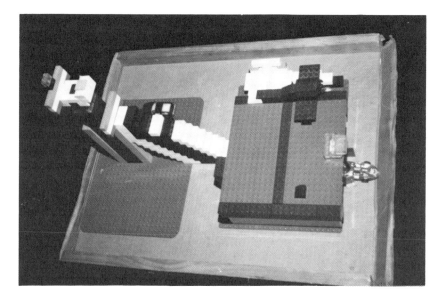

FIG. 12.4   Louis's Lego Service Station: Back Aerial View

2. Concrete Beginnings, Reality Orientation

Once engaged in an activity or headed in a direction, Louis characteristically proceeds by taking small, discrete steps. The source of his activities and projects is typically something Louis saw, did, or otherwise experienced. From such palpable beginnings, he goes on to create his own rendition, typically retaining the gist of those origins—the source of his activities is seldom obscured by subsequent modification. This tendency to begin with something already there holds for both the ideas that guide the projects and their eventual physical manifestation.

His teacher captures the essence of this quality, thinking of Louis as ''a rooted person; he is really rooted in reality.'' Louis's writing testifies to this quality. His stories tend to summon up real events, told in a matter-of-fact tone (see Writing section). His journal entries are sometimes based on a word found in the dictionary or on the writings displayed in the classroom.

The clearest evidence, again, comes from the building activities that compose a large portion of Louis's self-selected work. The very choice of materials that come in ready-made units such as Lego, blocks, and logs (rather than the alternatives offered by clay and woodworking, where the basic units have first to be fashioned) exemplifies his preference for working with elements that offer a guiding infrastructure. The ''content,'' or subject, of the constructions is similarly rooted in reality, tending to represent familiar objects in recognizable and authentic detail.

> In Lego he builds without the benefit of the models provided, yet his structures are of real objects, mostly vehicles . . . precisely, carefully constructed, very much as if a model was used. [January, 1st grade]

> Working with Lincoln Logs, he begins by making an addition to someone's barnyard, later contributes a variation on a stockade fence added by another boy. In blocks, he and a group of kids built a city. [October, 2nd grade]

> Given an oportunity to explore math materials, Louis chooses pop-up beads, filling paper cups with beads of uniform color. At the suggestion of another boy, he declares they are in a bakery, and the cup filled with red beads are cherry pies, the cup with blue beads, blueberry pies. He has a problem with pink filled cups.]October, 2nd grade]

> He uses Cuisinnaire rods to build a complex of bridges, with intricate undergirding. Blue rods are used to suggest a river flowing below. [October, 2nd grade]

Some of Louis's projects are inspired by something observed or suggested. As an example, after seeing a film about a boy who made a construction out of junk and other objects, Louis embarked on a similar project of his own (March, 2nd grade). Occasionally, Louis uses books for directions or as a source of ideas for an activity. He makes an Indian headband from a pattern, and he takes home a

Starter book, following its instructions for planting seeds in a grapefruit rind (2nd grade).

Louis's drawings, with few exceptions, also depict what he has seen or done. A life-size tracing of himself on brown paper is carefully drawn and the shape colored in. He looks at himself to see what he is wearing, then reproduces the color of his clothes on the cut-out (October, 2nd grade). The drawings that record an event usually show one object or one specific episode in realistic fashion. A visit to the puppet theater is summarized by a drawing of the stage and shows a scene from the performance. Another class trip to the Academy of Natural History, where the class sees a trained hawk, results in a drawing of the children watching the demonstration. The drawings, although relatively few, exemplify and illuminate Louis's approach to the world around him, as the following summary suggests.

Summary of Drawings.   A dozen or so drawings represent nearly all Louis's artwork in school—although he is reported to draw at home frequently. In addition to these drawings made on individual sheets of paper, there are drawings in Louis's writing journal and in the books he has made over the 2 years. Done in various colors of crayon and occasionally in pencil, they tend to represent what Louis has seen or done, and they do so predominantly through discrete objects. The drawings lack documentary backgrounds and imply no narrative. Thus, a visit to a puppet theater is summarized by a depiction of the stage and shows a scene from the performance. The rectilinear drawing faithfully reproduces the tripartite construction of the stage, each portion outlined and filled in with a different color. The drawing is symmetrical, centered on the page, but not anchored, and shows the stage from the audience's perspective.

As a group, the pieces are characterized by a general economy of expression. The focus is on the essential realistic quality of the objects depicted, details being emphasized selectively, judiciously, and quite effectively. For example, the demonstration of a trained hawk is recalled by the images of four figures: the trainer, the hawk, and two children. The trainer stands center page, unrelated to any background, and the hawk, the size of the trainer's head and torso, is perching on her outstretched arm. Both figures are cleanly outlined shapes, filled in selectively; the hawk is done in pencil, except for a large yellow beak. In the foreground, with backs to the viewer, two children sit, one on each side of the trainer, facing her. Although no background or foreground is indicated, the position of the children's hands and knees suggests a cross-legged posture and gives the appearance of their being well planted on the floor. On a separate sheet of paper, the legend is: "This is our class and we're getting ready to pet the hawk. And she is telling us about the hawk before we pet the hawk."

Expression in the drawings does not derive from gestures or facial expressions as much as from composition. The most effective drawings show a grouping of elements, often the same ones, repeated. These groupings are not symmetrical but are arranged in configurations that produce impressive effects. Two outstanding examples are a grouping of nine bees, arranged as if in a phalanx; the lead bee is followed by three rows of bees all flying in the same direction—a rather menacing effect that makes the repeated caption most plausible:

> I hate bees
> I hate bees

In contrast, a grouping of nine variously colored ice-cream cones spreads across horizontally but unevenly; they produce a summery, lighthearted air, confirming the declaration: I LIKE WATER ICE.

While the drawings of single objects centered on the page without background make the objects appear to float in space, the configurations created by groupings and repetition imply the whole page to be the setting and serve thus to frame and anchor the composition.

The drawings depict vehicles, insects, animals, and occasionally, people. The drawings of animals are more expressive, more detailed, and more spirited than the drawings of people. A subtheme in the drawings relates to supernatural creatures: ghosts, Dracula, Wolf-man, and various monsters. Many of these are in the form of "shape books," cut from a template representing a ghost. These paper cutouts are drawn over, each figure varied somewhat. The Dracula book, for example, has a cape-like attachment stapled to the ghost shape. The record also contains a few action pictures, mainly of battles.

The predominant line in the drawings is straight, and edges are invariably clean. Over time, curved lines appear more often. Some of the drawings are reminiscent of Lego structures, seemingly assembled of component parts. Outlined units are filled in with color and placed adjacent to each other. Motion is depicted directly in only one exceptional drawing of a person in a wheelchair careening down a ramp. The drawing was made after the class observed a racing event that featured handicapped persons in wheelchairs. The drawing emphasizes the chair rather than the person in it. It is a profile view, characteristic of some of the other drawings suggesting motion.

Many of the drawings are accompanied by text, usually a narrative of the event depicted. The drawings are often done first and serve as the stimulus for the text.

3. Sensitive to Situational Specifics, Rule-bound

Another, more elusive aspect of the literal quality that is evident in Louis's style of work is his predisposition to interpret rules and instructions more narrowly than broadly, to respect the letter of the law. He appears to prefer the definite, the clear, and the certain to having to choose among many options of dimly prefigured ends. It is a quality that makes Louis appear rule-bound and situationally sensitive yet gives him a concomitant understanding of rules, instructions, and situational boundaries.

Louis knows and understands rules and tends to abide by them. His teacher notes:

> When we're having reading, the rule is that you work independently, not bother [others]. Unlike some other children, he does not interrupt, just stands there, waits patiently, and succeeds in getting attention. Always knows what the directions are. Knows what pages to do next, what you are supposed to do with your finished page. If he does not understand something, he asks me for help, not other children. Very rule conscious. [October, 1st grade]

His sensitivity to situational boundaries emerges in several ways. He is seen to respond differently to the same person in different contexts, as, for example, to one of his teachers, who also happens to be his neighbor:

> He lives next door to her, goes to her house quite often, and behaves much more freely with her there than he does at school, where he is more reserved, almost awed by her. [October, 1st grade]

He respects role differences even in his mother. She is in school regularly, as a reading aide. When she is in that role, he "does not usually stick to her." When, however, his mother comes to school expressly for him, his behavior is quite different:

> His mom comes in and sits down. Louis goes over to her, turns his back to her and leans affectionately against her. She reaches for his paper. He teases her and holds the paper away from her, saying "Nope, nope." They then begin to look at, and talk about, the paper. [January, 1st grade]

He maintains a separation between home and school: only on rare occasions does he mention his family or talk about his life at home in school; these themes do not figure much in his writing or his conversation in class. Yet he is reported to have a close and warm relationship with his family, as is evident from the episode with his mother. Some of Louis's activities also vary across situations. He is reported to draw a lot at home but relatively little at school. There is, on the other hand, no report of his doing constructions at home, yet construction is a predominant activity in class.

His judgments regarding the equivalence of situations or materials show a sharp awareness of "correct" form. His teacher reports:

> His mother wrote a note to me recently, saying that Louis wants to have word cards to practice with, but did not find the ones she made acceptable. She was asking me

to make some for him, and to reassure Louis that his mother's are okay. I made some for him. [October, 2nd grade]

4. Knowledgeable Expert

The incremental manner and the concrete beginnings that are typical of much of Louis's way of working do not directly indicate the considerable knowledge and skill that he reveals in the process of working. In some of his activities, Louis's manner suggests the expert, the specialist at work. He selects his materials carefully; he proceeds by successive elaboration; he understands the requirements of the task at hand; he stays with an activity over time; he has a sense of a finished product. Together, these qualities give some of his activities a certain clarity of purpose and elegance of process that characterize the expert.

The record points to several areas where Louis has more than perfunctory knowledge:

He knows how things work, is aware how bombs drop out of the bottom of airplanes. [October, 1st grade]

He knows how things look and is able to recreate objects without the benefit of blueprints. [January, 1st grade]

He knows his materials and has a thorough familiarity with the available supplies. He can distinguish the Lego pieces that belong to the "space set" from those of the "regulars" when they get mixed up. [January, 2nd grade]

Louis knows the rules of many games, and he occasionally referees games played by others. "You can't do that—you gotta do this—if you get the same number, you're shot" is an example of his contributions to a game of Battleship, which involves estimating coordinates. [October, 1st grade]

He is knowledgeable about classroom routines and is aware of the class schedule. [March, 1st grade]

Louis acquires knowledge from many sources. Books clearly serve as a source of information, although not necessarily through textual content. He studies informative illustrations, such as pictures of machinery (February, 1st grade). He follows directions for making things, such as Indian gear (January, 2nd grade), and also uses dictionaries for spelling patterns and story starters (June, 1st grade).

Louis's drawings testify to his good eye and to his ability to retain images and reproduce them in distilled form. He can also recall, with remarkable accuracy, where and when he has learned a word. (See Reading History.)

Finally, Louis consolidates his skills through practice and growing familiarity. He likes to use what he knows, to point out familiar words, to relate familiar events, to reread familiar passages, thus providing himself with ample opportunity to solidify his knowledge base.

5. Fantasy, Imagination, Whimsy

The image of Louis as rooted in reality, as favoring the concrete and the literal, emerges forcefully and constantly from the record. Yet his teacher makes occasional references to his whimsy. Indeed, a close reading of the record uncovers instances of fantasy, humor, and imagination, and suggests that there is a counterpoint to that strong theme. Although examples of imaginative thought and play are not numerous, they do add up to an unmistakable subtheme.

Several strands make up the subtheme. In greatest contrast to Louis's generally appropriate and relevant responses to his environment stands his occasional production of pure nonsense. His teacher refers to the odd jokes he makes that do not make sense, examples of which she cannot recall. Then there are his odd comments. One of these is made toward the end of first grade, during a class discussion of how old each of them will be in the year 2000. Louis announces that he will be "coockoo man." Another time, he interjects into a conversation (in which a boy boasts about the eight TV sets in his house): "Oh I know where they are—they are all over the walls." Louis is also observed making silly asides in an attempt to insinuate himself into an ongoing Lincoln Logs project (February, 1st grade).

Imaginative play also surfaces during construction activities, when Louis realizes some uncommon possibilities in materials. While working on a Lincoln Log barnyard, he turns the roof into a sliding board for the animals (March, 1st grade). In a less spontaneous situation, the elaborate Lego construction that began as a gas station envolves to have an airfield on its roof, and in time acquires a massive control tower in the area adjacent to it.

Although Louis does not participate in the dramatic play that is often going on in the dress-up and housekeeping areas of the classroom, the record shows scattered instances of his playacting. Louis is seen crashing a Lego vehicle (rocket ship?) against a Lego building, simulating half a dozen crashes, complete with sound effects (November, 1st grade). He engages in a mock sword fight, using a sword made of two Lincoln Logs, and holds his side in a dramatic gesture when hit by his opponent (March, 1st grade). Missing a driver in a Lego vehicle, he places a piece in the driver's seat and calls it "Daddy" (January, 1st grade).

The closest Louis comes to trying out roles is wearing costumes. During the school year he occasionally comes in wearing a Dracula cape, a mechanic's suit, a fringed vest, thus suggesting an awareness of the dramatic value of clothing.

Other than the jokes that fail to come off, there is one outstanding example of verbal humor in the record:

Louis starts to enjoy a giggle with the child next to him over something the child has said. Ms. Green encourages him to share what he's laughing about. Louis does a more or less on-key version of the following song (to the tune of "On Top of Old Smoky") so that it's not much above audible and a bit slurred: On top of the school house/all covered with sand/I shot my poor teacher/with a rubber band.

An aspect of Louis's expressive works that is less whimsy or fantasy than unusual imagination shows him to be capable of effective, even powerful expression and representation of images and ideas. Several drawings are outstanding in their parsimony of line and power of expression; examples of writing are of similar quality, such as these opening lines to two journal entries:

—I like soccer. Soccer is part of my life.

—Today it is raining and it is a drowsy day.

The special flair and spirit of these bits of writing, and some of the drawings (the wheelchair race, the trained owl demonstration) are particularly interesting, for they show an integrative leap of the imagination that differs markedly from the incremental, bit-by-bit assembling of wholes that characterizes so much of Louis's other work.

6. Cautious, Unwilling to Venture

A cautious, prudent manner typifies Louis's engagement of tasks and people. He appears reluctant to take risks, even to guess; he does not leap into the unknown. This prudent aspect of Louis's way of dealing with his surroundings is indeed salient. However, a question may be raised about the interrelationship of the incremental style favored by Louis and the quality of caution, since a step-by-step process necessarily appears careful and relatively "safe." Is the incremental style a consequence of a cautious predisposition, or merely its artifact? The direction of the relationship remains moot.

An unwillingness to venture, a paucity of bold initiatives describes Louis's social and academic behavior. At the beginning of first grade, he stays at the periphery of the class and does not reach out to anyone. He does not volunteer or initiate much during class discussions, nor does he share his Lego constructions with his classmates when the opportunity is offered. His teacher comments that he is careful not to place himself in situations where he might be excluded by others, even if the likelihood is small.

Observed during recess in the school yard, Louis studiously avoids a gang of boys who are on the rowdy side (March, 1st grade). He generally avoids confrontations with his peers, rarely getting into fights. When the potential for conflict arises, Louis relies on one of two main strategies to avert it. He either acquiesces or moves to the side, working around the situation. He tends to acquiesce when the rules favor his opponent or when he perceives his opponent as more powerful than he. For example, he relinquishes a Lego piece because another child has first claim on it. He also defers to Stephen's plans to construct a building rather than the horse Louis suggests—Stephen plays a leading role in the Lincoln Log work party Louis is trying to enter (March, 1st grade). In another episode, he also gives in to his friend, Terry:

> Terry goes with his book (Richard Scarry's *The Best Word Book Ever*) to sit next to Louis. Each boy seems to be vying for control of the situation by trying to interest the other in his book. Eventually Louis gives up and attends to Terry's book. [February, 1st grade]

There are more subtle signs of Louis's timidity. When a child blocks his view of the teacher, he peers around him, rather than asking him to move. During a math period, when he is to paste paper pattern-blocks on a sheet, he waits for the teacher to bring him the paste that another boy is using, rather than asking for it directly. In a rather unusual episode, when he joins in an anti-school song with the class, he changes the words from first-person singular to neutral third-person:

> When I shot my . . . when the person shot the teacher/meatballs grew on her head. [February, 1st grade]

Louis's understanding of rules provides an interesting perspective on his caution and on its polar expression: an assertive, standing-his-ground quality that is also in evidence in his behavior with the children. Not only is he knowledgeable about rules in the classroom, he also tends to observe them. Being a "good citizen" may sometime contribute to his apparently cautious demeanor but it also occasions some bolder initiatives, as when he offers unsolicited advice about how to do things and about what may or may not be done in the class.

Similarly, Louis protects his own interests if the rules are on his side. When the boy he is sharing a book with tries to snatch it, he roars, "Stop it! I want to look at it" (February, 1st grade). In another episode:

> Louis (to boy picking up Lego construction): "That was mine. I made that; it got broken."
>
> He goes to the teacher, who directs the boy to give Louis the construction.
>
> Louis takes the toy from the boy, saying "Aha" with satisfaction. [October, 1st grade]

His teacher's comment incorporates both Louis's caution and his assertiveness:

When he wants something, he makes sure that he gets it. When we're having reading, the rule is that you work independently. . . . Unlike some other children, he does not interrupt, just stands there, waits patiently, and succeeds in getting attention. [October, 1st grade]

Thus there appears to be a general tendency on Louis's part to move only where he can be sure of his footing, i.e., when the consequences of his actions are reasonably clear to him. Whether he appears timid or assertive is context-dependent. When he is sure of his ground, he protects it. Given Louis's sensitivity to circumstances, it is not surprising that, while his reluctance to enter problematic situations may not alter, Louis's behavior in the classroom does. As he becomes more familiar and comfortable with his surroundings, his teachers, and his classmates and can better predict responses to his behavior, he becomes more active in classroom life. He occasionally gets rambunctious, allows himself to begin a mock fight, makes overtures to other boys, occasionally becomes more talkative, and contributes more than he once did to class discussion. He appears more confident and more venturesome by the time second grade draws to a close.

REPORT FROM THE READING RECORD

The essential inference to be drawn from Louis's reading history is that he learns to read in much the same incremental way he learns everything else in the classroom. As noted earlier, Louis shows considerable analytic skills in several areas, but seems a less powerful integrator. His analytic capacity enables him to identify materials and activities that are congenial to his preferred manner of work, and he therefore engages in many productive enterprises. Learning to read, however, is not an optional activity in the classroom, and the record testifies to both the supportive and the counterproductive consequences of Louis's resources and learning style as they are brought to bear on reading tasks. The discussion of Louis's record is organized according to the following headings.

1. Incremental Approach to Reading
2. Unwillingness to Guess, To Err, To Venture
3. Supports for Learning to Read
    Conceptual understanding
    Interest in books
    Interpretive capacities
4. Oral Reading
5. Writing

1. Incremental Approach to Reading

Both the teacher's accounts and the oral reading samples reflect Louis's predominant approach to reading. He progresses in small steps, treating letters and words as discrete units, assembling them one by one. This particular style enables his teacher to track his progress in uncommon detail:

—Louis knows the uppercase letters and most lowercase letters except for *g,v,d,* and *b*. He doesn't show evidence of knowing any beginning sounds. He knows five sight words from his Bank Street reader: *one, two, three, house,* and *making.* [October, 1st grade]

—Recognizes some beginning letters. Knows all the words from the Bank Street reader, 23 in all. [January, 1st grade]

—He knows almost all beginning sounds now, with the exception of letters like *g* and *z*. Can read all of the first Bank Street reader, but not the second book in the same series. He knows the word family *at.* [February, 1st grade]

—Knows all the words in the first three Bank Street Readers. [May, 1st grade]

At the beginning of first grade, Louis relies mostly on sight-word recognition. By the middle of the year, he uses beginning sounds (initial consonants). The productive use of picture clues becomes apparent in the fall of second grade, and later that year his repertoire expands to include the use of context clues.

The taped reading samples confirm and illuminate these reported observations. They indicate that although Louis has constructed more than one knowledge resource relevant to reading, he has difficulty using more than one in an integrated way. In a sample taken in January of first grade, he reads a selection from his instructional text with few errors until he encounters the word *good* in the phrase *good night.* The illustration on the page shows two children in their nightclothes looking out on a dark cityscape. Louis attempts to use picture clues, offering first *bed,* then *pajamies* as possibilities. By this time he knows the sounds of all the letters, and has begun to use initial consonants, yet he does not use this knowledge to modify his guesses.

An oral reading sample in April of first grade also reveals Louis's tendency to focus on single elements as well as his analytic capacity and his continuing difficulty with integration. Louis is painfully reading an unfamiliar few lines in a book entitled *The School:*

> When I go to school
> I learn to read
> and to write

With frequent help from the teacher, he arrives at the word *write* and gets completely bogged down. The teacher suggests that he look at the picture, which in fact depicts a boy at a desk writing. Louis offers *drawing* and *painting*. He then reverts to using letter sounds and asks the teacher what *i* sounds like ("sounds like *eye* sometimes") and what *e* sounds like ("that is a silent *e*"). When further encouraged to guess, he comes up with *wort*.

This example of a persistent though unsuccessful effort suggests that Louis is aware that he knows the sounds of *r* and *t*. Yet when he is supplied with the sounds of the vowels, he cannot put them together with the sounds he already knows or combine the clues with information gleaned from the illustration. Equally suggestive is Louis's failure to use his facility with language or the rhythm of the lines to connect *write* with *read*. The source of the difficulty appears to be his rather narrow and alternating focus that precludes an effective orchestration. It is not a failure to analyze the problem or to identify the components.

All the same, Louis continues to progress—incrementally. He begins the first year by learning everything he is taught. By midyear, his teacher comments that he knows more than she has taught him directly but still needs to have new words introduced to him. In the middle of the second year he begins to read independently, and he also starts to read at home.

That Louis tends to regard letters and words as discrete units may be inferred from the way he acquires them, as well as from other incidents:

—Taking the required California Achievement Tests, he picked out words he knew, such as *city, street, . . .* putting those in his answers more frequently than words he is less familiar with. [February, 1st grade]

—He knows with certainty the words he can read and those he cannot, and will not attempt the latter. [May, 1st grade]

—He recognizes words out of context easily, likes to pick out words he knows from texts. [May, 1st grade]

—He asks for word cards so he could practice single words. [October, 2nd grade]

—He likes books that present words and concepts individually, with minimal context, such as word books and dictionaries. [March, 1st grade]

—In writing, he assembles words letter by letter, looks for words to copy from signs in the room, books, other pieces of writing. [May, 1st grade]

—Has an interest in riddles and rhymes, which often pivot on the more mechanical aspects of language not involving connected discourse. [March, 1st grade]

An interesting indicator of the high salience that individual words held for Louis is found in an oral sample taken in January, first grade. He is reading from his instructional text with his teacher, who asks him from time to time how he knows a particular word. Louis's responses reveal an ability to identify the time and place he has heard, seen, or learned a word:

school—my Mommy gave me that on a word card
street—some kids in the reading group knew it
Night—they say that on Sesame Street
light—just trying to guess—I thought its name and I finally said it
Lights—I read it in a book a couple of days ago
houses—I knew that a long time ago
people—you know those kids that worked at that square table—they had this book
     and were reading it. [January, 1st grade]

Yet another example of Louis's sensitivity to boundaries and of his narrowed focus is found in a later oral reading (April, 1st grade). He begins to read a story about Mr. Pines, the sign maker. The format of the first page is shown in Fig. 12.5. Louis reads all the words except those demarcated by the sign shapes. When his teacher asks him if that makes sense, and points him to the signs, he reads them correctly.

2. Unwillingness to Guess, to Err, to Venture

A corollary to Louis's incrementalism is a reluctance to guess and to move into areas of uncertain knowledge. While the same tendency does not seem to handicap him in other areas such as construction projects, it does seem to slow his progress in reading. His teacher, on the basis of other indicators, expects him to move faster and comments at length on Louis's caution:

Louis's unwillingness to guess holds him back, in both reading and writing. He gets new words easily; after they had been introduced, he can put them to use right away. But he still needs to have every new word introduced, he won't tackle them on his own. His reluctance to guess keeps him from going ahead on his own. [June, 1st grade]

His reading is confined mostly to *Around the City*. I think he could read such books as *Go Dog Go*, but he hesitates to do it. I am not concerned that he won't learn to

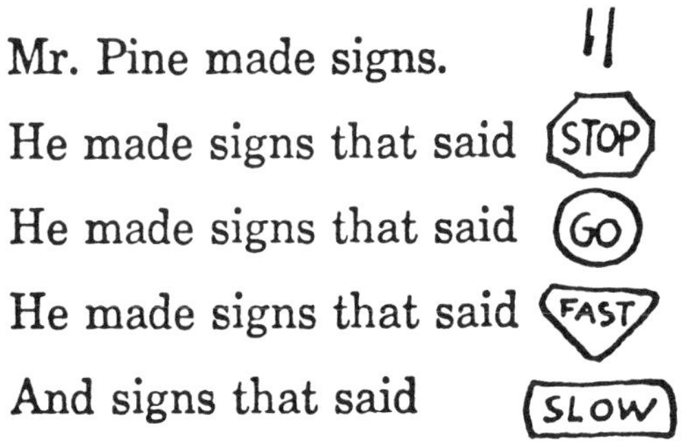

FIG. 12.5   Text from *Mr. Pine's Signs*

read, but that he could be further along than he is if he were bolder in attempting what he doesn't know with certainty. He is the best among the group. I still introduce words to him one at a time. He is good with workbooks, can figure out directions, and does them correctly. [June, 1st grade]

The oral reading samples confirm Louis's unwillingness to exhibit partial knowledge. The readings contain innumerable examples of Louis's simply stopping and waiting for the teacher either to supply him with the word or to give him a signal to skip. Although this characteristic is mitigated considerably during the second year, when he is more willing to brave error, Louis could be described at the end of the second grade as a cautious reader.

3. Supports for Learning to Read

The paced accumulation of knowledge that marks Louis's progress in reading is supported by a set of attributes and interests that more than balance the less facilitative aspects of his approach. Most have already been mentioned in the themes drawn from the total record. Here, they will be related to reading and writing.

Conceptual Understanding.   Louis brings to beginning reading a set of understandings and attributes that are critical resources for learning. His teacher reports:

—He pays close attention to directions, and always knows what they are—knows what pages to do, and what he is supposed to do with the finished page. [October, 1st grade]

—He has a clear grasp of the concept of reading, he knows what words are, and that words make sentences. He caught on to this from the beginning, unlike some of the other children. [January, 1st grade]

—He understands the nature of sequencing—he always does his work in the correct sequence and saves a task for the last if asked to do so. [January, 1st grade]

—On a workbook page, when the task suddenly shifts from identifying words by their beginning sounds to sorting by ending sounds, Louis was able to do the assignment correctly. Many of the children got confused. [February, 1st grade]

Louis also handles formal test situations well. After watching him take the California Achievement Tests, his teacher comments:

The CAT is a good indicator of the children's ability to tune in to what the nature of the task is, in what order to read it, how to follow along. They can get a lot of it right, even if they can't read the actual words, if they have the orienting skills. Louis does have them. [February, 1st grade]

The clear and accurate grasp that Louis has of task requirements is complemented by his generally responsive, responsible attitude toward classroom work. He is sensitive to contexts, to the demands implicit in different situations, and he accepts and abides the work orientation of the classroom environment. His thorough knowledge of classroom rules and customs enables him to fulfill his obligation and also pursue his interests. Learning to read is "work" in Louis's view, judging by the fact that he does not choose to do it when other options are available. He gives it the serious attention that work demands, learning what is taught, doing assignments, and staying with the task even when it gets difficult.

At a more general level, Louis's reading is also supported by his language capacity. Although he uses words sparingly, and dislays no extraordinary verve or fluency in language, he shows himself to be a competent user, with the capacity to make language serve his needs in the classroom. To illustrate:

—He comes to school with a good vocabulary, understanding words like *hoe* and *magnet*. [October, 1st grade]

—He tends to speak in complete sentences. [January, 1st grade]

—He knows the specific names of things, and identifies them with precision. [March, 1st grade]

Louis also uses language more privately to give expression to his thoughts and reactions, or just to play with sounds of his own making. In the following examples, Louis is heard talking to no one in particlar, i.e., to himself:

—During a reading group activity, when the children are asked to identify objects that start with the letter *s*, Louis says 'ssss'' quietly as the teacher holds up a soda bottle. [January, 1st grade]

—During a music lesson while "who has the penny" is being played, Louis says to no one in particular "I know who has it." [May, 1st grade]

A segment from an observation during math period contains several incidents of language use for his own purposes:

The teacher is passing out materials.
     Louis: "I'm gonna use a pencil for my lines. Do we have to use a crayon for our lines?" [The teacher says that a pencil might go through the paper.]
The other kids are kneeling and lying about on the floor.Louis is walking around behind them. Louis (to himself):

        "I don't even know where to sit."

The teacher gives instructions, telling the children that on the first line they are to draw one face, on the second line two faces, and so on. Louis is keeping up, drawing 1, 2, then 3 faces. Then he says, "I know what to do." . . . He counts aloud as he numbers the circles he has drawn (the two rows of ten) at the bottom. [June, 1st grade]

Interest in Books.   More specific to his progress in reading is Louis's well-documented interest in books. From the start, he is attracted to books, yet a paradoxical picture emerges from the record regarding the meaning that books and reading hold for Louis. While drawn to books, he does not appear equally interested in reading. The appeal that books have for him surfaces in several ways:

—The very first observation finds Louis and a friend absorbed in *Ghastly Ghostly Riddles.* The boys are looking at the pictures, commenting on and conversing about them. Louis offers an explanation apropos of a picture showing a man: "He loves someone 'cause he got hearts on his underpants." Louis is willing to share the book, but he keeps control of it when the other boys try to snatch it. [October, 1st grade]

—Louis repeatedly chooses *Machine Books* during quiet reading time. He pores over these large, lavishly illustrated books which depict vehicles and heavy machinery in rich and realistic detail. The text accompanying the pictures is compact and technical, much beyond Louis's capacity to read, and he does not even attempt it. [January, 1st grade]

—He loves to look at the *Bank Street Reader,* which serves as the instructional text in reading groups. He will occasionally look ahead, but does not try to figure out new words for himself. [January, 1st grade]

—Pop-up books and mix-and-match books, which have segmented pages, are well liked. Louis also enjoys the *What's Missing?* books. All of these books permit manipulation and rearrangement on the part of the reader. [January, 1st grade]

—Louis enjoys word books, dictionary-type books. An observation in the spring of the first year shows him and his friend Terry going over Richard Scarry's *Best Word Book Ever* with interest and animation. [March, 1st grade]

—Occasionally, Louis will use books for directions. He made an Indian headband following a pattern, and planted seeds in a grapefruit rind following instructions out of a book. [October, 2nd grade]

Louis is thus drawn to books that are factual, depict real objects, or offer directions to make something. He also enjoys books that can be said to have moving parts, books that can be physically rearranged, or that require the reader to supply parts, such as the *What's Missing?* books. In summary, Louis favors books that invite high reader participation without necessarily requiring a careful reading of the text.

These signs of interest in books stand counterposed to the activities Louis freely chooses in the classroom. These rarely, if ever, involve books. He reads only during instructional periods, and looks at books only during time slots designated for that purpose. His difficulties with deciphering written words, and his focus on that process to the detriment of gaining meaning, make reading text hard for him and for a while, relatively unrewarding work. Louis thus seems to differentiate between doing things with books—such as looking at pictures or conversing about dictionaries—and reading them.

Although Louis does not read many storybooks or other narratives on his own (and probably cannot do so), his responses as a listener bring to the fore a well-developed understanding of stories and their implications.

Interpretive Capacities.   Louis listens with rapt attention to the variety of stories his teacher reads to the class. In the discussions that usually follow, he does not initiate much but is responsive to questions, and his comments are always to the point. Some of these conversations reveal Louis to have reflected on and interpreted the story with uncommon understanding.

> Recently, I read the story of *Three Billy Goats Gruff* to the class—told from the point of view of the troll. When the kids discussed whose version was right, Louis said, ''It is really hard to tell.'' He has a good sense that there can be two sides to a story. [June, 2nd grade]

Louis's approach to books and his understandings of them are illustrated by his responses during the taping of the standard oral reading sample. He is reading with one of the research staff. The book is *Big Dog, Little Dog,* chronicling the adventures of two dogs not only discrepant in size but having different tastes and experiences. The opening conversation establishes the degree of Louis's familiarity with the book:

> T: Did you have this book in class Louis?
> L: Yeah.
> T: Did you ever read it before?
> L: Uh-uh. I can't read any books.
> I: You want to look at the pictures and tell me about them?
> L: Okay. (He turns pages) I haven't read this but I've seen the top of it.
> I: Can you read any of these words?
> L: I can read *and* and *dog.*
> I: How about telling me about the pictures?
> Louis goes on to comment on each page:
>> (to a page depicting the two dogs):
>>> ''Short and long''
>> (to a page showing small dog under umbrella, big dog getting rained on):

"Dry and wet."
(One dog playing the flute, the other the tuba):
"Soft and loud."
(Dogs at table, one handing the other a plate of food):
"Eating. Got and giving."
(Dogs painting a house, one using red paint, the other green):
"Red and green."

The underlying concept of oppositions is clearly grasped by Louis, and he can clearly, if sparsely, articulate it. He is in fact "reading" the book without benefit of the text.

4. Oral Reading

The regularly taped oral reading samples shed light on some of the resources Louis brings to the challenge of learning to read. The particular constraints and demands of the oral readings, however, make them a poor showcase for Louis's skills and strengths. Instead, they reveal some of the counterproductive consequences of his style. Absent are the sense of involvement, absorption, directionality—the knowledgeable "expert" tends to get obscured by the cautious neophyte of modest skills and little boldness. There is a plodding, dispirited quality to many of the readings. Louis works hard, persists, sustains long silences, but only occasionally gives signs of satisfaction or accomplishment. He is not reading for himself on these tapes, but doing schoolwork.

This characterization of the oral readings is valid for many, but not all, of the tapes; the source of the difference thus is interest. Familiarity shows up as a major variable. His readings come to life somewhat in selections from the *Bank Street* readers, his instructional text that he encounters daily. Under these circumstances, Louis is at ease and does a creditable job.

Louis's reading at the beginning of first grade was confined to a few sight words. Thus, for the first oral reading samples taped by his teacher, he is asked to retell a story that was read in class, with the book in front of him. Louis retells the story of Mr. Miacca, a fairly complex story involving dangerous adventure that hinges on attention to some critical details. His narrative does not flow smoothly, but he recaptures the essential meaning of the story. Louis sounds comfortable in the situation, and appears involved in the retelling. When he can't answer a question, he says "I don't know," an admission that occurs several times. He claims the story did not scare him.

During a later oral reading sample (April, 1st grade), Louis is asked to retell the plot of *Blackboard Bear* to an adult he has just met, after hearing the story for the first time. He undertakes the task, but with little enthusiasm. He grasps the story, which is told partly in pictures and partly in words, keeping some of the original words intact in his reconstruction. With the text before him, he seems reluctant to paraphrase, even though he is retelling, not reading.

The first time Louis is heard reading connected text is in January, first grade. The selection is from the first book of the *Bank Street* series, his instructional text. Louis is on familiar territory. He gives a virtually flawless performance of the approximately 150-word selection containing about 15 separate words. His is a largely word-for-word rendition, and the intonation suggests that he values precision more than flow. Yet the reading is not without expression or occasional sounds of liveliness.

The few deviations from the text are not a rich source of information about the strategies Louis invokes to help him control the text. He skips one word, *up,* but reads it when the teacher points to it. He substitutes *might* for *light* when the teacher asks him to compare the two words. The one word he is unable to decipher without considerable help is *good* (see previous comments). Louis thus seems in this reading to rely predominantly on his memory of whole words. He seems unable, in this instance at least, to integrate his knowledge of letter sounds with information gleaned from pictures. The tonal quality of the reading suggests the inference that what Louis has learned so far is to recognize words—there is no indication that he has memorized the text, an alternative strategy beginning readers often use.

Reading unfamiliar material, even of comparable level of difficulty, is clearly a trial for Louis. Here the disadvantages of an incremental, rather narrowly focused process becomes most apparent. Louis tends to focus on one word at a time, hardly looking either forward or backward. The words he knows he recognizes in or out of context, but he can apply few productive strategies to deciphering new words. The strategies that he has available he can use only one at a time. His early readings thus have an all-or-none quality about them, as ''He can either read the lines, or not.'' In the latter case he is often unable to get past the first unfamiliar word on his own. He simply stops, skipping the word only when his teacher tells him to do so.

The absence of forward thrust in Louis's oral reading is matched by a lack of backward looks. He rarely self-corrects or rereads a phrase after he deciphers a word or is provided with one. He does not seem to try to recoup the meaning of the sentence after it gets lost in the silences of waiting for a word to come.

Later in the first year, but more during the second year, Louis acquires a few handles to deal with text, and his reading exhibits more forward motion. He will slur words he cannot securely pronounce, even substitute and skip on his own. He also uses the strategy of repeating a beginning phrase several times in order to gain time, without losing momentum, to decipher the word ahead. Yet even this strategy does not seem to propel his reading much. Louis's attention seems mainly directed at the surface structure of the text.

There is ample independent evidence that Louis has the capacity to comprehend meanings rather more complex than those offered by the passages he reads aloud. Thus, his abandonment of meaning is likely related to his difficulties in mastering the intricacies of writing and to the situational characteristics of oral reading.

One source of difficulty may be the way memory is developed during oral reading, in contrast with its role in the construction process Louis excels in. In the case of assembling and fitting together units of a concrete material such as Lego, the material itself provides a running record of the history of the structure. The work in process is continuously available, effectively eliminating the need for a memory trace in the mind of the builder. In reading, however, given the perishable nature of the spoken word and the limitations of short-term memory, no concrete residue of the textual meanings remains. Unless reading proceeds apace and the reader uses the variety of mnemonic devices available to fix meaning—i.e., repetition, self-correction, summarizing, and so forth—meaning will not be retained. Since Louis seems to make little effective use of such mental devices in his early reading, and since his insistence on accurate rendering causes his pace to falter, oral reading, in its early stages, is for him largely devoid of meaning. It is essentially a task of decoding single words.

The last reading sample, taped in June of second grade, bears witness to Louis's progress. In his reading of an unfamiliar book, there are continuities as well as changes to note. When he encounters difficulty with a word, his tempo slackens, his voice changes to a lackluster monotone. He does, however, try in several ways to keep the flow going. The first page of the book is reproduced and discussed below, his rendition on this page being fairly typical of his rendition throughout the first five pages that he read for the sample.

> WALTER was a whale. He was young, but big. He lived in the ocean with his mother.
>
> He splashed in the salty, blue-green water. And his mother told him everything a whale needs to know—how to dive to the bottom to get nice fresh squids for dinner; how to come up and blow a spout in the air; how to sleep in the water, rocking gently on the waves.
>
> Walter was very curious, and he asked lots of questions.

Louis repeats the first sentence of the passage three times (''Walter was . . . Walter was a whale . . . Walter was a whale''), most likely to gain time enough to identify *young*. He slurs over the phrase containing *young,* saying something that sounds like ''in was wild.'' But he then pronounces the second sentence forcefully and correctly in response to the teacher's prompting to look again. He makes semantically reasonable and graphically approximate substitutions—reading *steady* for *salty* and *shrimp* for *squid*—thus giving evidence of having integrated two cue systems. His next difficulty is with the word *gently,* on the last line of the second paragraph. Again, in an apparent effort to gain time, he repeats the preceding word twice. When his teacher says, "Take the best guess you can and go ahead," Louis sounds out the word with reasonable success: "gg . . . gil . . . g-en-tul on the waves." He substitutes *cross* for *curious* in the next line ("Walter was very cross"), but at the teacher's signal that something is wrong, he produces "curiss." Louis's last mistake on the page and his comment about his correction are especially interesting. He reads *squids* for *questions* ("and he asked lots of squids"), a substitution which prompts the following exchange.

> Teacher: Do you think you can figure that sentence out now—"Walter was very curious, and he asked lots of———"?
> Louis: Questions.
> Teacher: How did you figure that out?
> Louis: It seemed like it.
> Teacher: How did it seem like it? From the way the word looked or the sense of the sentence?
> Louis: The way the word looked.

The impression from this last interchange is that Louis got the word from the meaning of the sentence, yet he specifically states that he derived the word on the basis of how it looked. Nonetheless, lots of changes are noteworthy in this last reading. Louis gives evidence of reading ahead in the text by his repetitions, of using multiple cues and strategies to spur his performance, of attempts to guess, even of slurring over words. As a result, there is a forward motion to his reading, along with signs of attention to meaning. In sum, the tape indicates that Louis has integrated some of the skills he acquired piecemeal and is now able to put them to use in oral reading.

Writing

Louis's approach to writing also bears his personal stamp. During his first 2 years in school, he does virtually no spontaneous writing; his writing record is consequently sparse, consisting of a few dictated stories, journal entries, captions accompanying drawings, and a few books on a unified theme. Most of these writings are a result of classroom assignments, some of them rather specific—writing about a classroom trip or event—others more general, responsive to the teacher's expectation that entries will be made in the writing journal regularly.

The mechanical aspects of writing are hard for Louis, and his writing remains rather labored to the very end. He assembles words letter by letter, asking his teacher for the correct spelling or using other sources of writing available in the room, like dictionaries or signs, often copying from these models. The painstaking work of forming letters and words is not always reflected in the finished writing: Louis organizes the space on the page decisively and economically, writing on the line, observing margins and skipping lines appropriately. In his journal, he makes two entries on each page, even when writing them a week apart.

The teacher offers a concise comment about Louis's own expectations of his writing: "He likes what he writes to make sense, and his spelling to be correct" (May, 1st grade). She elaborates later:

> His reluctance to guess keeps him from going ahead on his own. This is also evident in his diary and other writing. He will not write a word unless he is entirely sure of the spelling, or can find it around the room and copy it. He had a terrible time recently trying to write the caption: *The spider sings for the love monster.* When I asked him to sound out *spider,* instead of just spelling it for him, he was ready to abandon the effort. It was like pulling teeth to get him to do it. [May, 1st grade]

Louis's writing thus proceeds slowly, with numerous corrections, erasures, and pauses in between. Yet he has a sense of the whole that gives his writing continuity, even when the entries are composed over several days.

During the fall of first grade, Louis dictates several stories that prove to be prototypical of his dictation and of some of his own writings as well. The earliest one available dates around Halloween, and is inspired by an assignment involving a set of sequence cards that the children were supposed to order and then comment on. The four pictures, as aligned by Louis, show (1) a pumpkin in the field, (2) a pumpkin in the store, (3) a pumpkin half carved, and (4) a fully carved pumpkin in a window. The story reads:

> I went to the farm and I helped my father take it to the store and we saved it for Halloween. And we took it home Halloween. [October, 1st grade]

The realistic quality of the story, relating an event that did happen or could have happened and told in a matter-of-fact, lucid manner, is like that of many stories Louis dictates. The pumpkin story is especially characteristic of the concrete origins of much of Louis's writing. Most often, Louis bases his writing on a drawing of his own, or uses a trigger such as a word or picture in a dictionary. His drawings and writing are highly interrelated. One of the few class rules he consistently violates is the proscription against drawing in the journal.

> I went to camping and I went past a store and my father said, "Okey Dokey, we're here and I started to play and it was fun and in the afternoon I asked my father if I could go to the store. [November, 1st grade]

Reality is suspended from time to time in Louis's writing, as it is in his constructions, and a bit of fantasy emerges:

> Once upon a time, there was a pumpkin and he got married with Melody the Pumpkin. The(y) got killed. Their friend made a statue of both of them and put it in his window. The End [November, 2nd grade]

Violent images or thoughts are not a frequent presence in Louis's writing but when they occur, they are sharply expressed, as in the short announcement harboring violent intentions:

> I want to kill Ann ANd
> Melody ANd Jessie A. ANd
> Jessiea O. So I Will [April, 2nd grade]

An interesting contrast between Louis's writing and dictation is presented by an entry that begins with Louis doing the actual writing, and continues with him dictating the rest of the story:

Ships

> This.is.a Ship
>   With things escape with and kill other ships
> This is ship
> (dictated)
> Lots of people go on this big ship because it is a ship for carrying people to the other country. This is a very fast boat and it is a motor boat that is in lots of races.
> (back cover:) The End [September, 2nd grade)

One of the few instances of writing that Louis elects to do on his own occurs around Halloween of the first year. He makes a series of shape-books, in the form of a ghost, cutting the pages to fit a template. The identically shaped pages are differentiated by the drawings on them and by the pasted or stapled bits of paper on the front or back pages. The most elaborate of these books is the Count Dracula book, which has a cape-like attachment stapled on the back. The title page in Louis's writing reads:

Coun
t Dra
cula

The text on the following pages was dictated by Louis to his teacher:

(p. 1) Count Dracula's bats and Count Dracula is up near the moon and all the other bats are next to the haunted house (drawing of house, bats, blue streak in sky—moon)

(p. 2) Count Dracula turned back into Count Dracula and now he is not near the moon (the Count and the moon)

(p. 3) This is a dragon and a cat and they are happy. The dragon is green and he gots a brown face and he gots green points on his back (as described)

(p. 4) This is Count Dracula turned back into a bat and this is a haunted house with a broken window (as described)

(p. 5) This is Dracula's castle. And The End of Dracula

During this same period supernatural beings are the topic of a few other pieces of writing. One of the longest stories in this first writing book, which describes the drawing that precedes it, also has one of Louis's more successful opening lines:

> I'm on the railing and my uncle went outside and when he got outside he saw this spider and he saw 3 monsters. One was big, one was little and one was middle size and that was the end of Halloween day. [October, 2nd grade]

The quality of expression varies considerably in Louis's writing. On occasion, as in the story cited above, he shows a capacity for effective verbal expression. Two other examples of notable opening lines come from his second writing book. A portrait of himself playing ball is the occasion for the lines:

> I lik soccer, Soccer is.
> Part of my life. [September, 2nd grade]

Mood is conveyed effectively by a longer story:

> To Day it is rain'ning
> And iT is a drowsey
> Day and it is not
> Fan at School but iT is r
> Fanr at school The END. [April, 2nd grade]

In contrast with these vivid phrases and passages, the writing book contains its share of rather perfunctory writing on common themes:

> The cowboy is very
> Dongs there is a
> cowboy and hi
> naMe is cowboy and
> he has A frind. and
> his naMe is Indan

The indan is very dongs
and Some of The
cowboys and Idan
fight. [January, 2nd grade]

at Easter i got a
Socker ball and i
love it it is very fan
To play with and i am
going too play Hockey [April, 2nd grade]

In the last half of the second year Louis produces a piece of expository writing, in response to a classroom assignment, that integrates his knowledge and expressive skill:

A reptile has it's
baby in a egg
not born all by
itself A reptile
has no hair

In this succinct description of reptilian essence Louis's interest in factual information and accurate depiction converges with writing sufficiently skilled to accord with his own standards for competence. Under these circumstances, and only then, does Louis's performance lose its plodding quality and assume an air of confident mastery.

13 Tim

Anne M. Bussis, Virginia S. Cramer, and Beth Alberty
Teacher: Marjorie Robinson
Grades Covered by the Study: First and Second

SYNOPSIS

Tim is fairly tall for his age, well proportioned, slender but not thin. He speaks in a soft, sometimes husky voice, and his temperament matches his low-keyed tones. Although he converses easily with both adults and children, he uses words economically, rarely elaborating his thought and often not articulating it fully.

Though his manner is unobtrusive, Tim's presence is keenly felt in the classroom. He tends to assume command of free-play situations, continually channeling and directing his classmates' activity in the enactment of space and superhero dramas. Moreover, he does so without engendering strife. As an "upperclassman" in the second grade, he is often accorded the role of arbitrator and helper. The themes that emerge from Tim's record not only characterize his learning, they also illuminate the nature of his leadership.

Tim deploys attention on many fronts, and he appears to process diverse information in parallel fashion. He displays sensitivity to the individuality of peers and to differences in social settings, while simultaneously pursuing his own purposes. In reading, he scans pictures and text for clues to words, both at the point of difficulty and on surrounding pages. Sometimes the clue he uses is obvious in the substitution he offers, but often it is not. He seems to operate on several clues at once and to make inferences and leaps of thought in the process. When asked to focus on single letters and to blend their sounds sequentially, he tries to respond but is usually unsuccessful.

In his dramatic play and artwork, Tim reveals an encompassing and complex view of the world. He combines elements from different realms (earth, space, superhero) in unique ways, yet imbues each setting with its own rules and reality

317

constraints. In short, he generates interesting ideas that hold the attention of his friends. His view of books is similarly broad and differentiated. He regards some books as authoritative sources of knowledge, some as guides to be used as long as they are helpful, and some as grist for his own elaboration of story plots. In scanning text, his eye seems to take in broad spans of print while differentiating individual letters.

The attitudes that serve to distance Tim from situations also pervade his social and intellectual functioning. He is impartial in judging and reporting events, and he doesn't fuss about technical details or human foibles. Together, these characteristics earn him the reputation of being a "fair" person. When it comes to reading, he evidently equates "details" with troublesome words. Tim will improvise or skip words but refuses to get bogged down by them. His impartial attitude extends to his own ability in the sense that he makes accurate judgments about what is difficult or easy for him to read. He also distances himself by not investing high personal stakes in any particular product or performance. If one effort fails, he tries again or starts on a different tack. He is not easily discouraged or impeded.

Tim's progress in learning to read is steady and even, unmarked by plateaus or sudden advances. At the beginning of the record, he is in an early stage of formal reading; at the end, he is a competent reader of difficult texts.

INSTRUCTIONAL ENVIRONMENT AND READING PROGRAM

Tim's teacher throughout the duration of the study is Marjorie Robinson, a woman with several years experience teaching a combined first- and second-grade class. The group size ranges between 29 and 36 over the 2 years, and the composition divides about equally between grade levels and between sexes. Although Ms. Robinson remains solely responsible for the class, she does have some part-time adult help. Student teachers successively come under her guidance and assist in the classroom, some for only a few weeks and one for as long as 4 months. She also has the help of two classroom mothers on a fairly regular basis—one mother who comes for part or all of the day on Wednesday, and another who is there on Thursday afternoons.

Classroom Provisions and Activities

The classroom is situated at the end of a second-floor corridor in a solid-looking building, typical of the many city schools constructed during the period following World War II. The building houses approximately 1,000 students in grades K–6. The room itself is fairly large, with carpeted areas in two corners. These are fixed areas: one for block construction and dramatic play, the other primarily for reading and class meetings. A third corner contains a sink and cabinets of paint and other arts and crafts supplies. Aside from a sofa and several bookcases and storage cupboards, which remain stationary most of the time, the furniture consists of movable desks and tables that accommodate a flexible use of space. Most often, the children's desks are arranged in three or four large clusters, with eight to ten desk units pushed together to form a single cluster. (See map of classroom arrangement at the end of this section.)

The room is well supplied with sturdy building blocks of varying shapes and sizes, stored in shelves that line one wall of the block corner. A large Lego set enhances the general building capacity in the classroom. The sink area is supplied with paint and diverse construction material for arts and crafts. Provisions for math include individual workbooks, several types of manipulatible math materials (e.g., cubes), and various games that involve logic or number concepts. Toward the end of Tim's first-grade year, Ms. Robinson introduces a water tub and provides materials for working with water—e.g., funnels, measuring cups, hoses for syphoning. Although she had provided both sand and water in previous years for the children in her class, she is in a transition of phasing out these materials during the time that Tim is in her classroom.

The daily schedule of activities is generally "tighter" at the beginning of each school year, and loosens up as the children progressively learn to take more responsibility for their work, for each other, and for the smooth functioning of the group as a whole. Thus, at the beginning of Tim's first grade, activities generally conform to the following schedule:

9:00– 9:15	Morning meeting
9:15–10:15	Reading groups
10:15–10:50	Break: Children go to the yard or to gym, hear a story, or have a sing.
11:00–11:15	Writing time
11:15–11:50	Clean up and meeting. If the children haven't been read a story yet, Ms. Robinson usually reads at this time.
11:50–12:35	Lunch
12:35– 1:10	Quiet reading time
1:10– 1:50	Math groups and workbooks
1:50– 2:40	Choice time
2:40– 3:00	Clean up and meeting; story if not in the morning.

By the middle of the year, the class meets a longer time in the morning to discuss work assignments for the day (reading, writing, math) and whatever other matters need attention. The day then breaks up mainly into work periods during which the children tackle their assigned work in whatever order they decide and engage in choice activities.

Choice activities in the class include drawing (always), painting (when there is another adult in the room to help), various craft activities, games, reading, working with Lego or other small unit building materials, and large construction work and dramatic play in the block area. Because the block area is so popular, the children form self-selected block groups, and each group has assigned times in the area during the week. The children may also devise their own games and craft activities during choice times; they are not confined to the available commercial games or to adult suggestions about craft projects. All the children attend movement classes in the gymnasium, under the direction of a dance and movement teacher. Otherwise, their play in the gym and yard is of their own making. Ms. Robinson supervises the activity during these periods, but she does not direct it.

Two projects involve the whole class during Tim's first-grade year. One is the making of an animated film about creatures from outer space. The other project is a seven-act dance/movement performance. The performance was rehearsed for several weeks and put on twice: once for the class parents and once for other children in the school.

Marjorie has always had a personal interest in music and drama, and she possesses an exceptionally good singing voice. During Tim's second-grade year, she decides to resume professional singing lessons, and her enthusiasm carries over to the classroom. More and more, she teaches children words to songs (as an alternative to reading stories), and more and more the children become involved in group singing.

The Reading Program

Tim commences reading instruction with Ms. Robinson as a member of what she calls "The Beginning Level Reading Group." She makes rough estimates of reading levels at the beginning of the year and, for working purposes, mentally divides the children into three groups: The Beginning Level or "Readiness" Group, the "Breaking Through" Group, and the Fluent Group. These groups are not formally constituted but exist as temporary designations in Marge Robinson's mind, with individual children shifting levels as appropriate. She then differentiates her work with each group in the fall of the year according to the following general plan.

Beginning Level Reading Group ("Readiness").   These children do a lot of homemade books. Marjorie begins by reading "little books" to them (e.g., books in the *Breakthrough* series) that they can use as models. She tells the children that they can make their own books by drawing a picture and then saying what's happening, and she or the student teacher will write it down. When these children meet as a group, each child tells about a book he/she has made. Marjorie tries to get as much "fullness" of story as possible during these times. She also works on sounds with this group. Although she has never before emphasized a phonic approach to beginning reading instruction, Tim's entering first-grade class presents her with an unusual situation and something of a problem. Most of these children had received special instruction during kindergarten in a "decoding program" (initiated by the school the previous year) that stressed the various sounds of individual letters. When Tim's class came to her as first-graders, she didn't feel she could just ignore their previous instruction, so she made an effort to reinforce it. Throughout the fall, she therefore devises many formal lessons and informal games that emphasize beginning, ending, and medial letter sounds.

Breaking Through Group.   Children in this group also make their own books, but Ms. Robinson reads a lot with them as well. Books available for their use include several sets of "easy readers," which are color-coded with green tape and kept in a special bookcase. All the children are allowed to read these books, however, and many fluent readers do so. Marjorie usually spends concerted time with children when they are just on the verge of "breaking through." When she thinks a child is at this point, she may read every day with the child for 3 or 4 weeks.

Fluent Reading Group.   At the beginning of Tim's first grade, this group consists entirely of second-graders in the classroom. Ms. Robinson holds individual reading conferences with these children periodically, but they work mainly with the student teacher on any special projects. During the fall, the special project that Marjorie plans with the student teacher is on African folk tales.

By January, many of the children in the beginning group (including Tim) have shifted to more actual reading of simple books, unceremoniously joining the ranks of the "Breaking Through" group. Now, Ms. Robinson brings subgroups of six to eight children on the rug and reads with each individually. Also in January, she eases up on the sound instruction, giving formal lessons only once a week or less. (As noted in the "Report from the Reading Record," she drops this emphasis altogether with Tim by the end of January and adopts different strategies when reading with him individually.)

In conjunction with her work with groups and individuals, Marjorie stresses the importance of every child having a book to read or to look at during quiet reading period each day. She starts quite formally in the fall, recording each child's book on a 3 x 5 index card. Every time the children change books, they must come and report it to her. In this manner, she keeps a running record of the books children read, even though she doesn't read every single book individually with every child, and she generally gets the message across that each child must "have" a book. By mid-spring of the year, this strict accounting system becomes more lax. The children begin to keep their own records and may change books without reporting every change to the teacher.

The room is well stocked with reading material when Tim enters the class in the fall. There are books without words and several series of books at approximately the same level—the *Scott Foresman Reading Systems, Breakthrough* books, the *Monster* series, *Bright and Early* books, Dr. Seuss books, the *I Can Read* series, *Little Golden Books,* and the *Bill Martin Readers.* In addition to these series, there are story books, counting books, alphabet books, science books, animal books, and poetry. In the spring of the year, Marjorie bolsters the book collection by adding another (2nd level) set of the small, hard-bound *Bill Martin Readers.* She also adds about 50 *Scott Foresman Reading System* paperback books at the yellow, green, and orange levels. By this time, the children are also visiting the school library once a week to get books. As each child finishes his or her library book, the book is returned to a large crate (to keep them separated from the classroom books) for other children to read during the week.

At the start of Tim's second grade, Ms. Robinson adds another set of books that the children generally like and that Tim, in particular, reads avidly. This is a set of 48 *Wonder-Starter Books* (paperbacks) which Marjorie found during the summer for the bargain price of $.79 per book. Although she had to reinforce the spines of the books, she reports that it was well worth it. The books are written at approximately the second-grade reading level and range over a variety of nonfiction subject matter. Tim goes through the following titles in the set by mid-February: *Dogs, Cats, Rocks, Horses, Tigers, Fish, Clothes, Trees, Ants, Mountains.*

Ms. Robinson also makes extensive use of the SRA Reading Laboratory, a series of stories at different levels that fit in a self-contained file box. Each story is color coded as to level and accompanied by a set of vocabulary and comprehension questions geared to the story. The children usually work independently with these SRA materials, showing Ms. Robinson their finished set of questions. Occasionally, she will ask a child to read one of the SRA stories at an individual reading conference.

Another set of commercial reading materials is mandated for classroom use in the spring of Tim's first grade. This is an Individual Criterion Referenced Testing package (ICRT). The system breaks reading down into 340 discrete skills, with a skill card for each one. There is a box of cards, referred to as "benchmarks," for every two teachers in the school. The teacher is supposed to work with every child on each skill, using the benchmark card as a test when she thinks the child knows the skill well enough. Marjorie makes an effort to work the ICRT system into her reading program, but she uses the benchmark cards "straight off," without working on the skills beforehand. She talks with each child about skills that are failed.

Finally, Ms. Robinson's reading program emphasizes reading to children as much as children reading for themselves. As mentioned previously, Marjorie begins to alternate reading books with teaching songs to the class during Tim's second grade. She writes out the words to a song (usually a several-verse ballad), so that the children may "read along" as they learn the melody and words.

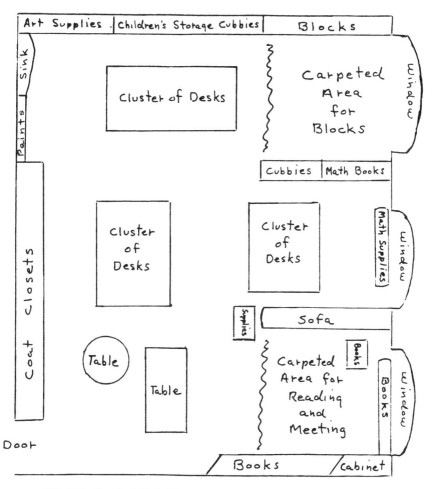

FIG. 13.1   Sketch of Tim's Classroom

REPORT FROM THE TOTAL RECORD

An initial reading of Tim's record prompts impressions of his quickness and "early bird" tendency, his consuming interest in space and superheroes, and his versatility in expressing this interest, especially in dramatic play. The dramatic play episodes in the documentation reveal him time and time again directing activity or turning the situation to his own purposes, but without recrimination from his peers—a fact that raises the question of how he manages to avoid conflict. This question became the basis for the first exhaustive charting of data about him under the heading, "Handling of Potential Conflict."

The themes that ultimately emerged from data integration clarify both Tim's learning and the question originally posed. They are as follows:

1. Wide Scope and Manifold View
2. Simultaneous/Parallel Processing
3. Quick, Easy-Going, Economical
4. Distanced, Impartial, Unimpeded
5. Enlivening, Courteous, Responsive

1. Wide Scope and Manifold View

Tim's formal knowledge and vocabulary lie well within the expected bounds of an attentive 6- to 7-year-old. According to his teacher, he expresses himself "adequately . . . with a little above average vocabulary." Neither precocious nor particularly gifted with words, he nonetheless projects a comprehensive and complex view of the world in his work and actions.

In art, for example, his graphic representations span dimensions of time and space, just as they traverse realms of fantasy and reality. The many drawings he produced at free moments during the spring of first grade are especially notable in this respect. Futuristic figures and objects from outer space are coupled with prehistoric, dragon-like creatures in his most usual combination, but other elements also appear together: spacemen with medieval helmets and swords, robots sitting at a modern lunch counter, space figures with comic book superheroes (see Figures 13.2 through 13.5).

FIG. 13.2   Tim's Pencil Drawing, (Sample A)

FIG. 13.3   TIM's Pencil Drawing (Sample B).

He also sees possibilities for creating unusual meaning by capitalizing on "artistic mishaps" and by transforming conventional or static images and ideas.

—A mottled, blotchy patch in the center of Tim's drawing paper vaguely suggests the upper part of a human silhouette. (The blotch is magic marker bleeding through from a figure of Batman on the reverse side of the paper.) Added to the blotch are two arms, two legs, and a cape sticking out from the torso. Tim's dictated caption for the picture—"Robin is being shadowed"—is perfectly attuned to the weird effect he has created. [From the drawing/dictation book entitled *Batman and Robin*, November, 1st grade]

—When Sam shows the group his tunnel construction, Tim immediately sees in it the possibility of a "Cylon base." [March, 1st grade]

—There is an argument among other boys at Tim's table about whether someone can call a particular piece of Lego a "muffler." Finally, Tim says: "You can make it what it is. He can call it a muffler." [October, 2nd grade]

—Tim starts his painting by outlining a spaceship and planet in blue and filling the interior of the space with white. Suddenly he scrubs white over the ship until he has obliterated its distinct outline, and all that remains are two white cloudish spots. Then he scrubs blue on the paper. When Raphael criticizes, saying the spaceship Galactica doesn't look like that, Tim explains: "It's in light speed." Raphael still

FIG. 13.4   TIM's Pencil Drawing (Sample C)

seems unconvinced, so Tim more aggressively adds, "Haven't you heard of the Galactica and light speed?" Raphael asks about the blue, and Tim says, "That's the space." When Raphael questions blue space, Tim sputters a bit about blue space, purple space, and so on. Then he cleans his brush and loads it with white, dripping a zigzag line and then individual spots all over the background—"Stars," he says, "Look stars!" [From an observation, April, 1st grade]

In the observation of the spaceship painting above, Tim's transformation seems guided by certain "reality standards" of space fantasy movies. The *Star Wars* movies, for instance, always depict the motion of light speed as a whitish blur that rapidly recedes into an inky blue, star-sprinkled galaxy. In a similar vein, Tim continually seeks to establish the limits of possible and permissible functioning within each realm that he differentiates along the reality/fantasy

FIG. 13.5   TIM's Pencil Drawing (Sample D)

continuum (earth, outer space, and superhero realms). The following excerpts illustrate this concern for constraining imagination with realism. They are taken from two observations and a conversation that occurred during the period March through May of first grade.

—Tim explains some interpretation of the Galactica characters and plot to Jamal, apparently in an effort to correct some misstatement about them.

—The boys make use of tiny, plastic teddy bear figures in their space play, assigning various roles to them (e.g., Muffin, the pet robot dog). During a conversation ostensibly centered on Muffin, Tim suddenly corrects Jamal "There is no such thing as a real life teddy bear. A real one, no—a fake one, yes."

—"No, that can't do. That has to stay there" . . . referring to the reality of a cardboard base station that Manuel is lifting in the air.

—"He don't have no cannon on his tail!"

—Tim suddenly turns into the area to correct something Manuel claims about one of the figures. According to Tim, the figure "can't fly."

—In maneuvering a Spiderman doll around the heads of two friends, Tim abides by Spiderman's constraints—moving the doll along lines determined by the (imaginary) web Spiderman throws.

—In a conversation about Tim's ambition to be an astronaut, the interviewer poses the possibility of going to Mars. Tim expresses doubt, referring to the actuality of the situation.

> Tim: "Nobody ever went to Mars! ! !"
> AB: "How do you know?"
> Tim: "Well, 'cause Mars is way far away."

—During an oral reading, Tim remarks that the boys' guns depicted in the book *Blackboard Bear* aren't real guns. And he exclaims with some delight about the picture of the chalk bear walking off the blackboard: "Now that's unbelievable—nobody could do that!"

Like millions of other children, Tim has assimilated popular space and super-hero fantasies of the day. Unlike many children however, he treats these imagined realms as potential extensions of the world, having their own inherent integrity and truth requirements. For him, fantasies mingle intimately with constructs about the real world.

The record also indicates a breadth of understandings and intentions. Tim thus appears to have many handles on the world—several points of entry for exploration and expression. Although he most often presents himself as a person in action, the evidence testifies to a careful observer who deploys attention on many fronts and is therefore alert to meaning in the smallest particulars as well as in the overarching properties of things. This tendency is illustrated in part by the examples given above, but there are other indications too.

—He can, and often does, depict detail with great care in his drawings of figures and objects. These include details of facial features and expression; costumes; vehicles and equipment; and, occasionally, background setting (e.g., a picture of plants on the classroom windowsill, with the wall thermometer clearly in evidence).

—He seems intent on keeping the flow of the story moving when he reads aloud, yet will often latch on to some minute pictured detail as the clue to an unknown word.

—The fact that he engages children differentially in dramatic play indicates that he takes in both obvious and subtle cues from the social environment. (See documentation under heading 2.)

The overall collection of Tim's artwork suggests versatility of style and purpose. There is elaboration of detail in some drawings (figures and objects) and almost total disregard of detail in others (action scenes). Line is likewise varied. There are curved and circular lines, lines following in opposition, angular and zigzag lines, stripes, and intersecting lines that form grids. Some lines are sketchy and tentative; others are sure and bold. Lines are used to show the motion of objects dropping down and of figures springing or flying upward. Zigzags, grids, scallops, and webbed lines are used to depict detail. Where backgrounds occur, diverging lines are often used to give the illusion of depth.

2. Simultaneous/Parallel Processing

Dual focusing enables a person to attend to one activity while monitoring other activities in the background. (Several instances of such background monitoring occur in Tim's record, but they are not of concern here.) Less common is the ability to focus on two or more matters of central importance. When such multiple focusing occurs, and when it is sustained over time, it suggests the more complex act of simultaneous or parallel processing of information. Tim displays evidence of this capacity by differentially engaging children in the dramatic play of the block area. He simultaneously exercises social judgment (to minimize conflict) while pursuing the goal of "good drama" (to enhance his own purposes and meanings).

Unless otherwise noted, all the illustrations that follow are taken from three extended observations of play in the block area made during March and April of the first grade. Observations of that particular activity were deliberately scheduled because Tim's decided preference for dramatic play had become clear by midyear, and because his success in guiding the action without arousing dissension was puzzling.

In interactions with *Eddie, Manuel,* and *Donald,* Tim asserts his purposes very directly by commanding and taking charge, but he does so within the framework of the drama. He rarely exhorts, urges, or nags them as individual persons to do his bidding.

—"You don't wanna attack yet!"—to Manuel.

—He dives Muffin (the robot dog) into Manuel's toy figure.

—"OK get those" . . . "Those!" . . . "Those!" . . . "Now give me the . . ." "No, the long one."—to Donald as his helper in building.

—"Give me a teddy bear or you're OUT!"—to Manuel, who says "OK" and trots off to get the teddies.

—"Get 'em up here (to the) ship!"—apparently warning Donald and Manuel about some danger. Manuel snaps back a very military "Yes sir!"

—"I'm the leader you guys"—to Donald and Manuel. Manuel asks: "What about me? I'm the lieutenant." There doesn't seem to be any disagreement over these roles, and Donald eventually assumes the position of sergeant.

—"You're the good guys. We're the bad guys"—to Eddie.

He also commands *Raphael* within the context of dramatic play, but there is more evidence of both give-and-take and minor disputing.

—He listens to Raphael explain about his block arrangement.

—He sits back and watches as Raphael adds a ramp to his building. Tim keeps watching. Then suddenly: "Lemme build the bottom."

—He disputes Raphael's claim to be the leader.

Toward *Jamal*, he behaves quite differently. Jamal is a large, strong-willed boy who can become difficult when crossed. Although he is not a member of Tim's assigned block group, he occasionally joins or asks to join the group when his work for the period is finished. He owns some of the popular space figures. Tim will correct Jamal about the Galactica plot or about matters of fact ("There is no such thing as a real life teddy bear"), but he never commands Jamal in play the way he does other boys. He will suggest, try to negotiate or bargain, sometimes plead. He asks permission and in other ways acknowledges Jamal's proprietary rights. If Jamal is pursuing his own line of play, Tim does not try to engage him but maintains congenial contact. If Jamal directly requests or demands something of Tim, Tim usually complies.

—Both Tim and Jamal have finished their assignment early, and Jamal has taken out the Lego. Tim takes a few pieces from the Lego bin and casually leans over Jamal while they talk. Jamal apparently agrees to share them, for Tim brings over a chair and immediately begins some fantasy play with the Lego. [November, 1st grade]

—Tim evidently has Starbuck in mind as the role he would prefer to play with the aid of Jamal's toy figures. He first asks Jamal:

"Am I gonna be him?" pointing to one of the figures. Then immediately, "I'll be Muffin, OK?"

Later: "You're Starbuck, right?"

Still later: "I wanna be Starbuck, please?" He repeats this several times and offers to bring in another toy tomorrow.

—Tim follows Raphael to the block area, but then circles back to Jamal's desk. After some joking negotiation, he borrows a small spaceman.

—Tim refuses Jamal's request to join the assigned block group but offers an idea for future play: "Tomorrow I'll bring Chewbacca and you can play with him . . . or Luke."

With *Kevin*, who is small, compact, and notoriously rough, Tim remains firm in denying him access to the block area. On the other hand, he accepts and directs Kevin in dramatic running games enacted in the gym or yard.

—When Kevin tries to enter the play of the block area: ''No!'' ''Three's enough!'' ''No! Now go away.''

—Marge Robinson's account in May of first grade: ''A fabulous game in gym today! Kevin, Raphael, Sam, Tim and a couple of other boys playing super-heroes. . . . Kevin was the Incredible Hulk. . . . The whole play was beautiful—exciting and active, but no bad feelings. It didn't get out of hand. . . . Tim's role was definitely some kind of leader—he would come up with strategies for captur-ing Sam, and he directed the Hulk's action at times.

Although *Sam* also has a reputation for roughness (and is large), Tim interacts with him—acknowledging, challenging, trying to lure, testing limits, backing off.

—Sam challenges Tim's statement that Muffin doesn't have a gun. Tim counters: ''Wanna bet?'' He then ignores Sam's apparent willingness to bet and, instead, turns back to play.

—When Tim sees possibilities for a prop (a Cylon base) in Sam's tunnel construc-tion, he immediately tries to engage Sam in the play: ''You wanna play with me?'' He seems to remember in midstream whose ''prop'' it is, for he quickly adds, ''Sam, can I play with you?'' Receiving no response to his request, Tim tries to engage Sam by plunging into play, stating that the tunnel is a Cylon base and placing a Cylon on top of it. Again no response from Sam. Tim walks off and zooms the Cylon in the air, talking about its radar attack. Still no response. He tries to elicit direct confirmation of his wishes: ''This is a Cylon base, right Sam?'' When all fails, Tim finally retreats from his effort and walks back to play with the others.

The effectiveness with which Tim orchestrates his play with the several chil-dren in and around the block area may be gauged from the fact that he never sparks disruption. Only once are there complaints.

—In Tim's absence one day, the boys in the block group made musical instru-ments. When the teacher praised their efforts, the ensuing discussion unearthed resentments: ''When Tim's here, all we can do is spaceships. . . .'' ''Yeah, we can't do anything else, only what Tim wants.'' [December, 1st grade]

In retrospect, this singular episode may be considered further evidence of Tim's successful orchestration, for complaints about his activity in the block area do not recur during the rest of the period covered by the record—and the block group keeps on enacting space and superhero dramas.

Tim's artwork also hints of his ability to process information in parallel fashion. Most of the drawings he produced during free time for his own enjoy-ment have the look of an artist's working sketches. There is more than one picture on a page, most of the scenes lack a background, figures and scenes are crossed out, and both sides of the drawing paper are used. As already mentioned, many drawings also combine people and creatures from different realms and times. These several features suggest that Tim does not focus solely on the representational aspect of drawing. Rather, the drawings serve to introduce characters and/or condensed elements from story plots he is constructing in his imagination.

This inference about his drawings receives considerable support from an observation of Tim in the process of painting. The painting in question was executed immediately following his rendition of the spaceship Galactica ''in light speed.'' (See Figures 13.6 + 13.7). On the surface, at least, it is an obscure picture and not a particularly attractive composition. The observation clarifies some of Tim's meaning but does not fully disclose it. The following is a synopsis of the observation.

—In preparing to start this picture, Tim announces twice (in the general direction of Manuel and Raphael) that he plans to draw Starbuck and some sort of blasting or shooting action. He begins by painting the center red oval with grid lines inside. There is talk with Manuel about his (Manuel's) painting of Muffin. Tim then paints a blue oblong line that surrounds the lower portion of the oval and its enclosed grid, announcing that this addition is Starbuck's jail. Then he extends the blue line to fully encapsulate the oval/grid and fills the space from the oval to the blue line with solid blue. After he has filled in this space, he takes green paint and in the lower left makes a squiggly circle with a dot in it. (He does not paint as carefully as he did with the red and blue.) He makes shooting noises to accompany the green painting, and then suddenly he draws the green brush upward into the red area, exclaiming: ''Look, Look! P-ugh, p-ugh! ! !'' He next gets orange and fills in in the area outlined by the green line within the red interior, creating a vivid, fiery look. With

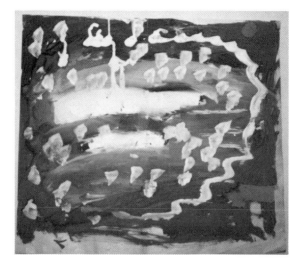

FIG. 13.6   Painting: The Spaceship Galactica in ''Light Speed''

FIG. 13.7   Painting: An Action Story

this, he is apparently finished and gives the painting to the paraprofessional. [April, 1st grade]

Finally, Tim displays evidence of parallel processing in his reading. This documentation appears in the report on the reading record and is not duplicated here.

3. Quick, Easy-Going, Economical

Quickness pervades virtually every aspect of Tim's functioning. He completes assigned work promptly, usually finishing before the allotted time is up. He swiftly executes shifts in movement, materials, or direction of work during an activity. He is responsive and alert in interchanges. He is an "early bird," minimizing periods of inactivity by starting work ahead of time.

—When he dictates, he seems to know exactly what he wants to say—no hesitation. [Interview: November, 1st grade]

—Speedily, he lays the sheet on the desk behind the teacher's chair, where she has told the children to leave them. Tim's is the first there. [Observation: November, 1st grade]

—Tim has been handed his math book and has gotten a pencil from his coat. He sits and begins working right away, though others are still settling around him and the teacher has not yet given any signal to begin. [Observation: November, 1st grade]

—Tim has very quickly built the more elaborate structure. [Observation: April, 1st grade]

—Before the teacher calls for silent reading period, Tim is singing out the words from a beginning page in his book. [Observation: April, 1st grade]

—Working with Lego, Tim quickly builds a frame around the edge of half of the flatbed. [Observation: October, 2nd grade]

—Tim begins reading right away, before the rest of the class has settled. [Observation: October, 2nd grade]

Though Tim works quickly, he is not hurried or precipitous. He takes time to work carefully when and where care is demanded. His shifts of direction in an activity (dramatic play or block building) and his maneuvers through the room are accomplished without tripping over objects, bumping into them, or knocking them over. And most of his interactions with children are without actual physical contact. In all these respects, his physical functioning is marked by an easy, fluid quality.

Tim also functions with emotional and temperamental ease in most situations. At the very beginning of the record, the teacher notes that "Tim is playful . . . has a good time . . . will cut up." Ms. Robinson has to speak to him as much as to anybody else with such reminders as "turn around" or "look at me." But it is easy for him to cooperate when she speaks to him. In the March interview (attended by the observer as well as the teacher), the observer comments that she has seen Tim ask for attention from other children several times and in several different ways, and that he can wait for it. He doesn't get distracted but patiently maintains his focus and purpose. Marjorie Robinson agrees with this—"He doesn't frazzle."

His patience is especially evident in episodes where he lures children into play rather than insisting or getting angry and frustrated when they do not respond to his wishes immediately. The episode in which he tries to lure Sam into making the tunnel a Cylon base has already been described. Another observation is also telling.

—Tim drops to his knees behind Eddie and Manuel, who are playing in the shelf space of the block area. He grins, partially joining them; they are absorbed. He begins maneuvering a Spiderman doll on the periphery of the shelves—first flying it behind their heads, then edging it down the wall above the shelves, then lighting it onto the shelves themselves. (There is an interruption when Donald comes over to complain about something.) Eddie and Manuel resume work, and Spiderman resumes its activities behind them. It turns head over heels in the air, zooms head first in straight paths in and out of the shelf environment. Tim is now in the thick of the boys' play, and there are some negotiations about the plot. [April, 1st grade]

Tim's patience and easy cooperation wear rather thin in only one context: periods of enforced inactivity. Unless he is intrigued with the topic of discussion or absorbed in listening to a story, he often appears fidgety, restless, at loose ends during meeting time. Sometimes he blatantly violates rules, though he usually moderates his misconduct so as not to disrupt others or call attention to himself—i.e., so as not to get caught. Moreover, these are the only times when Tim initiates physical contact with other children. The following excerpts from an observation of a class meeting capture this restless quality well. The teacher has been going over the sequence of parts for a movement performance the class is to present. She first asks them to recite the sequence of acts. Then the mood and pace of the meeting intensify as she plays the record and asks the various groups of performers to stand when their music comes on. Some of the children begin spontaneously rehearsing the movements, as they had done earlier in the morning at a formal rehearsal.

> —Tim plays with a pencil, sliding it along the top of the cabinet, trying to fit it into the recessed handles and lock. . . . He talks softly with Kevin. . . . He works on his shoes and only mutters the list as the others recite. When Tim stands with his group, he momentarily joins in the movement but with restrained gestures (unlike his earlier performance at the actual rehearsal). Then he starts fencing wth Sam who also has a (forbidden) pencil. . . . He continues fencing and banging pencils with Sam. . . . When another group rises, he exaggerates his motion and playfully bumps Allison. . . . He shoves Sam's head. . . . He and Sam struggle over the pencil. . . . Unlike the rest of the class, he does not watch the performance. . . . He watches without comment as the teacher takes Sam's pencil away. . . . Then he leans over the back of the couch to play with various math materials. . . . After a small tussle with another boy on the couch, he begins trying to stab Sam in the rump with his pencil. [January 1st grade]

This restlessness at meetings takes on added significance when one considers Tim's general reaction to times of transition—he avoids them as much as possible. His "early bird" tendency to start work in advance of the teacher's official signal to begin extends to the period before 9:00, when children are drifting into the room. Most children socialize at this time, but Tim usually works on something. When he finishes assignments before a period is over, he draws or builds with Lego during the interim. And when activities extend over a whole period (e.g., quiet reading, choice time), he keeps himself occupied the entire period. Nowhere in the record is he seen in any sustained interval of rest, reflection, observation, daydreaming, or total idleness.

The two major transitions of the day (entry into the classroom and dismissal) are noteworthy. Tim starts the year handling the first transition in a rather unusual manner. He formally shakes hands with Ms. Robinson. Although the handshaking doesn't continue for very long, he always makes sure to speak with the teacher when he enters the room. Dismissal is the only time that occasions serious distress for Tim. On and off during the fall of first grade, he collapses in tears just prior to 3:00—either because he wrongly anticipates the time and thinks his grandmother (who picks him up every day) is late, or because the class is in the schoolyard, and he fears she will not find him. These are emotionally intense crying incidents, sometimes developing into an uncontrollable sobbing and heaving. He finally gets his anxiety in check with Ms. Robinson's help, and later is able to do so on his own. But dismissal remains a shaky time for him, and his restlessness at meetings continues throughout the second grade.

Although Tim keeps himself continually engaged, there is no sense of "busyness" about him. To the contrary, he displays an economy of effort. He doesn't waste motions; he knows how to use resources efficiently; and he doesn't verbally elaborate his ideas much beyond the essentials, sometimes not fully articulating a thought. In trying to persuade Raphael that he is painting a spaceship in light speed, for example, his explanations are notably terse. The details he finally adds to the painting (presumably to accommodate Raphael's objections) are offered with the ultimate rationale: "Stars. Look, stars." Further documentation of Tim's economical verbal expression is presented in the report on reading. The instances below illustrate his regard for economy of physical effort.

—The children are coloring a ditto sheet filled with irregular designs that look like a jigsaw puzzle. The sheet contains instructions to fill so many patches with red, so many with blue, and so on. Tim starts by alternating colors, outlining a patch and then filling it in from the edges. Soon, he notices a much faster strategy another boy is using—making adjacent patches the same color, up to the number specified. Tim begins speeding up his work in a similar fashion. Having finished a patch of red, he spills it immediately into the adjacent patch. [November, 1st grade]

—The class is making cards for the two student teachers who are leaving. Tim makes one card and includes both names on it. When James notices this and asks who is going to get the card, Tim replies with unconcerned confidence, "They'll both read it." [January, 2nd grade]

—While reading an excerpt from *All About Prehistoric Cavemen,* Tim decides he wants to show the interviewer a certain picture. He flips through the book momentarily but then abandons this strategy, turning instead to the table of contents. He finds the chapter he wants, goes to the page indicated, and quickly finds the picture within the chapter. [June, 2nd Grade]

4. Distanced, Impartial, Unimpeded

For all that Tim is actively engaged in situations, he tends to distance himself from them. It's not a matter of being uninterested or uncaring, but rather of granting a separate identity and integrity to the things of the world. Fantasy play may not follow just any whim of the actors as far as Tim is concerned; inherent constraints in the world of spacemen and superheroes must be honored. The realities of the here-and-now world should also be recognized and honored. ("There is no such thing as a real life teddy bear." "Nobody ever went to Mars! ! !") And people, too, have their own individual identities and make-up that deserve individuated response.

Within the framework of this distancing perspective, Tim acts with impartiality. He commands and corrects with an appeal to authenticity rather than to personal authority. He refuses without malice or moralizing. In at least one instance, he resolves a situation with impeccable, if somewhat legalistic, equity.

—"Who wants to play with Luke?" Tim asks the group (Raphael, Donald, Manuel, and Eddie). All activity in the area stops as the other boys face Tim, raising their hands. Eddie raises two hands. "I'll give it to Eddie." Tim decides. [April, 1st grade]

Tim also distances himself from conflict. On the few occasions when major fights and arguments do break out, he leaves the scene. Often, however, he tries to steer the group around potential conflict by assimilating unpleasantness within the context of the drama.

—Eddie (who has come into the block area to complain) starts stealing some teddies from Donald and Tim. Tim cries: "Stop attack! Stop attack!" Then, with an aggrieved edge to his voice: "I said 'Stop attack,' Eddie." Eventually, Tim mutters to himself, "Gotta set 'em up again," followed immediately by "No, I don't wanna play." He retreats to the back of the area. In the meantime, Eddie accuses the others of messing up his shelf environment. Tim hangs back, appearing to ignore the dissension. Then, with a burst of energy, he begins picking up the teddies off his building. Cutting through the discord, he asks—"You gonna attack us, or we gonna attack you?" [April, 1st grade]

As an "upperclassman" in the second grade, Tim's qualities of impartial leadership become more evident. Now, he sometimes refuses both Kevin and Sam entry into the dramatic running games of the yard, unless and until the teacher tells him they have to be included. As Marjorie Robinson describes it: "The kids say, 'Tim won't let me play'—so he's definitely in charge. He's taken seriously by the others." Ms. Robinson thinks he excludes Kevin and Sam because they tend to get too rough in their pushing and shoving. But as soon as she says something to Tim, the other two boys are back in the games, apparently with no quarrels. Twice after reentering the games, Kevin has been so rough that Ms. Robinson has had to pull him out herself.

Despite these challenges to Kevin and Sam (and perhaps partially because of them), Tim is regarded as a "fair" and "trusted" person by the other children. There is usually a great deal of agreement with Tim's version of things. In fact, Ms. Robinson cannot remember any time when a child has felt that Tim was "telling something wrong." [February, 2nd grade]

Among the younger, first-grade children, Tim exercises both a controlling and helpful influence. The composition of his assigned block group is mainly first-grade boys, and he generally takes charge of the activity there. With respect to his commanding role, however, there are no complaints from the younger boys about Tim being unfair or bullying them. He is also reportedly patient and helpful in his volunteer role as a word helper to the younger children in reading. Occasionally, he takes on the mantle of arbitrator.

> —Tim gets up to inquire about an argument among a group of girls working in the reading area just to his right. "Girls! Girls!" He arbitrates, demonstrates, returns to his own desk. There, he advises Nancy about a spelling word and watches the reading area group somewhat abstractedly for a moment. Then he continues his work. [January, 2nd grade]

Tim's distanced perspective on life includes a tolerance of imperfection and incompleteness. For one thing, he realistically assesses his abilities and achievements. In reading, for example, he gives quite accurate estimates of whether a book is easy, too difficult, or "so so." And he is not wed to his own products. As mentioned previously, many of his drawings lack the completeness of a background setting and have the somewhat messy look of working sketches. If, for some reason, he can't build the particular object he has set out to construct, he builds another. If one line of dramatic play begins to disintegrate, he improvises another. He is not heavily invested in any single product as the ultimate expression of any single idea. This particular kind of detachment also means that Tim doesn't fuss unduly about minor problems or obstacles. There is an unimpeded quality to his functioning.

> —Someone points out that Tim and James don't have the right roof for the Lego house they are constructing. Tim: "We don't have to make it that color . . . well, we'll find some." [October, 2nd grade]

> —When Tim's chair is swiped at the Lego table, he looks around for it a minute but then sits on the edge of the table and continues building with concentration. [October, 2nd grade]

Tim also displays tolerance of others' foibles and idiosyncrasies. He may reject Kevin's and Sam's roughness in play, but he doesn't reject them as persons. His acceptance takes the form of being good-humored, patient, "a good sport." Sometimes he goes out of his way to mend fences.

> —"A little while ago, Tim taught Deron how to play checkers. He was good with Deron in this situation . . . was relaxed and not fussy-picky. Generally speaking, Tim is a good sport in such things as being willing to play with someone who doesn't know a game. Not all the kids would do that." [Interview: March, 1st grade]

> —Naomi (at Tim's table) has been reading her book out loud to another girl during the entire reading period. When she starts humming a drone for some reason, Tim finally comments. There is a minor exchange which ends when Tim urges her good-humoredly to "C'mon, finish reading." Later, Naomi refers to their in-

terchange and says, "I'm not gonna read it (aloud), Tim." Tim replies "Good" and concentrates on his own book. Within a few minutes, however, he turns to Naomi, urging her to read and prompting her by reading a line from her book. When she resumes reading, Tim lies across his desk momentarily to watch and, apparently, to listen. [May, 1st grade]

5. Enlivening, Courteous, Responsive

Enough has already been said to support the notion that Tim engages children in play and is full of ideas. Since the other boys usually endorse his ideas with enthusiasm, one may infer that the ideas are lively and interesting. Only once in Tim's absence do the others seem to realize that they have valid interests aside from space and superheroes, but they never repeat their apparent resentment of that one day. Tim's own enthusiasm comes through the pages of the record contagiously—"C'mon, let's play!"

His oral reading is usually rendered with expression and in ways that make him fun to listen to. Although writing is not a preferred medium for Tim, and he never elects to do it on his own, he nonetheless manages to introduce some life and lightheartedness into his assigned writing tasks. (Specific documentation is contained in the reading report.) Occasionally, he sparks the atmosphere with an element of surprise.

> —Tim normally speaks in a soft, low-pitched voice. One day, out of the blue and apparently referring to one of the space figures, he announced in a voice loud enough to be heard across the room—"Look what I did. I shot him in the ass!" [March, 1st grade]

Not only is Tim responsive to play, he is responsive to the feelings of others. He usually says "please" and "thank you" to other children (always to adults) and frequently extends his courtesy well beyond.

> —When the lights go out, indicating clean-up, Tim zooms his ships into the Lego bin, crushing them apart with his fist. Then he rather tenderly places Jamal's structure, complete, in the bin. [November, 1st grade]

> —A search for a missing space figure leads to a tall, gaily painted, cardboard structure, obviously made by another child. Tim advises the other boys that the figure is stuck in one of the slit holes of the cardboard structure. But when the boys take the construction off the bookcase and begin turning it in ways that look too rough, Tim cries: "Put it back up." [April, 1st grade]

Finally, Tim's responsiveness seems to take the form of a genuine liking of others. He will listen with appreciation to what others have to say, and he will unpretentiously demonstrate a concern for their welfare.

—Tim and Manuel are engaged in a cozy conversation about "damages" they will inflict on one another. ("Not if I get your toes and eat them." "You're going to die if. . . ." "You'll be sorry.") There is a brief digression, and then the conversation returns to a long story about some shocking thing that happened to Manuel's little brother. For the most part, it is Manuel who talks. Tim draws a bit, then stops to follow Manuel's story more closely. When Manuel finishes, Tim goes back to drawing. He announces with satisfaction: "I love those good stories." [January, 1st grade]

—Another boy had a drastic change in his pick-up schedule after school and became rather anxious about it. One day, Tim was in earshot of a conversation between Ms. Robinson and the boy about putting the card on the door. (The card indicates where the class may be found if they are not in the room—yard, library, gym, etc.) Tim offered a note of reassurance:

"Yeah, I used to worry like that all the time. But if you put the card on the door, they know where you are." [Interview: March, 1st grade]

—Tim and some other boys have finished their assigned work early and spent the last 15 minutes in the block area. When the teacher calls for clean-up, Tim puts the Spiderman doll away. Raphael is still working on his assignment as Tim approaches and says: "Raphael, you can rest now. It's time to stop." [April, 1st grade]

REPORT FROM THE READING RECORD

The initial interview depicts Tim as someone in the early stages of formal reading. He can recognize repetitive phrases in a beginning reader (e.g., "my mother") but misses words like *at* and *gets*. He knows certain letter sounds but is not yet able to use such knowledge effectively. For his first oral reading tape in December, Tim chooses a familiar and relatively easy Bright & Early book (*Hand, Hand, Fingers, Thumb*). He reads the first several pages of this book carefully and, for the most part, accurately but stumbles toward the end on pages he has not practiced. From these beginning forays, Tim makes consistent progress throughout the record. The last taping in June of second grade reveals him to be a fairly competent reader of text approximating adult vocabulary, grammar, and format (*All About Prehistoric Cavemen*).

Although Tim's progress is consistent, the books he chooses (or is asked) to read at any given time cover several levels of difficulty. This fact is fortunate, because it is the more difficult books Tim reads that most clearly disclose his style and strategies. What remains a mystery is how he began to read in the first place, considering his experience in kindergarten.

Tim is one of many children in Ms. Robinson's classroom who were exposed to intensive instruction in letter-sound correspondence during kindergarten (as part of a special school program instituted the previous year). Similar to Getagno's method, the program emphasized various sounds of the individual letters and of letter combinations, or blends. Instruction lasted 10 to 15 minutes a day and was conducted throughout the year. Although a stong phonic emphasis is not Ms. Robinson's preferred approach to beginning reading instruction, she felt obliged to honor and to reinforce this kindergarten program during the first half of the year. She did so by means of formal exercises and lessons in letter-sound correspondence and by informal rhyming games.

The difference between the two study children in Ms. Robinson's class is striking enough to deserve comment. Tim's counterpart, Rita (who also had the kindergarten instruction), displays a sophisticated understanding of phonics— perhaps the most advanced knowledge of any child in our research. She not only possesses the knowledge, she can use it to good advantage, confidently unlocking difficult new words like "occasionally" with speed and little audible struggle. Tim, on the other hand, can read next to nothing by blending sounds, and he seems utterly paralyzed when asked or required to use this approach. How he gained his first handle on print—despite the kindergarten experience—remains unanswered in the record. One can only make an educated guess based on strategies that are evident in his documented progress.

Thematic headings that organize this report are listed below.

1. A Differentiated View of Books
2. Difficulty with Linear Processing and Sequential Word Analysis
3. Scanning for Spelling Patterns
4. Scanning for Clues in Pictures
5. Parallel Processing with a Focus on Story Line and "Story"
6. Tolerant of Imperfection, Unimpeded, Relaxed
7. Economy of Effort and of Expressed Thought
8. Entertaining as a Writer and Oral Reader

The first heading concerns Tim's perspective on the world of books. The second deals with the albatross of his beginning reading efforts. His difficulty with linear processing and sequential word analysis is apparent throughout the record, but it is especially prominent in the beginning months of first grade. In fact, evidence about what is a hardship for Tim constitutes most of the information contained in his January oral reading tape. (After January of first grade, Ms. Robinson no longer urges a phonic approach in support of his reading.) The third and fourth headings focus on discrete strategies that can be isolated in the data. The fifth heading describes how Tim typically appears to function when he reads. Together, these first five headings reflect variations, specific to reading, of characteristics that were evident in the first report—the characteristics of parallel processing and wide scope of attention deployment. The last three headings also mirror themes from the total record. They are refrains of his distanced perspective, his economical style, and his enlivening personality.

1. A Differentiated View of Books (books as props, guides, authoritative sources, and vehicles of practice)

The report on themes from the total record describes Tim's view of the world as "manifold." He can readily transform situations by pushing aside conventional templates ("You can make it what it is"), yet he injects an aura of realism into fantasy play. His conceptual processes seem to function in different gears at different times. (He tranforms his spaceship into light-speed velocity in a drawing but tells the interviewer that "Nobody ever went to Mars!") And he engages children differentially, depending on the child and the setting. A similar kind of differentiation is reflected in his view of books.

In some instances, Tim regards books as props for his own imaginative expression. Although his precise meanings may not always be apparent, his use of books for fantasy seems clear.

> —He revolves the Atlas in order to see the maps from different angles. He turns the pages with great authority and similarly points and comments. The observer, however, has no sense that he understands what the maps actually are. [Observation: November, 1st grade]

> —Tim leafs through the book *Behind the Wheel*, which has many illustrations of vehicles. He makes motor noises while pressing his thumbs on a picture of a steering wheel and twisting them as if he is turning the wheel. [Observation: January, 2nd grade]

> —If a difficult book captures his imagination, as *The King's Shadow* seemed to do, he may even treat the text as a kind of prop. Words he tries to identify appear to become both the prompts and the means for expressing his own version of the story. His own substituted version may be nonsense, but it is nonsense in the style of Lewis Carroll. In two readings of *The King's Shadow*, he offers the following errant renditions of sentences:

>> It was twitching to the size of a house and had a rumble, trumble, pumble. [June, 1st grade]

>> He had splat the worse day bringing fire on hackets. [September, 2nd grade]

Tim also views books as guides, using them as long as they are helpful and discarding them when they are not. For example, he refers to a book of Lego models to direct and judge his building work, but he doesn't let it constrain his purposes. Eventually, he abandons the book altogether. The following excerpts of this incident come from an observation in October of the second grade.

> —"The book. Where'd the book go?" Tim discovers the book right next to him. He looks at it and then declares: "I'm going to make a fire engine."

—"Now I need . . ." he mutters to himself. He gets up and searches the Lego box, adding a flat piece to his fire engine. He bends over the picture and compares it to the fire engine in his hand. After this inspection, he takes a red piece off.

—Later, he and James leaf through the book and Tim chooses a picture of a two-story house. When someone points out that they don't have the right roof for that house, Tim says, "We don't have to make it that color—well, we'll find some."

—He consults the picture of the first step, which shows the foundation of the house, and compares it to what he has built. He mutters: ".and then I need one of those." He looks through the box and continues muttering. In the end, he is defeated by the lack of a door for the house.

—Tim again consults the book and decides to build an airplane. He works preoc-cupied for several minutes. Then: "Dumb airplane, I can't do it . . . I can't find that," and he points to the picture. As he works to detach some of the airplane pieces, he begins modifying the structure. From this point on, he is the only one of the group who works from scratch. When the period is up, he has produced an authentic looking van, complete with a transparent cab window.

Other books are taken quite seriously by Tim. They are neither props nor guides, but authoritative sources of knowledge. These include information books in the classroom as well as certain books at home.

—Tim tells the interviewer that although nobody has ever been to Mars, people can use space probes and *see* what's on Mars. When he continues about dogs being sent on the space probes, the interviewer asks him how he knows all this. He says he knows from his space books at home that "show how the rockets are built and things like that." [May, 1st grade]

—Discussion in the same conversation shifts to the topic book on horses that he recently completed. The interviewer inquires if he has horse books at home. Tim replies:

> No, I have encyclopedias about horses. I know how many teeth they have— they have 44. And they have one toe on each foot. . . And they're amphibi-ans—they eat only grass, they don't eat meat . . . they're vegetarians.

—During a reading conference with Ms. Robinson on the book *Mountains,* Tim offers to show her a picture, saying: "They even believed God lived on the mountain, and they have a picture of it!" [November, 2nd grade]

—For his last oral taping in June of second grade, Tim reads *All About Prehistoric Cavemen.* When he has finished, the interviewer questions him to see if he under-stands the last paragraph. The passage in question describes how scientists and lay people alike rejected the first discovery of a prehistoric skull bone, because they didn't want to believe humans had evolved from ape-like ancestors.

> Interviewer: Well, do you get what they're talking about there . . . people didn't want to think that—
> Tim: —that it was real, but it *was!*

Books are also the means of practicing one's skill in reading. Although Tim does not return to the same books over and over again, as some children do in their practice efforts, his view of books definitely includes a practice component. This conception is made explicit during a conversation with the teacher in June of first grade.

—Tim brings *Victor Makes a TV* to his reading conference, and Ms. Robinson asks him if he has read it yet.

> Tim: Yeah, I read it over and over.
> Teacher: Why?
> Tim: Because I wanted to practice.
> Teacher: Why do you practice?
> Tim: Because I want to read it good.

Perhaps because he has many views of books, Tim seems to gravitate toward reading materials that vary in difficulty. Within any given time period, he will sample books that consist mainly of pictures, books at his general instructional level, and books that challenge his capabilities as a reader.

2. Difficulty with Linear Processing and Sequential Word Analysis

Expressed language (speech and writing) necessarily conforms to an irreversible ordering through time and space, but Tim does not always honor this constraint. He seems to construe and to process linguistic information in large chunks, often transposing the individual elements. As long as a basic meaning is grasped from the components of language, the significance of their particular ordering eludes him at times. The documentation contains several instances of reversal that support this interpretation of Tim's linguistic processing. Although rotation and reversal of individual letters is common in young children's reading and writing (e.g., mistaking *p* for *d* or *d* for *b*), these are not the kind of errors Tim makes. Rather, his reversals involve larger units than individual letters.

—Three misspellings in his handwriting appear to be letter transpositions (similar to inadvertent typing errors) rather than attempts to invent appropriate spelling for words:

> *fo* for *of* (his "Plant Book," spring of first grade)
> *calssroom* for *classroom* (twice in Year I Journal)
> *namde* for *named* (Year I Journal)

—In one drawing, he depicts Batman pointing to a saucer-shaped object and saying "OFU." Tim's general knowledge of space terminology suggests that he would know the proper sequence of "UFO." [Fall, 1st grade]

—His dictated caption for one picture in a drawing/dictation book is curiously worded—"Robin is using his shoe jets," rather than" jet shoes." [Fall, 1st grade]

—The cover of his topic book on horses, produced in the spring of first grade, features a detailed drawing of a horse in the center of the page. The title and by-line above this drawing indicate that his sequence of writing was upward, toward the top of the paper. It appears as follows:

Tim

by

Horses

—On two occasions, he reverses word order in oral reading and goes back to self-correct. It should be noted that whole-word reversals are relatively rare, both in the experience of the collaborative research study and in the published data on oral reading miscues. Both these reversals (shown below) occurred in June of first grade, but in separate texts.

Text	*Tim*
You look just like. . .	You just look like. . .
suit of shiny armor.	suit of armor shiny.

When Tim deliberately focuses on letter sounds and tries to blend them, he sometimes reverses the sound sequence. In May of first grade, he is observed reading *Mr. Brown Can Moo, Can You?*, a book about animal noises that Mr. Brown can imitate. When he comes to the sounds "HOO HOO HOO HOO," he tries various pronunciations. Among them are: *uhug* and *ow-oo*. The clearest instances of blending reversals, however, are found in the abbreviated excerpts below, taken from his oral reading tape of January, first grade. The word he is trying to decode is *know*.

Ms. Robinson	*Tim*
What can you do with this word (*know*)?	Try to spell it out, with sounding the names.
OK, let's hear it.	ka—nnn—wa
What sound is after *n*?	oo (as in moo)
How does it all go together?	Could
. . . . (other interim attempts)	
Would it help if I told you the *k* was silent . . . then what?	Won
You have to start with the *n* sound.	
What sound does *n* make?	Ow (as in cow)
N makes *ow*?!	(Tim makes an "n" sound)
The teacher asks again about the *o* – *w* sound.	Wa
O is the first letter.	Wow?
What sounds can the letters *o* – *w* make? (Remember, from kindergarten, etc.)	I don't remember (very softly)

Tim doesn't always reverse sounds, but he is consistently stymied by the teacher's requests to analyze a word sequentially. Even if he succeeds with a phonic approach, he doesn't seem to recognize the word he has produced. He usually cannot (or will not) blend individual letter sounds, and, in at least one instance, he apparently cannot see the difference between words with similar letters. When called upon to produce blends, he typically comes out with a whole word. The first three examples below are taken from his reading of *A Rock Fence* on the January oral reading tape (1st grade). The last two are from an observation of his reading the same passage with the teacher on the day after his taping session.

—After prodding on the word *many*, Tim haltingly produces a word that sounds like "mainy." The following exchange then takes place:

> Teacher: What word is that close to . . . say it again.
> Tim: Many (sounding more like the word *man* plus *e*).
> Teacher: That's it!
> Tim: Many? (Again, the emphasis is on *man*.) He obviously doesn't hear or conceive that he has said the English word *many*.

—Again, in the same passage, he encounters the word *large* and says "like." The teacher blends the *lar* sound for him after he stabs at it unsuccessfully. When she indicates she wants the final syllable, Tim says "ga" (hard *g* sound). She asks for an alternative, and he says "je" (soft *g* sound). When she then asks for the whole word from the beginning, Tim produces "larje," pronouncing a vowel sound after the soft *g* (as he did when he articulated the sound originally). The teacher finally tells him the *e* is silent and pronounces the word for him.

—Later in the same passage, Tim says "go" for *grow*, but immediately says he knows this is wrong. When the teacher asks for the *o-w* sound, he remains silent. She asks for the *gr* blend, and he produces a hard *g* and some vowel sound. She asks him to try again, putting the two letters (*gr*) together quickly. Obligingly, and with some degree of confidence, Tim bursts out-"great!"

—Tim is observed reading the same passage to Ms. Robinson the next day. He reads the title and the first three words correctly but stops at the word *large*. He cannot come up with the *ar* sound, saying "er" instead, and a prompt about the initial consonant produces nothing. The teacher tries another tack for awhile and then goes back to the *ar* sound. Tim says softly, "I forgot from yesterday." She goes over the sounds of the individual letters *a* and *r*, but Tim doesn't get it.

—He stumbles and stops at the word *where*. Ms. Robinson asks him if he sees any similar word, and Tim indicates *were*. Despite much good-humored urging, she cannot get him to identify the difference between *were* and *where*.

3. Scanning for Spelling Patterns

It would be a mistake to assume that the difficulties documented above signal little or no phonic knowledge on Tim's part, for he actually understands a great deal about letter sounds. Even his faltering efforts with Ms. Robinson attest to such knowledge. The more telling evidence, however, lies in the orthographic similarity of his miscues to the actual text word. Many of his oral reading errors after January and continuing throughout the record suggest that he has transposed or slightly transformed spelling patterns. The list of examples below is by no means exhaustive.

Tim	Text	Book	Date
black	back	Big Dog, Little Dog	May, 1st grade
looked	took	I'm Terrific	"
walking	talking	"	"
blump	blurp	Mr. Brown Can Moo . . .	"
funiness	fussed	In the Night Kitchen	June, 1st grade
cracket	racket	"	"
rest	rise	"	"
want	went	Baby Monkey	"
want	what	"	"
almost	among	"	"
off	for	"	"
white	while	Cowboy on the Trail	"
palace	place	The Little Tailor	"
places	palace	The King's Shadow	"
heard	head	"	"
last	least	"	"
still	silly	"	"
tried	tired	"	"
black	block	Machine	September, 2nd grade
bun	Bud	Circus	November, 2nd grade
inside	instead	Mountains	"
screeching	searching	Prehistoric Cavemen	"
left	felt	"	"
center	certain	"	June, 2nd grade
blug	bulge	"	"

It would be almost impossible to produce errors like those shown above if one had no working knowledge of the sounds that letters and letter combinations represent. Tim's problem in analyzing words according to a phonic method seems to stem from two sources. First, the knowledge of letter sounds he possesses is more tacit than conscious. To the extent that he attends mainly to visual spelling patterns, his knowledge operates at a subsidiary level of awareness. When called upon to make this knowledge explicit, he either fumbles self-consciously or loses it altogether. His second source of difficulty follows from the first. To the extent that his eye takes in patterns, he finds it exceedingly hard to proceed in the step-by-step manner required by sequential analysis. His cognitive processes seem to range freely within the sweep of his eye—forward, backward, and skipping about. These are hypotheses, of course, but they fit well with other evidence that indicates he scans text for spelling patterns.

Another form of supporting evidence is the fact that he occasionally substitutes one word for two, in what seems to be an over-hasty scanning and anticipation of orthographic patterns. Fatigue may well account for the first such error, which occurs in December of first grade on his initial oral reading tape. The pictured heroes of his book (*Hand, Hand, Fingers, Thumb*) are a band of monkeys who engage in various actions—drumming on drums, picking apples and plums, and so on. The book has no more than four short lines of text per page. Tim makes very few errors through the first 21 pages, reading the word *monkey* and the word *monkeys* correctly several times. When he comes to page 22, he immediately says "monkeys" for *many more* and then sticks with this pattern, appearing to sense his error on the last line but petering out. The text and Tim's final rendition of it are as follows:

Text	Tim
Many more fingers	Monkeys finger
Many more thumbs	Monkeys thumb
Many more monkeys	Monkeys monkey
Many more drums	Monkey moyr . . . monkey . . . (voice trailing)

Tim's second error of substituting one word for two seems attributable mainly to haste. Interestingly, however, the error involves a configuration of letters similar to that involved in the first error. For his last oral reading tape in June of second grade, he reads several pages from a sophisticated information book (*All About Prehistoric Cavemen*) that he has studied over the course of the year. For the most part, he reads very rapidly and very accurately. One of his few errors occurs in the opening line of a paragraph. Although clearly wrong, it does little damage to the overall contextual sense of the chapter.

> Text: Now many scientists all over Europe, including. . .
> Tim: Memory scientists all over Europe, including. . .

Tim's miscues are critical indicators of orthographic anticipation, but one incident in the record provides convincing proof that he attends to spelling patterns (as contrasted with phonic patterns). The incident is a connection he makes between the words *know* and *grow,* which he encounters in consecutive selections read in January of first grade.

In the first selection, *The Clumsy Cowboy,* Tim breezes through several pages without error, until he comes to the word *know.* His attempts to sound the word (which end in reversals of the *o-w* and *n-o-w* sound sequence) were illustrated previously. After these unsuccessful efforts, Ms. Robinson asks him to skip the word and try guessing from context. In this case, however, context is of little help (''I know I can stay on you''), and Tim doesn't solve the problem. Finally, the teacher tells him the word, and they decide to go on to the next selection.

The next selection, *A Rock Fence,* is more difficult than the first and is one that Tim has never seen before. The reading is a painful experience for them both, because Ms. Robinson urges him to use phonic analysis to unravel the unfamiliar words—including *many, large,* and *grow* (all illustrated previously). In the midst of his struggle with the word *grow,* Tim suddenly makes an unexpected announcement that triggers the following exchange:

> Tim: If there was an *n* there, I would know.
> Teacher: What would it be if there was an *n* there?
> Tim: know.
> Teacher: I guess I don't know what . . . Where would the *n* be if it was?
> Tim: The *r* wouldn't be there; the *n* would be there.
> Teacher: And what would the first letter be?
> Tim: A *k.*
> Teacher: Oh! So you're talking about the word *know,* huh? Okay, maybe this rhymes with *know.* Could you make it rhyme with *know* but start it with *gr?*
> Tim: Grow?
> Teacher: It certainly would—good job!

This exchange occurs several minutes and many struggles after Tim's initial stumbling on the word *know* in *The Clumsy Cowboy.* At the time, Ms. Robinson doesn't understand the connection he is making back to the previous text, and it seems unlikely that any adult would grasp it under the circumstances. Indeed, a long history of experimental evidence on inhibition (loss of information recall after an interim of distracting events) points to the improbability of such a backward leap. Tim must be attending to spelling patterns quite consciously in trying to steer his course through text.

4. Scanning for Clues in Pictures

Pictures constitute an important source of meaning clues for Tim, but he uses this resource with discretion. Rather than making wild stabs, he seems to know when

FIG. 13.8   Page from *Hand, Hand Fingers Thumb*

a picture contains helpful information and when it does not. And he can readily spot even small details that suggest the clue to a word.

—In reading *Hand, Hand, Fingers, Thumb,* he obviously "reads" the picture to come up with the word *violins* for the text word *fiddles.* [December, 1st grade]

—In *Big Dog, Little Dog,* he reads the word *spinach* correctly, then stops for a moment to examine the picture more carefully. After this brief inspection, he announces "Yeah, spinach." [May. 1st grade]

—He spontaneously describes a futile search for picture clues in *The King's Shadow.* When he stops at the word *fight,* Ms. Robinson comments for the benefit of the tape recorder: "Tim is studying the picture now." Upon hearing this comment, Tim offers a progress report—"The only thing I see are his eyes sticking out." He never does produce a substitution based on the picture. [June, 1st grade]

—One illustration in *The King's Shadow* is dominated by a fierce-looking dragon, spread out over two pages. A burning haystack is shown in the lower right corner of the picture. Tim apparently latches on to this part of the illustration to come up with the word *sizzled* for *slain.* The sentence reads: "Now this was no ordinary dragon, or an ordinary knight could have slain him." [June, 1st grade]

5. Parallel Processing with a Focus on Story Line and "Story"

Tim's reading (as opposed to his phonic struggles) is usually guided by semantic anticipation. Only once on the oral tapes does he read something so far over his head that he loses meaning completely. Ms. Robinson judged the book (*Cowboy on the Trail*) would be too difficult, but she wanted to check; and in response to her direct inquiry, Tim says his reading isn't making sense. Aside from this incident, however, he keeps meaning in tow—or at least in sight—as he reads along. Several miscues indicate semantic anticipation based on his understanding of a specific sentence or of the general story line. The fact that many of these substitutions also approximate the graphic and/or spelling pattern of the text word suggests that two or three related lines of thought (graphic features, orthography, semantics) are operating simultaneously, in parallel fashion.

> Text: I'm a terrific worker, Jason said.
> Tim: I'm a fantastic worker, Jamison said. [May, 1st grade]

> Text: My mother mixes it . . . and calls it Green Cloud Supreme.
> Tim: My mother mixes it . . . and calls it Green Cold Superpie. [May, 1st grade]

> Text: There's a fiery dragon loose in your kingdom.
> Tim: There's fire dragons lost in your kindom. [June, 1st grade]

> Text: . . . the shadow was attached to his feet.
> Tim: . . . the shadow was actually to his feet. [September, 2nd grade]

The word "Story" (in quotation marks) is used in this heading for good reason. Some of Tim's most interesting miscues occur in two separate readings of *The King's Shadow*, a book that is difficult but certainly not impossible for him. He keeps the thread of meaning alive in both readings, but he often treads the text rather lightly. Again, his anticipations seem based on a combination of orthographic and semantic cues. With this book, however, the semantic cues appear to derive partly from the actual text and partly from a story stimulated by the text but spawned in his own imagination. The examples below are from his reading in June of first grade.

> Text: So the little king called in his wise men.
> Tim: So the little king called in his wischief men.

> Text: "Your Majesty," he cried.
> Tim: "Your Mischief," he cried.

> Text: . . . they dressed the trembling king in a suit of shiny armor.
> Tim: . . . they decided to trumble king in a suit. . .

Text: He was twice the size of a house. . .
Tim: It was twitching to the size of a house. . .

Text: . . . and had a terrible terrible temper.
Tim: . . . and had a rumble trumble pumble.

Tim's next reading of this story at the beginning of second grade is much faster and more accurate than the first reading, but he still invents part of the drama in a manner that ingeniously approximates the spelling of text. At a glance, the first error shown below seems to bear little resemblance to the text word. More careful examination reveals that it contains all the letters of the text word, along with an added element of the letter c.

Text: "Burn it at the stake,"
Tim: "Burn it at the casket,"

Text: He had spent the whole day breathing fire on haystacks.
Tim: He had splat the worse day bringing fire on hackets.

Other miscues in oral reading indicate Tim's awareness of syntax. If he ignores punctuation, for instance, he often attempts to recoup some reasonable sentence from the violated structure. Or, he will insert a word to maintain syntax after an error. His efforts in this respect are not always successful, but they reveal him engaged in a juggling act—trying to reconcile considerations of grammar and meaning on the one hand with graphics and spelling on the other. In the first example below, he apparently tries to make two words ("Ted shouted") both the end of one sentence and the beginning of another. This maneuver becomes necessary because he ignores the period at the end of a sentence. The sentence, however, is characterized by an unusual structure; it has an implied subject pronoun ("You") rather than an explicitly stated subject. Moreover, the sentence is preceded by several language structures similar to Tim's attempted manipulation (i.e., "Fred said to Ted" or "said Fred to Ted"). In the second example below, his insertion of the word *to* succeeds up to a point, but it eventually fails to maintain sense through the end of the sentence.

Text: Just switch rooms. Ted should sleep upstairs.
Tim: Just switch rooms, Ted shouted,—sleep upstairs?

Text: He says he won't leave.
Tim: He says he wants to leave.

Standard oral reading texts were given to all children in May of first grade. These texts ranged from a relatively easy book in the style of phonic/linguistic readers (*Ben Bug*) to a relatively difficult and sophisticated story (*I'm Terrific*). Tim made his way through all the books, though with much help from the interviewer and frequent approximations ("Green Cold Superpie") in the hardest text. The style of the first book in the series causes Tim some problems, and his reading is more jerky and less continuous than usual. The first book also affords one of the most convincing and interesting glimpses of Tim's ability to process different kinds of information simultaneously. In effect, it is an example of inferential reasoning carried out while in the process of negotiating text. The book and the incident are described below. The actual text and pictures are shown in Fig. 13.9.

An outline picture on page 1 shows Ben Bug and his hut. On page 2, raindrops fill the sky, and Ben's hut has noticeably diminished. The indication of rain is somewhat confusing, however, because the facing picture on page 3 features sunshine. The text in question is as follows:

> Page 1 Ben is a big bug.
> Ben has a mud hut.
>
> Page 2 Ben is sad.
> His mud hut got wet.
> The hut is a lot of mud.

At the first encounter of the word *mud* (p.1), Tim tries unsuccessfully to sound it out and then just skips it. At the second encounter (p.2), he tries *met* and *make* and then skips it. Then, looking at the picture, he suddenly asks: "What melts?" When the interviewer doesn't answer this question, he moves on with the reading. On the third encounter (p. 2, line 3), he finally gets it right and repeats the word with enthusiasm.

> Mud! Mud! Mud! Now I got it!

The interviewer asks how he got it, and Tim continues with his line of reasoning about melting.

> Well, mud melts in hot weather and it could melt in rain.

Although his reference to mud and hot weather is somewhat obscure (perhaps he means the mud that comes with spring thaws), the gist of his mental processing seems crystal clear. Moments later (while reading page 3), he nods back to the picture on page 2 and, as if to verify his reasoning, asks—"Is it raining here?"

For all his juggling and approximations, Tim's spontaneous comments and answers to questions indicate that he maintains some handle on meaning even when he reads through passages that are very difficult for him. In books he has practiced and reads quite well, these indications show a firm grasp of meaning.

—The last line of text on one page of *The King's Shadow* reads: "But when the king did, his shadow followed." Tim draws out the final word with a mysterious, slightly menacing expression: "*foll*—ow. . . d!"

—Another page of the same book ends with the line: "I'm m-m-m-m-much more afraid of a dragon than I am of my shadow,' said the king." Before turning the page, Tim lowers his voice and says—"I'm scared to see the next page."

Ben is a big bug.
Ben has a mud hut.

Ben is sad.
His mud hut got wet.
The hut is a lot of .mud.
Ben can not get in it.

Ben had to get a hut.
It is hot in the sun.

FIG. 13.9   Pages from *Ben Bug*

—His response to the interviewer's questions reveals a partial grasp of what he read in *I'm Terrific*. He understood the bear's basic conceit but not the implication that the other animals really resented it.

—A paragraph in the last chapter of *All About Prehistoric Cavemen* tells about the discovery of a skull bone, which some scientists claimed belonged to a prehistoric man. The emphasis of the paragraph, however, is on the fact that most scientists and laymen rejected such an interpretation, not wanting to believe that humans could have had ape-like ancestors. The paragraph concludes: "Many years passed before that bone was accepted as part of the skeleton of a Neanderthal man."

> Interviewer: Well, do you get what they're talking about there . . . people didn't want to think that—
> Tim: —that it (the bone) was real, but it *was!*

6. Tolerant of Imperfection, Unimpeded, Relaxed

Nowhere in the record does Tim render a word-perfect reading. He may make only minor miscues that do not alter the meaning of a text in any significant way, but he never achieves 100% accuracy. When he reads aloud to Ms. Robinson at a slow and steady pace, he undoubtedly intends to "read it good," as he once expressed it. He does read accurately by semantic standards at these times, but small deviations from the print ("Oh, me!" for "Oh, my!") simply don't register with Tim.

Much of the time, he seems more concerned with moving on in his reading than with striving for perfection. He will try to get words he doesn't know, but he usually won't belabor them or fuss over them. He makes approximations (as illustrated above) or he skips. The only time his reading comes to a grinding halt is early in the record, on those occasions when Ms. Robinson urges him to use a phonic strategy. Interestingly, his preference for skipping words is expressed only when he reads by himself or to the interviewer; he evidently does not perceive this to be an appropriate tactic when reading to the teacher.

—Tim is observed reading aloud to himself during quiet reading time. He reads the first and second lines of the page up to the word *wonder*. He pauses, then skips over it to the third line. [May, 1st grade]

—In reading the first selection at the standard oral reading session (conducted by ETS staff), Tim struggles with the word *always*. When the interviewer suggests he skip it, he seems only too glad to take this advice and to continue applying it. In all, he skips nine words during the course of the session, often giving a verbal ''flag'' that this is what he intends to do.

> Text: Why make big problems. . .
> Tim: Why make big—(''forget it . . . poles? . . . nay!)
>
> Text: Jason Everett Bear and his mother lived in a tidy. . . .
> Tim: Jamison Everett Bear and his mother lived in a . . . . (I'll skip it.'')

Tim sometimes appears totally unaware of minor omissions or substitutions in his reading, but when he omits or substitutes in order to ''get on with it,'' he seems fully cognizant of his track record. He is realistic in appraising his skill as a reader and accepts limitations. His voice may be subdued and convey hints of disappointment, but he exhibits no signs of defeat or great distress.

—When Tim is encouraged to try a word, he usually does so, but he often offers his own assessment of the situation—''I don't know that word.'' [Oral reading tapes]

—After reading *Big Dog, Little Dog*, Tim assesses the book and his performance with considerable accuracy: ''It's a little hard, but I can read it okay.'' [May, 1st grade]

—The teacher starts to get another book and Tim indicates that he has read it before. She asks if it was too hard or too easy. Tim replies, ''Too hard.'' [June, 1st grade]

—Tim's second reading of *The King's Shadow* is much more accurate than his first reading, but he violates meaning in the very first paragraph (reading *places present* for *palace parades*). He pauses after this mistake and then comments softly to himself: ''I don't know. . . . I'll try to go on. . . .'' [September, 2nd grade]

It is fortunate that Tim seems to accept the notion of imperfection, because he necessarily registers a great deal of negative feedback from his phonic attempts. This does not mean that the teacher's reinforcement is punitive or disparaging (Ms. Robinson tries to encourage him at every point); it means simply that he *knows* his attempts are unsuccessful. Even in the second grade, long after Ms.

Robinson has dropped phonic strategies with him, Tim has a continuing reminder of his shortcomings. This reminder is an Individual Criterion Referenced Test (ICRT) series—a program mandated throughout the district. During the final interview of the study, the teacher reports that Tim completed one of the test exercises perfectly. However, about ICRT #165 she says:

> —This was the short *i* vowel sound. The exercise shows two pictures of things that have identical vowel sounds, and the child is supposed to pick one word from four alternatives that has the same vowel sound. It was hard for Tim. [February, 2nd grade]

Tim's acceptance and realism, together with his refusal to let difficult text discourage a reading effort, contribute to the impression of him as a relaxed and confident reader. He is not, however, a nonchalant or blasé reader. He persists in every aspect of reading. From the middle of November through the end of January (second grade), for example, he persists in a long and technical book that is not easy for him (*All About Prehistoric Cavemen*). On one occasion when Ms. Robinson asked where he was in the book, Tim didn't give a page number but replied with some sense of pride in his voice, "Chapter Nine!" He also persists in practicing books and getting the teacher to hear him read. During the spring of first grade, there is a prolonged period in which Ms. Robinson doesn't read with Tim. At his first reading conference after this hiatus, Tim explains that he has had the same book out for some time, "because you didn't have me read (it) to you." Tim also persists during quiet reading time. He may engage in side excursions with other children during these observed periods in the record, but he always comes back to the task at hand.

7. Economy of Effort and of Expressed Thought

A certain brand of economy marks Tim's approach to reading and writing, just as it characterizes most of his functioning in the classroom. When he can get help from another child with a reading or spelling word, without waiting for "official assistance" from the teacher, he does so. He knows exactly what he wants to say in his early dictation books and doesn't hesitate or waste words saying it. He usually begins work while others are still settling in and often finishes assignments before the allotted time period is over. He knows how to use resources to find information quickly. For example, he uses the table of contents to locate a picture rather than wasting time flipping through the pages. Sometimes he cuts corners.

> —Tim makes one card for the two student teachers who are leaving and includes both of their names on it. When James notices this and asks who is going to get the card, Tim replies, "They'll both read it."

Most distinctively "Tim," however, is his economical, rather clipped style of expressing thought. He is neither nonverbal nor reticent to respond, but he doesn't volunteer every thought, and he doesn't engage in many extraneous comments or elaboration. He is a person of pointed words.

—He looks at pictures but doesn't comment on them when he is reading.

—When Ms. Robinson asks how he is trying to figure out a word, he typically replies, "I'm thinking."

—Most children announce the title of the story they are reading; and some will repeat the title as many times as it appears (on the cover, the title page, the first page of the text), almost as a "get-set" or warm-up exercise. Tim usually skips titles and just starts reading. Also unlike many children, he doesn't read captions to pictures.

—An entry in his homework book appears as follows:

I was named after
my grandfather
And he was named
after his, and so on. [January, 2nd grade]

—His spontaneous comments and answers to questions about his work are unembellished, concise, sometimes skeletal in nature. Many of these have already been illustrated.

"It's a little hard, but I can read it okay."
"I don't know that word."
"If there was an *n* there, I would know."
"The *r* wouldn't be there; the *n* would be there."
"Well, mud melts in hot weather and it could melt in rain."

One episode captures both his admiration for economical effort and his abbreviated style of communication.

—Tim advises his younger friends, James and Mike, that their assignment is supposed to be done in cursive writing. They balk, and all the boys go off to the teacher to settle the issue. Tim's judgment is evidently upheld. Upon returning to the table, he tells James reassuringly—"Cursive is faster." [January, 2nd grade]

In a record that generally coheres, one of the few puzzling and discordant notes occurs in this theme. Although everything else about Tim bespeaks economy, his own learning of cursive writing is peculiarly labored. For a long time during the spring of first grade, he writes in unconnected script and has to be reminded of the proper format by Ms. Robinson. Many of his work samples show this unusual combination of cursive letters spaced in the manner of printing.

8. Entertaining as a Writer and Oral Reader

Writing is not a preferred mode of expression for Tim, and most of his written work is done only in response to assignments. Even so, he often manages to liven up his assigned writing tasks.

—The *Plant Book* (spring, first grade) is an assigned record of observations reporting on the growth of a popcorn seed, which every child in the class had planted. Many children completed this assignment with deadly repetition (e.g., "My plant did not grow today"), but Tim exhibits some imagination. On the very first page, he writes as if he has an audience in mind and provides a courtesy illustration.

> I planted a
> plant on Monday
> April 30th. it
> was fun. I will
> show you how
> I did it.

A portion of this text, written in Tim's unconnected script writing, is shown in Fig. 13.10. In all, 10 of the book's 13 pages (spanning the month of May) contain detailed pencil drawings to go with the text. And within the confines of the observation, he tries to vary the wording—e.g., "Friday I had no luck."

—He also provides courtesy illustrations for several entries in his journals and homework books, and he sometimes turns phrases in interesting ways or injects an "offbeat" idea.

> On Mother's Day I gave
> my mother a dollar and she
> gave me a big hug and kiss.
> P.S. The rest of the day was
>   terrible   [Journal: May, 1st grade]

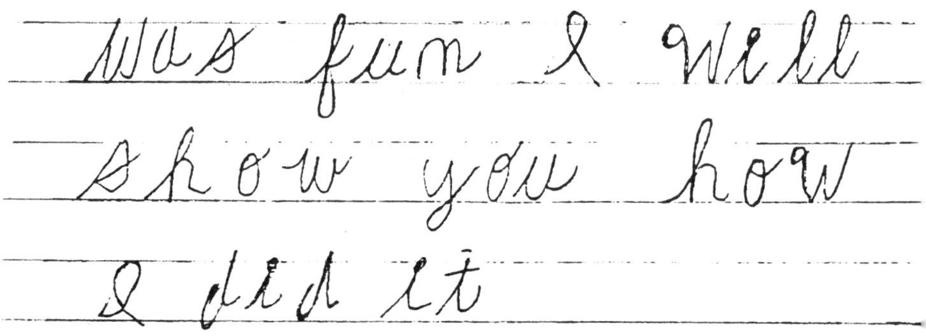

FIG. 13.10   Tim's unconnected script writing

> Tomorrow I am going
> to the zoo
> I will not bite   [Journal: September, 2nd grade]

As an oral reader, Tim is similarly lively and entertaining. His voice, which is pleasantly soft-pitched to begin with, often takes on an expressive lilt as he reads. Although he doesn't always honor the rhyme in rhyming texts, he frequently picks up the inherent rhythm in narrative and dialogue. Other factors also contribute to the entertaining quality of Tim's reading. He reads "alertly" and with apparent enthusiasm and enjoyment, even though his public stance toward reading aloud with the interviewer is one of qualified enthusiasm—"It's okay." He sometimes hums to himself in an amusing way as he examines a picture or turns pages. Occasionally, he makes interesting side comments about a book ("Now that's unbelievable!"); and his discussions with the interviewer and teacher are spirited, if brief. His tendency to move on with a reading and not fuss over it makes him an easy child to listen to. Finally, adults in the data integration group enjoyed Tim's substitutions. The consensus in many instances ("Green Cold Superpie," "It was twitching to the size of a house and had a rumble trumble pumble," "He had splat the worse day bringing fire on hackets") was that his imagination equaled that of the author.

Adults' views may admittedly be biased toward Tim's style of oral reading, but adults are not the only ones who find him an entertaining reader. Children do as well.

—Tim read *Ten Apples Up on Top* with expression and rhythm. There were several kids around the desk waiting to have their reading checked, and they listened entranced to Tim read. [Interview: November, 2nd grade]

—Donald specifically asked if he could accompany the interviewer and Tim to another room for the taping of Tim's last oral reading. When queried as to why he wanted to go along, Donald said that he thought Tim was a "funny" (i.e., "amusing") reader. [June, 2nd grade]

Ms. Robinson notices too. Toward the end of the record, she specifically comments that Tim seems to like to read to her and that he gives "a lively and enthusiastic reading."

Author Index

Numbers in *italics* indicate pages with complete bibliographic information.

A,B,C

Adrian, E., *21*
Allport, G., 10, *21*
Amarel, M., *24*
Athey, I., 9, *21*
Austin, G., 10, *21*, 140, *145*
Barr, R., 80, *111*
Bartlett, E., 94, *111*
Bever, T., 8, *21*
Bellugi, U., 8, *21*, 82, *111*
Biemiller, A., 80, *111*, 144, *145*
Bissex, G., 97, *111*
Bloom, L., 8, *21*
Bobrow, D., 11, *21*
Bremer, F., *21*
Brewer, W., 11, *21*
Brown, R., 8, *21*, 82, *111*
Bruce, B., 11, *22*
Bruner, J., 10, *21*, 140, *145*
Burke, C., 54, *55*, 80, *111*, 131, *145*
Bussis, A., 8, *21*, *24*
Carini, P., 44, 52, *55*
Cazden, C., 3, 8, *21*
Chein, I., 3, *21*
Chittenden, E., *21*, *24*
Chomsky, C., 8, *21*, 101, *111*

Chomsky, N., 7, *21*, 101, *111*
Clay, M., 54, *55*, 80, 97, *111*
Collins, A., 11, *21*
Courtney, R., *21*

E,F,G

Elkind, D., *22*
Flavell, J., *22*
Fodor, J., 8, *21*
Freedle, R., 11, *21*, *22*, *112*
Furth, H., 9, *21*
Galanter, E., 10, *21*
Garrett, M., 8, *21*
Keislar, E., *21*
Gibson, E., 86, *111*
Goodman, K., 54, *55*, 80, *111*
Goodman, Y., 54, *55*, 80, *111*, 131, *145*
Goodnow, J., 10, *21*, 140, *145*

H,J,K

Halle, M., 101, *111*
Hawkins, D., 3, *21*
Henderson, E., 97, 98, *111*
Hibbard, A., 90, *111*

Subject Index